North Korean House of Cards
Leadership Dynamics Under
Kim Jong-un

Ken E. Gause

Committee for Human Rights in North Korea

Committee for Human Rights in North Korea
1001 Connecticut Avenue, NW, Suite 435
Washington, DC 20036
P: (202) 499-7970

ISBN: 9780985648053
Library of Congress Control Number: 2015954268

Ken E. Gause

TABLE OF CONTENTS

I. ABOUT THE COMMITTEE FOR HUMAN RIGHTS IN NORTH KOREA (HRNK)

HRNK is the leading U.S.-based bipartisan, non-governmental organization in the field of North Korean human rights research and advocacy, tasked to focus international attention on human rights abuses in that country. It is HRNK's mission to persistently remind policy makers, opinion leaders, and the general public in the free world and beyond that more than 20 million North Koreans need our attention.

Since its establishment in October 2001, HRNK has played an important intellectual leadership role in North Korean human rights issues by publishing twenty-three major reports (available at http://hrnk.org/publications/hrnk-publications.php). Recent reports have addressed issues including political prison camps, North Korea's state sponsorship of terrorism, the role of illicit activities in the North Korean economy, the structure of the internal security apparatus, the *songbun* social classification system, and the abduction of foreign citizens.

HRNK was the first organization to propose that the human rights situation in North Korea be addressed by the UN Security Council. HRNK was directly, actively, and effectively involved in all stages of the process supporting the work of the UN Commission of Inquiry on North Korean human rights. Its reports have been cited numerous times in the report of the Commission of Inquiry and the reports of the UN Special Rapporteur on North Korean human rights. On several occasions, HRNK has been invited to provide expert testimony before the U.S. Congress.

II. PREFACE

After his seminal 2012 report *Coercion, Control, Surveillance, and Punishment,* which lifted the curtain on North Korea's internal security apparatus, Ken Gause continues his collaboration with HRNK through the publication of *North Korean House of Cards,* a pivotal book exploring the distinctive features, dynamics, and style of leadership under Kim Jong-un.

In February 2014, a UN Commission of Inquiry on the situation of human rights in North Korea (UN COI) established by consensus of all 47 members of the UN Human Rights Council released its report, following a year-long thorough investigation. The UN COI concluded that crimes against humanity have been and continue to be committed in North Korea pursuant to policies established at the highest level of the state.

These crimes and other egregious human rights violations do not happen in a vacuum. They span almost seven decades and are an intrinsic part of the Kim regime's *modus operandi,* situated at the very core of the apparatus that has maintained the family in power. In order to understand the mechanisms, lines of responsibility and individuals liable for the crimes committed, one needs to understand the relationship between the officials at the very top of the regime all the way down the chain of command to those who actually perpetrate widespread violations on the ground. Gause's book significantly contributes to this understanding by investigating North Korea's command and control structure and by profiling many of the people at the apex of the regime. *North Korean House of Cards* decidedly enables the reader to understand the motivations behind the regime's deliberate commission of crimes against humanity.

From the State Security Department (SSD)'s Seventh Bureau (Prisons Bureau), tasked to administer North Korea's political prisons, to the SSD's Central 109 Inspection Command in charge of cracking down on information from the outside world, to the Ministry of Public Security (MPS)'s Anti-Socialist Inspection Team, responsible for suppressing religious activities, the book provides the details about the chain of command liable for criminal offenses. This will ultimately help to establish the full connections between those in charge and the crimes committed on the ground, in particular those perpetrated inside North Korea's political prison camp system.

The book raises critical questions about the political and economic stability of the Kim Jong-un regime, now in power for almost four years. It shows how the regime reaches out to the international community while also intensifying repression to a level not seen since the 1950s. And it challenges expert assumptions. The reader, for example, learns that the political maneuvering behind the second hereditary transmission of power began not after Kim Jong-il's stroke in 2008, but six years earlier after first son, Kim Jong-nam was expelled from Japan and disgraced. The book delves into the intricate dynamics of regime consolidation under Kim Jong-un, from family intrigue and tension between Ko Yong-hui, Kim Jong-un's mother, and Jang Song-taek, the leader's uncle and only son-in-law of Kim Il-sung, to competition and disputes between different departments of the Korean Workers Party (KWP), namely the Organization and Guidance Department (OGD) and the Administrative Department.

While the purge of Jang Song-taek in December 2013 was a shock to people inside North Korea and also to North Korea watchers outside the country, Gause reminds the reader that, according to his sources, it was not entirely unexpected. In Kim Jong-il's will, the current leader's father allegedly warned that Jang's continued presence at the height of power would eventually threaten Kim family rule. *North Korean House of Cards* also reminds the reader that Jang's purge extended to associates and relatives, thus confirming that the *yeon-jwa-je* system of guilt by association is still applied in Kim Jong-un's North Korea. To some experts, the purging of Jang indicated that Kim Jong-un was firmly in control, but his indictment exposed possible weakness at the core of the regime. That indictment also provided unprecedented insight into the indecently lavish lifestyle of Jang and other members of the elite, in sharp contrast with the dire humanitarian situation of the majority of North Koreans.

North Korean House of Cards shows that with Jang's purge and execution, the regent structure in place after Kim Jong-il's death vanished, leaving Kim Jong-un as Supreme Leader surrounded by a group of key advisors in the top echelon and continuously evolving down the second, third, and fourth echelons of power. However, the extent of Kim Jong-un's power remains unclear. What he appears to lack is the unquestioned, absolute, and enduring loyalty of the leadership and the population. Indeed, *North Korean House of Cards*' author cautions that Kim Jong-un's ability to deliver on his policy agenda will ultimately affect his ability to consolidate his power. Farther removed from Kim Il-sung's revolutionary credentials than his father, his policy decisions will play a greater role in maintaining his legitimacy, at least from the perspective of the country's elites.

Kim Jong-un's tactics are shown to vacillate between *fearpolitik* reaching an intensity on a par with grandfather Kim Il-sung's purges of the 1950s and *giftpolitik* attempting to exceed father Kim Jong-il's generosity extended to those perceived as the most loyal and most needed by the regime. The magnitude and intensity of the purges may well have to do with Kim Jong-un's having to establish a power base in

Ken E. Gause

a hurry, not having had two decades to prepare like his father. Gause also reminds the reader that many are purged because of Kim's preference for blunt tactics, due to his lack of experience and inability to manipulate the levers of power. It is yet not clear if the purges are a sign of despondency, cruelty, erratic behavior, or part of a deliberate stratagem to keep the top echelons of leadership off balance and uncertain of their future.

North Korean House of Cards emphasizes that North Korea's apparatus of power is not static. The author points out that for Kim Jong-un to survive and strengthen his grip on power, he will continue to need the support of all four fundamental building blocks of the regime: the Korean Workers' Party (KWP), the Korean People's Army (KPA), the internal security agencies, and the inner core of the Kim family. With the role of control tower presumably restored to the Supreme Leader, he will continue to rely on his Personal Secretariat, the Royal Economy, and the Internal Security Apparatus as pillars of regime sustainability.

An overview of the biographies of members of inner circles of power reminds the reader that their average age is 70. The age gap between 30-year old Kim Jong-un and the Politburo is significantly greater than it was under Kim Jong-il, or under Kim Il-sung, who was approximately the same age as his close advisers. Gause reveals that North Korea's third and fourth echelons of power, generally unknown to North Korea watchers, comprise many of the fourth-generation apparatchiks, currently in their 30s and 40s, who will emerge as key players in the next few years. Many of them were selected by Kim Jong-un for important positions within the regime, or have a personal relationship with the new leader. When senior officials at the core, including some of the offspring of Kim Il-sung's fellow partisans, disappear, it is the fourth-generation officials Kim Jong-un will ultimately have to rely on to perpetuate his legitimacy.

For the time being, expert views will continue to span a broad spectrum, ranging from a despotic, firmly established Supreme Leader to a mere puppet controlled by the true power brokers behind the scenes. *North Korean House of Cards* suggests that despite rumors of power struggles and competition for resources, the regime does not show any blatant signs of weakness within the leadership. However, while the Kim regime may not be on the brink of collapse, it may continue in a state of perpetual uncertainty, with the possibility of collapse ever present. The day the regime crosses the point of no return could be more than a remote possibility.

Greg Scarlatoiu
Executive Director
Committee for Human Rights in North Korea
October 30, 2015

III. ABOUT THE AUTHOR

Ken E. Gause is the director of the International Affairs Group at CNA, a nonprofit research and analysis organization located in Alexandria, VA. He also oversees the Foreign Leadership Studies Program.

For the past two decades, his area of particular focus has been the leaderships of countries including North Korea, China, Iran, Syria, and Russia. Mr. Gause's work in this area dates back to the early 1980s with his work on the Soviet Union for the U.S. government. He has produced organizational studies on the leadership institutions associated with the Russian and North Korean ballistic missile programs, and an assessment of how North Korea develops its military doctrine. He has published numerous articles on leadership structures for such publications as Jane's Intelligence Review, RUSI's China Military Update, and the Korean Journal for Defense Analysis.

In addition to his CNA work, Mr. Gause has published widely on the North Korean leadership. In 2006, the Army War College's Strategic Studies Institute published his book, *North Korean Civil-Military Trends: Military-First Politics to a Point*. He is also the author of HRNK's *Coercion, Control, Surveillance, and Punishment: An Examination of the North Korean Police State* (2013) and *North Korea Under Kim Chong-il: Power, Politics, and Prospects for Change*, which was published by Praeger in 2011. His recent research interests include: North Korean succession politics; the North Korean police state; and North Korean civil-military relations.

IV. ABOUT THIS STUDY

There are numerous questions surrounding the regime of Kim Jong-un. Does he have a desire to take the country in a new direction, or will he follow in his father's footsteps? Is Kim Jong-un in control, or is he being manipulated from behind the scenes? Did his proclamation about the people "no longer hav[ing] to tighten their belts" really mean anything, or will "Military First" (*Songun*) continue to be the central organizing concept around which resources are distributed? Are the stories of widespread purges nothing more than rumors, or indications of serious challenges inside the regime?

Coercion, indoctrination, information control, and a highly centralized leadership system, which cannot function without a member of the Kim family ruling at its apex, have kept three successive generations of the Kim family in power. From the outside world's perspective, nothing seems to have changed. Many of the human rights problems in North Korea under Kim Il-sung and Kim Jong-il persist under Kim Jong-un. In fact, Kim Jong-un's actions suggest a leadership style that is much more overtly brutal than that of his father, characterized by public purges, the likes of which have not been seen since Kim Il-sung's consolidation of power in the 1950s and 1960s. This begs the question: why? Is it a necessary evil of the power consolidation process? Is it particular to Kim Jong-un's personality and leadership style? Will it become a characteristic of the Kim Jong-un regime, or is it a stage that will pass as the new leader matures into his position?

This study focuses on the tensions that Kim Jong-un is facing within the regime. In particular, it examines three narratives: 1) Kim Jong-un's attempts to consolidate power; 2) the regime's increasing desperation to secure hard currency; and 3) an evolving internal security apparatus dedicated to ensuring stability. In many ways, these narratives overlap and influence each other. The fall of Jang Song-taek is at the intersection of these three narratives.

V. ACKNOWLEDGEMENTS

In additional to the original research, this study makes use of some close monitoring of the North Korean leadership being done by a young, up and coming generation of Pyongyang-watchers. Michael Madden runs the well-respected blog *North Korea Leadership Watch*, which tracks leadership events and appearances. Nick Miller and a group of young Pyongyang-watchers are using network analysis software to analyze the North Korean leadership over the past fifteen years. These analysts are doing vital work that gives the Pyongyang-watching community institutional memory on issues related to the North Korean leadership.

The author would like to express his gratitude to Nick Miller, his research assistant in the United States, and to Sylas Lee and Jiwon Kwak, his research assistants in Seoul, who facilitated three sets of meetings in 2012, 2013, and 2014 and conducted additional research in support of this book. Without their assistance, this endeavor would not have been possible.

The author would also like to thank CNA and, in particular, the former vice president for communications, Connie Custer, for providing funding to put together the author's various notes and analysis that served as early research for this study. This analysis appeared in the two CNA manuscripts mentioned above.

Finally, the author would like to thank HRNK for the resources, encouragement, and editorial and research support it provided throughout the lifespan of this project. This is the second book the author has written for HRNK and both have been an enjoyable experience. In particular, the author would like to thank Board reviewers, including Co-chairs emeritus Roberta Cohen and Andrew Natsios, Nicholas Eberstadt, David Maxwell, Kevin McCann, Marcus Noland, and Jacqueline Pak, as well as UCSD Professor Stephan Haggard for their assistance in reviwinging the report and providing invaluable insight; HRNK Executive Director Greg Scarlatoiu for finalizing and ensuring the publication of this book; HRNK Director of Programs and Editor Rosa Park for editing and designing the book, as well as photographing the cover image; HRNK Project Officer Amanda Mortwedt Oh, who assisted with the executive summary and edited the book; HRNK Office Manager and Outreach Coordinator Raymond Ha, who edited the book and standardized Korean romanization throughout; HRNK interns Madeline Purkerson and Christopher Motola for editing the book; HRNK intern Amy Lau for her drafting of the bibliography; HRNK intern Brian Delmolino for his assistance with standardizing the romanization of North Korean terms; HRNK intern Suhwan Seo for his compilation of North Korean military ranks; and HRNK intern Grace Wright for her assistance with the photography of the cover image.

VI. EXECUTIVE SUMMARY

Merriam-Webster defines a "house of cards" as "a structure, situation, or institution that is insubstantial, shaky, or in constant danger of collapse."[1] As with many things in North Korea, its own house of cards is slightly unique, slightly less precariously balanced, but still in danger of collapse. North Korea's house of cards consists of the uppermost echelons of the country's leaders, with the "Supreme Leader," Kim Jong-un, situated at the top. This book, *North Korean House of Cards: Leadership Dynamics Under Kim Jong-un*, is centered on the regime and the leadership dynamics within it, and develops a model to make sense of a totalitarian system built on over sixty years of the Kim family dictatorship.

A critical component to reading this book and gaining insight into North Korea is to understand that the "who's who" in North Korea play a key role in the overall function and operation of the regime. Any aperture must look beyond just Kim Jong-un the person to the various leaders, leadership groupings, the Leader's decision making, and motivations behind actions in order to begin to understand the regime. Actions of the moment, such as a person being purged or demoted, offer very little in the larger context of how North Korean leadership dynamics operate. Therefore, a variety of different sources were consulted for this research, including: sources inside the North Korean regime; very high-level defectors; regional experts on the North Korean regime and leadership; and North Korea's own media and various reports showing the regime's perception of itself.

What this book tries to show is that the regime is going through a transition not just of the Supreme Leader, but also the wider apparatus of power that supports him. While Kim Jong-un is most likely the ultimate decision maker, his decisions are based on diverse processes supported by a large personal apparatus of power, as well as a larger leadership structure. For now, it appears that the young Leader has seized the reins of power and managed to build a network that is loyal to him. However, the leadership system as a whole is made up of many critical nodes where the messages up to Kim Jong-un and down the chain of command can be manipulated for personal gain. Recognition of this systemic flaw may prompt Kim's constant reshuffling of the leadership, as well as his draconian punishments for violating his instructions. As Kim Jong-un and the regime wrestle with the continuing reverberations of the transition of power, it should not come as a surprise that there are seemingly contradictory narratives about the nature of

---

1   "House of Cards," *Merriam-Webster.com*, accessed October 19, 2015, http://www.merriam-webster.com/dictionary/house of cards.

North Korea. If and when Kim consolidates his power, the narrative may become more focused and coherent.

The major question facing this regime in the next two to five years is whether it can ensure the continued survival of the "Leader" (*Suryong*) based system and Kim family rule. In this period, Kim Jong-un must consolidate his power or face systemic challenges, both economic and political, that he most likely cannot overcome. As a third-generation leader, Kim cannot rely on the inherent legitimacy of his grandfather. He cannot bend the system to his will, as his father did, because he lacks the web of connections that fosters loyalty secured through battles fought inside the system for decades. Instead, he must slowly build his own system of rule, while implementing successful policies at the same time. If he fails, he may survive as the Supreme Leader, but his ability to dictate the course of the regime will be compromised. He will have to negotiate with other powerful elements in the regime. The notion of Kim family rule will become a ruse used to justify the regime, not the driving force behind the regime.

As such, the Kim dynasty may be living on borrowed time. The regime has entered into its third generation, which is unheard of in the annals of recent political history. Totalitarian regimes may be ruthless and draconian, but are built on weak foundations. They are the result of informal alliances that are forged at a moment in time. As time marches on, these alliances become weaker as they are replaced again and again. North Korea is no exception. The Kim regime lacks the vigorous mandate it once had when Kim Il-sung was the "living embodiment of the Korean people," a fatherly figure. Now, this figure is a man in his early 30s whose existence was not even known to the North Korean people six years ago. The apparatus of power continues to create the image of a new, great, and powerful leader, all-knowing and omnipresent. However, the message does not carry the same weight as it did for his grandfather and father, which puts Kim Jong-un in a very difficult situation. If he attempts to continue along the same path as his grandfather and father as an unwavering tyrant, the system will eventually falter. If he chooses to pursue reform and tries to reinvent the regime by departing from totalitarianism, the regime could collapse into chaos. Whichever path Kim Jong-un follows, the rights of the North Korean people are likely to continue to suffer.

This book examines the leadership of the first three and a half years of the Kim Jong-un era. In addition to charting the rise and fall of the core group of leaders who make up the circles of power around the new Supreme Leader, it lays out a model for how the regime operates based on the major events from the end of 2011 through the summer of 2015. This model argues that Kim Jong-un is the ultimate decision maker and sole source of legitimacy for the regime, although he has yet to fully consolidate his power.

This book takes the author's years of study and research on the regime and consolidates it into two major sections. Section One describes the present leadership dynamics at play under Kim Jong-un since the transfer of power from Kim Jong-il. It outlines the leadership dynamics inside the regime at the beginning of Kim Jong-un's reign and through the power struggles and machinations leading up to the purge of Jang Song-taek, Kim Jong-un's uncle.

This book also provides an unprecedented, open source look into the men and women who comprise the "who's who" of the four echelons of Kim's leadership and delivers detailed biographies of these key advisors to the Supreme Leader. Names, positions, and little-known information on these individuals are organized in highly useful tables within the book.

Section One concludes with the implications of Jang Song-taek's purge on the wider leadership, including the fall of the regent structure and the makeup of the four echelons of power around Kim Jong-un. It argues, for one, that the answer to Jang's purge likely lies in a decision largely driven by the Kim family, as it is directly tied to Kim Jong-un's consolidation process. This has been the most severe purge since Kim Jong-un took power and was done because Jang was becoming a threat within the regime, able to create a second center of power. Jang had become a liability. He could not be trusted to uphold the best interests of the Kim family above all else. However, power struggles at the second echelon of power between Jang and other powerful interest groups undoubtedly accelerated his downfall and may have even contributed to his final fate. Other leaders, such as the Minister of the People's Armed Forces, Hyon Yong-chul, were purged and presumably executed in order to reshape the leadership and stop power struggles happening at the second and third echelons.

Section Two of this book focuses on the major components of Kim Jong-un's apparatus that are most critical to his success or failure as a third-generation Supreme Leader: the Personal Secretariat, the Royal Economy, and the internal security apparatus. In the Royal Economy chapter, the author provides timely examples of Kim Jong-un's incredible gift-giving operations to maintain loyalty, as well as names and titles of Kim regime members with ties to the Korean Workers' Party Organization and Guidance Department under the internal security apparatus chapter. These three vital parts of the apparatus—the Personal Secretariat, the Royal Economy, and internal security—are highlighted not only because of their inherent importance to the North Korean regime and how it operates, but also because they are important to the success of any totalitarian regime. These three elements are intertwined. If any one of these elements fails, it will place increasing strain on the others. If any one of these elements becomes corrupt and goes beyond the control of the Leader, it will severely compromise his ability to rule.

The book concludes with two informative appendices. Appendix A is comprised of detailed biographies of individuals in Kim Jong-un's inner circles of power. Best described as key advisors, these leaders often accompany the Supreme Leader. In addition to their formal positions, they most likely enjoy further influence by virtue of their proximity. This influence sometimes manifests when they are ranked above their cohorts on recent funeral committee lists, which Pyongyang-watchers use to identify the formal leadership ranking within the regime.

Appendix B provides tables on Kim Jong-un's gift-giving. While Kim is reported to continue to be buying and creating lavish gifts for select elites, Appendix B highlights an overall slowdown in the Royal Economy by showing that Kim's gift-giving operations are increasingly relying on beneficiary acts and expressions of gratitude to the North Korean leadership and people as opposed to actual gift-giving, which was more prevalent in the past. One example of this is a 2014 scientists' rest home provided by Kim Jong-un "to the scientists with loving care."

What does this all mean for the North Korean people? What does it say about human rights under this oppressive regime? Leadership dynamics inside North Korea are at the heart of the question of whether the regime can ever change in any meaningful way and respect the rights of the people. It is clear that the answer is currently no. In any country where one individual's control is dominant and pervasive, the needs of the people are disregarded in the near-term calculus. Kim Jong-un will do what he needs to do to stay in power. He will need to improve the economy if he is to consolidate power, and this will impact the lives of the people. Any such decisions, however, will be made out of necessity for the Supreme Leader's power, not the livelihood of his people. If economic improvement runs up against the needs of internal security, the arguments of the technocrats will lose. Unquestionably, economic reforms will not be permitted to infringe upon internal security.

For now, scholars and intelligence analysts can only observe and attempt to piece together the puzzle all the while sure of only one thing: as long as the regime continues to adhere to the tactics of a police state to hold onto power, human rights will continue to be violated in North Korea as the unfortunate citizens of the country continue to live in the shadows. As the United Nations Commission of Inquiry on human rights in North Korea determined in February 2014, some of these human rights violations constitute crimes against humanity and are being committed pursuant to policies set at the highest levels of the state. As a result, this book is a profound resource for future accountability of the regime's crimes against humanity; in order to understand crimes against humanity in their totality, the relationship between North Korea's house of cards and the people on the ground carrying out the crimes needs to be fully understood.

VII. ABBREVIATIONS

1. AKST: Association of Korean Scientists and Technicians in Japan
1. BT: Biotechnology
2. CMC: Central Military Commission
3. CNC: Computerized Numerical Control
4. CPRF: Committee on the Peaceful Reunification of the Fatherland
5. DFRF: Democratic Front for the Reunification of the Fatherland
6. FAD: Finance and Accounting Department
7. FSD: Finance and Supply Department
8. GC: Guard Command
9. GLD: General Logistics Department
10. GPB: General Political Bureau
11. GSD: General Staff Department
12. IAEA: International Atomic Energy Agency
13. IT: Information Technology
14. JVIC: Joint Venture Investment Commission
15. KAPPC: Korean Asia-Pacific Peace Committee
16. KCBS: Korean Central Broadcasting Station
17. KCNA: Korean Central News Agency
18. KCTV: Korean Central Television
19. KNIC: Korea National Insurance Corporation
20. KOMID: Korean Mining Development Trading Corporation
21. KPA: Korean People's Army
22. KPISF: Korean People's Internal Security Forces
23. KWP: Korean Workers' Party
24. LID: Light Industry Department
25. MID: Machine Industry Department
26. MPAF: Ministry of People's Arm Forces
27. MPS: Ministry of People's Security
28. MSC: Military Security Command
29. MSS: Ministry of State Security (Also known as SSD)
30. NDC: National Defense Commission
31. NEAB: North East Asia Bank

32. NIS: South Korean National Intelligence Service
33. NKSIS: North Korea Strategic Information Service Center
34. OGD: Organization and Guidance Department
35. PAD: Propaganda and Agitation Department
36. PSI: Proliferation Security Initiative
37. RGB: Reconnaissance General Bureau
38. SEC: Second Economic Committee
39. SEZ: Special Economic Zone
40. SGB: Security Guidance Bureau
41. SIC: Special Investigation Committee
42. SOCC: Secretarial Office of the Central Committee
43. SPA: Supreme People's Assembly
44. SPC: State Planning Commission
45. SPCSGC: State Physical Culture and Sports Guidance Committee
46. SRF: Strategic Rocket Forces (Command)
47. SSD: State Security Department (Also known as MSS)
48. UFD: United Front Department
49. UN: United Nations
50. UNESCO: United Nations Educational, Scientific and Cultural Organization
51. UNSC: United Nations Security Council

VIII. INTRODUCTION

Kim Jong-il's death in December 2011 brought about the hereditary transition of power to a third generation when Kim Jong-un, Kim Jong-il's youngest son, who is now in his early 30s,[2] assumed the mantle of Supreme Leader. In little over a year, he acquired all the titles of power, including Supreme Commander, First Secretary of the Korean Workers' Party (KWP), and First Chairman of the National Defense Commission (NDC). In December 2013, Kim Jong-un violently purged his uncle, Jang Song-taek, in a move that seemingly accelerated his power consolidation.

This book examines the leadership of the first three and a half years of the Kim Jong-un era. In addition to charting the rise and fall of the core group of leaders who make up the circles of power around the new Supreme Leader, it lays out a model for how the regime operates based on the major events from the end of 2011 through the summer of 2015. This model argues that Kim Jong-un is the ultimate decision maker and sole source of legitimacy for the regime, although he has yet to fully consolidate his power. While he may have been invested with inherent legitimacy by virtue of his position as Supreme Leader, he still needs to mature into the position and learn to effectively wield his power. This process of demonstrating capability and relationship building could take one to two more years. In fact, Kim Jong-un has rapidly moved into the final phase of power consolidation with the execution of his uncle.

The **first phase**, which began shortly after he was formally designated the heir apparent in September 2010, focused on stabilizing the three-generation hereditary succession. In this phase, potential opposition to the hereditary transition of power was eradicated through purges and retirements.

The **second phase**, which began in earnest in 2013, focused on Kim's steps to establish a power base that owes its loyalty directly to him. This patronage system was likely built to accommodate the regime philosophies of "Military First" (*Songun*) and creating a "Strong and Powerful Nation" (*Kang-seong-dae-guk*). It was likely that as Kim Jong-un began to exert his independence as a decision maker, the

---

2   Kim Jong-un's birth year has never been published in North Korean media. According to South Korea's Ministry of Unification, Kim was born on January 8th, but his birth year is assumed to be 1982, 1983, or 1984. Recently, Yoo Seong-Ok, the President of the Institute for National Security Strategy, a think tank associated with South Korea's National Intelligence Service (NIS), stated that Kim was born in 1984. However, Dennis Rodman, following his trip to North Korea in September 2013, said that Kim is 30 years old. This would mean that he was born in 1983. See Choe Sang-Hun, "Rodman Gives Details on Trip to North Korea," *The New York Times*, September 9, 2013.

regent structure would begin to change—something that could destabilize the upper reaches of the leadership.

The **final phase**, according to many Pyongyang-watchers, was supposed to begin in 2015 when Kim Jong-un would likely be able to assume the full responsibilities of his position as Supreme Leader. He would establish his own decision-making processes and would take more direct responsibility for policy formulation and execution. He would also most likely begin to marginalize his regents, which could intensify the instability in phase two.

The move against Jang Song-taek accelerated this timeline. Kim Jong-un has quickly moved to the final phase of power consolidation. The regent structure that Kim Jong-il put in place has nearly evaporated, and the remaining regents are more accurately described as senior advisors.

The model described here is, in many respects, tied to the motivation behind and timing of Jang Song-taek's demise. Some argue that Jang was brought down as the result of a power struggle at the second echelon involving institutions within the regime, such as the Party's Organization and Guidance Department (OGD), along with the military and the internal security apparatus. If so, this has serious implications for short-term stability as Kim Jong-un grapples with a system he does not control.

This study argues for another model that places Kim at the center, involved in the decision-making that brought another potential rival of power crashing down. The outcome has ensured short-term stability, but raises many questions about the future. It has also highlighted the need to examine the apparatus that upholds Kim Jong-un's role as Supreme Leader. As such, this study will devote several chapters to deconstruct this apparatus by examining three of its critical components: the Personal Secretariat; the Royal Economy; and the internal security apparatus.

- **Personal Secretariat:** This organization serves as Kim Jong-un's private office and center of operations. It coordinates his communications within the regime and sets the agenda for his decision-making. In many respects, it is the informal center of power within the regime and is home to many of his closest advisors. It is also closely tied to the OGD, which serves as the pre-eminent surveillance body for all aspects of the regime.

- **Royal Economy:** The North Korean regime is dependent on several economies. The national economy falls under the Cabinet. The Royal Economy serves the interest of the Kim family and, by extension, the defense-industrial complex. It is made up of organizations, such as Office 38 and 39, which are directly tied to the Supreme Leader's Personal

Secretariat. According to several sources, this apparatus is responsible for over $4 billion in hard currency—critical funding for Kim Jong-un to control the wider leadership.

- **Internal security apparatus:** With the death of Jang Song-taek, Kim Jong-un has assumed command and control responsibilities over the internal security apparatus, which is composed of the State Security Department (SSD),[3] the Ministry of People's Security (MPS), the Military Security Command (MSC), the Guard Command, and the KWP Organization Guidance Department. All five are critical to ensuring the loyalty of the population to the Kim family regime.[4] All are also involved in aspects of the Royal Economy.

A. Sources

The research for this study began in September 2010, when Kim Jong-un was formally announced as the heir apparent. The author interviewed skilled "Pyongyang-watchers" throughout Asia who are adept at interpreting the subtleties within the North Korean leadership.[5] Particularly useful was a trip to Seoul in April 2013, during which the author discussed recent North Korean leadership dynamics in depth with a number of experts in the government and leading think tanks. Some of these interviews were with defectors, who brought unique perspectives and fresh information to the discussions. These interviews added nuance to the study and placed arguments in context. The sources are not revealed because these discussions were off the record.

In December 2013, as the Jang Song-taek purge was unfolding, and again in May 2014, the author took additional trips to the region where he reconnected with many of the same sources to gauge their thinking on what the purge meant for North Korean leadership dynamics. At the time of this writing, there are many theories as to why Jang was purged and the implications this will have for the regime.

---

3   The SSD is also known as the Ministry of State Security (MSS).
4   In 2012, the author published a study on this apparatus. It was updated in 2013. See Ken E. Gause, *Coercion, Control, Surveillance, and Punishment: An Examination of the North Korean Police State*, 2nd ed. (Washington, D.C.: Committee for Human Rights in North Korea, 2013). This chapter updates the findings of that second edition.
5   The term "Pyongyang-watcher" is used in this paper to refer to experts who focus on the North Korean leadership, much akin to the distinction made in the Cold War when Kremlinologists were a subset of the broader community of "Sovietologists."

However, there is very little evidence. Therefore, parts of what is presented in this study is a snapshot in time that may or may not be grounded in truth.

This book leverages past research that the author has conducted on the North Korean leadership, which can be found in the following studies:

1. *North Korean Leadership Dynamics and Decision-making under Kim Jong-un: A Second Year Assessment* (Alexandria, VA: CNA Occasional Publication 2014-U-006988, March 2014).

2. *North Korean Leadership Dynamics and Decision-making under Kim Jong-un: A First Year Assessment* (Alexandria, VA: CNA Occasional Publication 2013-U-005684, September 2013).

3. *Coercion, Control, Surveillance, and Punishment: An Examination of the North Korean Police State* (Washington, DC: The Committee for Human Rights in North Korea, Second Edition, May 2013).

4. "North Korea's Political System in the Transition Era: The Role and Influence of the Party Apparatus," in Scott Snyder and Kyung-Ae Park, eds., *North Korea in Transition* (Lanham, MD: Rowman & Littlefield, 2012).

5. *North Korea Under Kim Chong-il: Power, Politics, and Prospects for Change* (Santa Barbara, CA: Praeger Publishers, 2011).

6. *North Korea After Kim Chong-il: Leadership Dynamics and Potential Crisis Scenarios* (Alexandria, VA: Center for Naval Analyses, November 2011).

7. "Can The North Korean Regime Survive Kim Chong-Il?" *Korean Journal of Defense Analysis* 20, no. 2 (June 2008).

8. *North Korean Civil-Military Relations: Military First Policy to a Point* (Carlisle, PA: Strategic Studies Institute of the U.S. Army War College, September 2006).

B. Organization

This paper is organized into two major sections. Section One describes the transfer of power from the Kim Jong-il regime to the Kim Jong-un regime. It outlines the leadership dynamics inside the regime at the beginning of Kim Jong-un's reign, through the power struggles and machinations leading up to the purge of Jang Song-taek, and concludes with the implications of the Jang purge on the wider leadership, including the fall of the regent structure and the makeup of the circles of power around Kim Jong-un. Section Two focuses on Kim Jong-un's apparatus of power. It delves into the decision-making structure that the new Supreme Leader uses and how it is evolving to fit his leadership style. The final three chapters cover the critical parts of Kim Jong-un's leadership apparatus: the Personal Secretariat, the Royal Economy, and the Internal Security Apparatus. There are three appendices. Appendix A provides additional biographical details of Kim Jong-un's advisors. Appendix B provides examples of gift-giving in the Kim Jong-un era. Appendix C provides North Korean military ranks and insignias.

IX. SECTION ONE: NORTH KOREAN LEADERSHIP DYNAMICS UNDER KIM JONG-UN

It has been nearly four years since Kim Jong-il died and his third son, Kim Jong-un, assumed the reins of power in North Korea. Early in this power transition, Kim Jong-un received the titles of Supreme Leader and Supreme Commander of the armed forces. In April 2012, at the Fourth Party Conference and the subsequent Supreme People's Assembly (SPA), he received the additional titles of power: First Secretary of the KWP, Chairman of the KWP Central Military Commission (CMC), and First Chairman of the National Defense Commission (NDC). But even with these titles of power, questions remain regarding Kim's ability to run the regime and the workings of the decision-making process within the North Korean leadership.

Since Kim Jong-un took power, his age and his capability to make decisions and manage the regime have been subject to speculation. North Korean political culture, which places extraordinary power in the hands of the Supreme Leader, has been weighed against powerful individuals and institutions that reside in close proximity to the young leader. Whether they have a decision-making role or simply serve as *consigliere* is unclear.

This section examines the leadership dynamics surrounding Kim Jong-un's first three and a half years in power in an attempt to piece together the picture of how the regime operates under the new leader. It consists of four chapters. The first chapter begins with the mourning period and discusses the evolution of the leadership in 2012 and 2013. It ends with a discussion of the role and function of the regent structure around Kim Jong-un. The second chapter is devoted to the narrative surrounding the purge of Jang Song-taek. It provides background on the power struggles and tensions that made Jang a threat to the regime. The third chapter covers the changes in the leadership since Jang's purge through the summer of 2015 and examines the key leaders around Kim Jong-un. The fourth chapter provides some concluding thoughts.

A. CHAPTER ONE: THE TRANSFER OF POWER

The process of power consolidation in North Korea is long and complex; it is not simply a matter of the Supreme Leader designating his successor and the leadership falling in line. In order to consolidate power, a leader must not only sweep away potential opposition and bind the wider leadership to him, but also solidify this allegiance by executing policies that reflect well on the regime and benefit his supporters. For Kim Il-sung, this process took nearly twenty-five years, ending with the adoption of the 1972 constitution that laid out his authority as the Supreme Leader. Kim Jong-il spent nearly twenty years preparing the way for his own succession with the support of his father. He consolidated his position in 1998, four years after his father's death, with the adoption of the "Socialist Constitution of the Democratic People's Republic of Korea" (Kim Il-sung Constitution) that laid the foundation for Kim family rule and the hereditary transfer of power.

Although Kim Jong-il took measures to pave the way for the transfer of power to a third generation, much still needed to be done when he died on December 17, 2011. During 2012 and into 2013, Kim Jong-un and his supporters embarked on a campaign to further transform the leadership. Surprising many Pyongyang-watchers, this exercise in power consolidation moved at a rapid pace and included purges of officials considered close to Kim Jong-il. Some old faces returned to the second and third echelons of power, which raised questions about Kim Jong-un's policy proclivities. However, in many cases, the rising stars were new officials whose direct loyalties were open to speculation.

1. THE MOURNING PERIOD

Although it was expected, the death of Kim Jong-il came suddenly. On December 19, 2011, the official *Korean Central News Agency* (*KCNA*) said he had "passed away from a great mental and physical strain" at 8:30 a.m. on December 17, 2011 while on a train for one of his "field guidance" tours. The report went on only to say that Kim died of a "severe myocardial infarction along with a heart attack." He was 69. A weeping announcer urged the people to follow Kim's youngest son and heir apparent Kim Jong-un.[6]

---

6   North Korean state media began to refer to Kim Jong-un as being "respected" (*jon-gyeong-ha-neun*), a clear sign that another hereditary power succession was under way in North Korea.

All Party members, military men, and the public should faithfully follow the leadership of comrade Kim Jong-un and protect and further strengthen the unified front of the Party, military, and the public.[7]

As Pyongyang-watchers scrambled to assess what would come next, the signals coming out of Pyongyang suggested continuity and a smooth transfer of power. The state media's coverage of Kim Jong-il's death and the first tentative moves of the new regime mirrored what had taken place seventeen years earlier when Kim Il-sung died.[8] The announcements of the death and official medical reports were eerily similar. The formation of the funeral committees and the communiqués indicated a leadership committed to Kim family rule. The order individuals are listed in the funeral committees is based on their attachment to Party, military, and state organs. The Funeral Committee list for Kim Jong-il was very similar to the Funeral Committee list for Kim Il-sung in 1994 in terms of the heir being catapulted to the top of the list, ahead of those who had previously outranked him. This was illustrated by Kim Jong-un's name being at the top of Kim Jong-il's Funeral Committee list, ahead of nominal head of state Kim Yong-nam, who previously outranked him in the formal hierarchy.[9]

One of the first acts of Kim Jong-il's Funeral Committee was to issue a communiqué setting the schedule for the mourning activities. The mourning period was set to run from December 17 to 29, 2011, with mourners being allowed to file by Kim Jong-il's coffin in the Kumsusan Memorial Palace from December 20 to 27, 2011.[10]

On December 20, 2011, Kim Jong-un and the senior leadership arrived at the palace and slowly filed past the body of Kim Jong-il, which was lying in state in a glass coffin. Kim Jong-il was dressed in his trademark khaki tunic, with most of the body covered by a red sheet. The still photographs show a somber, darkly-clad Kim Jong-un and others, some in military uniform, circling a flower-bedecked bier supporting the casket as honor guards with AK-47s stood silently at attention.

---

7   "'Notice to All Party Members, Servicepersons and People' on Kim Jong Il's Death," *KCNA*, December 19, 2011.

8   If there was any difference in the regime's handling of the initial death notification, it was in the timing. The regime waited fifty-two hours before pubilcly announcing the news of Kim Jong-il's death. This was eighteen hours longer than it had waited in 1994 to announce Kim Il-sung's death. This suggests that there could have been indecision within the leadership about how to handle the message. The decision to include a reference in the communiqué about a prior internal notification may have been done to justify the delay and deflect any speculation within the larger leadership that problems might be afoot.

9   "List of Names on DPRK State Funeral Committee for Kim Jong Il," *KCNA*, December 19, 2011.

10   Kumsusan Memorial Palace is also known as the Kumsusan Palace of the Sun.

The first set of mourners, who accompanied Kim Jong-un, included some of the most powerful men within the regime and some of the key administrators: Jang Song-taek (Vice Chairman of the NDC), O Kuk-ryol (Vice Chairman of the NDC), Ri Yong-mu (Vice Chairman of the NDC), Kim Yong-chun (Minister of People's Armed Forces (MPAF)), Ri Yong-ho (Chief of the General Staff Department (GSD)), Kim Yong-nam (Chairman of the SPA Presidium), Choe Yong-rim (Premier), Jon Pyong-ho (KWP Secretary for Defense Industry), Yang Hyong-sop (Vice President of the SPA Presidium), and Pyon Yong-rip (President of the State Academy of Sciences).

The next day, North Korean television continued its coverage of the mourning, which was not subtle in pointing out that the Kim family was in charge. Kim Jong-un, clad in a black Mao suit with tears streaming down his red face, shook hands with distraught visitors in dark attire or military uniforms, occasionally bowing to them. A young woman in a funeral *hanbok* stood behind him, crying.[11] This was his younger sister, Kim Yo-jong, assuming the ceremonial position that her aunt, Kim Kyong-hui, had held seventeen years earlier.[12] The symbolism was unmistakable.

Image 1: Kim Jong-un and Kim Yo-jong at the funeral ceremony for their father, Kim Jong-il (Source: KCBS, 21 December 2011)

A week later, the mourning shifted to the snow-covered streets of Pyongyang with the funeral procession. Wailing citizens and tens of thousands of troops bowed their heads as the cortège left the Kumsusan Memorial Palace. A car bearing a huge portrait of a smiling Kim Jong-il led the procession. Behind it was a hearse carrying Kim's coffin, draped with a red flag and surrounded by white flowers on its roof.

---

11   *Hanbok* refers to traditional Korean dress.
12   Kim Ok, Kim Jong-il's de facto fourth wife, was also spotted on television weeping in front of the body and bowing to Kim Jong-un. On December 24, 2011, Kim Kyong-hui appeared at the bier, standing three spots to her nephew's right.

Dressed in black, gloveless, and bare-headed despite the cold, Kim Jong-un walked beside his father's hearse, accompanied by key members of the Party and military. Directly behind Kim Jong-un were the Party representatives—his powerful uncle, Jang Song-taek, Kim Ki-nam, and Choe Tae-bok. On the other side of the hearse were the military representatives—GSD Chief Ri Yong-ho, Minister of People's Armed Forces Kim Yong-chun, General Political Bureau (GPB) First Vice Director Kim Jong-gak, and SSD First Vice Director U Tong-chuk.

Image 2: Kim and cohorts surround Kim Jong-il's hearse
(Source: KCNA, 28 December 2014)

Upon returning to the Kumsusan Palace, the hearse was met by O Kuk-ryol, other members of the leadership, and members of the Kim family, including Kim Yo-jong. The 105-minute ceremony had come to an end.

2. TRANSITIONAL LEADERSHIP

In the days after Kim Jong-il's death, the leadership configuration that would shepherd in the new regime came into focus. It seemed to be made up of several rings with ties to the Party and the high command. The inner core was composed of several gatekeepers who presumably had some involvement in decision-making:

- **Vice Marshal Ri Yong-ho**, Chief of the GSD, had operational control over the armed forces. A longtime associate of the Kim family, he oversaw one of the key support groups within the military that supported Kim Jong-un. This group was made up of officers in their 50s and 60s, generally considered to be the rising stars among the field commanders and high command. Many Pyongyang-watchers presumed that Vice Marshal Ri would be instrumental in keeping the military in check during the transition period.

- **General Jang Song-taek**, who had oversight of the internal security apparatus and the economy, was well situated to support Kim Jong-un in running the daily operations of the regime. He was well-versed in both policy execution and the machinations revolving around personnel appointments that would be critical for Kim Jong-un's power consolidation.[13]

- **General Kim Kyong-hui** jumped from 14th to fifth in the formal leadership rankings between her brother's death on December 17, 2011 and the final mourning ceremonies. She would likely play an advisory role and serve as a key arbitrator within the Kim family as well as the wider North Korean leadership.

- **General O Kuk-ryol** was a long-time Kim family loyalist. He, too, jumped within the power rankings from 29th to 13th. His primary responsibility would be to ensure regime stability. His input into decision-making would likely be limited, but his opinion could carry weight in deliberations involving tradeoffs between reform and security.

- **Kim Ki-nam** was Director of the KWP Propaganda and Agitation Department (PAD). He had forty-five years of experience in propaganda and masterminded the personality cult surrounding the Kim dynasty. Under his watch, the KWP PAD directed much of the

---

13   Jang Song-taek's special status within the leadership came into focus on December 26, 2011, when he appeared on state television as part of the mourning ceremonies at Kumsusan Memorial Palace. He was dressed in full military uniform as a four-star general for the first time. Until then, Jang had only been spotted in a suit and tie. Kim Jong-un and Kim Kyong-hui had already been promoted to four-star generals on the eve of the Third Party Conference in 2010.

choreography of the transfer of power, including the grooming of the heir apparent in the image of his grandfather, Kim Il-sung.

- **Choe Tae-bok** was Chairman of the SPA. He worked in education and science, and was likely entrusted with technological development. After Kim Jong-un was appointed as successor, North Korean media suddenly began to highlight science and technology. They began praising Kim Jong-un for fostering what it quaintly referred to as computerized numerical control (CNC). This was the new leader's own brand, in the same way that Kim Il-sung had the "Self-Reliance" (*Juche*) doctrine and Kim Jong-il had the "Military First" (*Songun*) policy.

The outer ring of this leadership configuration was apparently centered in the KWP CMC, which was made up of key second- and third-generation military and security officials from across the regime. Kim Jong-il's reinvigoration of the CMC at the Third Party Conference in 2010 had placed this body on par with the NDC in terms of reach and influence. Pyongyang-watchers believed that the CMC would most likely replace the NDC as the command post of "Military First" (*Songun*) politics under Kim Jong-un. It would be responsible for crafting the "Great Successor's" image, garnering loyalty towards the new regime, and running the country. In terms of Kim's relationship with the military, three CMC members were particularly crucial during the transition period. All three members accompanied Kim Jong-un as he escorted his father's hearse through the streets of Pyongyang:

- **Vice Marshal Kim Yong-chun**, Minister of the People's Armed Forces, oversaw the logistics and training of the military. Along with Jang Song-taek, he would serve as a key conduit to the NDC. In addition, he had past service in the KWP OGD and the KPA GPB, which gave him invaluable experience in detecting potential disloyalty within the armed forces. In this regard, his surveillance reportedly contributed to foiling a coup attempt by the Sixth Corps in the mid-1990s.[14]

---

14   The Sixth Corps incident refers to an attempted coup d'état by forces in North Hamgyong Province in 1996. The coup plot was led by political committee members and included commanders of battalions. The chief secretary of North Hamgyong Province, administrative cadres, vice directors of the provincial SSD, and other cadres were implicated. The group was apparently planning to start an uprising in North Hamgyong Province first and then head for Pyongyang. However, the plan was discovered by the MSC (with support from Kim Yong-chun, who helped oversee the dismantlement of the corps) and the ringleaders were rounded up. According to some sources, around forty were executed and a further 300 severely punished.

- **General Kim Jong-gak** was the acting head of the KPA G[...] sibility he assumed with the death of Jo Myong-rok. Accor[...] North Korean leadership protocol during the Kim Jong-il [...] director of the GPB, which is the lead agency for ensuring Pa[...] over the military, was the de facto third-ranking member in the command behind the heads of the MPAF and the GSD.

- **General U Tong-chuk**, First Vice Director of the SSD, oversaw the country's powerful secret police. General U was a leading member of a key support group for Kim Jong-un that was composed of general officers within the security services.

Other individuals with military/security portfolios also stood out and should be mentioned: O Il-jong (Director of the KWP Military Department); Kim Kyong-ok (First Vice Director for Security Affairs at the OGD); and Choe Ryong-hae (KWP Secretary for Military Affairs).[15] They had important roles to play in monitoring the loyalty of the armed forces and ensuring a smooth transition. They would also be critical in creating and facilitating a unified and centralized Party guidance system that would invest the "Great Successor" with the ideological authority that he would need to rule. However, initial media coverage did not suggest that they would be within Kim Jong-un's inner circle.

3. Purges, Demotions, and Promotions

There were significant changes over the next four months. Most striking was the fate of several leaders who accompanied Kim Jong-un alongside his father's hearse.[16] In March 2012, the South Korean press began to note that U Tong-chuk had not been seen in public since February.[17] Then, it was reported that he had

---

15   It is worth noting that Choe Ryong-hae, while being the son of a former minister of defense, lacked any background in military and security affairs. His promotion to four-star general and appointment to the Secretariat with a military portfolio was likely due to his ties to the Kim family, not his experience.

16   Lee Yong-Su, "North Korea's Kim Jong Un Replaces All of the Military Gang of Four Who Escorted Kim Jong Il's Hearse," *The Chosun Ilbo*, November 30, 2012.

17   Kim Hee-Jin, "In First Year, Taming The Army Was Kim's Goal," *Korea JoongAng Daily*, 17 December 2012. U Tong-chuk was last seen at the celebration of the Day of the Shining Star (Kim Il-il's birthday) on February 16. U was removed from the NDC in April 2012. Although not mentioned publicly, South Korean intelligence sources told the media that he was also removed from his Party positions in the Politburo and CMC at the Fourth Party Conference.

suffered a stroke.[18, 19] A month later on the eve of the Fourth Party Conference, Kim Yong-chun was relieved of his duties as Minister of the People's Armed Forces and given the less prestigious role as Director of the KWP Department for Civil Defense.[20] He was replaced by another member of the funeral procession, Kim Jong-gak, whose stature within the regime appeared to be on the rise in the months after Kim Jong-il's death.

At the Fourth Party Conference in April 2012, it became apparent that the leadership that had been in place when Kim Jong-il died would not remain static. The Politburo was altered. Four members moved up significantly and seven others were apparently removed. The major winner was Choe Ryong-hae, who rose from alternate Politburo status to a member of the Presidium. He was also made a Vice Chairman of the CMC. Shortly before the meeting, Choe was promoted to Vice Marshal and put in charge of the GPB, filling the post left vacant by Jo Myong-rok's death.[21]

The Fourth Party Conference had one obvious loser—Vice Marshal Ri Yong-ho, the Chief of the GSD. After rising dramatically through the leadership ranks at the Third Party Conference, he received no promotions or appointments. This led to many questions about his status, which were answered in July with the most visible purge within the high command in years. Vice Marshal Ri Yong-ho was removed from all of his posts, including member of the Politburo Presidium and Vice Chairman of the KWP CMC.[22] The *KCNA* announcement, which attributed

---

18   Kim Seung-Jae, "Kim Jong Un's Closest Confidant U Tong-chuk Collapsed From Cerebral Hemorrhage," *YTN*, April 29, 2012.
19   Lee Young-Jong and Lee Eun-Joo, "Weighing The Fall of Clique of U and Ri," *Korea JoongAng Daily*, July 23, 2012. There is a more nefarious story regarding U Tong-chuk's disappearance. According to South Korean intelligence sources, 69-year-old U emerged in September 2009 when Kim Jong-un was officially rising as the next leader of North Korea. Whether on Kim Jong-il's orders or on his own initiative, U began to construct a secret file on various North Korean leaders who could inhibit the heir apparent's rise to power. When Kim Kyong-hui learned of this secret file after her brother's death, she was surprised and apparently dismayed. She and her husband, Jang Song-taek, supposedly took measures to replace U and place the day-to-day control of the SSD (MSS) in the hands of Kim Won-hong.
20   Author's discussions in Seoul, 2012 and 2013. Kim Yong-chun, while having been demoted, retained a key position within the regime. He was trusted by the Kim family for his past service. In 1995, Kim, with the support of Jang Song-taek (as First Vice Director of the KWP OGD), suppressed the attempted coup d'état by the Sixth Corps. This formed a bond between the two. Even though Kim lost his portfolio as Minister of People's Armed Forces, the de facto number two position in the military, he retained his posts on the Politburo and the CMC, and that of Vice Chairman of the NDC.
21   Other winners included Kim Won-hong, Kim Jong-gak, Pak To-chun, and Hyon Chol-hae. Kim Won-hong, the new head of the SSD, and Hyon Chol-hae, Vice Minister of the People's Armed Forces, were appointed to full Politburo status. Kim Jong-gak, the new Minister of the People's Armed Forces, and Pak To-chun, KWP Secretary for Defense Industry, moved from alternate to full status in the Politburo.
22   The first indication that Ri's position was in trouble came in the weeks following Kim Jong-il's death. Ri figured prominently at the funeral ceremonies, walking alongside the hearse. However, rumors began to surface of Ri's growing appetite for power and his jaundiced view of Kim Jong-un as a viable Supreme Leader. Long considered an ally of Jang Song-taek, Ri was now increasingly described

his removal from power to illness, did not refer to his position as Chief of the GSD. However, the appointment of Hyon Yong-chol to this post made it clear that Ri no longer was a member of the high command.[23] Later reports suggested that Ri's dismissal was due to his opposition to the June 2012 economic measures and the transfer of various hard currency operations from the military to the Cabinet.[24] This was a clear move to shift away from "Military First" (*Songun*) politics, which had served as the operational doctrine for the regime under Kim Jong-il.[25] Rumors appeared in late 2012, indicating that Ri was currently under house arrest somewhere in North Hamgyong Province.[26]

In November 2012, an even more surprising reshuffle occurred when Vice Marshal Kim Jong-gak was replaced as Minister of the People's Armed Forces by General Kim Kyok-sik, a Vice Chief of the GSD. Kim Jong-gak, while a fixture

---

by many Pyongyang-watchers as a competitor for influence over Kim Jong-un. Whether accurate or not, these stories spread quickly in the aftermath of the April 2012 leadership events in which Ri received no promotions, not even to the NDC, the one leadership body to which he did not belong. In addition, the new head of the GPB, Choe Ryong-hae, surpassed Ri in the formal rankings as he assumed key positions in the Politburo, the CMC, and the NDC. The GSD was no longer seen as the pre-eminent military body. It now took a back seat to the organization responsible for political indoctrination and ensuring the loyalty of the armed forces. Ri Yong-ho, however, continued to appear in public and even participated in the annual memorial ceremony commemorating Kim-Il-sung's death on July 8, 2012.

23   General Hyon Yong-chol's rise was closely linked with Kim Jong-un's rise. He had almost no public profile before September 2010 when he was promoted, along with Kim Jong-un, to four-star general. He appeared on the state Funeral Committees for Kim Jong-il and Jo Myong-rok. At the Central Committee Plenum in March 2013, he was appointed to the Politburo as an alternate member.

24   The so-called June Measures allegedly evolved out of a speech Kim Jong-un gave to the Party leadership on June 28, 2012. They were circulated at a meeting of the SPA. The measures touch on changes in the agricultural, mining, and industrial sectors. In agriculture, the government appears to be taking its cue from the first phase of the Chinese reform experience, reducing the size of work teams on state-run farms from ten to twenty-five people to only four to six. Reports have also suggested that the government will fix the state's take of the harvest. In effect, this could grant farmers fixed-rent tenancy, under which they would have full ownership rights on production exceeding their quotas. In industry, the measures reportedly allow state-owned enterprises to retain 30 percent of their earnings—again, a crucial reform of incentives. The government might also permit private investments in joint ventures with state entities, as long as they are appropriately registered.

25   "Top NK General Ousted For Debating Economic Reform," *Dong-A Ilbo*, July 31, 2012. According to defectors associated with *NK Intellectuals Solidarity*, a research organization formed by North Korean defectors in South Korea, Ri Yong-ho was purged at a meeting of the Politburo on July 15, 2012. At the meeting, there was a heated discussion on the "New Economic Reconstruction Policy," specifically on transferring economic projects from the Party and military to the Cabinet, and reducing of the number of workers at collective farms, among other issues. Jang Song-taek was briefing the policy when Ri pushed back, saying, "The policy is an ill-advised idea that denies the socialist principles that our previous supreme leaders followed and seeks to introduce capitalism instead. It is a plot aimed at funneling funds for modernization of the military for revolution to other uses." Jang responded by saying that the policy was formulated under Kim Jong-un's direct guidance and accused Ri of challenging Kim's leadership. Kim Jong-un then stood up and stripped Ri of his title and rank on the spot and had him arrested, saying, "I cannot work for revolution with someone who doesn`t follow me."

26   "Kim Jong-un Still Trying to Get Control of The Military," *The Chosun Ilbo*, November 19, 2012.

at the GPB in the Kim Jong-il era, began to rise within the high command soon after Kim Jong-un became heir apparent. He was appointed an alternate member of the Politburo and member of the KWP CMC at the Third Party Conference in 2010. On April 10, 2012, the eve of the Fourth Party Conference, he was appointed Minister of the People's Armed Forces, replacing Kim Yong-chun. In the days that followed, at the Fourth Party Conference and SPA, Kim was made a full member of the Politburo and a member of the NDC. His rank within the leadership rose from 24th to seventh. He was one of several officers with ties to the GPB to be appointed to high office, leading to speculations that Kim Jong-un was setting up a counterweight to Ri Yong-ho within the high command.[27] He was included in a growing clique of younger-generation military officers and Party cadre tied to Jang Song-taek.[28] At a ceremonial wreath-laying before the anti-Japanese revolutionary Cho Kwang-su's statue on October 30, 2012, North Korean media suddenly stopped referring to Kim Jong-gak by his title of Minister of the People's Armed Forces, simply referring to him as "comrade Kim Jong-gak." Kim then disappeared from public view until December 17, 2012. He was mentioned as part of the delegation that accompanied Kim Jong-un and his wife, Ri Sol-ju, to the renovated Kumsusan Palace of the Sun to pay respects to Kim Jong-il on the first anniversary of his death.[29] While Kim lost his seat on the NDC at the Seventh Session of the 12th SPA in April 2013,[30] he continues to attend leadership functions and is rumored to currently hold the post of President of Kim Il-sung Military University, a trusted position from which to educate and influence the upcoming generation of military leaders.[31, 32]

27   "NK Names Armed Forces Minister to Keep Army Chief in Check," *Dong-A Ilbo*, April 12, 2012.
28   Author's interviews in Seoul, November 2012. Kim Jong-gak's ties to Jang Song-taek were more as a cohort than a protégé. Both entered the Politburo as alternate members at the Third Party Conference. Pyongyang-watchers did not tie Kim to Jang's patronage system, but assessed that Jang controlled Kim through his position as Vice Chairman of the NDC.
29   "Kim Jong Un Pays Respects to Kim Jong Il," *KCNA*, December 17, 2012. At this event, it was revealed that Kim Jong-gak had been reduced in rank to general. At a sports match on April 16, 2013, Kim Jong-gak again wore the rank of Vice Marshal. See also "Appearance of former Minister of People's Armed Forces Kim Jong-gak in Nodong Sinmun Photo Draws Attention," *Yonhap News Agency*, April 16, 2013.
30   *KCNA*, April 1, 2013. While not disclosed by North Korean media, it was assumed that Kim Jong-gak also lost his Politburo position and possibly his CMC position. This assumption was based on his fall in the leadership rankings.
31   "Appearance of former Minister of People's Armed Forces Kim Jong-gak in Nodong Sinmun Photo Draws Attention," *Yonhap News Agency*, op. cit.
32   Given Kim Jong-gak's low profile since his demotion as the Minister of the People's Armed Forces, it was surprising to see him on the leadership rostrum during the 70th anniversary of the founding of the Party on October 10, 2015. This could be an indication that his career will be resurrected.

There was a great deal of speculation within Pyongyang-watching circles regarding these purges of military leaders in 2012.[33] One theory was that Kim Jong-un was trying to bring the high command under the Party's control. Another was that he was paving the way for what would likely be unpopular economic measures.[34] These may have been collateral motives, but an analysis of the high command appointments in 2012 suggests that Kim Jong-un was replacing those parts of the military leadership that were particularly close to his father. He put into place officers who owed their loyalty to him and with whom he had close relationships.[35] Under both Kim Il-sung and Kim Jong-il, the heads of the GSD, MPAF, and GPB were critical to controlling the military. Kim Jong-un, working closely with Kim Kyong-hui and Jang Song-taek, engineered the most sensitive move within the high command when he appointed Choe Ryong-hae as Director of the GPB. Choe's elevation at the Fourth Party Conference to the Presidium of the Politburo and Vice Chairman of the CMC placed the GPB ahead of the MPAF and GSD in the high command's hierarchy, setting the subsequent changes into motion.

Kim Jong-un chose Ri Yong-ho's replacement, Hyon Yong-chol, from obscurity, likely with Choe Ryong-hae's support. Hyon's rise from Eighth Corps Commander to Chief of the GSD suggested close ties to the center of the regime. His rise through the ranks began in 2010 with the announcement of his promotion to four-star general alongside Kim Jong-un, Kim Kyong-hui, and Choe Ryong-hae. He was ranked 83rd on the funeral list for Jo Myong-rok, former Director of the GPB, and 77th on the funeral list for Kim Jong-il. He also received the Order of Kim Jong-il as part of the ceremonies commemorating the late leader's 70th birthday in February 2011. He was promoted to Vice Marshal only days before Kim Jong-un received the title of Marshal at the end of July 2012.[36]

While it predated Kim Jong-un's appointment as heir apparent, Kim Kyok-sik's career was tied to the succession. He was apparently demoted in February

---

33   According to South Korean sources, thirty-one senior-level military officers had been demoted or removed from their posts since Kim Jong-un came into power.

34   Park Chan-Kyong, "Kim Eyes Reform in Purge of N. Korea Old Guard," *AFP*, July 19, 2012.

35   It should be noted that even Kim Jong-un's apparent appointees were not beyond punishment. Choe Ryong-hae was demoted from Vice Marshal to General in December 2012 and re-promoted to Vice Marshal in February 2013. Hyon Yong-chol was demoted from Vice Marshal to General in October 2012. Kim Yong-chol was demoted from General to Colonel (or Lieutenant) General in 2012 and re-promoted to General in February 2013. It was rumored that Choe Pu-il, the recently appointed Minister of People's Security, was demoted from General to Colonel General in 2012. In April 2013, he was again listed as a General.

36   *KCNA* announced Kim Jong-un's appointment as Marshal on July 18, 2012, one day after Hyon Yong-chol's promotion to Vice Marshal. For reasons still unclear, Hyon was demoted to a four-star General in October 2012.

2009 from Chief of the GSD to Commander of the Fourth Corps, one month after Kim Jong-un was announced as heir apparent within the North Korean leadership. Nevertheless, Kim Kyok-sik oversaw the operations tied to the heir apparent's rise to power. From his position as Commander of the Western Front, Kim Kyok-sik may have played a role in both the sinking of the *Cheonan* and the shelling of Yeonpyeong Island. The first event was critical to the succession and the second was designed to bolster Kim Jong-un's credentials as a military leader.[37] Between these two events, he was made an alternate member of the KWP Central Committee at the Third Party Conference in September 2010. In November 2011, he returned to the GSD as Vice Chief. According to defector sources, following Kim Jong-il's death, he also moved into Kim Jong-un's Personal Secretariat as a military advisor, a position he held until taking over the MPAF.[38] At the Central Committee Plenum and SPA in 2013, he was made an alternate member of the Politburo and a member of the NDC.

As noted above, the reshuffle extended beyond the military leadership to include senior officers responsible for internal security. Kim Won-hong's rise through the ranks began shortly after Kim Jong-un's designation as heir apparent. In February 2009, Kim Won-hong, the previous Commander of the Military Security Command (MSC), became the Director of the Organization Bureau of the KPA GPB as part of Kim Jong-il's plan to build support for his successor within the military elites. At the Third Party Conference, he was appointed to the KWP CMC. On the eve of the Fourth Party Conference, Kim Won-hong was identified as the Director of State Security (Minister of State Security).[39] At this Party Conference and the subsequent SPA meeting, Kim Won-hong became a full member of the Politburo and a member of the NDC.[40]

In 2013, appointments to the military and security leadership took an unexpected and complicated turn. Officers who had just emerged in key positions in 2012 were replaced. Kim Jong-un and his regents reorganized the military leadership, bringing a mix of trusted officers and a new generation to the forefront of the high

---

37   While it was the prevailing view among Pyongyang-watchers that Kim Kyok-sik had knowledge of the operational planning regarding the sinking of the *Cheonan*, there is little evidence to suggest that he had direct operational involvement. At most, he was aware of the operation in order to respond to any South Korean retaliation. The operation itself was most likely overseen by the Reconnaissance General Bureau (RGB).

38   Author's interview in Seoul, April 2013.

39   Kim Won-hong's appointment as head of the SSD was significant because North Korean media had previously avoided publicly identifying the official in charge of the secret police.

40   Author's interviews in Seoul, 2012 and 2013. According to some sources, Kim Won-hong's exponential rise is due to the influence of Kim Kyong-hui, not Kim Jong-un. His role within the internal security apparatus suggests Jang Song-taek's influence as well.

command.[41] One long-trusted officer was Choe Pu-il, whose ties to the Kim family date back to the early Kim Jong-il era. Choe was appointed Minister of People's Security, replacing Ri Myong-su. At the Third Party Conference, Choe was made a member of the KWP CMC, to which Kim Jong-un was appointed Vice Chairman.[42] At the Central Committee Plenum on March 31, 2013, Choe was elevated to alternate member of the Politburo. Two days later at the SPA, he was appointed a member of the NDC.

Colonel General Ri Yong-gil was identified by North Korean media as the Director of the GSD Operations Bureau in March 2013.[43, 44] He appeared in a photograph of a briefing that Kim Jong-un was receiving on operations associated with the evolving March/April crisis.[45][46] Ri's name first appeared in North Korean media with the announcement of his promotion to Lieutenant General as part of the April 2002 promotion list. It is rumored that he assumed command of the Third Corps, which is one of the operational units directly responsible for the protection of Pyongyang.[47] Like Choe Pu-il, Ri Yong-gil was made an alternate member of the Central Committee at the Third Party Conference. Before his current posting, Ri

---

41   In 2012 and 2013, the demographics of the high command began to shift. Flag officers in their 60s and older were almost, but not entirely, supplanted. At the same time, the appointments appeared to signify a move in favor of military leaders with field experience.

42   According to South Korea's Ministry of Unification, Choe was demoted in October 2012 from General to Colonel General. It was speculated that this was connected to the defection of a North Korean soldier stationed near the Kaesong Industrial Complex. This was also tied to Hyon Yong-chol's demotion. Choe's official biography, released at the time of his appointment to Minister of People's Security, did not mention this demotion.

43   *Nodong Sinmun*, March 29, 2013. It was not clear when Ri assumed the post of Director of the Operations Bureau.

44   Jeong Yong-Soo, "To Curb Jang Song-taek's Influence, Kim Jong-un Completely Reshuffles Core of the Military," *Korea JoongAng Daily*, July 3, 2012. According to some sources, Kim Myong-guk was replaced as Director in 2012. Some reports stated that he had been replaced by Choe Pu-il. Therefore, Ri replaced either Kim Myong-kuk in 2012 or Choe Pu-il in 2013.

45   The story associated with the picture lists three-star Colonel General Ri Yong-gil as the Director of the Operations Bureau. Previously, North Korean media had never identified a current occupant of this position. The only time the Operations Bureau was mentioned was in profiles of officers who had held the position in the past. This story was also the first time that North Korean media identified the existence of the RGB and its Director General Kim Yong-chol, and of the Strategic Rocket Forces (SRF) and its Commander, Lieutenant General Kim Rak-gyom.

46   The March/April crisis refers to the tension and escalation that surrounded the Korean Peninsula in the spring of 2013. In response to the annual Foal Eagle/Key Resolve combined U.S.-ROK military exercises, North Korea raised tensions on the peninsula and threatened provocations.

47   The Third Corps, along with the Pyongyang Defense Command, plays important Praetorian Guard functions and is dedicated to the protection of the capital. As such, both commands are headed by politically reliable commanders with ties to the senior leadership. If Ri was a Commander of the Third Corps, it suggests that he has had long-standing ties with the Kim family.

had been the Fifth Corps Commander from 2007 to 2012.[48] He was cast in the limelight when he spoke at the Military Loyalty Pledge for Kim Jong-un, held on the one-year anniversary of Kim Jong-il's death. His name also appeared alongside Choe's in the Kim Jong-il Funeral Committee list.[49]

At the end of the March/April crisis, three additional changes occurred in the high command. First, Colonel General Pyon In-son, the Commander of the Fourth Corps, was replaced by Ri Song-guk. Pyon had steadily climbed up the military ranks for two decades, becoming a Vice Minister of the People's Armed Forces in 2010. He took command of the Fourth Corps at the end of 2011. He also became a member of the KWP Central Committee in 2010 and his name appeared on both the Jo Myong-rok and the Kim Jong-il Funeral Committee lists. This suggested that his ties to the regime were established in the period during the emergence of Kim Jong-un as the successor.[50] He also had a high profile during the March/April crisis, accompanying Kim Jong-un on a visit to the two islets in the West Sea, something that could have contributed to his removal.[51] On July 25, 2013, North Korean media, in a report of wreath-laying for fallen Chinese fighters, noted that Pyon had returned to his post of Vice Minister of the People's Armed Forces.[52] In August 2013, he was identified as the Director of the GSD Operations Bureau.[53]

Not much was known about Ri Song-guk when he replaced Pyon. His only previous appearance in North Korean media was when he accompanied Kim

---

48   In the Kim Jong-un era, the Fifth Corps seems to be a way station for military leaders coming from and returning to the senior leadership. In addition to Ri, Hyon Yong-chol was demoted from Chief of the General Staff to commander of the Fifth Corps before returning to the senior leadership as Minister of the People's Armed Forces in 2014. Jang Jong-nam, when he was replaced by Hyon, was demoted to commander of the Fifth Corps.

49   KCNA, December 19 2011. Colonel General Ri Yong-gil was also a member of the Jo Myong-rok Funeral Committee.

50   However, Pyon In-son fell outside of the generational cohort that Kim Jong-un appeared to be trying to bring into the high command. He became a Lieutenant General in 1997 and a Colonel General in 2003, when he took command of the Seventh Corps. He was also a delegate to the 11th and 12th SPAs, which suggests that his ties to Pyongyang were developed before Kim Jong-un became heir apparent.

51   Initial analysis showed that the regime appeared to be reshuffling commanders tied to the more strident actions that the regime took in the recent past. The fact that Pyon In-son and Kim Kyok-sik were replaced within days of the end of the March/April crisis suggested that the regime wanted to move in other policy directions—diplomatic and economic—without being weighed down by recent events. Kim Kyok-sik's appointment as Chief of the GSD called this analysis into question.

52   "Wreaths Laid Before Cemetery of Fallen Fighters of CPV," KCNA, July 26, 2013.

53   This timeline is based on Ri Yong-gil's appointment as Chief of the GSD, leaving the Operations Bureau post vacant. In addition, film footage of the military parade and demonstration on the 65th anniversary of the country's founding on September 9, 2013 shows a KPA officer who resembles Colonel General Pyon briefing Kim Jong-un during the Worker-Peasant Red Guards' parade, a position normally reserved for the Director of the Operations Bureau.

Jong-un at a live-fire exercise aimed in the direction of South Korean islands in the West Sea in March 2013.[54] Due to the fact that the Fourth Corps is in charge of an area that could be a flashpoint in inter-Korean relations, he is, presumably, a third-generation military leader with considerable operational experience.[55]

At a performance of the Korean People's Internal Security Forces' Dance Ensemble on May 13, 2013, Colonel General Jang Jong-nam was identified as the new Minister of People's Armed Forces, replacing General Kim Kyok-sik.[56] This was the third appointment to this post in little over a year.[57] Jang Jong-nam was the former Commander of the First Corps, which is responsible for guarding the front lines in Gangwon Province.[58] This continued a series of appointments designed to bring a new generation into the high command.[59] He was one of four corps commanders to speak at a loyalty rally of KPA service members and officers on the one-year anniversary of Kim Jong-il's death.[60, 61] He also spoke at a Party-army solidarity rally in July 2011, three months after he was promoted to Lieutenant General on Kim Il-sung's birthday in April 2011.[62]

---

54   *KCNA*, March 14, 2013.

55   Jeong Yong-Soo, "North Replaces Commander of Key Frontline Unit," *Korea JoongAng Daily*, April 30, 2013.

56   Kim Kyok-sik was last mentioned as Minister of the People's Armed Forces in a Pyongyang radio report on April 23, 2013 about a banquet to commemorate the eighty-first founding anniversary of the KPA. Given the fact that he was appointed to both the Politburo and NDC in 2013, his removal from the MPAF was obviously not tied to issues of loyalty.

57   According to one source, the fact that the MPAF had four ministers since the beginning of 2012 (Kim Yong-chun, Kim Jong-gak, Kim Kyok-sik, and Jang Jong-nam) may have been an indication that the senior ranks of the armed forces were unstable.

58   According to North Korean media, Jang Jong-nam was promoted to a one-star General (Major General) in 2002 and two-star general (Lieutenant General) in 2011. At the performance on May 13, 2013, the photograph shows Jang with three stars (Colonel General) on his epaulets.

59   Jang Jong-nam was in his 50s, while Kim Kyok-sik was 75.

60   Many in the international media speculated that Kim Kyok-sik was removed because he was "hawkish." This was a fundamental misreading of the North Korean high command, where "hawkishness" is a matter of degree. Corps commanders have been highly indoctrinated, especially those from the third generation such as Jang Jong-nam. At a massive rally in Pyongyang in July 2011, Jang spoke forcefully against what the regime believed were provocations by South Korea: "Now that South Korean confrontation maniacs without equals in the world dared to perpetrate such extreme provocations as not ruling out even a war against the DPRK, there remains between the North and the South only physical settlement of returning fire for fire." See "Massive N. Korean Crowd Takes Part in Rally Against S. Korea," *Yonhap News Agency*, July 4, 2011.

61   Mo Gyu-Yeop, "Kim Jong-un Replaces More Than Half of Corps Commanders Over Four Months in 2013," *Kukmin Ilbo*, August 8, 2013. It should be noted that, according to some sources, at least four corps commanders (First, Second, Fourth, and Fifth Corps) have been replaced since the beginning of 2013. Most of this reshuffle was tied to the senior-level appointments made at the end of April and the beginning of May 2013.

62   "N. Korea Replaces Hawkish Armed Forces Minister," *Yonhap News Agency*, May 13, 2013. Like Ri Yong-gil, Jang Jong-nam was promoted to Major General in April 2002. This suggests that Kim

Days after Jang Jong-nam was identified as the new Minister of the People's Armed Forces,[63] North Korean media identified Colonel General Jon Chang-bok as the new First Vice Minister during coverage of Kim Jong-un's visit to the February 20 Foodstuffs Factory of the KPA.[64] Jon replaced Vice Marshal Hyon Chol-hae, long-time Kim family associate and Kim Jong-il military aide.[65] Hyon had been appointed First Vice Minister and Director of the KPA General Logistics Department (GLD) in April 2012 and elevated to full membership in the Politburo and the CMC.[66] Jon Chang-bok was Hyon's predecessor as Director of the KPA GLD and, in August 2011,[67] he led a delegation of KPA logistical personnel to China and held talks with Defense Minister Liang Guanglie.

In media accounts of "special envoy" (*teuk-sa*) Choe Ryong-hae's departure for China on May 22, 2013, Kim Kyok-sik was identified as the Chief of the GSD, replacing Hyon Yong-chol, who became the Commander of the Fifth Corps.[68] Kim held this position from 2007 to 2009, when he was moved out of Pyongyang to take over the Fourth Corps. This move, while highly unusual, appeared to bring to a close the reorganization of the high command that began with Ri Yong-ho's dismissal. Hyon Yong-chol was most likely a placeholder until Kim Jong-un felt comfortable enough in his relations with the military to put his close aide, Kim Kyok-sik, into place. In addition, if the regime decided to shift away from "Military-First" (*Songun*) and toward diplomacy and economic development, having a noted hardliner with Kim Kyok-sik's operational credentials as head of the GSD, to compensate for Choe Ryong-hae's lack of credentials, would make it harder for

---

Jong-un is drawing from the cohort of officers in their 50s, 60s, and the third generation to staff the high command.

63   Jon Chang-bok's profile began to rise in 2010 when Kim Jong-un made his official debut. He was promoted to Colonel General in April 2010, and in September of that year, he was made a member of the Central Committee of the KWP. He was a member of both the Jo Myong-rok and the Kim Jong-il Funeral Committees. He began to accompany Kim Jong-un on visits to military and economic units in April 2012.

64   *KCNA*, May 16, 2013. See also No Jae-Hyeon, "North Korea Replaces Vice Minister of Defense," *Yonhap News Agency*, May 17, 2013.

65   "North Korea replaces Vice Minister of People's Armed Forces," *The Chosun Ilbo*, May 17, 2013. There is only one first vice minister in North Korean ministries. Therefore, it appears that Hyon Chol-hae might have retired. South Korean reports suggest that Hyon Chol-hae was replaced for health reasons. However, he continued to appear at leadership functions.

66   Hyon (81) was regarded as one of the North's top military figures who helped support Kim Jong-un following the death of Kim Jong-il.

67   Jon Chang-bok was Director of the GLD from August 2011 to April 2012.

68   *KCBS*, May 22, 2013.

the military to push back.[69] However, it did raise a question about the relationship between Kim and Choe Ryong-hae.

In August 2013, the saga revolving around the post of Chief of the GSD continued when indications surfaced in North Korean media that Kim Kyok-sik had been replaced by Ri Yong-gil. In a report about a soccer match on August 29, 2013, attended by Kim Jong-un and the leadership, Ri Yong-gil was listed fourth, after Jang Song-taek and before Minister of the People's Armed Forces Jang Jong-nam. This position is normally reserved for the head of the GSD.[70] Kim Kyok-sik was not identified as one of those in attendance. Additionally, Ri Yong-gil and Jang Jong-nam were shown wearing four stars, the appropriate ranks for the Chief of the GSD and Minister of the People's Armed Forces.[71] While the reason for this apparent reshuffle was the subject of widespread speculation in South Korean media, it did not appear to be the result of a purge.[72] It suggested that Kim Jong-un was continuing to populate the formal political and military leadership with individuals who owed their allegiance directly to him. At the same time, he moved more senior leaders, who had ties to both him and his father, into the background. If this were true, Kim Kyok-sik would most likely continue to play a vital role as an advisor behind the scenes, possibly within Kim Jong-un's Personal Secretariat.[73]

---

69   The return of Kim Kyok-sik to the GSD, albeit temporarily, served as notice that the regime intended to be much more aggressive in controlling the operational commands, where much of the pushback came from the aftermath of the Ri Yong-ho dismissal. It was unclear whether Hyon Yong-chol had the gravitas and influence throughout the high command to enforce such control.

70   Park Seong-Guk, "Lee Young Gil On The Rise," *Daily NK*, August 30, 2013. According to one senior Pyongyang-watcher, "In North Korea, the listing of chief-of-staff and armed forces minister could be flipped, but there is no way the director of operations should be mentioned before the minister."

71   *Korean Central Television* (*KCTV*), August 29, 2013.

72   This speculation is supported by the fact that Kim Kyok-sik attended the CMC meeting that took place earlier in August 2013. He was seated in the first row of military leaders next to Jang Jong-nam.

73   Kim Kyok-sik's removal from such a prominent position within the high command could also assist in the regime's diplomatic outreach, which was probably undermined by his association with the events of 2010.

4. Civil-Military Relations by Mid-2013

By mid-2013, Kim Jong-un's control over the military was still debatable.[74] He oversaw a reorganization of the high command that appeared to unfold in two stages. In 2012, officers seen as obstructive or more loyal to Kim Jong-il than to Kim Jong-un were replaced. This was followed in 2013 by reappointments to critical positions as well as the continuation of bringing officers with allegiance to Kim Jong-un into the high command. These moves challenged rumors about Kim Jong-un being controlled by the military, especially in the wake of the March/April crisis. Moreover, there were no overt signs of disloyalty within the high command.

The removal of members of the high command and appointments of relatively unknown and politically weak officers seemed to bolster the power of the GPB, which is responsible for ensuring the high command's loyalty to the Party and Supreme Leader.[75] Appointing trusted aides, such as Kim Kyok-sik, would not only ensure a politically astute command and control mechanism over operational forces,[76] but would also allow Kim Jong-un to build relationships with the second- and third-level members of the officer corps with the GSD's assistance. This was critical because if Kim Jong-un were ever to fully assume the role of Supreme Leader, he would need the unwavering support of the military.[77]

---

74   There are several patronage systems that make up the high command. These systems are headed by officers close to the Kim family. At the beginning of the Kim Jong-un regime, the major patronage systems were tied to O Kuk-ryol, Hyon Chol-hae, Ri Yong-mu, and, to a lesser extent, Ri Yong-ho. Before his purge, some argued that Jang Song-taek, vis-à-vis his late brothers who were military officers, also had a patronage system. If this speculation was true, Kim Jong-un, perhaps with Jang Song-taek's support, may have dismantled the patronage systems tied to Hyon Chol-hae and Ri Yong-ho. Ri Yong-mu has been retired in place for years, and his patronage system may have diminished. The important question is whether O Kuk-ryol has been marginalized or remains a critical player inside the regime. The South Korean Pyongyang-watching community is sharply divided on this issue.

75   Cheong Seong-Chang, *DPRK Leadership Under Kim Jong-un* (Seoul: Sejong Institute, 2012). According to several sources, Kim Jong-un and his advisors were thrown off balance by the blowback from the purge of Ri Yong-ho. This accounts for the lack of follow-through with the June Economic Measures in 2012 and the spike in references to the "Military First" (*Songun*) in North Korean media.

76   While Kim Kyok-sik disappeared from public view, it is likely that he continued to wield influence from the shadows.

77   Stephan Haggard, "Military Promotions in the DPRK," *North Korea: Witness to Transformation*, Peterson Institute for International Economics, August 13, 2013. This blog entry's command and control chart shows the trends of major military promotions from 1997 to 2013. Since 2010, when the regime began to lay the foundation for the Kim Jong-un succession, there had been 206 major military promotions. Since Kim Jong-un came to power in 2012 (up to August 2013), there had been 148 major promotions.

5. Role of the Regents

Following the Fourth Party Conference and into 2013, the power structure around Kim Jong-un came into clearer focus. Many of the leaders who had played prominent roles during the transition period following Kim Jong-il's death faded from the scene. At the same time, stories began to emerge from Pyongyang about a meeting that took place in 2008 that established the inner core of the leadership.[78]

As Kim Jong-il was recuperating from his stroke, he convened a meeting with his sister, Kim Kyong-hui, and her husband, Jang Song-taek, to discuss the upcoming succession. In addition to securing their support for his choice of Kim Jong-un as the heir apparent, Kim Jong-il asked them to establish a regent framework around Kim Jong-un to assist in his decision-making and instruct him in the art of conducting politics inside the North Korean regime. Kim Kyong-hui and Jang Song-taek were later joined by Choe Ryong-hae, most likely in 2010, as the three regents who served as the gatekeepers. They ensured Kim Jong-un's situational awareness, assisted him in developing critical relationships, and guided his decision-making.[79] All three played a role in the leadership machinations described above, especially the purge of Ri Yong-ho. Additionally, all three had their own functional responsibilities and influence.

---

78   Author's discussions in Seoul, 2012 and 2013. This meeting apparently took place in September 2008, one month after Kim Jong-il's stroke. During that period, Kim Kyong-hui, Jang Song-taek, and Kim Ok assumed the day-to-day roles of running the regime.

79   "The Rise of Moderate and Hardline Factions in North Korea," *Sankei Shimbun*, August 1, 2013. This is only one theory of how power politics works at the highest leadership level around Kim Jong-un. It is based on the notion that senior-level command and control had carried over from the Kim Jong-il era, where there was no viable opposition to the Supreme Leader, only degrees of influence. As mentioned earlier, this theory was opposed by another that came out of North Korea through informant channels soon after Kim Jong-un took power, which argued that there were confrontations within the senior leadership over how to proceed within Kim Jong-il's guidelines. The moderate faction, headed by Kim Kyong-hui and Jang Song-taek, reportedly stressed the importance of developing the economy as the best strategy for achieving a "Strong and Powerful Nation" (*Kang-seong-dae-guk*). The hardline faction, led by elements within the KWP OGD and the military, insisted on developing the country's critical defense systems, both missile and nuclear, in the name of "Military First" (*Songun*). Both of these lines were emphasized in Kim Jong-il's policies toward the end of his life. This could account for the new "Dual Development Strategy" (*Byeong-jin*), which stresses the need to make progress on both the economic and nuclear fronts. This theory contends that while the moderate faction ascended early on in the Kim Jong-un era, the missile and nuclear tests (at the end of 2012 and beginning of 2013) indicated that the hardline faction had gained influence. This theory suggests that while Kim Jong-un may have been surrounded by regents from the moderate faction, the individuals and institutions directly responsible for his personal protection fell into the hardline camp. The stories of factionalism inside North Korea should be read with caution. While this could be a new phenomenon that is emerging in the Kim Jong-un era, it runs counter to much of the Pyongyang-watching community's understanding of North Korean politics in the recent past. As one South Korean intelligence official and long-time Pyongyang-watcher once noted, "Inside the North Korean leadership, there are no factions, only winners and losers."

- **Kim Kyong-hui (69)** was the premier regent and wielded the most influence over Kim Jong-un.[80, 81] According to one source, she was the only person allowed to verbally discuss policy with Kim Jong-un; others had to make their suggestions in written form.[82] She was responsible for coaching Kim Jong-un on how to conduct politics and took the lead in ensuring that he developed the critical relationships he would need in order to rule on his own. As a blood relative and the keeper of Kim Jong-il's last will and testament, she was responsible for ensuring that the Kim family equities were respected and protected. In this capacity, she had veto power over all decisions, except those made by Kim Jong-un himself. Whether she used this veto power on her own or through Kim Jong-un was unclear.[83] Her health was rumored to be worsening, although she still managed to make appearances at critical leadership events until September 2013.

---

80   "Kim Jong-un's Aunt Critically Sick," *The Chosun Ilbo*, July 22, 2013. In July 2013, reports began to surface in South Korean media that Kim Kyong-hui was critically ill. She has a history of alcoholism and depression, which was exacerbated in the mid-2000s with her marital problems and the death of her daughter, Jang Kum-song, who committed suicide in 2006. Some reports claim that she is also suffering from hypertension and diabetes. At that time, she had not been seen in public for over eighty days. On July 8, 2013, she did not attend the important memorial event at the Kumsusan Palace of the Sun for the 19th anniversary of Kim Il-sung's death.

81   "Kim Jong-un's 'Sick' Aunt Resurfaces," *The Chosun Ilbo*, July 26, 2013. She eventually reappeared as part of the celebration ceremonies for the 60th anniversary of the armistice that ended the Korean War. On July 25, 2013, at the opening ceremony for the Fatherland Liberation War Martyrs' Cemetery in Pyongyang, she stood two spaces to the left of Kim Jong-un, next to Premier Pak Pong-ju. She has again disappeared and has not been seen in public since September 2013.

82   Kim Yun-Sim, "The Life and Times of a Kingmaker: Kim Kyung-hee in Close-up," *Daily NK*. Kim Yun-Sim was born in Pyongyang and came to South Korea in 2012.

83   Author's discussions in April 2013 with South Korean Pyongyang-watchers and senior-level defectors.

Image 3: Kim Jong-un and Kim Kyong-hui at the National Light Industry Meeting in March 2013.
(Source: KCTV)

Kim Kyong-hui's formal power was revealed at the Fourth Party Conference. She was elevated within the Central Committee apparatus from Department Director to KWP Secretary for Light Industry. She also became a full member of the Politburo at the Third Party Conference. Her position within the formal leadership ranking moved from 14th to sixth, which was confirmed by her ranking on Kim Kuk-tae's Funeral Committee list in December 2013. Additionally, it was rumored that Kim Kyong-hui was the Director of the powerful KWP OGD.[84] There was no evidence to support this view except that Kim Jong-il may have believed that only his sister had the experience and relationships necessary to ensure Kim family rule through this department.[85] According to South Korean sources, she worked behind the scenes to engineer the promotions of several other Party, military,

---

84   "The Rise of Moderate and Hardline Factions in North Korea," *Sankei Shimbun*, op. cit. If the factionalism theory discussed above is true, it is highly unlikely that Kim Kyong-hui occupies the directorship of this powerful organization.

85   In terms of the succession, placing Kim Kyong-hui as head of the OGD would make sense. From this post, she would be better equipped to engineer the necessary turnover throughout the leadership to guarantee that Kim Jong-un could establish his legitimacy and rule effectively. Giving this position to Kim Jong-un, with his inexperience in the finer points of how the regime operates, could have undermined the succession process. However, he will eventually have to take this post, if he has not already, in order to consolidate his power.

and government leaders to key positions within the leadership. These leaders included Choe Ryong-hae, Kim Won-hong, Pak Pong-ju, and Kwak Pom-gi.[86]

• **Jang Song-taek (67)** was, for all intents and purposes, the number two leader within the regime until his execution at the end of 2013.[87, 88, 89] Up until his death, there was a consensus within the South Korean Pyongyang-watching community that he served as the "Control Tower" (*Chong-kwal-bon-bu*).[90] He reportedly saw most, if not all, of the reports and message traffic earmarked for Kim Jong-un. He was allowed to prioritize this paperwork, but could not alter it in any way. He interacted with various task groups to discuss policy options and reach a consensus for Kim's final decision.[91] In this regard, he worked closely with Kim's Personal Secretariat. Jang maintained control over the economy and the internal security apparatus. He also had input in foreign policy, especially vis-à-vis China and inter-Korean relations. Given his apparent meetings with two private U.S. delegations to

86   Author's discussions in Seoul, April 2013.

87   "Interview: Unprecedented insights into North Korea's military structure," *New Focus International*, January 11, 2014. This is an interview with Choe Ju-hwal, "the highest-ranking military defector in South Korea." In formal rankings, Kim Yong-nam, the President of the SPA Presidium, holds this position, but Jang Song-taek eclipsed Kim in terms of power and authority. According to some senior defectors, informal power rankings are a foreign concept in North Korea; there is the Supreme Leader and everyone else.

88   *KCBS*, November 4, 2012. However, in 2012, a special meeting of the Politburo created the State Physical Culture and Sports Guidance Committee (SPCSGC) and appointed Jang as the Chairman. This organization cemented Jang's status as the de facto "second in command." Most of the senior leadership was included in the SPCSGC. Although the goal of founding the SPCSGC was, in principle, "holding and guiding the general work of the physical culture and sports of the country in a unified manner," Jang Song-taek would be able to take charge of the affairs of the Party's Secretariat through the SPCSGC if Kim Jong-un or Kim Kyong-hui were unable to carry out their duties.

89   *KCTV* film footage of the opening ceremony for the Fatherland Liberation War Martyrs' Cemetery, July 25, 2013. South Korean press speculated about Jang Song-taek's standing within the leadership given his reduction in public appearances in 2013 versus 2012. The decrease could have been due to Kim Jong-un's need to be seen as the leader, as well as Jang's heavy workload. Jang continued to make appearances at high-level events such as the opening ceremony for the Fatherland Liberation War Martyrs' Cemetery in Pyongyang on July 25th, where he stood two spots to Kim Jong-un's right, next to Choe Ryong-hae.

90   In North Korean terminology, the "Control Tower" (*Chong-kwal-bon-bu*) is the locus for day-to-day administration of the regime. When he was still alive, there was no question that Kim Jong-il was the "Control Tower."

91   These issue groups are apparently developed on an ad hoc basis to examine policy issues and develop options for the "Control Tower." Some, such as the one that focuses on relations with South Korea, is long-standing and composed of Party and government offices tied to foreign affairs. Others are apparently created to deal with short-term policy issues.

Pyongyang in 2012,[92] he may have also influenced North Korean relations with the United States, although this was likely the purview of Kang Sok-ju, the longtime foreign policy advisor to the Kim family.

Image 4: Jang Song-taek and Kim Jong-un at the April 2013 Eunhasu Concert to mark Kim Il-sung's birthday, the Day of the Sun. (Source: KCTV)

At the Fourth Party Conference, Jang Song-taek was elevated from alternate member to full member of the Politburo. He was also a Vice Chairman of the NDC, as well as the Director of the KWP Administrative Department, which oversees the organizations responsible for internal security. He reportedly oversaw one of the largest and most diverse patronage systems within the North Korean leadership.

- **Vice Marshal Choe Ryong-hae (65)** was the junior member of the regents surrounding Kim Jong-un.[93] His role was to ensure the loyalty

92 Ken Dilanian and Barbara Demick, "Secret U.S.-North Korea diplomatic trips reported," *Los Angeles Times*, February 23, 2013.

93 Cheong Seong-Chang, "The Importance of Choi Ryong Hae," *Daily NK*, August 19, 2013. In a system where blood lines and familial heritage are of great importance, Choe Ryong-hae's high status stems from his connection to the anti-Japanese partisan revolutionary line, which is superseded in importance only by the Mt. Paektu line of the Kim family itself. Therefore, in order to understand Choe's status in the North Korean regime, one must look at the relationship between the Choe and Kim families. Choe's family has a long-time relationship with the Kim dynasty. Choe's father, Choe Hyun, who died in 1982, was a friend of North Korean founder Kim Il-sung during the early years of the anti-Japanese

of the military. More than that of any other figure, Choe's status was catapulted at the Fourth Party Conference, when he moved up the formal leadership rankings from 18th to fourth. Already an alternate member of the Politburo since the 2010 Third Party Conference, as well as the KWP Secretary for Military Affairs, Choe was further elevated to the Politburo Presidium.[94] He also became Vice Chairman of the CMC. Although he lacks military experience, Choe was Vice Marshal and Director of the GPB,[95] the Party's surveillance organ within the armed forces.[96] Choe apparently had a direct channel to Kim Jong-un; his reports were not subject to vetting by Jang Song-taek. While the relationship between Choe and Jang was unclear,[97,98] Kim Jong-un, with Kim Kyong-hui's assistance, could have played the two against each other in order to expand his own power and influence within the inner core of the regime.

---

guerrilla movement. He later served as North Korea's Defense Minister. Choe Hyun's family is known as a "family of loyalty" in North Korea.

94   In March 2015, evidence appeared in North Korean media that Choe Ryong-hae had lost his position on the Politburo Presidium. In a report by *KCBS* on an event celebrating International Women's Day that was held in Pyongyang on March 8, 2015, Choe Ryong-hae was referred to as just a member of Politburo. In mid-February, personnel matters were discussed at an expanded meeting of the Politburo. At that time, Choe was either demoted, or it is possible the Politburo Presidium was abolished. See "Choe Ryong-hae, Close Aide to Kim Jong-un, Possibly Demoted to Only Member of Party Politburo," *Kyodo Clue IV*, March 8, 2015.

95   Choe had effectively become the regime's top military authority after Kim Jong-un.

96   According to the factionalism theory discussed above, the KWP OGD and the military high command allowed Choe's appointment out of respect for Kim Jong-il's wishes and the strong relationship that once existed between Kim Il-sung and Choe's father. His appointment also took place during the period when the moderate faction was gaining influence within the regime.

97   Author's interviews in Seoul, April 2013.

98   Lee Mi-Young and Park Seong-Guk, "Defector Claims Jang-Choi in Military Battle," *Daily NK.* The relationship between Choe Ryong-hae and Jang Song-taek was the subject of much debate within the South Korean Pyongyang-watching community. Some believed that close ties between the two from their days in the Kim Il-sung Socialist Youth League created a bond that continued. They pointed to the fact that Choe was demoted from his position around the same time that Jang Song-taek disappeared from public view in 2004. Choe also re-emerged upon Jang's return to prominence. Others believed that Choe was closer to Kim Kyong-hui than to Jang Song-taek and that Kim used Choe to keep her husband in check. They argued that Jang used his ties with the high command to undermine Choe and keep him politically unbalanced.

Image 5: Choe Ryong-hae receiving a gift from Kim Jong-un at the enlarged meeting of the KWP CMC in February 2013. (Source: KCTV)

The regime structure in the early years of Kim Jong-un's reign was one in which the Supreme Leader operated within a highly structured circle of gatekeepers. His interactions outside of this circle were somewhat managed, for instance through guidance inspections, but he had the ability to reach out to the wider North Korean leadership to access reservoirs of information, receive advice, and build relationships.

This structure changed faster than most Pyongyang-watchers believed possible. In December 2013, any discussion of regents ceased with the very public purge of Jang Song-taek. While the outside world may have been caught by surprise, the story had been unfolding behind the scenes for nearly a decade.

B. CHAPTER TWO: THE PURGE OF JANG SONG-TAEK AND THE DESTRUCTION OF THE REGENT STRUCTURE

While the regent structure appeared solidly in place in 2012, as shown by the apparent engineering of the removal of Ri Yong-ho, the following year revealed some cracks in the edifice of power around Kim Jong-un.[99] As the year progressed, outside media began to focus on Jang Song-taek's declining presence at Kim's guidance inspections at a time when Choe Ryong-hae was on the rise.[100] Another story centered on Kim Kyong-hui's disappearance from the public spotlight. Although the media treated these two stories in isolation, a much bigger story was unfolding behind the scenes in Pyongyang that would eventually lead to a transformation in how the regime is run.

1. The Seeds of Jang's Demise

The succession of power from Kim Jong-il to Kim Jong-un did not begin in 2008 with Kim Jong-il's announcement of his decision on his heir to Kim Kyong-hui and Jang Song-taek. In fact, it began six years earlier when Kim Jong-il's wife at the time, Ko Yong-hui, and her supporters began plotting a co-regency similar to the one that had paved Kim Jong-il's rise to power. In 2001, Kim Jong-il's first son, Kim Jong-nam, was expelled from Japan and publicly disgraced. A year later, an idolization campaign began to take shape inside the regime around Ko Yong-hui.[101] The campaign to construct a cult of personality around the "respected mother" was engineered by elements within the high command and the KWP OGD, namely Ri Je-gang and Ri Yong-chol, both of whom were close to Ko and fierce opponents of Jang Song-taek. While Jang and his wife, Kim Kyong-hui, were close to Kim Jong-nam, Ko's allies led an effort to inaugurate a succession centered on her children, most notably Kim Jong-chol. By 2004, the political space around Kim Jong-il was dominated by those close to Ko Yong-hui.[102]

---

99   Unlike his father, Kim Jong-un did not have decades of experience in running the regime. Many Pyongyang-watchers believed he would need a regent structure around him for at least another year or two until he managed to consolidate his power, probably in the late 2014 to 2015 timeframe.
100   Lee Mi-Young and Park Seong-Guk, "Defector Claims Jang-Choi in Military Battle," op. cit. Choe Ryong-hae accompanied Kim Jong-un on his site visits more often than any other official in the first half of 2013. During this period, he appeared at seventy-two out of ninety-five such public appearances. Conversely, Jang, who appeared the most in 2012, appeared only twenty-five times in the first half of 2013.
101   Ken E. Gause, *North Korea Under Kim Chong-il: Power, Politics, and Prospects for Change* (Santa Barbara, CA: Praeger, 2011).
102   This became clear when Jang Song-taek disappeared, apparently purged and sent off for re-education after attending a wedding ceremony of one of his protégés in violation of regime rules that

However, Ko Yong-hui died of breast cancer in 2004 at a hospital in Paris. Within a year, Kim Jong-il put a halt to any discussion of succession within the regime. This decision was largely driven by two considerations: 1) his desire to avoid the creation of a second center of power and 2) the need to prevent the growth of factions within the military and Party centered on potential successors. It was apparently his fear that the eventual heir apparent could become mired in regime politics, compromising his ability to consolidate power.

Simply stopping these discussions within the regime would not be enough. Regime dynamics in the mid-2000s were unbalanced in favor of a politically active OGD and a military leadership that was becoming increasingly powerful under "Military First" (*Songun*) politics. Kim Jong-il decided to deal with the situation by resorting to one of his preferred strategies—creating a counterweight. In order to keep the military and the OGD in check, he reached out to the part of the Kim family that had competed with Ko Yong-hui, namely Kim Kyong-hui and Jang Song-taek. First, he brought Jang Song-taek back from political exile in 2006 and, shortly thereafter, made him the head of the newly created KWP Administrative Department, which had been carved out of the OGD.[103] This not only weakened the OGD as an institutional actor, but also created a blocking mechanism within the Central Committee apparatus to keep the OGD in check.[104] Second, Kim Jong-il elevated Jang to Vice Chairman of the NDC and authorized him to oversee and restructure the military's trading rights. This move gave Jang the authority he needed to build his own economic empire, at the expense of many existing military hard currency operations. Finally, Kim turned over the responsibility for overseeing the eventual transfer of power to Kim Jong-un to Kim Kyong-hui and Jang Song-taek, essentially sanctioning what Ko's allies secretly tried to do just years before.

With this authority, Jang Song-taek's influence began to grow within the regime. In addition to his oversight of the internal security apparatus, he also played an increasingly important role in managing relations with China within the regime. This became clear shortly after his return to power in 2006, when he led a delegation to China to observe the special economic zones (SEZs) Kim Jong-il had visited three months earlier. The delegation was entrusted with the mission of formulating policy alternatives to address the economic difficulties in North Korea. The trip

---

prevented the gathering of senior leaders without Kim Jong-il's authorization. According to some sources, Ri Je-gang engineered Jang's removal from the center of politics in 2004.

103   The KWP Administrative Department had once been an independent Central Committee department before it was absorbed into the KWP OGD in the early 1990s.

104   While on the surface this seemed like a typical power move on the part of Kim Jong-il to balance power within the Party apparatus, in truth, it was a very sensitive move that by weakening the OGD risked undermining Kim's own control on power.

afforded Jang the opportunity to meet with the Chinese leadership and forge relations that later became suspect to those closest to Kim Jong-un.

In the following years, Jang was portrayed by international media as a proponent of free markets and the official responsible for implementing Kim Jong-il's second phase of economic reform.[105] However, this optimism gradually faded. Jang was linked to even more drastic measures to restrict markets, such as banning private hiring and tightening age and gender restrictions on those who could participate in market activity.[106] By 2009, he was considered a proponent of a constricted economic policy that stressed social stability.[107] His meager reform goals were focused on the SEZs along the border with China where he could conduct any number of hard currency operations that fed into his growing empire.[108]

Jang's wife, Kim Kyong-hui, reappeared in public in 2009 after a long hiatus. This not only signaled that the forthcoming succession would be handled by the Kim family, but it also created the space for Jang to enhance his own power at the expense of his rivals. As Kim Jong-il began to rely more on Jang Song-taek in the aftermath of his stroke in 2008, Jang was able to expand his patronage system and tie it into his ever-expanding hard currency operations. This was made clear in early 2010, when Jang took on the currency operations of his rival O Kuk-ryol by creating a trading firm called the Korea Daepung Group.[109] His growing power and influence manifested with the deaths of his two principal rivals in the OGD, Ri Je-gang and Ri Yong-chol, both of whom passed away in 2010 on the eve of Jang's elevation to Vice Chairman of the NDC.[110]

---

105   Seo Jae-Jin, "Significance of Jang Song-taek's Visit to China," *Korea Institute for National Unification: Online Series* 06, No. 3 (March 31, 2006).

106   Choi Jin-Wook, "The Changing Party-State System and Outlook for Reform in North Korea," *International Journal of Korean Unification Studies* 18, No. 1 (2009). Choi Jin-wook is the current acting Director of KINU.

107   Park Hyeong-Jung, "North Korean Conservative Policy Since 2006 and Jang Song-taek: Looking at 2009," *Korea Institute for National Unification: Online Series* 08, No. 72 (December 23, 2008).

108   Following Kim Jong-il's death and Kim Jong-un's announcement of the June economic measures in 2012, many began to re-evaluate where Jang stood on reform. Maybe he was a closet reformer. The view of his desire to use his relationship with China to increase his own power did not change.

109   Lee Young-Jong, "O Kuk Ryol, Who Returned Around the Time of Jang Song Taek's Downfall," *Korea JoongAng Daily*, December 25, 2013.

110   Ri Yong-chol died on April 27, 2010 of a heart attack. Ri Je-gang died a little over a month later on June 2, 2010 in a mysterious car accident. Jang Song-taek was promoted to Vice Chairman of the NDC on June 7, 2010.

Military First and Hard Currency Operations

In the late 1990s, the North Korean military began to use the governing doctrine of "Military First" (*Songun*) to improve its access to resources. By 2009, news of the imbalance in hard currency operations within the regime began to trickle out to the international community. On the occasion of O Kuk-ryol's appointment as a Vice Chairman of the NDC in April, articles discussing his family's ties to the counterfeiting of $100 "supernotes" emerged. For decades, O reportedly played the central role in printing and circulating counterfeit U.S. $100 bills known as "supernotes," as well as planning and supervising overseas counterfeiting operations. His family was also involved. His son, O Se-won, was one of two key overseas officials involved in counterfeiting. Another relative, Ri Il-nam, was a Councilor at the North Korean Embassy in Ethiopia and operated as a "supernote" courier, traveling between Pyongyang, Beijing, and Addis Ababa.

Much of this hard currency activity became centered in the Central Committee's Operations Department, which O Kuk-ryol oversaw.[111] In the mid-2000s, this department siphoned off personnel and South Korea-focused responsibilities from the KWP United Front Department (UFD) and Office 35, which are responsible for espionage activities aimed toward South Korea. With this growth, the Operations Department also increased its access to resources and funding streams tied to South Korea and Japan.

In May 2009, the regime streamlined hard currency operations by removing them from the Party apparatus and placing them under the newly enhanced RGB, which reports directly to the NDC, and O Kuk-ryol in particular.[112] As part of this reorganization, the KWP Operations Department and Office 35 were shifted from the Party

---

111   Kim Jong-il once proclaimed, "the Operations Department is my 'flying column' (*byol-dong-dae*)." As Director of this Operations Department for twenty years, O Kuk-ryol was the confidant most trusted by Kim Jong-il. He is the son of O Chung-song, who was one of the famous five brothers of the anti-Japanese guerrillas.

112   "North Korea Integrates Maneuvering Organs Targeting the South and Overseas Into RGB," *Yonhap News Agency*, May 10, 2009.

and merged into the RGB as Bureaus 1 (Operations Department) and 5 (formerly Office 35).

Jang's assault on the "Military First" (*Songun*) claim to resources began in 2010 with his elevation to Vice Chairman of the NDC. He used this position to target hard currency operations, which had shifted from the Party to the military beginning in the 1990s. Critical to this strategy was Jang's cooptation of Department 54. Originally part of the MPAF, Department 54 supplied electricity, coal, fuel, clothes, and other necessities to the military. Jang shifted its chain of command from the MPAF directly to the NDC. In addition, he linked the department to the Party apparatus, placing it under the control of Jang Su-kil, one of his protégés and Vice Director of the KWP Administrative Department. Under this new structure, Department 54's mandate spread as it took over numerous hard currency operations tied to the growing Jang empire inside North Korea and China.[113]

2. THE ROLE OF THE CONTROL TOWER

In addition to his growing economic power, Jang Song-taek's political influence inside the leadership was unparalleled. He was one of the few leaders with access to Kim Jong-un on a regular basis. He was also involved in running the day-to-day operations of the regime.

The term "Control Tower" (*Chong-kwal-bon-bu*)[114] came into North and South Korean lexicons during the Kim Jong-il period. It was a term well-suited to Kim's "hub-and-spoke" leadership style. While the term was sometimes attributed to the Party, it was generally understood that the "Control Tower" resided in the Supreme Leader, who provided command directives and guidance to the core entities of the Party, government, and military. However, early in his tenure as Supreme Leader, many Pyongyang-watchers speculated about Kim Jong-un's ability to smoothly

---

113   "Purge of Jang Song-taek Triggered by Supply Corruption," *The Chosun Ilbo*, December 12, 2013. Under KWP Administrative Department control, Department 54's responsibilities shifted from military supply to a number of different ventures, including running department stores in Pyongyang and Wonsan, as well as controlling mines, power plants, cement factories, and agricultural distribution networks throughout North Korea. In 2011, when North Korea faced a food shortage, Jang ensured that Department 54 imported 50,000 tons of corn and distributed it to military units around Pyongyang and the residents of the capital. Despite its support for broader regime needs, Department 54 officials were also implicated in corruption in the running of a chain of restaurants overseas, primarily in China, under the name Haedanghwa. Please refer to the chapter on the Royal Economy for more details on the expansion of Department 54 operations.
114   The literal translation is "Chief Command Headquarters."

control the various agencies focused around the "Control Tower."[115] The absence of a strong central "Control Tower" could thus become, as one Pyongyang-watcher noted, "the greatest source of uncertainty as the Kim Jong-un regime ventures into the unknown without a manual."[116]

In 2012, many Pyongyang-watchers believed that with Kim Jong-il's death, the "Control Tower" role did not pass to Kim Jong-un, but to Jang Song-taek.[117] This would not be surprising given the role Jang played in the months after Kim Jong-il's stroke in 2008, when he worked with Kim Kyong-hui and Kim Ok to assume much of the "Control Tower" responsibilities. According to one source, Jang's role during this period was to receive orders from Kim Jong-il and channel them to state agencies,[118] acting like a stand-in coordinator for day-to-day state affairs. This ensured that if Kim died, the notion of the "Control Tower" would not collapse. In addition, economic cooperation with China was a critical factor in stabilizing the regime during the transfer of power. Since Jang already managed relations with China, this was a logical addition to the "Control Tower" responsibilities.

In the first few years after Kim's death, the North Korean media's treatment of Jang Song-taek was unique and, in many respects, unprecedented. In November 2012, an enlarged meeting of the Politburo established the State Physical Culture and Sports Guidance Committee (SPCSGC), a thirty-two-member organization responsible for managing sports and athletics in North Korea.[119] Jang Song-taek was appointed Chairman of the Committee. While North Korean media described the mission of the new Committee as, "to control the overall sports work of the country in a unified manner," an examination of its membership revealed the most senior leadership in the Party, Cabinet, and military. Moreover, some Pyongyang-watchers suggested that it was a shadow government that allowed Jang to convene official meetings of senior leaders without being accused of trying to undermine the legitimacy of Kim Jong-un, who was not a member.

Several months later, Jang Song-taek's position within the regime began to be heralded in the popular media as second only to Kim Jong-un.[120] He was referred

---

115   With intensifying competition among the elites to display loyalty, Kim Jong-un may not be able to restrain them from engaging in destabilizing power struggles.

116   Choi Jin-Wook, "The Dawn of the Kim Jong Eun Regime and the Choice for North Korea," *Korea Institute for National Unification: Online Series* 12, No. 17 (May 15, 2012).

117   Author's interviews in Seoul, April 2013.

118   "DPRK Leader's In-Law Gaining Power," *AFP*, November 11, 2008.

119   "Report on Enlarged Meeting of the Political Bureau of the Workers' Party of Korea Central Committee," *KCBS*, November 4, 2012.

120   This view was generally not reflected in the discourse within the Pyongyang-watching community, which viewed Kim Jong-un as the undisputed leader. The notion of a number two leader was for the most part reserved to discussions on leadership ranking, not power.

to as the *éminence grise*, who was at ease with his power. At the Fourth Meeting of Party Cell Secretaries in February 2013, Jang was caught on state television sitting with his left arm leaning against the armrest of his chair or staring off into the distance as Kim Jong-un delivered a speech. This apparent lack of interest in the proceedings was in stark contrast to the rest of the leadership on the podium, who sat stiffly, looking straight ahead. According to one South Korean Defense Ministry official, "We've frequently spotted Jang Song-taek looking unfazed by Kim Jong-un's presence and we are repeatedly hearing rumors that he is the person who is really in power in the North."[121]

Image 6: Kim Jong-un speaking at the Fourth Meeting of Party Cell Secretaries. Jang Song-taek is highlighted with circles. (Source: KCNA)

There was a great deal of speculation about Jang's daily role and function as the "Control Tower," but there was little information. His main responsibility was to oversee the implementation of the Supreme Leader's policy decisions.[122] He interacted with various policy task forces, making the necessary decisions to keep policies on track.[123] This was something Kim Jong-il would have done in the past. Decisions were frequently not made in a timely manner because of the amount of documents generated to ensure that the regime would continue to function. Since Kim Jong-un was still learning how to manage the regime's politics, it is unlikely that

---

121   "N. Korea's Eminence Grise at Ease in Power," *The Chosun Ilbo*, February 1, 2013.
122   Author's interviews in Seoul, April 2013. According to one South Korean Pyongyang-watcher, the "Control Tower" under Jang Song-taek was not a decision-making post, unlike under Kim Jong-il. While it retained many of the "hub-and-spoke" administrative functions, final decisions rested with the "royal family"—Kim Jong-un and possibly Kim Kyong-hui.
123   Author's interviews with senior-level defectors in Seoul, April 2013.

he played this role.[124] To ensure that Kim was informed he received reports from all sectors of the regime, including the Party, military, and security services.[125] Jang received these reports first with the possible exception of military reports. He was allegedly allowed to provide comment on them and even work with Kim Jong-un's Personal Secretariat to prioritize them.[126] Whenever the Supreme Leader's decision was needed to embark on a new policy line or to resolve conflicting policy options, Jang Song-taek presumably advised his nephew on the courses of action and helped him through the decision-making process. According to numerous sources, the Supreme Leader's reporting and approval systems were still in place. This would suggest that all documents carried Kim Jong-un's, not Jang Song-taek's, signature—a vital practice to ensure the legitimacy of the "Leader" (*Suryong*) system.[127, 128]

3. JANG SONG-TAEK'S FALL FROM GRACE

By early 2013, rumors spread that Jang Song-taek's influence was waning. He was no longer as visible as he had been the year before. As noted earlier, the number of times he accompanied Kim Jong-un on guidance inspections began to decrease. Still, he did not appear in imminent danger. According to several sources from inside the regime, Jang's power was much more precarious behind the scenes. While he remained part of the inner circle around Kim Jong-un, his activities came under scrutiny in light of a warning that Kim Jong-il had alluded to in his will.

---

124   Park Hyeong-Jung, "One Year into the '6.28 Policy Directives': Contents and Progress," *Korea Institute for National Unification: Online Series* 13, No. 18 (28 June 2013). However, there were some indications that Kim Jong-un occasionally established special working groups to provide advice and options on matters of policy, perhaps through Jang Song-taek. In the days after Kim Jong-il's death, it was rumored that Kim Jong-un instructed the Cabinet to establish a "study group to prepare for reforms in the economic management method." This group produced recommendations and policy directives that would set the foundation for the June 28 policy directives.

125   Ibid.

126   Ibid. According to one source, "Jang Song-taek shares major documents that are reported to Kim Jong-un and appears to be deeply involved in major policy decisions, advising Kim on all state affairs." This most likely reflected his dual role as a senior regent to Kim Jong-un and the "Control Tower." See "N. Korea's Eminence Grise at Ease in Power," *The Chosun Ilbo*, op. cit.

127   Author's interviews in Seoul, April 2013.

128   Please see Section Two of this paper for a description of the "Leader" (*Suryong*) system.

a. Kim Jong-il's Will

In 2012, defector sources secured copies of Kim Jong-il's last will and testament.[129] He dictated his will to his daughter, Kim Sol-song, and shared it with his sister and executor of the will, Kim Kyong-hui, in the months before his death.[130] In his will, Kim Jong-il outlined policy prescriptions that Kim Jong-un, his successor, should adhere to. These prescriptions covered everything from domestic and foreign policy to internal Kim family relations. Within the wishes Kim put forth for his family, he stressed that Kim Jong-un should put his trust in Kim Kyong-hui and his half-sister, Kim Sol-song. He also urged that Kim Jong-nam be left alone and not targeted or harassed by the regime. Jang Song-taek is not mentioned, although the will warns against sectarianism arising from powerful elements within the Party.

According to defector sources, Kim Jong-il held a series of private conversations with his sister and executor of his will, Kim Kyong-hui. He warned her that Jang's continued presence at the pinnacle of power would eventually threaten Kim family rule. While he apparently did not provide a deadline for dealing with Jang, he noted that Jang would eventually become a second center of power if nothing was done. This would not only undermine the Supreme Leader's position, but could also make the Kim family irrelevant within the wider leadership.

Thus, from the onset of the Kim Jong-un era, Jang Song-taek's fate was not a matter of if, but a matter of when. It did not take long for Kim Kyong-hui and Kim Jong-un to become suspicious about Jang's motivations.

b. Jang's Ill-Fated Trip to China

On August 13, 2012, Jang Song-taek arrived in China on a hastily organized trip. He was the highest ranking North Korean official to visit Beijing since Kim Jong-il in May 2011, when Jang accompanied him. The official reason for the trip was to attend the third session of the joint North Korea-China Guidance Committee on the development and management of the Rajin-Sonbong economic and trade zone and the Hwanggeumpyeong-Wihwa SEZ.

---

129   It should be stressed that at the time of this writing, analysis of various copies of the will is still underway and debate continues over whether they are authentic.

130   Lee Yun-Keol, *The Contents of Kim Jong-il's Will: The Blueprint of Kim Jong-un's Regime and Possibility of Change* (Seoul: NKSIS, 2012). One source of Kim Jong-il's will is Lee Yun-Keol, a high-profile North Korean defector and head of the NK Strategic Information Service Center (NKSIS), a Seoul-based think tank. In April 2013, the author held interviews with NKSIS and other defector sources on various aspects of the will.

On the surface, the trip was a success. According to the Chinese Ministry of Commerce, both sides made progress on setting up developmental guidelines and systems for the promotion of projects. They also announced the formation of management committees for the two zones. A deal was signed on forming an economic, technological, and agricultural alliance; operation and management of the committees; power supply; and the establishment of a company in the Rason zone.

What was not mentioned in the press was the secret reason for Jang's trip. Kim Jong-il's will implies that for a successful transfer of power, Kim Jong-un would need access to regime funds to build his patronage system. It calls for all Kim family funds, both domestic and international, to be placed under Kim Kyong-hui's control, presumably until Kim Jong-un was ready to take over management himself. Chinese authorities had reportedly frozen approximately $1.7 billion of the Kim family's funds that were allegedly in banks in Hong Kong, Macau, Shanghai, and Guangzhou. Kim Kyong-hui and Kim Jong-un instructed Jang Song-taek to use his connections with the Chinese leadership to unfreeze these funds and transfer them to Kim family accounts inside North Korea.

According to sources inside China, Jang Song-taek failed to secure these funds. Beyond the reason that his request was denied by China's leaders, two rumors for why he was unsuccessful have emerged in defector circles.[131] The first suggests that Jang had entered into an agreement with Chinese authorities to withhold the funds, forcing the North Korean regime to embrace Chinese-style economic reforms. Furthermore, Jang sent a letter to the Chinese leadership in 2013, explaining his desire to be an agent for change, gradually shifting power away from the KWP to the Cabinet. The letter was intercepted by the SSD and was included in the investigation report on Jang as evidence that he had established a confidential liaison with China outside the purview of the Supreme Leader. Sources point to Jang's indictment that accuses him of "anti-Party and anti-revolutionary acts" as a veiled reference to his attempts to co-opt the political process and set himself up as the de facto Premier.[132]

---

131   Discussion with defector in Seoul who has close ties to Korea-watchers in China, May 2014. According to one Chinese source close to Hu Jintao, the Chinese leadership's view was that Jang's power in August 2012 was not as profound as it once was. He was seen as a messenger, not a power broker. If this is true, it lends credence to the theory that his fate had been sealed much earlier in 2011 when Kim entrusted his will to his sister, Kim Kyong-hui, despite Jang's dramatic rise in status following Kim Jong-il's death.

132   "Exclusive: Jang Song-thaek was executed following his letter to Chinese leadership," *New Focus International*, June 30, 2014. In the letter, Jang reasoned that "Kim Il-sung ruled through a government overseen by the Premier and Cabinet in order to develop the nation's light industry and agriculture, while maintaining the military industry as top priority." Jang reportedly eschewed the idea that he wanted to replace Kim Jong-un. On the contrary, he explained that he wanted to develop the

A second rumor suggests that Jang's actions were more self-driven and less tied to a secret alliance with China. If he could deny the Kim family funds to Kim Jong-un, the new leader would become more dependent on Jang and his considerable resources. This would make Kim more pliable, allowing Jang to expand his empire along with Kim Jong-un's overall consolidation process. By the time Kim was firmly established as the Supreme Leader, Jang would be the immovable power behind the throne.

Regardless of the reason, Jang's inability to secure the funds from the Chinese banks allegedly raised suspicions about his loyalty towards the regime in the eyes of Kim Kyong-hui and Kim Jong-un. Although Jang continued to be a visible force within the regime, his actual power began to diminish from this point on. This made him vulnerable to other forces inside the leadership that had been looking for an opportunity to attack.

c. Jang under Investigation

Jang Song-taek's influence and position within the regime was not something he achieved in his own right, but came from the fact that he was the husband of Kim Kyong-hui. He was consequently viewed as a "side branch" by members of the Kim family and their key allies within the leadership. His ability to maneuver and thrive within the regime depended on his wife's support. While this support waxed and waned over the years, Kim and Jang operated as a "power couple." Their patronage systems were linked, but not intertwined. When Jang came under threat from other elements within the regime or was even purged, Kim Kyong-hui protected him from permanent damage. This began to change in the fall of 2012.

In September, reports about Kim Kyong-hui's health began to surface in South Korean media.[133] Speculation increased after she did not attend a highly unusual second session of the SPA, which convened at the end of September.[134] The other two regents, Jang Song-taek and Choe Ryong-hae, were prominently featured, making her absence even more noticeable.

According to information that has recently emerged from defector channels, Kim Kyong-hui suffered a minor stroke around this time.[135] She was bedridden, but

---

North Korean economy using the Cabinet and government as a pivot, in order to stabilize Kim Jong-un's rule and maintain the current regime.

133   Kim Young-Jin, "N. Korean Leader's Aunt in Ill Health," *The Korea Times*, September 7, 2012.
134   "Kim Jong-un's Aunt Seriously Ill," *The Chosun Ilbo*, September 28, 2012.
135   There is debate over when this minor stroke occurred. Some sources claim it occurred in early January 2013. If this is the case, she made a remarkable recovery, since she appeared at the Fourth Meeting of Party Cell Secretaries held on January 29, 2013.

conscious and able to function. Given the growing suspicion surrounding Jang, the decision was made—either by Kim Kyong-hui, Kim Jong-un, or both—to place him under surveillance. Since Jang was a senior Party member, the KWP OGD was tasked with this operation.[136]

For the next several months, Jang Song-taek's activities were tracked and examined. From the outside perspective, Jang maintained his busy public profile. As December came around, he topped the list of cadres accompanying Kim Jong-un, attending 100 out of 143 events.[137] Earlier in the year, Kim introduced Jang as his "closest revolutionary comrade."[138]

In March 2013, the KWP OGD presented its findings to Kim Kyong-hui. Not surprisingly, the report revealed his infidelity, a long-standing problem that had plagued the marriage for decades. The report noted that he had allegedly been seeing seven women.[139] According to defector reporting, Kim Kyong-hui was outraged by the report and vowed to carry out her brother's wishes to ensure a smooth power consolidation for Kim Jong-un.[140] This presumably included agreeing to remove Jang Song-taek from the political scene.[141]

It reportedly took two months for the Kim family to make the final decision regarding Jang. Whether the decision included his ultimate fate is unknown, but it was determined that he could no longer remain in the central leadership. In May 2013, Kim Jong-un convened a task force composed of elements within his Personal Secretariat, which presumably included his half-sister, Kim Sol-song, the

---

136   Ken E. Gause, Coercion, *Control, Surveillance, and Punishment: An Examination of the North Korean Police State*, 2nd ed., op. cit. Only the KWP OGD is authorized to investigate senior members of the Party. Below the central Party level, other investigative organs, such as the SSD and the MPS, have authority to carry out investigations.

137   "Who Runs N.Korea?" *The Chosun Ilbo*, December 18, 2012.

138   Ibid.

139   Discussion with a senior-level North Korean defector, May 2014. This report may account for the insertion of language about Jang's infidelity into the list of charges made against him.

140   Kim Kyong-hui was the guarantor of the Kim family equities within the regime and had engineered her nephew's consolidation up to this point. She established the ideological foundation through the revision of the "Ten Principles for a Monolithic Ideological System" into the "Ten Principles for a Monolithic Leader Ideological System," which strengthened the rationale for continued Kim family rule.

141   "Covert Organization that Holds the Key to Finding Out the Whole Picture of the Abductions—Study of North Korea's Ministry of State Security," *Sentaku Magazine*, August 2014. If the OGD did produce a report on Jang Song-taek's activities, its contents need to be examined with a certain amount of skepticism. According to other defector reports, members of the military, the OGD, and the SSD met in Samjiyeon in March to plot the downfall of Jang, the same month that the report was presented to Kim Jong-un and Kim Kyong-hui. Whether the report was an output of this meeting or an actual investigation remains unclear. Since that time, this coterie of people from these three organizations has been known as the "Samjiyeon Group."

KWP OGD, and the SSD, to construct a report justifying the need to remove Jang Song-taek from power.

This report was much more thorough than the previous surveillance report of March 2013 and delved deeply into Jang's actions since returning to the leadership in 2006. The primary investigation was conducted by the KWP OGD under the direction of First Vice Directors Kim Kyong-ok and Jo Yon-jun, and Vice Director Min Pyong-chol,[142] with support from the SSD. The report revealed Jang's efforts dating back to Kim Jong-il's stroke in August 2008 to build a stronghold of power throughout the regime, separate from that of the Supreme Leader.[143] This process was somewhat hidden from Kim Jong-un because of the deterioration of the surveillance apparatus inside the regime, most of which reported directly to Jang. The investigation also found that Jang had fabricated documents and manipulated evidence in order to remove his rivals, such as Ri Je-gang and Ri Yong-chol of the KWP OGD. The report was submitted to Kim Jong-un in October 2013.

d. The Purge Unfolds

With this evidence and Kim Kyong-hui's acquiesence, Kim Jong-un entrusted his half-sister, Kim Sol-song, to develop the strategy for the purge in concert with a special task force made up of Guard Command and SSD personnel.[144, 145] The plan was to first go after Jang's key lieutenants, Jang Su-gil and Ri Yong-ha. This would remove an important support mechanism for Jang by cutting off his ties within the KWP Administrative Department, the center of his growing empire.

As it would happen, Jang's lieutenants had come to Kim Jong-un's attention in September 2013 for their role in a struggle for control over profits from North

---

142   Kim Jeong-U, "A Full Account of the Purge of Jang Song-taek," *Chosun Monthly*, January 2014. One theory purports that the OGD's investigation of Jang Song-taek began in December 2011, soon after Kim Jong-il's death.

143   The Politburo readout of December 8, 2013 notes, "Jang desperately worked to form a faction within the Party by creating illusion about him and winning those weak in faith and flatterers to his side." Furthermore, he tried "to increase his force and build his base for realizing it by implanting those who had been punished for their serious wrongs in the past period into ranks of officials of departments of the Party Central Committee and units under them." Jang also apparently sought to dismantle the personality cult of the Kim dynasty and impede the Party's campaign to build Kim Jong-un's personality cult, considering the Politburo accused him of "shunning and obstructing in every way the work for holding President Kim Il-sung and Kim Jong-il in high esteem for all ages."

144   "Jang Song-thaek's Purge was Expected a Long Ago," *NKSIS*, December 10, 2013.

145   Lee Yun-Keol, "Kim Jong Un and His Brother Kim Jong Chol Picked Their Uncle Jang Song Thaek as a 'Prey' to Maintain the 'Kim Dynasty Regime' in North Korea," *NKSIS*, December 10, 2013.

Korea's most lucrative exports—clams, crabs, and coal.[146, 147] Kim Jong-un ordered North Korean military forces to retake control of the seafood farms, one of the sources of these exports, that Jang Song-taek had seized from the military when he became Vice Chairman of the NDC. In the battle for control of the farms, the emaciated, poorly trained North Korean forces were beaten badly by Jang's loyalists. When Kim learned of the rout, he was outraged that his orders were ignored by the Fisheries Office responsible for these resources, presumably acting on orders from Ri Ryong-ha and Jang Su-gil. Kim Jong-un sent more soldiers to the area, who enforced his will.

Image 7: Ri Ryong-ha (left) and Jang Su-gil (right) are reported to have been publicly executed in November 2013 as part of a purge of political figures close to Jang Song-taek. (Source: KCNA/KCTV/North Korea Leadership Watch file photos)

In mid-November, a joint SSD-Guard Command task force placed Ri Ryong-ha and Jang Su-gil under arrest.[148] At this time, the OGD informed Jang Song-taek that he was confined to his home, essentially placing him under house arrest. According to later reports, Jang apparently tried to contact Kim Jong-un,

---

146   "N. Korea purge sparked by mineral disputes: Seoul official," *AFP*, December 23, 2013. In a testimony to the South Korean National Assembly, the Director of the NIS, Nam Jae-Joon, explained that "Jang intervened too much in lucrative state businesses...related to coal, which drew mounting complaints from other (related) state bodies...Kim Jong-Un was briefed about it... and issued orders to correct the situation. But many officials loyal to Jang [Ri Ryong-ha and Jang Su-gil] did not immediately accept his orders [saying they first needed to check with Jang Song-taek], which eventually led an angry Kim to launch a sweeping purge."

147   Choe Sang-Hun and David E. Sanger, "Korea Execution is Tied to Clash Over Businesses," *The New York Times*, December 23, 2013.

148   Some sources report the specific date as November 18, 2013.

but his pleas went unanswered. At the end of November, both Ri Ryong-ha and Jang Su-gil were branded as Jang Song-taek's "people" (*se-ryeok*) and publicly executed. [149, 150]

On December 9, 2013, North Korean media featured a lengthy report of an enlarged meeting of the Politburo that took place the previous day, at which a decision was made to dismiss Jang Song-taek from all of his positions. This included membership to the Politburo itself, as well as Vice Chairman of the NDC. The Politburo also removed Jang from the KWP. In unusually harsh language, the Politburo report stated:

The Party served warning to Jang several times and dealt blows at him, watching his group's anti-party, counter-revolutionary factional acts as it has been aware of them from long ago. But Jang did not pay heed to it but went beyond tolerance limit. That was why the Party eliminated Jang and purged his group. [151]

Image 8: Senior North Korean officials observe Jang's removal from the December 8, 2013 Politburo meeting. (Source: KCTV screen capture)

---

149   "Explosion of Soaring Rage of Millions of Soldiers and People, Traitor for All Ages Firmly Punished—Special Military Tribunal of the DPRK Ministry of State Security Against Jang Song Taek, Unparalleled Traitor for All Ages," *KCBS*, December 12, 2013. The Special Tribunal Report on the Execution of Jang Song-taek spelled out the regime's contempt for Ri Ryong-ha in particular. It noted that "every time the bastard [Jang Song-taek] was transferred to a different job since the 1980s, the bastard carried fawning bastard Ri Ryong-ha on his coattails and even elevated to the post of First Department Vice Director at the Party Central Committee the same individual who was kicked out for his factional behavior rejecting the Party's unitary leadership, thus making him the bastard's right-hand man."
150   Later reporting claimed that Pak Chun-hong, another Vice Director of the KWP Administrative Department, was also executed. This same reporting claimed that Ri Myong-su, the former Minister of People's Security, had either been placed under house arrest or executed.
151   *Nodong Sinmun*, December 9, 2013.

Departing from past handling of leadership purges, the media not only provided the litany of indictments against Jang in explicit detail,[152] but also provided photographs of him being arrested and forcefully removed from the Politburo meeting.[153] Not since the 1950s and Kim Il-sung's purges of factional elements within the leadership had the media used language, such as "anti-Party and counter-revolutionary factional acts," to describe Jang's political crimes.[154] With regard to the crimes in their totality and their public airing, this purge was unprecedented.[155]

Three days later, on December 12th, the media reported that a special military tribunal of the SSD tried Jang Song-taek on charges of perpetuating a "state subversive plot."[156] The court sentenced Jang to death, pursuant to "Article 60 of the Republic's criminal code," and his sentence was carried out immediately after the trial.[157] The readout from the trial was even harsher than that of the expanded Politburo meeting.[158] In language normally reserved for the regime's most vitriolic diatribes against South Korean leaders, the trial readout accused Jang of having "impeded the work of establishing the Party's monolithic leadership system." It

---

152   The indictments were not confined to political indiscretions, as has been the practice in the past when ranking officials were punished, but went beyond politics to include many salacious descriptions of his "dissolute and depraved life." They cited examples of his womanizing, drinking, drug use, and squandering of foreign currency in overseas casinos.

153   On December 9, 2013, *KCTV* aired two photographs of Jang's arrest. This was unprecedented in the North Korean media's treatment of a fallen senior official, not to mention a member of the Kim family. Later reports indicated that Jo Yon-jun, First Vice Director of the KWP OGD, orchestrated this event from the leadership podium.

154   *Nodong Sinmun*, August 11, 1953. In August 1953, the KWP's Sixth Central Committee Plenum accused Vice Premier and Foreign Minister Pak Hon-yong of being a "factionalist" who led a "clique of anti-Party, and anti-state spies" for the United States. He was removed from the Party and put on trial.

155   The only other senior official publicly removed under somewhat questionable circumstances during Kim Jong-un's tenure had been Ri Yong-ho. While some rumors contended that he was also removed from his positions at a Politburo meeting, the media only announced that he had retired due to illness. The reference to Ri as a "comrade" in the dismissal announcement was a sign of respect, although speculation was that he had been forced to retire and may even be under house arrest. See "Ri Yong-ho 'Relieved' of All Posts at July 15 Party Meeting," *KCBS Pyongyang*, July 15, 2012.

156   In the history of the regime, North Korean media has only reported on two other trials of senior leaders. Both were military tribunals that took place in the 1950s as Kim Il-sung struggled to eliminate factionalism within the ranks of the leadership. Following Pak Hon-yong's removal from the Party in 1953, he was handed over to a "special trial of the Supreme Court," which was presided over by Vice Marshal Choe Yong-gon, the Minister of Defense. *Nodong Sinmun* provided an account of the trial in 1955. Ri Sung-yop, a KWP Secretary, was also put on trial in 1953 for carrying out a "subversive plot against the Republic and espionage against the state" for the United States. While Pak was sentenced to death, the implementation of his sentence was never reported. *Nodong Sinmun* reported in August 1953 that Ri and others were executed soon after the verdict.

157   *KCBS Pyongyang*, December 12, 2013.

158   For a detailed analysis of the execution notice, see Adam Cathcart, "Thrice-Cursed Acts of Treachery? Parsing North Korea's Report on the Execution of Kim Jong-un's Uncle," *The Atlantic*, December 13, 2013. For the notice itself, see "Traitor Jang Song Thaek Executed," *KCNA*, December 13, 2013.

referred to him as an "unparalleled traitor for all ages" and "an ugly human scum worse than a dog." Unlike the more restrained Politburo report, which referred to Jang Song-taek by his full name, the trial indictment referred to him over twenty times as a "bastard."[159] *Nodong Sinmun's* report of the special military tribunal contained two additional photographs: one of the tribunal judges and the other of a handcuffed Jang, forced to bow his head by guards on either side of him.

Image 9: Jang Song-taek appears before a tribunal of the SSD on December 12, 2013.
(Source: Nodong Sinmun)

4. THE AFTERMATH OF THE PURGE

While Jang Song-taek's purge has not been ignored, North Korean statements have sought to downplay it over time, suggesting that the affair was easily contained. While defector sources talk of widespread purges at the lower levels of the regime throughout the country, North Korean media is mute on the matter. As for Kim Kyong-hui, her name was listed sixth on the Kim Kuk-tae Funeral Committee, although she has not been seen in public since September 2013.

The way in which Jang's purge was carried out suggests that the issue of internal stability requires close examination. What sets this purge apart from others

---

159   "DPRK Ministry of State Security Holds 'Special Military Tribunal' For Jang Song-taek," *KCNA*, December 12, 2013.

is not that it was tied to member of the Kim family, which is potentially destabilizing in itself, but how it was publicized. Kim Jong-un and his supporters took a risk in exposing weakness at the regime's core by openly discussing Jang's indictment in such detail. This was followed by an unusually swift execution. On both counts, the circumstantial evidence points to an internal power struggle—either between Kim Jong-un and Jang, Jang and other power brokers, or likely both—that needed to be quickly addressed. If this is the case, it is most likely that Kim Jong-un has not yet consolidated his power and achieving this goal may have become more difficult. Not only has Kim become the "Control Tower" before he was prepared to take on such responsibility, but he is now also directly exposed to the power struggles that have been churning within the regime since Kim Jong-il's death.

Nevertheless, Jang's high-profile purge likely froze the leadership in place for the moment. The wider leadership was now concerned about what happens next. The safest move would be to show unwavering loyalty to the Supreme Leader. This created a period of stability as the remnants of Jang's patronage network were either neutralized or co-opted.

C. CHAPTER THREE: NORTH KOREAN LEADERSHIP DYNAMICS POST-JANG SONG-TAEK

On December 24, 2013, Kim Jong-un reportedly issued orders to the SSD, MPS, and MSC to commence an investigation to root out "rebels" within the system and stabilize popular sentiment following Jang Song-taek's purge.[160] This led to harrowing stories over the following weeks of relatives of Jang Song-taek and those close to him being dragged from their houses and sent to prison camps. Stories also began to trickle out about senior-level leaders being absent from meetings and prominent events.

This chapter examines leadership dynamics in North Korea since Jang Song-taek's purge. It studies the reshuffling of portfolios in 2014 and the first half of 2015 and offers analysis on Kim Jong-un's evolving inner circle. Finally, it considers what these changes say about Kim Jong-un's strategy to consolidate power.

1. IMPACT ON POWER NETWORKS

In terms of the formal leadership structure, the overall rankings remained largely unaffected in the weeks after Jang's purge. A comparison between the leadership events surrounding the first anniversary of Kim Jong-il's death in December 2012 and leadership events in 2013, including Kim Kuk-tae's funeral, reveals that only a few leaders moved significantly in the rankings. Kim Yong-nam, Premier Pak Pong-ju,[161] and Choe Ryong-hae remained at the top of the formal leadership rankings behind Kim Jong-un.[162] Choe Yong-rim, the former Premier, and Hyon Chol-hae, the former First Vice Minister of the People's Armed Forces, fell several spots, most likely due to their retired status. Ju Kyu-chang, Director of the KWP Defense Industry Department, inexplicably fell six spots after the Founding Anniversary Parade in September 2013. Jo Yon-jun, First Vice Director of the KWP OGD, and Tae Jong-su, KWP Secretary, both rose in the rankings in

---

160   This information was provided to a senior defector in Seoul by way of a contact in the North Korean central government apparatus.
161   Oh Gwan-Cheol, "Keep an Eye on Premier Pak Pong-ju," *The Kyunghyang Shinmun*, December 19, 2013. While much of the media speculation at the time centered on Choe Ryong-hae, many Pyongyang-watchers contend that Kim Yong-nam and Pak Pong-ju remained two of Kim Jong-un's key advisors. While they occupied the second and third positions in the formal rankings, they were rumored to be key players within the informal power structure.
162   It is interesting to note the placement of Pak Pong-ju. Although he was only a member of the Politburo, he was ranked with both Kim Yong-nam and Choe Ryong-hae, who were both members of the Politburo Presidium. This suggested Pak's role as one of Kim Jong-un's inner circle of advisers.

October 2013 and then fell back in December 2013. Officials closely tied to Jang Song-taek, such as Ro Tu-chol, Chairman of the State Planning Commission, and Choe Pu-il, Minister of People's Security, remained in place. Choe rose in the ranks in October 2013 at the Party Anniversary Concert, only to fall back in December 2013.

The re-emergence of O Kuk-ryol was particularly notable. Although he played a prominent role in the aftermath of Kim Jong-il's death, his role within the leadership had been a matter of speculation among Pyongyang-watchers. Many believed that he had been retired in place even though he was a Vice Chairman of the NDC and an alternate member of the Politburo. In September 2013, at the anniversary of the founding of the state, he dramatically rose in the formal ranking.[163] Two months later, at a national meeting of scientists and technicians, he was not only listed third, behind Pak Pong-ju and Choe Tae-bok, but he was also the sole representative of the military at a non-military event. On the Kim Kuk-tae Funeral Committee list, he was ranked before Kim Won-hong, a full member of the Politburo, suggesting that O may have been elevated from alternate to full member status. [164]

---

163 Alexandre Mansourov, "North Korea: Leadership Schisms and Consolidation During Kim Jong-un's Second Year in Power," op. cit. This overlaps with Jang Song-taek's disappearance from key leadership meetings. He failed to appear at the 65th anniversary of the founding of the state (September 8), the 16th anniversary commemorating Kim Jong-il's election as the KWP General Secretary (October 7), Kim Jong-un's visit to Kumsusan Palace of the Sun (October 10), and Kim Jong-un's visit to Samjiyeon county in Yanggang province (November 30). He also missed lower-level military and security events: the Fourth Meeting of KPA company commanders and political instructors (October 22-29), which was attended by key individuals in his chain of command (Kim Won-hong and Choe Pu-il); the Fourth Meeting of KPA active service personnel for political work with the enemy (November 12); and the Second Meeting of KPA security personnel (November 21), which was led by Kim Won-hong and Jo Kyong-chol.

164 A reading of this Funeral Committee list would suggest other movements within the Politburo ranks. Ri Yong-gil and Jang Jong-nam appear to have risen to possible alternate membership status, while Hyon Chol-hae and Choe Yong-rim may have been demoted from full to alternate status. This is based on analysis done by Michael Madden, the author of *North Korea Leadership Watch*.

Image 10: General O Kuk-ryol with scientists in November 2013. (Photo: Nodong Sinmun)

The rise in O Kuk-ryol's profile, which overlaps with the timeframe of Jang's downfall, may not be coincidental, as the two were rumored to be rivals. As the patriarch of a powerful political family in North Korea, O Kuk-ryol was believed by some Pyongyang-watchers to be a counterweight to Jang Song-taek. Their rivalry apparently intensified after Jang became Vice Chairman of the NDC and began to create a hard currency operation that rivaled the one controlled by O.[165] In the wake of the Third Party Conference and the launch of the succession process, O faded into the background as Jang's profile began to rise. Therefore, it is not surprising that this powerful individual would return to prominence to fill the political vacuum created by the demise of his rival.

While the impact of Jang's purge on the formal leadership was barely perceptible and subject to interpretation, the informal networks of power were more directly affected. North Korean media only mentioned the execution of two members of Jang's faction, Ri Ryong-ha and Jang Su-gil.[166] International media speculated on the purge of other individuals who had once been close to Kim

---

165   Lee Young-Jong, "O Kuk Ryol, Who Returned Around the Time of Jang Song Taek's Downfall," op. cit. After entering the NDC as a Vice Chairman in 2009, O Kuk-ryol created an organization in charge of many military hard currency operations, the Korea International Company, which was ratified by the SPA. This apparently spurred Jang to launch the Korea Daepung Group in January 2010 in order to keep O Kuk-ryol in check. Jang also allegedly planted the story in North Korean media that the activities of the Daepung Group were based on orders directly from NDC Chairman Kim Jong-il.
166   "North Korea's Kim Jong-un Executes 1000 of Jang Song-taek's Associates in 20 Days," *Free North Korea Radio*, January 3, 2014. According to defector reporting, Ri Myong-su, the former Minister of People's Security, may have also been executed. He was inexplicably replaced by Choe Pu-il in 2013. Ri was rumored to be very close to Jang Song-taek and his older brother, Jang Song-u.

Jong-il, such as Ri Su-yong (Ri Chol)[167] and Kim Chang-son.[168] While these specu-lations proved to be false, it spoke to the rumor mill that was aimed not at the senior leadership, but at members of the second echelon. Finally, several North Korean ambassadors with ties to Jang were recalled and relieved of their posts, including: Jang Yong-chol, Jang Song-taek's nephew and the Ambassador to Malaysia; Jon Yong-Jin, Jang Song-taek's brother-in-law and Ambassador to Cuba; Pak Kwang-chol, the Ambassador to Sweden; and Hong Yong, North Korea's Deputy Permanent Delegate to the United Nations Educational, Scientific, and Cultural Organization (UNESCO). Subsequent reporting told of their families being sent to prison camps.

Of those who appeared to be rising within the informal ranks, the military officers were most visible. At a meeting of KPA security personnel in November 2013, the month before Jang was officially purged, Kim Jong-un was surrounded by six men on the leadership rostrum: Vice Marshal Choe Ryong-hae; General Kim Won-hong; Major General Ryom Chol-song, reportedly Vice Director of the GPB; Lieutenant General Jo Kyong-chol, the Commander of the MSC; Lieutenant General Kim Su-gil, Vice Minister of the People's Armed Forces; and Hwang Pyong-so, the Vice Director of the KWP OGD.[169] This reflects where Kim Jong-un's critical networks within the military lie. They are within those parts of the apparatus dedicated to surveillance, internal security, and propagation of the monolithic leadership model of regime maintenance.

Two weeks later, Kim Jong-un paid a special visit to the Kumsusan Palace to commemorate the 22nd anniversary of Kim Jong-il's appointment as Supreme Commander, accompanied by the leaders of the high command. In addition to some long-standing military leaders, such as Kim Jong-gak, Kim Yong-chol, and O Kum-chol, rising stars were also on full display: General Ri Yong-gil, Chief of the GSD; General Jang Jong-nam, Minister of the People's Armed Forces; Pyon In-son,

---

167   Koo Jun-Hoe, "Mainichi Shimbun: Ri Su Yong Executed," *Daily NK*, December 11, 2013. Ri Su-yong was appointed North Korea's Ambassador to Switzerland in 1988 and was guardian to the young Kim Jong-un during his period of overseas study. He is thought to have handled around $4 billion of Kim Jong-il's hidden funds under the assumed name Ri Chol. After returning to North Korea in 2010, Ri took orders from Jang and was charged with attracting foreign capital as the Head of the Joint Venture and Investment Commission. According to reports in December 2013, he was executed. This was later proved wrong as Ri was appointed Minister of Foreign Affairs.

168   There was speculation in South Korean media that Kim Chang-son, the Director of the NDC Secretariat, may have been purged. Although he was one of Kim Jong-un's gatekeepers, he had not been observed in the public media since late November 2013. His ties with Jang Song-taek and Kim Kyong-hui go back to the 1970s. He later made an appearance in 2014, suggesting that he may have been sent off for re-education, but not purged.

169   "Second Meeting of Security Personnel of KPA Held," *KCNA*, November 20, 2013. The meeting of the military intelligence officials was held abruptly for the first time in two decades. It is assumed by many Pyongyang-watchers to have been a prelude to the Jang purge.

Director of the GSD's Operations Bureau; So Hong-chan, First Vice Minister of the People's Armed Forces; Lieutenant General Kim Su-gil; and Major General Ryom Chol-song.[170] Vice Marshal Choe Ryong-hae was noticeably standing to Kim Jong-un's immediate left.[171, 172]

Below is a chart of leadership connections within the regime at the end of 2013. The solid lines represent direct connections to Kim Jong-un, while the dotted lines represent more indirect connections.

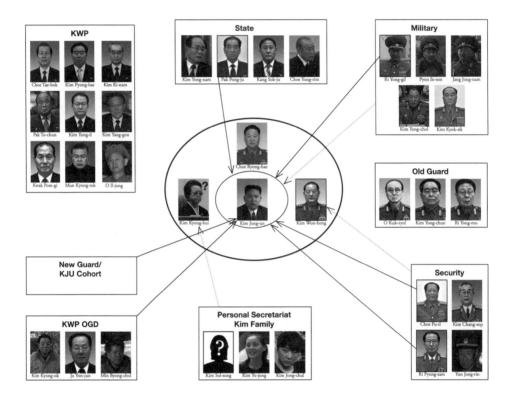

According to a South Korean intelligence report, Kim had begun a generational shift across the board, replacing many older figures with relatively younger

170   Lee Young-Jong, "Report Details North Korea's Rising, Falling 'Stars,'" *Korea JoongAng Daily*, December 19, 2013. These officers are part of a cadre of twenty-five senior generals who were newly appointed in the Kim Jong-un era. They mostly specialized in operations and have experience as field commanders.

171   Kang Seung-Woo, "Choe Solidifies Power Base," *The Korea Times*, December 24, 2013.

172   *Nodong Sinmun*, December 24, 2013.

ones, lowering the average age of the inner circle from 76 to 62.[173] Outside of the military figures mentioned above, four deputy ministerial-level officials from the KWP are worth noting: Kim Pyong-ho, Vice Director of the PAD; Pak Tae-song, Vice Director of the OGD; Hong Yong-chil, Vice Director of the Machine Industry Department (MID);[174] and Ma Won-chun, Vice Director of the Finance and Accounting Department (FAD). They frequently accompanied Kim Jong-un on his guidance inspections and he reportedly praised their work.

2. Leadership Dynamics in 2014/2015

In his 2014 New Year's address, Kim Jong-un hailed the execution of Jang Song-taek as the elimination of "factional filth." This was a brief reference to the events of December. The address was scrutinized by the international community for any signs of leadership changes after the purge, but none were apparent. The only other major event broadcast on January 1, 2014 was Kim Jong-un's visit to the Kumsusan Palace of the Sun. Coverage showed the North Korean leader flanked by his wife, Ri Sol-ju, and Chairman of the Presidium of the SPA, Kim Yong-nam, alongside political and military officials. Senior military officers stood to Kim Jong-un's right again, as they did on his visit to the same building on the anniversary of his father's death on December 17.

Contrary to much speculation in the Pyongyang-watching community, a full-blown purge and reshuffle of the North Korean leadership did not immediately follow the Jang Song-taek purge. What did happen over the course of 2014 and into 2015 was a careful reordering of the key individuals around Kim Jong-un. Much of this re-arrangement was only visible through a careful tracking of appearances by individuals in close proximity to the Supreme Leader.

3. The Regent Structure

Jang Song-taek's purge raised questions about the viability of the regent structure around Kim Jong-un. Over the next several months, the Pyongyang-watching community looked for signs regarding the fate of the other two regents, Kim Kyong-hui and Choe Ryong-hae.

As of the summer of 2015, Kim Kyong-hui has not appeared in public since September 2013, when she stood on the leadership podium during a military parade

---

173   Lee Young-Jong, "Report Details North Korea's Rising, Falling 'Stars'," op. cit.
174   Although it has not been mentioned in North Korean media, Hong Yong-chil's appearances in 2014 suggest that he may have replaced Ju Kyu-chang as Director of the KWP MID.

of the Worker-Peasant Red Guard Forces and a Pyongyang mass rally at Kim Il-sung Square to commemorate the 65th founding anniversary of the state.[175] While it is assumed that she is in poor health,[176] it is unclear whether she has been removed from politics. There are very few clues as to her current status in the regime.

Her name appeared sixth on the Kim Kuk-tae Funeral Committee list, which was announced shortly after Jang's purge, quelling initial speculation that she had also been purged. In February, however, she was deleted from a documentary of the leadership's tribute to Kim Il-sung and Kim Jong-il. It had originally aired, with her image included, on December 13, 2013, the day after Jang's execution. In May, after not appearing at the meeting of the SPA, she failed to appear in a re-run of the documentary.[177] Later that month, she appeared in another documentary entitled, "He Boosted Sports as a Nationwide Frenzy,"[178] praising Kim Jong-un's contributions to promoting the regime's sports industry.[179] The last indication of her status was her absence from Jon Pyong-ho's Funeral Committee list in July 2014.[180] Given her appearance on Kim Kuk-tae's Funeral Committee list, this was likely an indication that Kim Kyong-hui has left the political scene. Whether she retains any influence or has any contact with her nephew is unknown.

Like Kim Kyong-hui's status, Choe Ryong-hae's position within the leadership has been cloaked in mystery. Often perceived as a rival of Jang Song-taek, Choe's profile was expected to rise with Jang's purge. Many in the Pyongyang-watching community rushed to designate him as the new number two leader within

---

175   "Defector: Kim Jong-un's Aunt Killed Herself Last Year," *The Wall Street Journal*, November 26, 2014. In late 2014, Kim Heung-kwang, a defector, claimed that he received information from inside the regime that Kim Kyong-hui committed suicide by poison a few days after her husband's execution and on the second anniversary of her brother's death (December 17, 2013). He contends that this fact explains why Kim Kyong-hui was edited out of a documentary only to reappear during a rerun, something that would not have been allowed to happen if she were alive.

176   "U.S. Doctor Visits N. Korea To Treat Leader Kim's Aunt," *Yonhap News Agency*, October 2, 2014. According to South Korean reporting, an American cardiologist arrived in Pyongyang around September 28, 2014 to treat Kim Kyong-hui.

177   According to several Pyongyang-watchers, Kim Kyong-hui's status may account for the decision not to publicize the proceedings of the Politburo meeting on April 8, 2014. If a decision was made to remove her from the Politburo and Secretariat, this would send a dramatic signal to her powerful patronage system that she is no longer involved in politics. This could potentially be destabilizing since Kim Jong-un most likely needs access to this system to consolidate his power.

178   Lee Young-Jong and Kim Hee-Jin, "Kim's Aunt Makes Appearance in State Broadcast," *Korea JoongAng Daily*, May 2, 2014.

179   Kim Kyong-hui's disappearance and reappearance in North Korean documentaries has led to speculation that the removal of her image was not on purpose but tied to an effort to remove the image of Mun Kyong-tok. He was the former KWP Secretary for Pyongyang Affairs and a close ally of Jang Song-taek. Mun has not been seen in public since February 2014.

180   "DPRK Party Organ Carries Full List of State Funeral Committee Members for Late Jon Pyong-ho," *Nodong Sinmun*, July 9, 2014.

the regime. Throughout 2013, Choe accompanied Kim Jong-un on eighty percent of his guidance inspections. In January 2014, his status became uncertain.

The first indication that Choe's status might be falling occurred in January when he missed seven consecutive military-related public appearances with Kim Jong-un.[181] In February 2014, he disappeared for nearly a month, although he continued to appear in documentaries. He reappeared on March 7, 2014 as the first among nine officials accompanying Kim Jong-un on a military inspection.[182] The following month came with mixed messages for Choe. At the 13th SPA, he was promoted to Vice Chairman of the NDC, filling the vacancy left by Jang Song-taek. However, following a meeting of the KWP CMC at the end of the month, North Korean media announced that Choe had been replaced as Director of the GPB by Hwang Pyong-so, a First Vice Director of the KWP OGD.[183] Choe retained his post as Party Secretary, but his portfolio is unclear.[184] While most of the Pyongyang-watching community speculates that Choe Ryong-hae has lost power,[185] some Chinese sources believe that his power and responsibilities have shifted from the military to the Party apparatus.[186] He was ranked tenth on Jon Pyong-ho's Funeral Committee list.[187]

As 2014 progressed, Choe's status appeared to stabilize. He assumed the Chairmanship of the SPCSGC, a position once held by Jang Song-taek. Although Hwang Pyong-so replaced Choe as Vice Chairman of the NDC at the second meeting of the SPA in September, Choe's status appeared fully restored by October, when he surpassed Hwang in coverage of Kim Jong-un's guidance inspections.[188]

---

181   Since becoming Director of the GPB in 2012, Choe Ryong-hae had never missed more than four military appearances.

182   Documentaries from January showed Choe Ryong-hae walking with a limp, suggesting the possibility that his disappearance was due to health reasons.

183   Michael Madden, "The Fall of Choe Ryong Hae," *38 North*, May 2, 2014. This CMC meeting came only six weeks after another meeting of the body—an unusual occurrence—suggesting that it was convened to handle a special matter. Some Pyongyang-watchers have speculated that Choe was removed as head of the GPB because he had failed to boost the military's loyalty to Kim Jong-un.

184   Park Hyeong-Jung, "The Demotion of Choe Ryong Hae: Background and Implication," *Korea Institute for National Unification: Online Series* 14, No. 5 (May 21, 2014). Dr. Park Hyeong-Jung speculates that Choe no longer holds the position for military affairs to which he was appointed at the Third Party Conference in 2010. He is now the KWP Secretary for Workers' Organizations.

185   Michael Madden, "The Fall of Choe Ryong Hae," op. cit.

186   Discussion with a Chinese North Korea-watcher, August 2014.

187   "DPRK Party Organ Carries Full List of State Funeral Committee Members for Late Jon Pyong-ho," *Nodong Sinmun*, op. cit.

188   "Choe Ryong Hae Called Ahead Of Hwang Pyong So: NK's Power Ranking Shift?" *Dong-A Ilbo*, October 30, 2014. In an article on the completion ceremony of the May First Stadium on October 29, 2014, North Korean media listed Choe Ryong-hae before Hwang Pyong-so. The last time state media listed both Choe and Hwang as Kim Jong-un's accompanying officials was on October 22, 2014, when Kim Jong-un visited a scientists' rest home, and Hwang was listed before Choe. A few days

Since then, he has been a constant presence around the Supreme Leader.[189] Additionally, in November, he led a delegation to Russia to meet with President Vladimir Putin.

Kim Kyong-hui and Choe Ryong-hae's changing fortunes appear to indicate the end of the regent structure. As Kim Jong-un moves into his final phase of power consolidation, he has begun to transform the leadership model in order to maximize his direct control of the policy- and decision-making process.[190] Instead of regents, he is now surrounded by senior advisors, who have varying degrees of influence, but no ability to dictate policy.[191] While he continues to oversee formal leadership meetings, it is highly likely that he will adopt elements of his father's "hub-and-spoke" leadership style in interacting with the wider leadership. As a consequence, Kim Jong-un's Personal Secretariat will probably grow in size in order to accommodate the more informal aspects of his leadership style.

earlier at another guidance inspection, Choe's name was listed before Kim Ki-nam, KWP Secretary for Propaganda and Agitation. This led to speculation by some Pyongyang-watchers that Choe may hold an extremely important post in the Party, possibly KWP Secretary for Organization and Guidance. However, by March 2015, Hwang Pyong-so had again eclipsed Choe Ryong-hae. The North Korean media cited Hwang ahead of Choe when it reported on leader Kim Jong-un's visit to the Victorious War Museum in Pyongyang. See "Is Kim Jong Un Playing Musical Chairs At The Top?" *The Chosun Ilbo*, March 2, 2015. Pyongyang radio on March 8, 2015 reported that "Comrade Choe Ryong-hae, member the WPK CC Political Bureau," gave a report at the "central report meeting" held on the same day to mark the 105th anniversary of International Women's Day. Just a month before, Choe had been referred to as a member of the Politburo Presidium.

189   "Choe Ryong-hae to Second-in-Command with the Help of his Wife Who is Close to Ri Sol-ju - RFA," *The Chosun Ilbo*, November 6, 2014. According to rumors inside Pyongyang, Choe Ryong-hae's return to the center of power is due, to some extent, to his wife, Kang Kyong-sil. She is reportedly close friends with Kim Jong-un's wife, Ri Sol-ju. Kang's relationship with the ruling family goes back to Kim's mother, Ko Yong-hui. Kang was a member of the Pibada Opera Troupe, which frequently interacted with the Mansudae Art Studio, to which Ko belonged. Kang's two brothers are executives of a trading firm, which suggests that the family is held in high regard.

190   Ken E. Gause, *North Korean Leadership Dynamics and Decision-making under Kim Jong-un: A Second Year Assessment* (Alexandria, VA: CNA Occasional Publication 2014-U-006988, March 2014).

191   North Korean media treatment of Hwang Pyong-so and Choe Ryong-hae in the summer and fall of 2014 suggests that Kim Jong-un may be creating a rivalry to facilitate his own power consolidation.

4. Kim Jong-un and the Wider Leadership

With the removal of the regent structure, Kim Jong-un's relations with the wider leadership have become increasingly important. As the new "Control Tower," Kim's closest advisors most likely reside within his personal apparatus. But in order for the regime to operate, he will have to rely on connections on at least two levels: the second and third echelons.[192] These echelons include much of the senior leadership within the Party, military, and government. They also include the commanders, ministers, and directors responsible for domestic, foreign, and security policy execution.

Many of these individuals are tied to the Kim family through blood and family relations. Kim Jong-il's "hub-and-spoke" leadership style was based on clear lines of communication to these echelons. He often bypassed the chain of command to ensure orders were understood and carried out. It is not yet clear whether Kim Jong-un will run the regime in the same way that his father did, but relationships at these levels will be critical as he eventually consolidates his power. A fourth echelon of leadership, while still highly speculative, is worth analyzing because it may contain future key leaders.

Since the purge of Jang Song-taek, the regime has published extensive funeral committee lists for two senior leaders who have passed away: Kim Kuk-tae in December 2013, and Jon Pyong-ho in July 2014.[193] Jon's Funeral Committee is especially useful for the Pyongyang-watching community to better understand where power and influence lie. It reveals some emerging leaders and provides insight into the status of some previously high-profile officials. These lists, combined with recent reporting on Kim Jong-un's guidance inspections and information coming from senior-level defectors, provide insights into the emerging leadership structure that Kim Jong-un must manage as he consolidates his position as Supreme Leader.

---

192   There is much debate within Pyongyang-watching circles on which leaders should be included in which echelons. The author's opinion is based on discussions with numerous Pyongyang-watchers over the years.
193   "DPRK Party Organ Names Members on State Funeral Committee for Late Kim Kuk-t'ae," *Nodong Sinmun*, December 15, 2013. "DPRK Party Organ Carries Full List of State Funeral Committee Members for Late Jon Pyong-ho," op. cit.

a. Key Advisors

The purge of Jang Song-taek and the dissolution of the regent structure have increased the political space around Kim Jong-un, which has been filled by a handful of rising individuals. Best described as key advisors, these leaders often accompany the Supreme Leader. In addition to their formal positions, they most likely enjoy further influence by virtue of their proximity. This influence sometimes manifests when they are ranked above their cohorts on recent funeral committee lists, which Pyongyang-watchers use to identify the formal leadership ranking within the regime.[194]

Ironically, it is at this level where much of the turmoil within the leadership ranks has occurred in 2015. In February, the international media claimed that Pyon In-son, Chief of the General Staff's Operations Bureau was purged, allegedly for disregarding or taking exception to Kim Jong-un's orders.[195, 196] This was not confirmed in the North Korean press, although he was no longer highlighted as being part of Kim Jong-un's retinue during guidance inspections. In May 2015, the NIS claimed that it had intelligence that Hyon Yong-chol, the Minister of People's

---

194   The question many Pyongyang-watchers struggle with is whether any of these advisors impact policy or doctrine development, or are they irrelevant to the policymaking process? In other words, do they matter? In some cases, long-term advisors on critical policy areas, such as Kang Sok-ju, probably play a role in providing context and critical advice. Others, especially power brokers in the military and security apparatus, are less relevant to policymaking and, as such, more interchangeable in the balance of power inside the regime.

195   Colonel General Pyon In-son (69) was Director of the GSD Operations Bureau. He was part of the third generation of the military leadership. He was also a member of the KWP Central Committee and deputy to the SPA. He was promoted to Colonel General on July 25, 2003. Pyon's career was spent moving between Pyongyang and the field commands. His early career was primarily served in the MPAF headquarters before he assumed the command of the Seventh Corps in South Hamgyong Province in the late 1990s. In 2007, he returned to Pyongyang as a Vice Minister of the People's Armed Forces. Four years later, he was returned to the field as the Commander of the Fourth Corps in South Hwanghae Province. Following the March/April crisis, he returned to the center as a Vice Minister of the People's Armed Forces and Director of the GSD Operations Bureau (August 2013). He was ranked 43rd on Jon Pyong-ho's Funeral Committee list.

196   "Unidentified South Korean Government Official Says DPRK Kim Jong Un 'Removed' Two Aides," *NHK*, February 4, 2015. The media also speculated that Ma Won-chun, the Director of NDC Design Department, had also been purged. Later speculation said that he had either been executed or died before he could return to Pyongyang. In October 2015, Ma was identified as a member of Kim Jong-un's guidance inspection trip to Rason to examine how the North Korean city was recovering from Typhoon Goni.

Armed Forces,[197] had been executed by anti-aircraft fire for treason.[198] In the same timeframe, rumors emerged that Han Kwang-sang, the head of the KWP FAD, had been purged.[199] The removal of these key advisors, all of whom were presumably handpicked by Kim himself, raised questions about the process of power consolidation. Whether these moves were done out of desperation, malice, or part of a calculated strategy to keep the wider leadership off balance was not clear as this book went to print.[200] It is likely, however, that this group of close advisors will continue to evolve as Kim Jong-un moves to consolidate his power.

---

197   Colonel General Hyon Yong-chol (66) was the Minister of the People's Armed Forces, an alternate member of the Politburo (since 2013), and a member of the NDC (2014). His rise through the ranks paralleled the period in which Kim Jong-un became the heir apparent, which suggested that there might have been a relationship between the two. For reasons that are still unclear, he was replaced as Chief of the GSD, a month after being raised to the Politburo, in 2013 and appointed Commander of the Fifth Corps with a reduction in rank from a four-star to a three-star general. Nearly one year later, in June 2014, he was appointed Minister of the People's Armed Forces, replacing Jang Jong-nam. Hyon was re-promoted to four-star general. He was listed sixth on Jon Pyong-ho's Funeral Committee list. At the September 2014 meeting of the SPA, he replaced Jang Jong-nam on the NDC.

198   Yu Shin-Mo, Bak Eun-Gyeong and Yu Jeong-In, "Kim Jong-un's Reign Of Terror: North Korean Military's Second in Command Purged," *The Kyunghyang Shinmun*, May 14, 2014. An oddity surrounding Hyon's apparent purge is that he continued to appear in the North Korean media days after his apparent execution on April 30, 2015. He appeared in a documentary on Kim Jong-un's military inspections, which aired on May 5, 11, and 12. One explanation for this apparent departure in how the North Korean media handles leaders who have fallen afoul of the Supreme Leader is that the regime did not want to alert the outside world, and maybe the wider leadership, to Hyon's purge. Apparently, Kim Jong-un's ability to lead was challenged in the aftermath of the Ri Yong-ho purge, when the media announced his immediate retirement due to health issues, coded language that suggested he had been purged.

199   Han Kwang-sang (57) was the director of the KWP FAD. He emerged on the political scene in January 2010 as part of Kim Jong-il's guidance inspection of the Hyangsan Hotel. He was identified as a First Vice Director of the KWP. In May 2012, his name began to appear before the first vice directors of the KWP OGD and PAD, something that suggested that he had been promoted to a Director of a Central Committee department. The KWP FAD manages the Party's funds and assets and is responsible for the welfare of cadres and employees working for the central Party apparatus. As such, Han most likely had some access to Kim Jong-un, the extent of which is currently unclear. He was ranked 30th on Jon Pyong-ho's Funeral Committee list.

200   For more biographical details of these individuals, see Appendix A.

Table 1: Key Advisors to Kim Jong-un[201]

Name	Position(s)	Comments
Kim Family		
Kim Yo-jong (28)	• Vice Director of a KWP Department (since 2014)	Kim Yo-jong is Kim Jong-un's younger sister. She is rumored to be working in the KWP OGD or PAD and her brother's Personal Secretariat.[202] She was identified as a vice director of a KWP department in 2014. Since Kim Ki-nam's apparent retirement in place in 2015, some speculate that she is now directing the operations of the PAD. During Kim Ki-nam's withdrawal from the public spotlight in the spring of 2015, some speculated that she had taken over the day-to-day operations of the Propaganda and Agitation Department.[203]

---

201   For some biographies, there is a question mark (?) in the "Position(s)" column. This designates that this person may no longer occupy this position or is only rumored to occupy the position. The leadership around Kim Jong-un is shifting. Appointments to senior Party bodies have not been fully reported on by the North Korean media since 2012. Therefore, the author has used the question mark to reflect this lack of clarity.

202   "Kim Jong Un Gives Guidance at April 26 Cartoon Film Studio," *KCNA*, November 26, 2014. Kim Yo-jong was identified for the first time as a Vice Department Director of the KWP Central Committee in November 2014, as part of her brother's inspection of the April 26 Cartoon Film Studio. Based on the fact that the key cohorts accompanying Kim, Kim Ki-nam and Ri Jae-il, are from the KWP PAD, the South Korean government speculated that Kim Yo-jong was also with this Central Committee department. However, earlier speculation tied her to the KWP OGD. She is the youngest vice director of the KWP in the history of North Korea. Her father, Kim Jong-il, became the Vice Director of the PAD in 1970 when he was 28. Her once-powerful aunt Kim Kyong-hui became the Vice Director of the International Department when she was 30.

203   "NK Leader's Sister Seen as Playing Key Role in Propaganda Work," *Yonhap News Agency*, June 3, 2015. See also Lee Sang-Yong. "Kim Yo Jong in de facto power of PAD," *Daily NK*, July 20, 2015. Information from July 2015 suggests that Kim Ki-nam and Kim Yo-jong both continue to have roles in the PAD. Kim Yo-jong has been put in charge of idolization projects for the leadership, while Kim Ki-nam supports her in his role as Director of the KWP PAD, albeit a director who is essentially retired in place. As Vice Director of the PAD, Kim Yo-jong is personally responsible for leading idolization projects related to her brother.

Name	Position(s)	Comments
Kim Sol-song (41) (?)	• Member of Kim Jong-un's Personal Secretariat (?)	Kim Sol-song is the daughter of Kim Jong-il and Kim Yong-suk. She is Kim Jong-un's older half sister. Close to her aunt, Kim Kyong-hui, Kim Sol-song has reportedly taken over mentoring duties of Kim Jong-un and Kim Yo-jong. She also reportedly is a senior figure in Kim's Personal Secretariat.
Party		
Choe Ryong-hae (65)	• Member of the Politburo (since 2015) • KWP Secretary (since 2010, 2015)	Choe Ryong-hae is a former regent to Kim Jong-un. He now acts as a senior Party advisor. Although he suffered a demotion in 2014/15 with his removal from the Politburo Presidium and directorship of the GPB, he continues to occupy a position close to the Supreme Leader. He has been tasked to lead special missions to both China and Russia and appears to play a balancing role within the senior leadership. He has been a KWP Secretary since 2010—first for Military Affairs and more recently for Work Organizations. His second son, Choe Song, is reportedly married to Kim Yo-jong.
Kang Sok-ju (76)	• Member of the Politburo (since 2010) • KWP Secretary for International Affairs (since 2014)	Kang has been a major player in North Korean foreign policy since the 1980s, when he was in the Ministry of Foreign Affairs. He likely remains an influential strategist in helping Kim Jong-un maneuver within the international arena. His promotion to Party Secretary in 2014 ensures that he has direct talks with Kim Jong-un on a regular basis.

Name	Position(s)	Comments
Kim Yang-gon (73)	• Member of the Politburo (since August 2015) • KWP Secretary for South Korean Affairs (since 2010) • Director of the KWP United Front Department (UFD) (since 2007)	The UFD is the Party's intelligence agency dedicated to South Korean operations. Kim's role in facilitating dialogue between the two Koreas in the past was rarely acknowledged but highly significant. Kim Yang-gon is Kim Jong-il's cousin and was a close confidant. In October 2014, he was part of a three-person delegation, along with Choe Ryong-hae and Hwang Pyong-so, that visited Seoul in an effort to restart inter-Korean relations. In August 2015, he accompanied Hwang Pyong-so to Panmunjom to negotiate an exit from the inter-Korean crisis following North Korea's firing of artillery across the DMZ. In the same month, North Korean media referred to him as a full member of the Politburo. He was ranked 16th on both Kim Kuk-tae's and Jon Pyong-ho's Funeral Committee lists.
Jo Yon-jun (76)	• Alternate member of the Politburo (since 2012) • First Vice Director of the KWP OGD	Jo Yon-jun handles political and economic issues inside the OGD. He is believed to be one of Kim Jong-un's key allies within the OGD. He was ranked 24th on Kim Kuk-tae's Funeral Committee list and 22nd on Jon Pyong-ho's Funeral Committee list.

Name	Position(s)	Comments
Kim Song-nam (62)	• Alternate Member of the KWP Central Committee • Vice Director of the KWP International Affairs Department	Kim Song-nam is a renowned "China hand" who started working in the KWP International Affairs Department in the 1980s. He is one of Kim Jong-un's primary advisors on China affairs and allegedly has a direct communications channel with the Supreme Leader.[204]
Kim Su-gil (76)	• Chief Secretary of the Pyong-yang Municipal Party Commit-tee (since 2014)	Kim Su-gil replaced Mun Kyong-tok, who was reportedly removed because of his close ties to Jang Song-taek and the former KWP Administrative Department. It is highly likely that he has also replaced Mun as the KWP Secretary for Pyongyang Affairs. He is rumored to be affiliated with the GPB's Organization Department. He was listed 72nd on Jon Pyong-ho's Funeral Committee list.
Jon Il-chun (74)	• Vice Director of the KWP FAD • Managing Director of the State Develop-ment Bank	As a former head of Office 39, Chon's ties to hard currency operations would suggest that he has a direct channel of communi-cation with Kim Jong-un, as well as Kim Yo-jong and Kim Sol-song, who have re-sponsibilities for the Kim family funds. His leadership ranking rose from 41st on Kim Kuk-tae's Funeral Committee list to 35th on Jon Pyong-ho's Funeral Committee list.

204   It should be noted that Kim Song-nam last appeared in the North Korean media in November 2014 as part of a North Korean delegation that saw Choe Ryong-hae off at the airport on a mission to Russia.

Name	Position(s)	Comments
Military/ Security		
Vice Marshal Hwang Pyong-so (66)	• Director of the GPB (2014) • Member of the Politburo Presidium (2015) • Vice Chairman of the NDC (2014)	Responsible for securing the loyalty of the military to Kim Jong-un. Widely considered the second most powerful man in the regime, Hwang Pyong-so's rapid promotion suggests that he has become one of Kim Jong-un's most trusted advisors. His background in security affairs in the OGD has been most useful in his oversight of the military.
General Ri Yong-gil (60)	• Chief of the GSD (since August 2013) • Alternate Member of the Politburo (since April 2014)	Responsible for the operational status of the armed forces. As former Director of the GSD Operations Bureau, with a rapid rise into the inner circle, Ri was ranked fourth and fifth respectively on Kim Kuk-tae's and Jon Pyong-ho's Funeral Committee lists.
General Kim Won-hong (70)	• Member of the Politburo (since 2012) • Member of the CMC (since 2010) • Member of the NDC (since 2012) • Director of the SSD (since 2012)	Kim Won-hong's status has been tied to Kim Jong-un more than that of any other member of the North Korean leadership. He publicly appeared in leadership circles in 2010 and has been a frequent member of Kim Jong-un's guidance inspections, where he would have direct access to the Supreme Leader. He was ranked 15th on Jon Pyong-ho's Funeral Committee list, a rank that understates his real influence.

Name	Position(s)	Comments
Colonel General Jo Kyong-chol	• Commander of the Military Security Command (MSC)	As head of the MSC, he runs an organization that plays an important role in guaranteeing internal security. Because of its sensitive mission, the commander of the MSC reportedly has a direct line of communication to the Supreme Leader. Jo Kyong-chol was ranked 47th on Jon Pyong-ho's Funeral Committee list. He was also promoted to colonel general in February 2015.
Colonel General Yun Jong-rin (77)	• Member of the CMC (since 2010) • Director of the Guard Command (GC)	As Director of the Guard Command (GC), he is responsible for ensuring Kim Jong-un's protection. Therefore, he not only works with Kim's Personal Secretariat but also most likely has a direct line of communication to Kim that bypasses any gatekeepers.
Government		
Pak Pong-ju (76)	• Member of the Politburo (since 2013) • Premier (since 2013)	Responsible for managing the economic affairs of the "people's economy," Pak most likely interacts directly with Kim Jong-un. He was listed second and third, respectively, on Kim Kuk-tae's and Jon Pyong-ho's Funeral Committee lists.

Name	Position(s)	Comments
Ri Su-yong (Ri Chol) (75)	• Minister of Foreign Affairs (since 2014)	Normally a position of little influence, the foreign affairs position has likely taken on greater importance under Ri Su-yong, who has had close ties to the Kim family for decades. He managed Kim Jong-il's finances in Europe and oversaw the education of Kim Jong-chol, Kim Jong-un, and Kim Yo-jong when they attended school in Bern, Switzerland. Ri has also been tied to Kim Jong-un's Personal Secretariat and the secret family slush fund, worth billions, that is used to ensure the regime's support among the wider leadership.
Major General Ma Won-chun (59)	• Director of the National Defense Commission Design Department	Began to appear on Kim Jong-un's guidance inspections in May 2012 as a KWP vice director. Appointed as head of NDC Design Department in May 2014. Fell out of favor in late 2014 following Kim Jong-un's unfavorable inspection of the renovation of Pyongyang Airport. Allegedly purged but returned to favor in October 2015.[205]

b. Key Individuals in the Second Echelon of the Leadership

In addition to those closest to Kim Jong-un, the wider North Korean leadership is composed of echelons of power where many of the formal elite belong. The second echelon includes officials who hold critical positions within the leadership. They are responsible for relevant policy areas or have control over critical resources and patronage systems.[205] These officials can provide advice and intelligence, but

---

205   It should be noted that it is particularly difficult to identify individuals at this level of the leadership because their standing is tied to their posts within the formal leadership. In the case of the Party, appointments and retirements within the senior leadership bodies, such as the Politburo and CMC, have been largely hidden since 2012. In August 2015, for example, the North Korean media mentioned that several members had been dropped from the ranks of the CMC, however, it failed to identify these individuals.

have no decision-making authority. Many have also cultivated a close relationship with Kim Jong-un since 2010, when he became the heir apparent. Some within this echelon may occasionally be able to reach out to him directly, bypassing his gate-keepers.[206] As Kim Jong-un consolidates his power, many of these leaders will likely disappear from the leadership.[207] As of now, this echelon of the senior leadership includes the following individuals:

Table 2: Second Echelon of Power

Name	Position(s)	Comments
Party		
Kim Ki-nam (86)	• Member of the Politburo (since 2010) • KWP Secretary for Propaganda (since the 1990s) • Director of the KWP PAD • Rumored to be retired in place	A close associate of the Kim family, Kim Ki-nam is credited for creating the cult of personality around Kim Jong-il and praising Kim Il-sung's historic role as the founder of the regime. He was given a role in ensuring Kim Jong-un's succession and appointed to the Politburo in September 2010. He was one of only three civilian officials who accompanied Kim Jong-il's coffin during his funeral in December 2011. He was ranked seventh on Jon Pyong-ho's Funeral Committee list. According to defector reports, his day-to-day role in the PAD may have been taken over by Kim Yo-jong.

---

206   This ability to bypass the gatekeepers is likely tied to a person's relationship with Kim Jong-un. Blood relatives of the Kim family and close associates of Kim Jong-il may have a certain amount of access that is denied to others.

207   Nicolas Levi, "Analysis: Old Generation of North Korean Elite Remain Active," *New Focus International*, July 31, 2013. Some Pyongyang-watchers, such as Levi, caution against the belief that the old guard is being forced out. Many still continue to play important roles within the regime despite their age and health.

Name	Position(s)	Comments
Choe Tae-bok (85)	• Member of the Politburo (since 2010) • KWP Secretary • Chairman of the SPA (since 1998)	Along with Kim Jong-un and Kim Ki-nam, Choe Tae-bok was the only other civilian to accompany Kim Jong-il's hearse. Choe is a reported protégé of Yang Hyong-sop, the Vice President of the SPA Presidium and is tied to Kim Kyong-hui's patronage system. He was ranked eighth on Jon Pyong-ho's Funeral Committee list.
Pak To-chun (71)	• Member of the Politburo (since 2010) • KWP Secretary for Defense Industry (until 2015) • Member of the NDC (from 2011 to 2015) • Reported to be an advisor to Kim Jong-un on defense-related issues	Pak To-chun played a central role in the early Kim Jong-un era but was reportedly retired in 2015. Given the role that testing of critical defense systems, such as the nuclear and missile programs, plays in Kim Jong-un's reign, it is highly likely that Pak To-chun continues to have access to the Supreme Leader. He was ranked tenth on Jon Pyong-ho's Funeral Committee list.
Kim Kyo-ng-ok	• Member of the CMC (since 2010) • First Vice Director of the KWP OGD • Rumored to have retired for health reasons	Kim Kyong-ok was tied to the rise of Kim Jong-un dating back to the mid-2000s. Within the OGD, he has the portfolio for military and security affairs. In recent years, his patronage ties have been linked to Kim Sol-song and, according to some reports, they are married. He was last seen in the North Korean media in December 2014. He is rumored to be suffering from health issues and may have stepped down from his posts.

Name	Position(s)	Comments
Military/ Security		
General O Kuk-ryol (85)	• Alternate member of the Politburo (since 2012) • Vice Chairman of the NDC (since 2009)	O Kuk-ryol's ties to the Kim family date back to the 1930s. O sits atop one of the most prominent patronage systems inside the North Korean armed forces. He reportedly has responsibilities within the NDC for intelligence operations abroad as well as for crisis management. In periods of tension on the Korean peninsula, O's influence and access to Kim Jong-un and his advisors may increase. He was ranked 14th on Jon Pyong-ho's Funeral Committee list, which remained unchanged from his ranking in 2013 on Kim Kuk-tae's Funeral Committee list.
Vice Marshal Ri Yong-mu (90)	• Member of the Politburo (since 2010) • Vice Chairman of the NDC (since 1998)	Ri Yong-mu oversees one of the major patronage systems inside the military. His access to Kim Jong-un is unclear and most likely not on a regular basis outside of formal channels. It is also rumored that Ri suffers from cancer and therefore is limited in his ability to conduct politics. He was ranked 13th on Jon Pyong-ho's Funeral Committee list, which remained unchanged from his ranking in 2013 on Kim Kuk-tae's Funeral Committee list.

Name	Position(s)	Comments
General Ri Pyong-chol (66)	• Member of the CMC (since 2010) • Member of the NDC (since 2014) • Former Commander of the KPA Air Force (until December 2014) • First Vice Director of a KWP Central Committee Department (2015)	Ri Pyong-chol has spoken at a number of leadership events and has accompanied Kim Jong-un on a number of military-related guidance inspections. Ri's name has also been associated with the North Korean drone program. With his appointment to the NDC at the meeting of the SPA in September 2014, he most likely gained direct access to Kim Jong-un and no longer has to communicate through the GSD. In January 2015, Ri was identified as the First Vice Director of a KWP Central Committee department. According to South Korean media, he is attached to the KWP Military Department. He ranked 52nd on Jon Pyong-ho's Funeral Committee list.
Vice Marshal Kim Yong-chun (79)	• Member of the Politburo (since 2010) • Member of the CMC (since 2010) • Director, KWP Civil Defense Department (since 2012) • Possibly has been retired	Kim Yong-chun's ties to the Kim family go back to the 1980s, when he was Director of the GSD Operations Bureau. A member of the guard that accompanied Kim Jong-il's hearse, Kim Yong-chun appeared to play a critical role in the early Kim Jong-un period. However, rumors surfaced in 2013 that he had been retired from the leadership.

Name	Position(s)	Comments
General Kim Yong-chol (69)	• Member of the CMC (since 2010) • Vice Chief of the GSD (since 2013) • Director of the RGB (since 2009)	Kim Yong-chol's ties to Kim Jong-un allegedly date back to the early 2000s, when he oversaw Kim Jong-un's education at Kim Il-sung Military University. Previously, he was in the GC and served as a bodyguard to Kim Jong-il. The RGB has been tied to the 2010 sinking of the *Cheonan* and the 2015 landmine explosions along the DMZ. Formally, his access to the senior leadership would go through Chief of the GSD, Ri Yong-gil, and Vice Chairman of the NDC, O Kuk-ryol. However, Kim Yong-chol's long-time relationship with Kim Jong-un likely provides him with a private channel of communication, especially on issues related to South Korea and in times of crisis. He was ranked 54th on Jon Pyong-ho's Funeral Committee list.
General Choe Pu-il (71)	• Alternate Member of the Politburo (since 2013) • Member of the CMC (since 2010) • Member of the NDC (since 2013) • Minister of People's Security (since 2013)	A close associate of the Kim family for years, Choe Pu-il is rumored to be a favorite of Kim Jong-un. As Minister of People's Security, he reported up to Jang Song-taek and the NDC. This apparently has not hurt his standing within the leadership; however, he did disappear from public view for some time following the collapse of a housing unit in Pyongyang in 2014. He was ranked 20th on Jon Pyong-ho's Funeral Committee list.

Name	Position(s)	Comments
Government		
Kim Yong-nam (87)	• Member of the Politburo Presidium (since 2010) • Chairman of the SPA Presidium	As Chairman of the SPA Presidium, Kim Yong-nam is considered the de facto head of state of North Korea. His real power, however, comes by virtue of his close ties to the Kim family and relationships throughout the leadership. Kim Yong-nam has long played an intermediary role and a stabilizing force within the senior leadership. He most likely has a direct channel to Kim Jong-un. He was ranked second on Jon Pyong-ho's Funeral Committee list.

c. Key individuals in the Third Echelon of the Leadership

The third echelon is composed of bureaucrats, military officers, and technocrats who are responsible for executing operations—many of whom hold positions on senior leadership bodies. They may have decision-making authority over the operations of their institutions, but these decisions are guided by higher-level decisions. They have limited influence or contact with Kim Jong-un other than during guidance inspections and field exercises. He may reach out to them for subject matter expertise. This is the level at which many of the fourth-generation leaders, who are currently in their 30s and 40s, will appear in the next few years.[208] But for now, the more notable individuals in this echelon include those listed below.

---

208   While this may be the focal point for a future generation of leaders, it is not immune from purges. In the summer of 2015, South Korean media reported that Vice Premier Choe Yong-gon and Vice Director of the KWP United Front Department (UFD) Won Tong-yon had both been purged. Choe Yong-gon was reportedly removed and possibly executed for taking exception to Kim Jong-un's forestation program and Won Tong-yon, one of the negotiators of the Kaesong Industrial Complex, was caught up in a purge of figures deemed to be too close to South Korea.

Table 3: Third Echelon of Power

Name	Position(s)	Comments
Party		
Kwak Pom-gi (76)	• Alternate Member of the Politburo (since 2012) • KWP Secretary for Finance (since 2012) • Director of the KWP Finance and Planning Department (FPD) (since 2012)	Kwak Pom-gi's elevation to the senior ranks of the leadership was tied to Kim Kyong-hui and Jang Song-taek with the expectation that he could bring some pragmatism to the decision-making process on the economy. Following Jang's purge, he now most likely works directly with Kim or through Pak Pong-ju. He was ranked 18th on Jon Pyong-ho's Funeral Committee list.
Kim Pyong-hae (74)	• Alternate Member of the Politburo (since 2010) • KWP Secretary for Personnel (since 2010) • Director of the KWP Cadres Department (since 2010)	Kim Pyong-hae's portfolio will be critical in the coming years as the inevitable turn-over of the Party membership takes place. Kim Pyong-hae's relationship to Kim Jong-un is unclear. He allegedly belonged to a group of Party leaders that followed Jang Song-taek. That said, Kim Pyong-hae survived Jang's purge and remains in place. He was ranked 18th and 17th respectively on Kim Kuk-tae's and Jon Pyong-ho's Funeral Committee lists.

Name	Position(s)	Comments
Colonel General O Il-jong (61)	• Director of the KWP Military Affairs Department (since 2010) • Director of the KWP Civil Affairs Department (since 2013) (?)	The son of O Jin-u, one of Kim Il-sung's closest associates, O Il-jong supervises reserve forces, including the four million-strong Worker-Peasant Red Guards. In recent years, he has been identified as Director of the KWP Civil Defense Department, apparently replacing Kim Yong-chun. His ties to Kim Jong-un appear to be more direct in recent years, as he is a frequent cohort on Kim's guidance inspections. He was ranked 26th on Jon Pyong-ho's Funeral Committee list, up seven spots from Kim Kuk-tae's Funeral Committee list.
Ri Jae-il (80)	• First Vice Director of the KWP PAD	Ri was one of a group of core elites who laid the foundations for the Kim Jong-un succession, and he played a major role in constructing the public legitimacy campaign around the new leader. He was ranked 120th on Kim Jong-il's Funeral Committee list. His position jumped to 38th and then to 33rd on Kim Kuk-tae's and Jon Pyong-ho's Funeral Committee list respectively.
O Su-yong (71)	• KWP Secretary for Light Industry (since 2014) • Chairman of the SPA Budget Committee (since 2014)	O Su-yong's ties to the Kim family are vague at best, which is surprising since he succeeded Kim Kyong-hui in his current position. His formal rank within the leadership rose dramatically from 47th on Kim Kuk-tae's Funeral Committee list to 19th on Jon Pyong-ho's Funeral Committee list.

Name	Position(s)	Comments
Ju Kyu-chang (87)	• Alternate Member of the Politburo (since 2010) (?) • Member of the CMC (since 2010) (?) • Director of the KWP Machine Industry Department (MID) (since 2010)	Because of its responsibility for day-to-day oversight of the development of the regime's critical defense systems, the director of the KWP MID is probably one of the few director-level officials who has regular access to Kim Jong-un. Ju Kyu-chang was, however, dropped from the NDC in 2014, which suggests that his influence may have waned. His formal ranking within the leadership plummeted from 29th on Kim Kuk-tae's Funeral Committee list to 85th on Jon Pyong-ho's Funeral Committee list. Some have suggested that he has been replaced as Director of the KWP MID by Hong Yong-chil.
Tae Jong-su (79)	• Alternate Member of the Politburo (since 2010) (?) • KWP Secretary for General Affairs Department (since 2010) (?) • South Hamgyong Provincial Party Secretary (since 2012)	As Kim Jong-il was revitalizing the Party apparatus, he placed Tae Jong-su in the sensitive post as Director of the KWP General Department, which is in charge of the handling and transmission of Party documents. From this post, Thae would presumably have had direct access to Kim Jong-un, who began receiving reports from various parts of the regime, including the Party. In 2012, Tae Jong-su was sent back to the provinces to take up another sensitive post as Party Secretary of South Hamgyong Province, which is rumored to be a potential source of factionalism within the regime. While he remains within the leadership, his position in the formal ranking dropped from 25th on Kim Kuk-tae's Funeral Committee list to 73rd on Jon Pyong-ho's Funeral Committee list.

Name	Position(s)	Comments
Lieutenant General Choe Chun-sik (60)	• President of the Second Academy of Natural Sciences	Choe Chun-sik first appeared in North Korean media standing next to Kim Jong-un in December 2012. The Second Academy of Natural Sciences is the research and development wing of the North Korean defense-industrial complex. It exists within the Party apparatus and answers up the chain of command to the KWP MID and the Secretary for Defense Industry. Choe most likely has a channel of regular communication with the Supreme Leader on issues of weapons development. Whether that communication is directly with Kim Jong-un or through the KWP Secretary for Defense Industry is not clear. He ranked 86th on Jon Pyong-ho's Funeral Committee list.
Military/ Security		
General O Kum-chol (68)	• Vice Chief of the KPA GSD	A former Commander of the KPAF, O Kum-chol's portfolio within the GSD includes military strategy and planning, as well as relations with foreign militaries. He also participates in expanded meetings of the KWP CMC and the Politburo. He most likely has an occasional channel to Kim Jong-un. He was ranked 55th on Jon Pyong-ho's Funeral Committee list.

Name	Position(s)	Comments
General Pak Yong-sik	• Minister of People's Armed Forces (since 2015)	A former Vice Director of the GPB, Pak Yong-sik replaced Hyon Yong-chol as the Minister of People's Armed Forces in June 2015. Although he is a ranking member of the high command, General Pak's ties to and communication channel with Kim Jong-un are unknown. North Korea's elevated media handling of Pak Yong-sik since his appointment as Minister of the People's Armed Forces suggests he is second in the regime's military ranking behind Vice Marshal Hwang Pyong-so. This was reflected in his position on the leadership rostrum during the 70th anniversary celebration of the founding of the Party.
Colonel General Ro Kwang-chol	• First Vice Minister of the People's Armed Forces	Ranked 58th on the Jon Pyong-ho Funeral Committee list, Ro Kwang-chol began to attend guidance inspections with Kim Jong-un in 2015 and has been a part of several North Korean delegations in military-to-military talks with other countries. Whether he has achieved unfettered access to the Supreme Leader or must still go through the chain of command is currently unclear.
Vice Admiral Ri Yong-chu	• Commander of the KPA Navy (since 2015)	A former Vice Chief of the GSD, Ri Yong-chu has been a frequent cohort on Kim Jong-un's guidance inspections of military installations in 2015. He was ranked 61st on Jon Pyong-ho's Funeral Committee list.

Name	Position(s)	Comments
Colonel General Pak Jong-chon	• Vice Chief of the KPA GSD • Director of the Firepower Command Bureau (KPA Artillery) (?)	Pak Jong-chon has accompanied Kim Jong-un on inspections of artillery units since 2012. Given that Kim's own military training is in artillery tactics, it is likely that Pak has a special relationship with the Supreme Leader. Pak was promoted to Colonel General in May 2013, and he was ranked 56th on Jon Pyong-ho's Funeral Committee list.
Colonel General Ri Pyong-sam (72)	• Alternate Member of the Politburo (since 2012) (?) • Political Director of the Korean People's Internal Security Forces (KPISF) (?)	Ri Pyong-sam has served four MPS ministers, giving him a unique perspective on various patronage systems within the internal security apparatus. His line of communication to Kim Jong-un most likely goes through Choe Pu-il, the Minister of People's Security, although he may have an informal channel, given the apparent relationship he has developed with the Supreme Leader over the last two years. That said, the KPISF was closely tied to Jang Song-taek and, if tainted, could limit Ri's access. Ri has not been seen in public since February 2014.
Colonel General Choe Kyong-song	• Member of the CMC (since 2010) (?) • Former Commander of the 11th Corps ("Storm Corps")	In February, Choe Kyong-song, who had been demoted in 2014 to Lieutenant General, was replaced as Commander of the 11th Corps. Although it is not clear whether Choe has been transferred to another post, after his removal, he was again promoted to Colonel General (*Sang-jang*). This suggests that he may have moved into a more advisory role, possibly within Kim's Personal Secretariat.

Name	Position(s)	Comments
Colonel General So Hong-chan	• Member of the CMC (?) • First Vice Minister of the People's Armed Forces (since 2013) • Director of the General Logistics Department (since 2013) (?) • Director of the GSD Operations Bureau (2015) (?)	So Hong-chan began accompanying Kim Jong-un on guidance inspections in May 2013. He is rumored to also be a member of the CMC and head of the General Logistics Department (GLD). In late 2015, rumors surfaced that he may have replaced Kim Chun-sam as Director of the GSD Operations Bureau.[209] He was ranked 44th on Jon Pyong-ho's Funeral Committee list.
Lieutenant General Kim Chun-sam	• First Vice Chief of the GSD (since 2015) • Director of the GSD Operations Bureau (since 2015)	As the Director of the GSD Operations Bureau, Kim Chun-sam is responsible for the daily operational management of the armed forces and supervises the formulation and implementation of the KPA's training and contingency planning. From this position, he most likely has some routine contact with Kim Jong-un, especially as part of the latter's guidance inspections. Whether he has achieved unfettered access or must still go through the chain of command (i.e. Ri Yong-gil) is currently unclear.

---

209   "Kim Jong Un Says Recent High Level Inter Korean Meetings Could 'Bear Rich Fruit'," *Hankyoreh*, August 29, 2015.

Name	Position(s)	Comments
Lieutenant General Yun Yong-sik	• Director of the GSD Artillery Bureau (since 2015)	It is not clear whether the GSD Artillery Bureau replaced the Firepower Command Bureau, which is headed by Colonel General Pak Jong-chon. Yun Yong-sik has been a rising star within the high command having risen to a GSD post from a Fourth Corps brigade commander in 2012.
Lieutenant General Kim Yong-bok	• Commander of the 11th Corps (aka "Storm Corps") (since 2015)	The 11th Corps is a special warfare command in nature, but is much bigger and more diverse in the range of its mission. Experts estimate that it has a force size of 40,000 to 80,000. Kim Yong-bok's formal chain of command runs through the GSD, although he most likely also has a line of communication to O Kuk-ryol, who retains responsibility for crisis operations within the NDC.
Lieutenant General Kim Rak-gyom	• Member of the CMC (since 2012) • Commander of the Strategic Rocket Force (SRF) Command (since 2012)	According to some sources, Kim Jong-un has a special attachment to the SRF in that it reflects the high-tech part of the armed forces. The SRF Command is a unified command of all short-, medium-, and intermediate-range missile units under the NDC. Thus, Kim Rak-gyom most likely has direct channels of communication to a number of NDC members, including Kim Jong-un.
Government		
Yang Hyong-sop (90)	• Member of the Politburo (since 2010) • Vice President of the SPA Presidium (since 1998)	Yang Hyong-sop, who is related to the Kim family by marriage, has spent his career in the SPA apparatus. His ties to Kim Jong-un are likely occasional.

Name	Position(s)	Comments
Ro Tu-chol (71)	• Alternate Member of the Politburo (since 2012) • Vice Premier (since 2003) • Chairman of the State Planning Commission (since 2009)	Along with Pak Pong-ju, Ro Tu-chol is one of the "young" technocrats who is well versed in external economic affairs. His appointment to the SPC and the Politburo has been interpreted by many Pyongyang-watchers as an effort by Kim Jong-un to increase the level of pragmatism in leadership deliberations on economic development. He was ranked 23rd on Kim Kuk-tae's Funeral Committee list and 21st on Jon Pyong-ho's Funeral Committee list.
Jo Chun-ry-ong	• Member of the NDC (since 2014) • Presumed Chairman of the Second Economic Committee (since 2014)	Jo Chun-ryong's direct ties to Kim Jong-un are opaque, but his position on the NDC would suggest some regular contact. He was ranked 84th on Jon Pyong-ho's Funeral Committee list.
Kim Kye-gwan (72)	• First Vice Minister of Foreign Affairs (since 2010)	Kim Kye-gwan has been a leading figure in international talks over the country's nuclear weapons program, including the Six-Party Talks. While he presumably has formal meetings with Kim Jong-un, it is probably not one-on-one, but in concert with Kang Sok-ju. He did not appear on Jon Pyong-ho's Funeral Committee list.
Kim Chun-sop	• Member of the National Defense Commission (since 2015) • KWP Secretary for Defense Industry (since 2015)	Although Kim Chun-sop replaced Pak To-chun on the NDC, it is not clear if he has also assumed his role as Party Secretary for Defense Industry. In any case, he most likely has direct contact with Kim Jong-un on defense-industrial issues.

Name	Position(s)	Comments
Ki Kwang-ho	• Minister of Finance (since 2015)	Ki Kwang-ho has the reputation of a savvy finance expert who gets results. He is also linked to efforts to restructure the North Korean banking system.

d. Key Individuals in the Fourth Echelon of the Leadership

There are a number of functionaries, technocrats, and military officers far down the chain of command who are largely unknown to the Pyongyang-watching community, but play critical roles in the regime. These individuals are mostly in their 30s, 40s, and 50s. They have either been handpicked by Kim Jong-un for key jobs within the regime apparatus or have a personal relationship with the new leader, and thus, have some access to him in the course of their work.[210] These are the up-and-coming North Korean leaders who will likely assume critical positions as Kim consolidates his power. According to some reports, Kim Jong-un's Personal Secretariat is mostly populated with these bureaucrats in the fourth echelon. For now, they are note-takers and act as Kim's eyes and ears in various parts of the regime. In the future, they could form critical lines of communication and serve as trusted advisors. Table 4 lists some of the individuals believed to be part of this fourth echelon. Because it is difficult to identify North Korean individuals at this level, the list is speculative at best.

---

210   Many have developed their relationships with Kim Jong-un through the course of his guidance inspections. Some now frequently accompany him on his visits, which would suggest that they are particularly close to the new leader.

Table 4: Fourth Echelon of Power

Name	Position	Comments
Military/ Security		
Colonel General Jo Chang-bok	First Vice Minister of the People's Armed Forces	• A hold-over from the Kim Jong-il era • Responsible for the Rear Service General Bureau[211]
Colonel General Yun Tong-hyon	Vice Minister of the People's Armed Forces	• Received Kim Il-sung Order in 2007 • Became an alternate member of the Central Committee in September 2010 at the Third Party Conference • Ranked 108th on Kim Jong-il's Funeral Committee list • Spoke publicly on KCNA in 2012, vowing to destroy the South Korean regime • Delivered speech at the Pyongyang Army-People Joint Meeting on February 14, 2013 to mark the third nuclear test • Began accompanying Kim Jong-un on guidance inspections in March 2012 • Ranked 48th on Jon Pyong-ho's Funeral Committee list
Colonel General Kang Pyo-yong	Vice Minister of the People's Armed Forces	• Appointed an alternate member of the Central Committee in September 2010 at the Third Party Conference • Member of Kim Jong-il's Funeral Committee • Began accompanying Kim Jong-un on guidance inspections in February 2013 • Ranked 49th on Jon Pyong-ho's Funeral Committee list

---

211   Kim Jong-un has allegedly decided that positions responsible for military operations and rear area services should be retained by officers with authority and experience.

Name	Position	Comments
Colonel General Kim Hy-ong-ryong	Commander, KPA Second Corps	• Vowed to "blow up the Blue House" as part of loyalty pledge by the Second Corps in March 2012 • Ranked 50th on Jon Pyong-ho's Funeral Committee list
Colonel General Pak Tong-hak	Unknown (Military Officer)	• Promoted to Colonel General in 1999 • Began accompanying Kim Jong-un on guidance inspections in February 2013
Colonel General Ri Chang-han	Unknown (Military Officer)	• Appeared with Kim Jong-un at Kumsusan Memorial Palace in February 2012 on the occasion of Kim Jong-il's birthday • Frequent member on the leadership rostrum at Party and military events • Deputy to the SPA • An alternate member of the KWP Central Committee • Often seen in close proximity to Kim Jong-un at memorial and celebratory events • Ranked 60th on Jon Pyong-ho's Funeral Committee list
Colonel General Son Chol-ju	Vice Director for Organization and Propaganda, GPB	• Allegedly served on the political committee of a front-line unit before coming to the GPB • Began accompanying Kim Jong-un on guidance inspections in April 2012
Colonel General Pak Jong-chon	Vice Chief, GSD	• Frequent member of Kim Jong-un's guidance inspections of military units since April 2012 • Ranked 56th on Jon Pyong-ho's Funeral Committee list

Name	Position	Comments
Lieutenant General Kim Jong-kwan	Vice Minister of the People's Armed Forces	• First appeared as a speaker at a MPAF symposium in December 2013 • Elected as a deputy to the 13th SPA • Began accompanying Kim Jong-un on guidance inspections in May 2014[212] • Ranked 57th on Jon Pyong-ho's Funeral Committee list
Lieutenant General Kim Taek-ku	Vice Minister of the People's Armed Forces	• Began accompanying Kim Jong-un on guidance inspections in February 2013 • Elected as deputy to the 13th SPA • Ranked 64th on Jon Pyong-ho's Funeral Committee list
Lieutenant General Pak Yong-sik	Department Director, MPS	• Spoke at a conference of military propaganda officials, which was attended by Kim Jong-un, in March 2013 • Accompanied Kim Jong-un at the Kumsusan Memorial Palace on April 15, 2014 • Vice Chairman of the Special Investigation Committee (SIC) on Japanese residing in North Korea[213] • Ranked 45th on Jon Pyong-ho's Funeral Committee list
Lieutenant General Choe Yong-ho	Commander, KPA Air and Air Defense Forces	• Began accompanying Kim Jong-un in December 2014 on a visit to the Air and Air Defense Unit 458[214]
Lieutenant General Son Jong-nam	Ranking Officer, KPA Air and Air Defense Force Command	• Appointed an alternate member of the Central Committee in September 2010 at the Third Party Conference

212   He was a participant in Kim Jong-un's inspection of the newly built Satellite (*Wi-seong*) Scientists Residential District. This inspection took place in October 2014 after Kim Jong-un had been absent from public view for nearly forty days.

213   "On Organizing 'Special Investigation Committee' for All-Inclusive and Comprehensive Investigation Into All Japanese People [in the DPRK]," *KCNA*, July 4, 2014.

214   Choe was identified in his current position for the first time, having replaced Ri Pyong-chol.

Name	Position	Comments
Lieutenant General Ju To-hyon	Unknown (military officer)	• First public appearance was at a February 1, 2009 ceremony to vote for Kim Jong-il as a candidate to the 12th SPA, one month after Kim Jong-un was announced as heir apparent within the North Korean leadership • Began accompanying Kim Jong-un on guidance inspections in June 2013 • Ranked 59th on Jon Pyong-ho's Funeral Committee list
Lieutenant General Tong Yong-il	Unknown (military officer presumably affiliated with the GPB)	• Participated in a meeting between Choe Ryong-hae and the Vietnamese Director of the General Political Department in July 2013 • Attended the Eighth Meeting of KWP Ideological Functionaries in February 2014
Lieutenant General An Ji-yong	Commander, Island Defense	• Promoted to Major General in 2010 • Appeared on television as Deputy Fourth Corps Commander in March 2012 as part of an anti-South Korean media campaign • Began to accompany Kim Jong-un in August 2012 when Kim inspected island defense detachments stationed along the southwestern front • Part of Kim's cohort that inspected the Changjae Islet Defense Detachment and Mu Islet Hero Defense Detachment in March 2013 • Frequent cohort on inspections of island detachments • Ranked 69th on Jon Pyong-ho's Funeral Committee list

Name	Position	Comments
Lieutenant General Ryom Chol-song	Director, GPB Propaganda Department	• Began accompanying Kim Jong-un on guidance inspections in February 2013 • Part of a commemorative photograph taken in March 2013 with Kim and military propaganda officials, suggesting Ryom is affiliated with the GPB • Ranked 46th on Jon Pyong-ho's Funeral Committee list
Lieutenant General Jo Nam-jin	Director, GPB Organization Department	• Began accompanying Kim Jong-un on guidance inspections in November 2013
Vice Admiral Ri Yong-chu	Commander, KPA Navy	• Identified as KPA Navy Commander during Kim Jong-un's inspection of Unit 164 in April 2015 • Elected to the 13th SPA in June 2014 • Ranked 61st on Jon Pyong-ho's Funeral Committee list
Lieutenant General Ri Song-guk	Commander, KPA Fourth Corps	• Appointed to his post in April 2013 • Assumed to be close to Kim Jong-un but does not appear in the North Korean media as part of guidance inspections
Major General Rim Kwang-il	Unknown (Military Officer)	• Interviewed by KCNA in August 2012 in conjunction with Kim Jong-un's inspection of island defenses • Accompanied Kim on an inspection of a military exercise in February 2013 • Accompanied Kim on many military inspections related to coastal and island defense
Major General Jang Chang-hwa	Unknown (Military officer)	• Began accompanying Kim Jong-un in May 2015 at his inspection of the Sokmak Atlantic Salmon Breed-fish Ground and Raksan Offshore Salmon Fish Farm under KPA Unit 810

Name	Position	Comments
Lieutenant General So Tae-ha	Counselor for Security, NDC and Vice Director, SSD	• Heads the SIC on Japanese residing in North Korea[215] • According to South Korean sources, So is close to Kim Jong-un • He was promoted to Lieutenant General in April 2015
Kim Myong-chol	Counselor, SSD	• Vice Chairman of the SIC on Japanese residing in North Korea • Ties to Kim Jong-un are unclear
Kang Song-nam	Bureau Director, SSD	• Chief of the Panel for the Victims of Abduction for the SIC on Japanese residing in North Korea • Ties to Kim Jong-un are unclear
Party		
Han Kwang-bok (69)	Director, KWP Science and Education Department	• Has steadily risen through the leadership ranks. • She was ranked 36th on Kim Jong-il's Funeral Committee list, 32nd on Kim Kuk-tae's Funeral Committee list, and 25th on Jon Pyong-ho's Funeral Committee list • Assumed current post in 2014

---

215   "Late DPRK Leader's Ex-Chef on Abduction Probe Committee Chairman," *Fuji Television*, August 6, 2014. According to Kim Jong-il's former chef, Kenji Fujimoto, he saw So for the first time at a Party in 1995 that Kim hosted to entertain North Korean senior officials. In a television interview, Fujimoto noted that "Kim called some officials, including So to the Party room, and So poured some wine in Kim's glass and toasted with Kim." A co-worker told Fujimoto that So was highly "capable" and would likely be promoted.

Name	Position	Comments
Hong Yong-chil	Vice Director, KWP MID (?)	• Began accompanying Kim Jong-un on guidance inspections in February 2013, mostly to machine plants speculated to be associated with the defense industry • Rumored to hold a high-ranking position related to defense logistics in either the KWP MID or the SEC[216] • On March 17, 2013, North Korean media published a photograph of him sitting in the front row with Kim Jong-un and Pak To-chun at a "meeting of the Council of the Functionaries in the Munitions Industry Sector"[217] • Ranked 39th on Jon Pyong-ho's Funeral Committee list[218]
Ri Il-hwan	Department Director, KWP Working Organization Department	• Former KWP Secretary of the Pyongyang City Committee • Oversaw numerous rallies in support of Kim Jong-un in 2012 • Assumed current position in April 2014 • Ranked 23rd on Jon Pyong-ho's Funeral Committee list

216   Jang Cheol-Un, "Hong Yong-chil, New Face Who Frequently Accompanies the North's Kim Jong Un on On-Site Guidance Trips, Draws Attention," *Yonhap News Agency*, July 4, 2013. South Korean media have speculated that Hong Yong-chil is a Vice Director of the KWP MID or a Vice Chairman of the SEC in charge of manufacturing munitions.

217   Ibid. In his 50s, Hong allegedly came to the attention of the North Korean leadership in 2011 when he received the title of "Labor Hero," the highest honor in North Korea. It was conferred on him in February 2011 while he was working as the Party Committee Secretary of the Unsan Tool Plant, North Pyongan Province.

218   Given Ju Kyu-chang's decline in the formal ranking on this list to 85th, some have suggested that Hong may now be the new Director of the KWP MID. Since Jon's funeral, Hong has appeared at a number of defense industry events, while Ju has remained out of the public eye.

Name	Position	Comments
Kim Man-song	First Vice Director, KWP	• First appeared in North Korean media when he received the Kim Il-sung Order in April 2012 • Deputy to the 13th SPA • Ranked 40th on Kim Kuk-tae's Funeral Committee list and 24th on Jon Pyong-ho's Funeral Committee list
Choe Hwi	First Vice Director, KWP PAD	• Began accompanying Kim Jong-un on guidance inspections with the title of First Vice Director in May 2013 • Ranked 39th on Kim Kuk-tae's Funeral Committee list and 34th on Jon Pyong-ho's Funeral Committee list[219]
Pak Tae-song	Department Vice Director, KWP	• Received Kim Il-sung Order in April 2012 • Began accompanying Kim Jong-un on guidance inspections in August 2012 • Rumored to work in the KWP OGD
Ho Hwan-chol	Department Vice Director, KWP	• Began accompanying Kim Jong-un on guidance inspections in January 2013
Cho Yong-won	Department Vice Director, KWP	• Began appearing with Kim Jong-un on guidance inspections in December 2014 • Coverage of him in the North Korean media suggests he might be with the KWP PAD

219   It should be noted, however, that in 2015, rumors spread that Choe Hwi had been purged. He has not been seen in public since he attended a rally of the "18 June Shock Brigade" held on August 8, 2014. "North Korea's Power Trio Disappear From Public View," *Yonhap News Agency*, February 18, 2015.

Name	Position	Comments
Jo Thae-san	KWP Department Vice Director	• Began appearing with Kim Jong-un during guidance inspections in February 2015 • Coverage of him in the North Korean media suggests he might be with the KWP PAD
Kim Tong-il	Department Vice Director, KWP Working Organization Department	• Appointed an alternate member of the Central Committee in September 2010 at the Third Party Conference • Member of Kim Jong-il's Funeral Committee • Member of the SPCSGC • Began accompanying Kim Jong-un on guidance inspections in April 2013
Hong Sung-mu	Vice Director, KWP MID	• From the production and manufacturing side of the country's military and munitions industries[220] • Appeared at Kim Jong-un's meeting on January 25, 2013 with security and foreign affairs officials, days before the third nuclear test • Ranked 126th on Kim Jong-il's Funeral Committee list • Began accompanying Kim Jong-un on guidance inspections in January 2013 • Ranked 40th on Jon Pyong-ho's Funeral Committee list
Maeng Kyong-il	Vice Director, KWP UFD	• Maeng is a former councilor of the Korea Asia-Pacific Peace Committee • North Korean representative to the 16th North-South ministerial-level talks in 2005

---

220   Michael Madden, "Biographies: Hong Sung-mu," *North Korea Leadership Watch*, February 3, 2013. This is in contrast to his immediate superior, Ju Kyu-chang, who comes from research and development.

Name	Position	Comments
Kang Kwan-il	Vice Director, KWP Department	• Began accompanying Kim Jong-un on guidance inspections in May 2012 • Ranked 38th on Jon Pyong-ho's Funeral Committee list
Kim Tae-hui	Party Secretary, Kim Il-sung University	• Son of Kim Chol-man, former Chairman of the SEC
Huh Chol	Party Secretary, Ministry of Foreign Affairs	• Son of Huh Dam, former Party Secretary for Inter-Korean Affairs, and Kim Jong-suk, Chairwoman of the Committee for Cultural Relations with Foreign Countries
Kang Chi-yong	Director, Committee for the Peaceful Reunification of the Fatherland (CPRF) Secretariat	• Current position suggests he is also a Vice Director of the KWP UFD • Publicly vocal during the March/April crisis[221]
Pak Jong-nam	Chief Secretary, Gangwon Provincial Party Committee	• Served in the Gangwon Party apparatus, at least since 2001[222] • Rumored to have been brought to Pyongyang to support Choe Ryong-hae
Jon Yong-nam	First Secretary. Kim Il-sung Youth League	• Assumed current post in 2012 • Tied to youth issues, which are supported by Kim Jong-un • Played a key role in establishing Kim Jong-un's succession by mobilizing youth organizations • Son of Jon Chae-son, former Vice Minister of the People's Armed Forces

---

221   Following the Supreme Command's abrogation of the Armistice Agreement, Kang made a speech in which he said, "the Supreme Command spokesman's statement is a firm statement of the revolutionary strong army of Mt. Paektu for the final victory in the great DPRK-U.S. confrontation that has continued across a century." See *Nodong Sinmun*, March 6, 2013.

222   Kim Jong-un reportedly is showing favor to this province, where he was born.

Name	Position	Comments
Government		
Ri Yong-nam	Minister of External Economic Affairs	• Nephew of Ri Myong-su, former Minister of People's Security
An Jong-su	Minister of Light Industry	• Assumed post in June 2010 • Appointed alternate member of the Central Committee in September 2010 • Member of the SPCSGC • Penned article in *Nodong Sinmun* in support of Kim Jong-un's first New Year's Editorial (January 2, 2012) • Accompanied Kim Yong-nam to Southeast Asia in 2012 • Began accompanying Kim Jong-un on guidance inspections in October 2013 • Listed 96th on Kim Jong-il's Funeral Committee list
Ri Je-son	Minister of Atomic Energy Industry	• Assumed current post in April 2014[223] • One of five North Korean officials to be sanctioned by the UNSC after North Korea's second nuclear test in 2009[224] • Most likely oversees the Yongbyon nuclear facility and has ties to the KWP MID Munitions Bureau • Ranked 87th on Jon Pyong-ho's Funeral Committee list
Ri Song-ho	Minister of Commerce	• Son-in-law of Kim Yong-chun, Vice Chairman of the NDC

---

223   The Ministry of Atomic Energy Industry was set up in April 2013 to replace the General Department of Atomic Energy, where Ri served as Director-General.

224   Ri was banned from traveling and had his overseas assets frozen.

Name	Position	Comments
Ri Yong-ho	Vice Minister of Foreign Affairs	• Son of Ri Myong-je, a former KCNA Editor and Vice Director of the KWP OGD who served as a Deputy Director of Kim Jong-il's Personal Secretariat in the 1980s and early 1990s • North Korea's representative to the Six Party Talks • An alternate member of the KWP Central Committee • Third-generation elite • Protégé of Kang Sok-ju
Choe Son-hui	Vice Director, Ministry of Foreign Affairs	• Daughter of Choe Yong-rim
Kang Ki-sop	Director, General Bureau of Civil Aviation	• Member of Kim Jong-il's Funeral Committee • Began accompanying Kim Jong-un on guidance inspections in February 2013
Ri Myong-san	Vice Minister of External Economic Affairs	• Son-in-law of Kim Yong-ju, Kim Il-sung's brother • Leading diplomat for Southeast Asian affairs
Cha Tong-sop	Vice Minister of Commerce	• Son-in-law of Kim Yong-chun, Vice Chairman of the NDC
Ri Kwang-gun	Vice Minister of External Economic Affiars	• Son of Ri Yong-ku, Kim Jong-il's former doctor • Protégé of Jang Song-taek • Former Minister of Foreign Trade • Former Chairman of Joint Venture Investment Commission (JVIC)

Name	Position	Comments
Kim Chol-jin	Vice Director, State Economic Development Commission,[225] and Chairman, Pyonggon Investment Group	• Began accompanying Kim Jong-un to economic sites in September 2013 • Believed to be involved in economic affairs at a high level at least since the beginning of 2012 • Served at the Ministry of Foreign Trade and government agencies facilitating Chinese investment • Reported to have extensive business connections in China and experience trading with South Korea in the mid-2000s • One of the few experts in economic cooperation and trade in North Korea • Oversaw the import of materials for building houses in Pyongyang, the Munsu Water Park, and the Masikryong Ski Resort • Referred to in the South Korean press as an "economic tsar," along with Pak Pong-ju and Ro Tu-chol
So Ho-won	Vice Chairman, Committee for Cultural Relations with Foreign Countries	• Son-in-law of O Kuk-ryol, Vice Chairman of the NDC

There is another group of Kim Jong-un's cohorts who may belong to this fourth echelon. They are personal friends, mostly in their 20s and 30s, drawn from the children of the North Korean elite. While they may or may not hold key positions within the current leadership apparatus, their future rise within the official apparatus cannot be overlooked. However, it should be noted that their power is always vulnerable. If their parents get purged, they can lose all of their wealth and

---

225   Yun Il-Geon, "The Rise of Kim Chol-jin: North's Hidden Influence in Economic Development," *Yonhap News Agency*, February 19, 2014. The State Economic Development Commission was established in October 2013 under the control of the Cabinet. Although Kim Ki-sok is the Chairman of the Commission, many believe that Kim Chol-jin carries more influence.

influence instantly, and their lives can be put in danger. In the past, some of the princelings from the Kim Jong-il era have disappeared from the center stage after their fathers left the inner circle of the Supreme Leader.[226]

Table 5: Family and Same Generation Associates of Kim Jong-un[227]

Name	Relation	Comments
Kim Jong-chol (34)	Kim Jong-un's older brother	• Rumored to be working in the KWP OGD, Guard Command, or SSD[228]
Kim Hy-on-nam (44)	Illegitimate son of Kim Il-sung	• Rumored to work in the Ministry of Foreign Affairs as part of a division that handles Japanese and South Korean affairs • Allowed to return from exile • Relationship with Kim Jong-un unclear[229]
O Se-hyon	Son of NDC Vice Chairman O Kuk-ryol	• Rumored to be the head of the "Torch Group" (*Bong-hwa-jo*), which is involved in illicit hard currency operations[230, 231] • May be an employee in the Foreign Department of the Ministry of Commerce • Described in some reports as O Kuk-ryol's second son, O Se-won[232]

---

226   This also creates a compelling need for the highest-ranking cadres to absolutely obey Kim Jong-un. To do otherwise would jeopardize the family wealth. For them, defending the regime is the same thing as defending their right to survival and vested interests.

227   For more information on these connections, see Ken E. Gause, *North Korea Under Kim Chong-il: Power, Politics, and Prospects for Change*, op. cit.

228   In May 2015, Kim Jong-chol was seen in London attending an Eric Clapton concert. The fact that he was allowed to travel abroad in a period of tension within the regime following the purge of Hyon Yong-chol suggested to some Pyongyang-watchers that he does not hold a critical position within the regime.

229   "Kim Il-sung's Love Child Works for N. Korea's Foreign Ministry," *The Chosun Ilbo*, July 2, 2015.

230   Bill Gertz, "North Korea Elite Linked to Crime," *The Washington Times*, May 24, 2010.

231   "N. Korea's 'Bonghwajo' Club Doing Drugs, Counterfeiting," *Dong-A Ilbo*, April 18, 2011.

232   "Power Struggle Said Behind DPRK's Uncompromising Stance on Missile Launch," *Zakzak Online*, April 10, 2012. This article notes that O Se-won is the head of the Torch Group (*Bong-hwa-jo*), which is involved in illicit drugs. It also contends that O was allied with Ri Yong-ho, the former Chief of the GSD.

Name	Relation	Comments
Ri Il-hyok	Son of former Ambassador to Switzerland, Ri Chol	• Rumored to be involved with the Torch Group (*Bong-hwa-jo*) • Since his father became Minister of Foreign Affairs, Ri's status may have ascended.
Kim Chol	Son of SSD (MSS) Director Kim Won-hong	• Rumored to be involved with the Torch Group (*Bong-hwa-jo*) • Chairman of the Ryanggang Province People's Committee[233] • Head of the Chongbong Trading Company and referred to as "little MSS Director"[234, 235]
Choe Hyon-chol	Son of KWP Secretary Choe Ryong-hae	• Hard currency generator and Kim Chol's rival
Ri Yong-ran	Daughter of deceased OGD First Vice Director Ri Yong-chol	• Adopted daughter of Hwang Pyong-so • Rumored to have assumed the directorship of Department 54 operations since the purge of Jang Song-taek and the dismantling of the KWP Administrative Department, with her ties to this department going back to 1996[236] • Rumored to be allied to Hwang Pyong-so and a rival of Kim Chol

---

233   Ryanggang Province is home to much of North Korea's defense industry.

234   "The Emergence of an Elite More Feared than the Supreme Leader," *New Focus International*, December 9, 2014. Kim Chol is also referred to as the "Chungbong Bank" or "Kim Jong-un's Elder Brother" because he brings in millions of dollars of hard currency into the regime on an annual basis.

235   Kim Chol reportedly generates large amounts of money from investments in various areas including oil imports. North Korea annually imports about $600 million (about 709.4 billion Korean won) worth of oil from China. North Korea's oil import franchise used to be monopolized by Jang Su-kil, a vice director of the KWP Administration Department, the closest aide to Jang Song-taek. However, Kim Chol reportedly took over the oil import franchise after Jang Su-kil was executed in November 2013. See "Inheritance of Wealth' Among Children of People in Power in North Korea," *Dong-A Ilbo*, September 16, 2015.

236   Ibid. According to this source, Department 54 now resides within the GPB. It earns huge amounts of foreign exchange proceeds from selling coal and other minerals and fishery products to China.

Name	Relation	Comments
Kang Tae-sung	Son of Vice Premier Kang Sok-ju	• Rumored to be involved with the Torch Group (*Bong-hwa-jo*) • Head of a foreign trading corporation, dealing mainly with European countries
Kim Chol-un	Son of former Vice Director Kim Jung-il of Kim Jong-il's Personal Secretariat	• Rumored to be involved with the Torch Group (*Bong-hwa-jo*)
Kim Chang-hyok	Son of SSD Political Bureau Director Kim Chang-sop	• Rumored to be involved with the Torch Group (*Bong-hwa-jo*)
Kim Song-hyon	Grandson of SPA Presidium Chairman Kim Yong-nam	• No information available
Choe Jun	Son of KWP Secretary Choe Ryong-hae	• No information available
Jon Yong-jin	Husband of Jang Song-taek's elder sister	• Former Ambassador to Cuba • Previously served as Pyongyang's top envoy to Sweden and Iceland • Status unclear since Jang Song-taek's purge[237]

---

237   Jon Yong-jin is rumored to have been executed. Other family members of Jang Song-taek who have reportedly been purged include: Jang Kye-sun (sister; executed), Jang Un-sun (sister; executed), Jang Su-kil (foster son; missing), Jang Hyon-chol (Jang Song-u's eldest son; living in seclusion), Jang Yang-chol (Jang Song-u's second son; former ambassador to Malaysia; unemployed and living in Pyongyang), Jong Hye-yong (Jang Kye-sun's eldest daughter from previous marriage; in a prison camp), Chon Kum-yong (Jang Kye-sun's second daughter; in a prison camp), and Jon Chol-min (Jang Kye-sun's eldest son; in a prison camp).

Name	Relation	Comments
Cha Chol-ma	Son-in-law of late KWP OGD First Vice Director Ri Je-gang	• Rumored to be one of the richest men in North Korea • Serves in a top position at the Mansudae Assembly Hall, the seat of the SPA • Reportedly oversees a number of foreign currency-earning businesses run by the SPA's standing committees[238] • Reportedly the Director of the Mansudae Company

D. SECTION ONE CONCLUSION

Over the course of 2014 and 2015, the North Korean leadership has begun to change to reflect the preferences of Kim Jong-un and his ongoing strategy to consolidate power. The regent structure has evaporated, leaving Kim surrounded by a group of key advisors and continuously evolving channels into the second, third, and fourth echelons of power. While he has made swift strides in building a network within the high command that includes a number of two-, three-, and four-star generals, the power and influence around him appears to come through Party channels. Within these Party channels, figures such as Hwang Pyong-so and members of the old guard, including Choe Ryong-hae and Choe Tae-bok, continue to play an important institutional role. Technocrats within the Cabinet, such as Premier Pak Pong-ju, have access to the Supreme Leader, but their influence is unclear.

In terms of stability, the regime does not show any overt signs of weakness within the leadership, although rumors of power struggles and competition for resources persist. Contrary to much speculation, recent SPA meetings have not revealed a major revamping of the senior leadership. However, the extent of the Party reshuffles since 2014 remain obscured because North Korean media has yet to publish the full results of administrative decisions made at Politburo and CMC meetings. Both Kim Yong-nam, the 87-year old Chairman of the SPA Presidium, and Premier Pak Pong-ju have retained their posts despite widespread rumors from time to time that they would be replaced. This suggests that while Kim is willing to reorient the informal power structure, he values continuity within the formal ranks of power, most likely as a show of stability. One South Korean analyst noted:

---

238   "One of NK's richest men said to serve in assembly hall," *Yonhap News Agency*, February 19, 2012.

Kim Jong-un chose stability rather than change. He appears intent to minimize any internal instability that could be caused by the purge of Jang Song-taek and manage state affairs stably, while the regime continues to be isolated by the international community.[239]

As of the summer of 2015, the North Korean regime appears to be moving into the final phase of Kim Jong-un's power consolidation. Questions of regime stability remain a source of speculation and for good reason. Theories about the dynamics within the regime vary widely. Some Pyongyang-watchers contend that stability within the regime is tied to the fundamentals of how the Jang Song-taek purge continues to play out and will ultimately be resolved. They raise the high-profile nature of the purge and the unprecedented nature of this event, given its direct links to the Kim family. The decision to purge the "number two" member within the regime was risky and the reverberations continue to be felt inside the regime. The purge of Hyon Yong-chol was an effort to re-freeze a leadership that had grown complacent and to stave off dangerous power struggles, most likely within the military, that could interfere with Kim Jong-un's attempts to consolidate power.

Other Pyongyang-watchers agree that the Jang Song-taek saga was important, but it was only a part, albeit a key part, of a larger narrative that describes Kim Jong-un's inability to bring the regime entirely under his control.[240] They note that over seventy senior Party and military officials have been purged since Kim came to power. While generational changes and power struggles might explain some of the turnover, many leaders are disappearing from leadership roles because of Kim's lack of experience and basic inability to manipulate the levers of power. The North Korean regime may not be on the verge of collapse, but it exists in a state of perpetual instability, which could one day metastasize to a point of no return.

---

239   Kim Hee-Jin, "Inner Circle in Regime Mostly Stays Intact," *Korea Joongang Daily*, April 11, 2014.
240   Alexandre Mansourov, "North Korea: Leadership Schisms and Consolidation During Kim Jong-un's Second Year in Power," op. cit. According to Mansourov, the regent structure around Kim Jong-un began to unravel not at the end of 2013, but in 2012, with the purge of Ri Yong-ho. Jang's purge was just the *coup de grace* of an already evolving process. If this is the case, much of the reported North Korean political history from 2013 needs to be reexamined. It suggests the possibility that Kim Jong-un is more adept at manipulating the levers of power than previously believed. Kim may have taken measures beginning in early 2013 to marginalize Jang's influence and power. This may have been the reason why Jang Song-taek was not part of the January 26, 2013 meeting of the senior officials handling foreign and security policy in which the third nuclear test was allegedly discussed. It could explain the sudden replacement of Ri Myong-su as Minister of People's Security with Choe Pu-il, who is rumored to be close to Kim Jong-un. It might shed light on the re-promotion of generals in 2013 (Choe Ryong-hae, Kim Kyok-sik, Kim Yong-chol) who had been demoted in 2012. In other words, these occurrences may not have been random, but early indications of Jang's diminishing clout at the hands of his nephew.

While there is debate within the community of North Korea watchers regarding current and near term leadership dynamics, they largely agree on the fundamentals of the more distant future. The longer-term prognosis depends on Kim Jong-un's intrinsic leadership traits, as well as the system's ability to move forward with new faces at the fore. Provided that there has been no coup, as some suggest, the concept of monolithic leadership rule should enforce stability at the center. However, if policy failures begin to mount, Kim has left himself with little room to maneuver.[241] He lacks the legitimacy his father possessed, let alone that of his grandfather.[242] The Kim family itself has been wounded. If Kim Kyong-hui is out of the picture,[243] the connection to the Mt. Paektu bloodline, which created the foundation for the Kim regime's legitimacy, will begin to fade.[244] Instability could creep in and this could eventually lead to growing public agitation that the regime cannot control. This would allow the wider leadership more flexibility to go its own way, ignoring the demands from the center.

---

241   The biggest weakness for Kim as he marks his fourth year as leader is that he has been unable to accumulate startling achievements that would justify his position. "Quick wins" on the policy front are critical for building his legitimacy.

242   "Does Aunt's Absence Weaken Kim Jong-un?" *The Chosun Ilbo*, January 7, 2014. Kim Jong-un is not protected by former partisan soldiers like his grandfather, Kim Il-sung, and has been unable to build a strong base of supporters like his father, Kim Jong-il, who was groomed for twenty years to assume the throne.

243   In addition to reports about Kim Kyong-hui's health, there are also reports, primarily from Japanese and South Korean media, that she may be in Switzerland or Poland. This may be for medical treatment or due to a falling out with Kim Jong-un over her husband's execution. If the latter is true, which is still highly speculative, the potential for instability is real as news of a breach within the Kim family leaks out to the wider leadership.

244   Song Sang-Ho, "Absence of Kim's Aunt May Not Impact North Korea Leadership," *The Korea Herald*, January 13, 2014. Some Pyongyang-watchers doubt that Kim Kyong-hui's illness will have much impact on her nephew's power consolidation process, which is coming to a close. If she is unable to perform her Party and other official duties, these may fall to Kim Yo-jong, who appears to be following in her aunt's footsteps as a key advisor to her older brother.

SECTION TWO: KIM JONG-UN'S APPARATUS OF POWER

Kim Jong-un is the Supreme Leader, but he does not rule alone. Although he is the ultimate decision-maker, his power and authority rest upon a vast apparatus consisting of several institutions and individuals largely nested in the Party, but also spread across the regime. He depends on this apparatus to provide him with situational awareness, protection, and the funds he needs to rule unburdened.

The apparatus of power in any totalitarian regime is not static. It evolves to take on the character of the Supreme Leader. In North Korea, this apparatus changed dramatically from Kim Il-sung to Kim Jong-il. What was once a formal system in service of an all-powerful individual became a set of informal channels in service of an individual more comfortable wielding power behind the scenes. With the rise of Kim Jong-il, the role of the Personal Secretariat was dramatically enhanced and a special channel for funding the Kim family, widely known as the Royal Economy, was established. The internal politics of the security services also evolved to match broader political trends.

This section begins with a discussion of how the regime operates. The "Leader" (*Suryong*)-based system is designed to ensure that all power and authority flow from the Supreme Leader. The first chapter in this section discusses how the system evolved. This is followed by an examination of the steps that were taken to usher in the Kim Jong-un era, which includes an assessment of Kim's leadership style, how information flows throughout the leadership, and how decisions are made. The consequences of Jang Song-taek's purge on the *Suryong* system are also considered.

The section concludes with an examination of Kim Jong-un's apparatus of power itself. In particular, these chapters are devoted to three critical elements of the apparatus:

- **Kim Jong-un's Personal Secretariat.** This chapter will look at the role and mission of the Personal Secretariat, as well the Secretarial Office of the Central Committee (SOCC),[245] a larger apparatus tied to the KWP. It is from this inner sanctum that the Supreme Leader runs the wider regime.

---

245   It should be noted that the SOCC is not the KWP Secretariat. They are distinct bodies. The personnel in the SOCC are members of the Supreme Leader's personal staff that coordinates the functions of the Party and wider regime apparatus as it relates to the Leader. The KWP Secretariat is responsible for managing the implementation and enforcement of the Party's decisions. It manages the KWP's administrative, personnel, financial, and housekeeping needs through subordinate departments and bureaus.

- **The Royal Economy.** This chapter presents an overview of the organizations and processes used by the regime to raise hard currency for the Kim family. It explores how relevant bodies, such as Office 38 and Office 39, are linked into the wider regime and identifies the key individuals involved in these operations. Access to and control of these funds has driven much of the politics inside the regime for the last few years. It played a role in Jang Song-taek's downfall, and it will continue to influence how effectively Kim Jong-un can run the regime.

- **The Internal Security Apparatus.** This chapter updates and expands the author's earlier book *Coercion, Control, Surveillance, and Punishment: An Examination of the North Korean Police State*. In addition to updating the information on the SSD, MPS, and MSC, it explores the organization, structure, and missions of the GC and KWP OGD. Together, these five organizations guarantee the protection of the Kim family regime from all internal threats. They are the first and last lines of defense. They are also at the core of much of the terror and misery that is inflicted on the population every day.

A. CHAPTER FOUR: HOW THE REGIME OPERATES

Kim Jong-un's apparatus of power is rooted in a unique political culture. The North Korean system operates by a set of rules established in the Kim Il-sung period and adjusted to fit the style of rule under Kim Jong-il. At its heart, this "Leader" (*Suryong*)-based system is built around one individual's ability to make all of the decisions and command all of the power. This is an apparatus that has evolved over the decades. Through his first two years in power and well into his third, Kim Jong-un is growing into the role of Supreme Leader. He did not have the twenty years his father had to shape the regime to follow his lead. Kim Jong-un relied on the regent structure to educate him in manipulating the levers of power and building the relationships necessary for him to rule. Now that the regent structure has been dismantled, Kim must rely on the Supreme Leader apparatus to inform his decision-making and build and sustain the relationships he will need to govern on his own. The contours of this apparatus have changed to suit the Supreme Leader's leadership style.

This chapter outlines the theoretical construct of the *Suryong* system and examines Kim Jong-un's leadership style. The theory of whether other individuals or entities could seize the mantle of leadership will be examined, as well as Kim's evolving decision-making process. This will lay the foundation for the discussion in the following chapters of Kim Jong-un's apparatus.

1. THE *SURYONG* SYSTEM

One of the most peculiar features of the North Korean system is the supreme authority of the "Leader" (*Suryong*) in every domain, including ideology, law, administration, and regulations. [246] For this reason, the North Korean political system is often called a "Leader-dominant system" (*Suryong-je*) or a "Monolithic system" (*Yu-il che-je*). [247] In 1949, Kim Il-sung designated himself *Suryong* and began a campaign to eliminate all resistance to his position as the unchallenged leader of the nation. He started to construct the ideological foundation to support his status

---

[246]   This section of the paper draws from the author's previous work. See Ken E. Gause, "North Korea's Political System in the Transition Era: The Role and Influence of the Party Apparatus," in Scott Snyder and Kyung-Ae Park, eds., *North Korea in Transition* (Lanham, MD: Rowman & Littlefield, 2012).
[247]   Cheong Seong-Chang, "Stalinism and Kimilsungism: A Comparative Analysis of Ideology and Power," Asian Perspective 24, no. 1 (2000). It is important to note that the title "Leader" (*Suryong*) is reserved for Kim Il-sung. Kim Jong-il never adopted this title. In this paper, the word "*Suryong*" is used to denote the system within which Kim Jong-il operated and Kim Jong-un now operates.

within the leadership in the mid-1950s with the unveiling of a Marxist-Leninist model for self-reliance called *Juche*. This became the principal ideology for politics, economics, national defense, and foreign policy. It is still the foundation of the regime today. The *Juche* ideology served as a catalyst among North Koreans, whose history is rife with dominance and subjugation by other nations. This ideology became a rallying cry for nationalism and isolationism, allowing Kim both to distance himself from Moscow and Beijing and to undercut Party members more closely aligned with those two patron nations. By 1956, Kim achieved unchallenged dominance in the KWP, tightly controlling all aspects of both politics and society.[248] This was further solidifed in the late 1960s and early 1970s with the "*Suryong* Monolithic System of Guidance,"[249] which was designed to lay the groundwork for the transfer of power from Kim Il-sung to Kim Jong-il.[250]

As was made clear by North Korean propaganda, "The *Suryong* is an impeccable brain of the living body, the masses can be endowed with their life in exchange for their loyalty to him, and the Party is the nerve center of that living body."[251] This statement was clearly manifested during the Kim Il-sung era, when most policymaking at the national level was realized through official decision-making institutions that met on a fairly regular basis. At the top was the Party's Politburo, where senior-level debates were held and Kim Il-sung's thinking was translated

---

248   Cheong Seong-Chang, "Stalinism and Kimilsungism: A Comparative Analysis of Ideology and Power," op. cit. Kim Il-sung solidified his control over his own partisan faction by purging the *Kapsan* faction members in 1967. This spelled the end of all opposition within the Party to Kim's cult of personality. Afterwards, Party bureaucrats of the Manchurian guerrilla group, who were loyal to Kim Il-sung, took leadership positions. North Korean politics stabilized thereafter.

249   Ibid. The Monolithic Guidance System was created in the late 1960s by Kim Yong-ju, Kim Il-sung's younger brother and then Director of the KWP OGD. It was then adopted and modified in the 1970s by Kim Jong-il. North Koreans were called upon "to unconditionally accept the instructions of the Great Leader, and to act in full accordance with his will." Kim Il-sung also demanded that Party members "fight to the end to protect to the death the authority of the 'party center' [Kim Jong-il]."

250   Kang Mi-Jin, "NK Adds Kim Jong Il to 'Ten Principles,'" *Daily NK*, August 9, 2013. Central to the Monolithic Guidance System is the "Ten Principles for the Establishment of the One-Ideology System." The Ten Principles, which were formulated in the 1970s by Kim Jong-il as guidelines for Kim family rule, are defined in North Korean textbooks as "The ideological system by which the whole Party and people is firmly armed with the revolutionary ideology of the *Suryong* and united solidly around him, carrying out the revolutionary battle and construction battle under the sole leadership of the *Suryong*." Until recently, they were based on the thoughts and deeds of Kim Il-sung. According to defector reports, Kim Jong-il's name has been added to the description of this leadership structure. The second principle, which used to state that "We must honor the Great Leader comrade Kim Il-sung with all our loyalty" has been amended to state, "We must honor the Great Leader comrade Kim Il-sung and General Kim Jong-il with all our loyalty." This is most likely part of the regime's attempts to create the ideological foundation for Kim Jong-un's rule by creating the bridge between him and his grandfather.

251   Masayuki Suzuki, "Bukanui Sahoejeongchijeok Saengmyeongcheron" [The Theory of a Socio-political Organism in North Korea] in Han-Sik Park, ed., *Bukanui Silsanggwa Jeonmang* [North Korea in a Changing World Order] (Seoul: Donghwa, 1991).

Ken E. Gause

into policy decisions.[252] These decisions were enforced by the Secretariat through the unified *Juche* Party doctrine and the far-reaching Party committee structure.

It was within this leadership system that Kim Jong-il engineered his succession. This was made clear by the code phrase "Party Center" (*Dang Jung-ang*), used by the regime in the 1970s to refer to the heir apparent, Kim Jong-il.[253] Kim Jong-il started his career in the Party with his support network firmly entrenched in the Central Committee apparatus. His succession also took place within the Party structure.

As in other communist systems, a political party exists alongside the governing apparatus. While the government and the military can take part in the ruling of the country, power is defined by and emanates from the political regime. For communist systems, this political regime resides within the Communist Party. It is only through the Party apparatus that the heir apparent can learn how to wield power. In 1973, at the Seventh Plenum of the Fifth Central Committee, Kim Jong-il was appointed to the KWP Secretariat for both the PAD and the OGD, the two key posts within the Party apparatus. The former allowed him to craft the message of the regime, while the latter ensured that the regime would firmly adhere to the notion of Kim family rule and embrace the idea of a dynastic succession.

Ultimately, it was only through the Party apparatus that the heir could eventually consolidate his position as the future *Suryong*. At the Sixth Party Congress in 1980, Kim Jong-il moved into the upper echelons of the decision-making apparatus through appointments to the Presidium of the Politburo and the CMC. Only Kim Jong-il and Kim Il-sung held positions in all three of the KWP's leadership bodies: the Politburo, Secretariat, and CMC. While Kim Jong-il was officially ranked fifth within the North Korean leadership, his credentials as heir were readily apparent.

As Kim Jong-il inherited more of his father's power and authority, he changed the leadership system in important ways. Institutionally, Kim Jong-il shifted the center of gravity within the Party from the Politburo to the Secretariat, his

---

252   Hyon Song-il, *Bukanui Gukgajeollyakgwa Pawo Elliteu* [North Korea's National Strategy and Power Elite] (Seoul: Sunin Publishing, 2007). After Kim Il-sung's unitary ruling system was established in the late 1960s, the Political Bureau ceased to be a collective consultative body. It became a rubber stamp where only the voices of Kim's loyal supporters were heard. Nevertheless, it remained a body where "constructive opinions," which fit within the boundaries of Kim's own ideas, often broadened Kim's thinking.
253   "Anti-Japanese Guerrilla Instigation," *Nodong Sinmun*, February 13, 1974; Morgan E. Clippinger, "Kim Chong-il in the North Korean Mass Media: A Study of Semi-Esoteric Communication," *Asian Survey* 21, no. 3 (March 1981). The term "Party Center" (*Dang jung-ang*) entered the North Korean vernacular at the time of the Eighth Plenum of the Fifth Central Committee in February 1974. Before then, the phrase was rarely used in North Korean mass media. It later became personified as *Nodong Sinmun* increasingly cited the *Dang jung-ang* as the brain behind numerous socialist construction guidelines.

base of power.[254] Decision-making on all policies and personnel appointments was transferred to the Party Secretariat Office and specialized departments, while the Politburo was reduced to a rubber stamp for ratification.[255] It was within this transition period, as Kim Jong-il began to assume more responsibility for running the regime, that an additional system of command and control began to develop attached to the offices of the heir apparent. Of particular importance was the development of a Personal Secretariat and an apparatus for managing the Kim family finances, otherwise known as the Royal Economy, both of which will be discussed in more detail in the following chapters.

Kim Jong-il Reorients the System

It is one thing to consolidate one's power as heir apparent in North Korea's "Leader-dominant system" (*Suryong-je*). It is quite another thing to hold onto that power as the succession moves into its final phase. The heir has to assume more responsibility for running the regime and prepare to become the leader. In the case of Kim Jong-il, the final phase of the succession began in the early 1990s. During this phase, the regime transformed its operating procedures to prepare for the transfer of power and Kim Jong-il's ruling power began to eclipse that of Kim Il-sung. Kim Jong-il's situational awareness was further enhanced as he took control of the day-to-day affairs of the regime. While Kim Jong-il maintained Kim Il-sung's policies, he began to leave his own mark. These aspects of the succession were, for the most part, contained within the Party apparatus.

However, in order for the transfer of power to take place, Kim Jong-il needed to assert his control over the military. This could only be done by revising the North Korean political regime. The *Suryong* would no longer rule through the Party.[256] Now he would take a more direct role in ruling the government and

---

254   Lee Yang-Su et al., "Analysis of the DPRK Power Group (2)—Route to the Heart of Leadership," *Korea JoongAng Daily*, January 5, 2007. In 1994, twenty-nine out of fifty North Korean elites had worked for the KWP Politburo. This means that this body was an important stop on the road to advancement. In 2006, however, only eight members of the elite had served in the Politburo. As a South Korean intelligence official explained, "Since 1993, Chairman Kim has not reorganized the Politburo, which has a lot of empty positions due to deaths, purges, and defections. Furthermore, the Politburo itself is being overshadowed by the Secretariat."

255   Toward the end of the Kim Il-sung period, policy consultation within formal leadership circles became perfunctory. This was replaced by a reporting mechanism whereby policy drafts were drawn up by each ministry and department before being passed directly to Kim Jong-il's office. Here, they were prioritized and, if deemed worthy, passed to Kim Il-sung. The Political Bureau was convened only to ratify decisions that had already been made by Kim Il-sung and Kim Jong-il.

256   A number of epithets denoting Kim Jong-il's elite status began to appear in the months after his formal designation as heir apparent. North Korean media labeled him "Dear Leader" (*Chin-ae-ha-*

military. Only through an undiluted command and control system could Kim Jong-il ever hope to reach the level of his father in terms of garnering respect and asserting guidance. In 1991, Kim was appointed Supreme Commander of the Armed Forces. This was a technical violation of the 1972 constitution, which stipulated that this position was intrinsically linked to that of the President, a post still held by Kim Il-sung. This provision was removed during the 1992 revision of the constitution, which also elevated the NDC in status.[257] The year following the revision, Kim Jong-il became the Chairman of the NDC.

After Kim Il-sung's death, this division of labor became more entrenched in the system as Kim Jong-il was faced with a crumbling economy. It quickly became apparent that the Party was not capable of dealing with this crisis. In a speech to Party members in December 1996 at Kim Il-sung University, Kim Jong-il bitterly criticized the Party for being debilitated, using terms such as "Elderly Party" (*No-in-dang*) and "Corpse Party" (*Song-jang-dang*). According to defector reports, Kim even threatened to disband the Party during an informal meeting in 1997.[258] He also reportedly reproached the Party for "not dealing properly with the food shortages in the country," and contended that he "did not owe anything to the Party."[259] The Party's inability to function was revealed in October 1997, when Kim Jong-il bypassed established Party rules to assume the mantle of General Secretary of the KWP. This was not done through the convening of a plenary meeting of the KWP Central Committee, but through a joint endorsement by the Party's CMC and Central Committee.[260] By circumventing the Central Committee process and not accepting the title of General Secretary of the Central Committee, but rather taking that of General Secretary of the KWP, Kim placed himself firmly above the Party apparatus. This gave notice that, unlike his father, he would not rule through the Party.

---

neun Ji-do-ja) in November 1980, an apparent analog to his father's "Great Leader" (*Wi-dae-han Suryong*). According to the Open Source Center, other epithets followed, such as "successor" (*gye-seung-ja*) in May 1981, "respected and beloved Kim Jong-il" (*gyeong-ae-ha-neun Kim Jong-il*) in April 1982, and "father Kim Jong-il" (*eo-beo-i Kim Jong-il*) in January 1992. As noted above, Kim Jong-il never adopted the title "Leader" (*Suryong*), which was reserved for his father.

257   The Supreme Commander was now intrinsically linked to the post of Chairman of the NDC.
258   *Monthly Chosun*, April 1997.
259   Suh Jae-Jean, "Possibility for WKP to Take Back Role of Decision-making," *Yonhap News Agency Agency: Vantage Point* 33, no. 8 (August 2010).
260   The CMC's ability to endorse Kim Jong-il as General Secretary was apparently made possible by a revision to the KWP rules in 1982 in which the CMC was elevated in status equal to that of the Central Committee. However, some Pyongyang-watchers dispute the fact that because the CMC was now referred to as the Party CMC that meant it was no longer subordinate to the KWP Central Committee. Regardless of this issue, Kim Jong-il's assumption of this position seemed to violate Article 24 of the KWP Charter, which states that a plenary meeting of the KWP Central Committee should elect the General Secretary.

The Tenth SPA convened in Pyongyang on September 5, 1998. It had three items on its agenda: 1) revise the North Korean Constitution; 2) re-elect Kim Jong-il Chairman of the NDC; and 3) appoint officials to posts throughout the government. Although not described as such, the meeting ushered in a new ruling structure under Kim Jong-il.

The revised constitution made Kim Il-sung the eternal President (*Ju-seok*) of North Korea,[261] ending speculation on when his son would succeed him to this highest post. Instead, Kim Jong-il chose to continue the pattern established in 1992 of concentrating authority in the NDC. The new structure left little doubt that the NDC was Kim Jong-il's organizational base from which to implement "Military First" (*Songun*) politics. The NDC was elevated to the highest state body and the position of NDC Chairman to the highest position in government.[262] Many Pyongyang-watchers considered the status of the NDC Chairman to be as high as that of the Politburo. Kim Jong-il issued directives in the name of the NDC over the years, displaying its power.

The NDC assumed the responsibility for the defense and security of the country. Its members managed military affairs, the defense industry, and internal security. However, the emergence of the NDC as the highest body of state authority did not signify, as many thought, the creation of an official policymaking body to replace the defunct Party Politburo. No evidence, either through defector channels or in grey literature, suggests that the NDC ever met as a collective decision-making body. At most, instructions occasionally came down to the close aide network under the title "NDC Chairman's Order," which suggested that Kim Jong-il used NDC membership as a coordinating mechanism for particular national security-related issues.

261   "Kim Chong-il Inherits 'Great Leader' Title," *JoongAng Ilbo*, September 7, 1998. Thae abolition of the presidency did not mean the removal of the three Vice Presidents (Ri Jong-ok, Pak Song-chol, and Kim Yong-ju) from the leadership. Instead, they were appointed honorary Vice Chairmen of the SPA Standing Committee, which signaled their withdrawal from front-line political affairs.
262   Kim Yong-nam, "Achieving Ultimate Victory of *Juch'e* Revolutionary Cause While Highly Enshrining Beloved and Respected Comrade Kim Jong Il at Top Place of State Is Firm Resolve of Party Members, Korean People's Army Servicemen, and People," *Minju Joson*, April 10, 2009. Kim Yong-nam described the chairmanship of the NDC as being "the highest rank of the state," responsible for commanding politics, defense, and the economy, and as being a "sacred position signifying the dignity of the state."

2. The Leadership System under Kim Jong-un

In the months after Kim Jong-il's stroke in August 2008, the regime began to grapple with the implications of his leadership model, which was informal in its structure, tied solely to one man, and characterized by multiple lines of competing reporting chains that served the role of balancing power. How would it be possible to pass this model to a new leader who lacked Kim Jong'il's connections and power? When Kim's choice of his third son, Kim Jong-un, as his successor became known within leadership circles in 2009, these issues became magnified. Not only was Kim Jong-un only in his late 20s, but he had also only been involved in regime affairs for a few years.

a. Reviving the Party

In order to address this challenge, Kim Jong-il adopted a two-pronged strategy. First, he took steps to create a formal structure around the heir apparent by reviving the Party leadership apparatus.[263] The Third Party Conference in September 2010 announced new appointments to the Politburo, Secretariat, CMC, and the Central Committee. These new appointments revitalized the moribund Party structure and gave Kim Jong-un an extensive bureaucracy dedicated to policy oversight. The fact that these leadership bodies would now meet on a regular basis and issue directives would give an air of legitimacy to decisions that Kim Jong-un would make in the future.

The Party Conference also attempted to fuse *Songun* politics and the *Dang Jung-ang* to create a sustainable leadership that would support the succession.[264] The CMC was newly defined in the Party Charter as "organizing and leading all military operations."[265] Furthermore, the new charter stipulated that the Chairman of the Commission position would be concurrently held by the Party's General Secretary. This upgrade suggested that the Party's military body would become a critical institution from which the heir apparent might consolidate his power. The move would allow him to control both the Party and the military when he eventually became General Secretary. Finally, a reference to *Songun* politics was inserted into the charter, which then read, "the Party will establish military-first politics as a basic political

---

263   Cho Young-Seo, "The Distinctive Nature of the Kim Jong-un Regime in North Korea and Prospects for its Change," *Yonhap News Agency Agency: Vantage Point* 36, No. 9 (September 2013).
264   *Dang jung-ang* is the designation for the heir apparent.
265   The current status of the KWP CMC remains a point of contention among Pyongyang-watchers. Some believe that the CMC was placed back under the Central Committee.

system of socialism."[266] For many Pyongyang-watchers, this latter revision validated the transformation in the hierarchy of power from Party-government-military that existed under Kim Il-sung to the current Party-military-government.

As discussed earlier, the assumptions of this system, namely that the "Leader" (*Suryong*) would have years of grooming and preparation before assuming power, were dealt with through the creation of a regent system around Kim Jong-un. For nearly two years, this kept the system functioning as the young leader was educated on the finer points of governing a regime that has often been referred to as a "gangster state," where power is highly dependent on securing and leveraging relationships. With the sudden purge of Jang Song-taek and the disappearance of Kim Kyong-hui, the Pyongyang-watching community was faced with fundamental questions: had the *Suryong* system been discarded? Was Kim Jong-un the Supreme Leader or nothing more than a puppet? The answers to these questions are fundamental to understanding the long-term stability of the regime.

b. Has the *Suryong* System Collapsed?

Within months of Jang Song-taek's purge, a series of articles appeared in the defector-run media arguing that a coup had occurred inside the Hermit Kingdom. An alliance of anti-Jang forces headed by the KWP OGD had supposedly become the power behind the throne, making Kim Jong-un little more than a puppet.[267] If true, North Korea is no longer ruled by a single individual, but a collective group of leaders from different institutions, particularly the OGD, military, and internal security apparatus. This would spell the end of the *Suryong* system and have implications for how the regime is ruled.

The KWP OGD undoubtedly could be considered a victor with the removal of Jang Song-taek. There is a good deal of circumstantial evidence to suggest that the OGD and military were actively engaged in a political struggle with Jang Song-taek and the KWP Administrative Department in the final year of Kim Jong-il's life. In December 2011, the publication of the former OGD First Vice Director, and adversary of Jang, Ri Je-gang's book, *Reflecting the Times of Strengthening Purity of the Revolutionary Organization*, signaled to the larger leadership that the struggle that existed around the succession in the early 2000s had returned. The signals continued throughout 2012 with the idolization of Ko Yong-hui, Kim Jong-un's mother and

---

266   Korean Workers' Party (KWP) Charter (*Jo-seon Ro-dong-dang Gyu-yak*), September 28, 2010, as published in *North Korea Tech*, January 22, 2011.
267   "Exclusive: 'Kim Jong-un is a Puppet' in the Eyes of North Korean Elite," *New Focus International*, March 7, 2014.

ally of the OGD against Jang, and the airing of the documentary of Ri's book on *KCTV*.[268] In 2014, five months after Jang's downfall, Hwang Pyong-so, an OGD First Vice Director, assumed control of the military's most powerful agency, the GPB.

The argument that the Pyongyang-watching community must resolve in order to understand the nature of the system is whether or not this elevation of the OGD's status has translated into decision-making power. Proponents of the theory that Kim Jong-un is a puppet argue that the *Suryong's* word was law under Kim Il-sung and Kim Jong-il. It was enough to ensure that orders were executed and enforced. They argue that Kim Jong-un does not command the same authority. Policy decisions are ultimately made at enlarged Politburo meetings. Real power has transferred to the OGD, which ensures policies are carried out. It is even suggested that an OGD "mafia" may guide the decision-making process by lobbying its own agenda.[269]

In all likelihood, the reality is much more complex. To suggest that Kim Jong-un is a puppet ignores many of the tenets of the system that remain even if one Supreme Leader has died and been replaced by a weaker heir. On the other hand, to suggest that Kim Jong-un is able to assume the mantle of power that his father held, to say nothing of his grandfather, sells short those aspects of legitimacy that the *Suryong* must earn. This is a position that he must grow into.

While the absolute truth on leadership dynamics inside North Korea is not possible to determine at this time, certain assumptions can be drawn from the regime's political culture and the public events surrounding Kim Jong-un. One assumption is that Kim Jong-un is the ultimate decision-maker in a system that can only function with one leader at the top from whom all legitimacy and power flow. Along these lines, Kim Jong-un may have become the Control Tower with the purge of Jang Song-taek. His personal apparatus of power must grow in order to allow the Supreme Leader to fulfill this role.[270] Instead of being a puppet, Kim Jong-un is an inexperienced leader who must take advantage of a leadership infrastructure placed around him by his father to grow into his role as Supreme Leader. Once he has achieved this, he will fully consolidate his power.

It can also be assumed that, following the purge of Jang Song-taek, the wider leadership is frozen in place.[271] It is locked in step behind the Supreme

---

268   Park Hyeong-Jung, "The Purge of Jang Song-taek and the Competition for Regency During the Power Succession," *Korea Institute for National Unification: Online Series* 14, No. 3 (February 27, 2014).
269   "Kim Jong-un: North Korea's Supreme Leader or State Puppet?" *The Guardian*, May 27, 2014. This article provides a useful overview of the theories about how North Korea is ruled.
270   See the next chapter for an examination of Kim's Personal Secretariat and apparatus of power.
271   The phrase "frozen in place" does not mean that the maneuvering and struggles for influence have ceased within court politics around Kim Jong-un. Instead, it refers to the dose of caution that has been injected into those dynamics. Individual leaders continue to promote themselves around the Su-

Leader. However, this will not last. If Kim Jong-un is unable to succeed in the policy paths he has established, especially those tied to the "Dual Development Strategy" (*Byeong-jin*), natural rivalries within the regime could re-emerge. If Kim is unable to manage these power struggles, his position as *Suryong* could become vulnerable.[272]

A collective leadership composed of elements of Kim's retinue is hard to envision. Not only would this faction have to lead through Kim for its policies to have legitimacy, but they would also be vulnerable to the Supreme Leader's whim. The surveillance system in place reports directly to the Supreme Leader from a number of different channels, making the formation of any faction nearly impossible.[273] For Kim Jong-un to fully achieve his role as Supreme Leader, he will need to be able to manipulate his retinue as well as the wider leadership. Kim Jong-un's advisors are invested with key portfolios across the policy spectrum. They have the latitude and influence to operate within the policy environment, but not as much as was enjoyed by the regents. It is Kim's job to balance these divergent interests through the acceptance or rejection of recommendations.

3. THE DECISION-MAKING PROCESS

One of the central questions regarding the Kim Jong-un regime is how decisions are made. The process appears to have changed from Kim Il-sung to Kim Jong-il, and presumably has changed again under Kim Jong-un. It is a process that is impacted by how the Supreme Leader utilizes the wider leadership environment, as well as by his leadership style. After a year in power, the growing consensus among Pyongyang-watchers was that Kim Jong-un is the final decision maker. However, there was fierce debate over how the decision-making process functioned. Does Kim Jong-un control the decision-making environment and determine the agenda, as is

---

preme Leader, and may even try to undermine their rivals, but they appear to now refrain from the fierce power struggles that characterized the period before Jang Song-taek was purged.

272   Author's interviews in Seoul, May 2014. According to numerous Pyongyang-watchers in South Korea, Kim Jong-un must consolidate his power over the next couple of years. Policy failures stretching into the two to five year timeframe could be detrimental to the regime.

273   "Kim Jong-un: North Korea's Supreme Leader or State Puppet?" op. cit. Michael Madden, the author of *North Korea Leadership Watch*, observes that Kim Jong-un inherited a hyper-vigilant system put in place as Kim Jong-il's health was declining. During this period, Kim Jong-il strengthened the Supreme Leader's lines of communication with the surveillance apparatus and Praetorian Guard. These channels are not easily co-opted by Kim Jong-un's retinue and some channels are designed to keep others under observation. According to some sources inside Pyongyang, this includes multiple channels within the KWP OGD, which allows this organization to conduct internal surveillance.

his right under the dictates of the *Suryong* system?[274] Or, as some would argue, is he being coerced by competing forces within the regime, such as the military?

What follows is an analysis of how decision-making appears to work in the Kim Jong-un era. It examines what can be seen on the outside and speculates, based on interviews of numerous defectors and experienced Pyongyang-watchers, how the system has evolved since Kim Jong-il's death. The shifting role of the Control Tower acts as a breaking point between the way the system operated before and after the purge of Jang Song-taek.

a. Glimpses into the Process

Kim Jong-il's decision-making process took decades to develop and was dependent on wide-ranging relationships across the regime. It was unlikely that Kim Jong-un could have easily stepped into his father's leadership model, since it was so dependent on Kim Jong-il's personality and required profound inside knowledge of regime politics, policies, and processes. He was only designated his father's successor in 2009. In other words, he had a handful of years to learn on the job, whereas Kim Jong-il had nearly thirty years between the time he entered the Party apparatus in the early 1960s and Kim Il-sung's death in 1994. Yet, the regime went to great lengths during Kim Jong-un's first years in power to show him as the Supreme Leader and ultimate decision maker.

In January 2012, North Korean media unveiled photographs of Kim Jong-un's signature and noted that he would continue his father's practice of directly reviewing and signing off on policy recommendations and other internal reports.[275] As the year came to a close, North Korean television broadcasted a documentary that showed Kim Jong-un chairing a Politburo meeting in which he conveyed the news of Kim Jong-il's death.[276]

274   Author's interviews in Seoul, April 2013. The author was privy to an extraordinary debate at the Korea Institute for National Unification that laid out the two leading theories on North Korean decision-making.

275   Alex Melton and Jaesung Ryu, "Wanted: Handwriting Analyst," *North Korea: Witness to Transformation*, Peterson Institute for International Economics, February 5, 2012; "Kim Jong-un's Handwriting Shows Chip Off the Old Block," *The Chosun Ilbo*, January 4, 2012. Photographs of Kim Jong-un's signature, attached to loyalty pledges from various institutions throughout the regime, appeared for the first time in *Nodong Sinmun* on December 2, 2011. The regime probably decided to release the photographs in order to show that Kim Jong-un was in control and was the ultimate decision-maker, even if a collective group of advisors had significant input into the policy deliberation process. This was not the first instance of North Korean media revealing the Supreme Leader's signature. There were at least 100 cases dating back to 1981, when state media showed Kim Jong-il's signature on internal reports.

276   Michael Madden, "Film Released to Mark 1 Year Anniversary of KJI's Death," *North Korea Leadership Watch*, December 13, 2012. The Politburo scenes are in the fourth part of the documentary

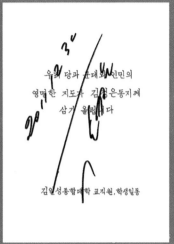

Image 11: Kim Jong-il's signature is on the left and Kim Jong-un's is on the right. (Source: KCNA, Nodong Sinmun)

Image 12: This is reportedly a Politburo meeting from December 2011 when Kim Jong-un announced his father's death. (Source: KCTV/KCNA screenshot as appeared on North Korea Leadership Watch)

---

film, *We Will Hold the Great Leader Comrade Kim Jong Il in High Esteem Down through Generations*. The ninety-minute fourth installment of the official documentary film series chronicled the death and funerary rites of Kim Jong-il during December 2011. Entitled *The Great Leader Comrade Kim Jong Il Will Live Forever*, it was released to mark the one-year anniversary of Kim Jong-il's death.

On January 27, 2013, *Nodong Sinmun* reported that Kim Jong-un had convened a meeting of national security officials two days earlier to discuss "the grave situation prevailing in the DPRK."[277] This was the first time that North Korean media had made such a leadership meeting public.[278] The report was accompanied by photographs showing Kim Jong-un sitting around a conference table with General Choe Ryong-hae, Director of the KPA GPB; General Hyon Yong-chol, Chief of the KPA GSD; General Kim Won-hong, Director of the SSD; Pak To-chun, KWP Secretary for Defense Industry; Kim Yong-il, KWP Secretary for International Affairs; Hong Sung-mu, KWP Vice Director of the MID; and Kim Kye-gwan, First Vice Minister of Foreign Affairs. During the meeting, Kim Jong-un was briefed about "the new situation and circumstances prevailing on the Korean Peninsula and in its vicinity." In response, "[he] expressed the firm resolution to take substantial and high-profile important state measures in view of the prevailing situation as the stand had already been clarified by the NDC and the Foreign Ministry of the DPRK through their statements that powerful physical countermeasures would be taken to defend the dignity of the nation and the sovereignty of the country. He advanced specific tasks to the officials concerned." Many believe that this was the meeting in which the upcoming third nuclear test was discussed.[279]

---

277   The meeting reportedly focused on the international community's reactions to the April 2012 and December 2012 launches of the Unha-3 rocket and the subsequent UN sanctions.

278   Cheong Seong-Chang, "Process for Policymaking Regarding National Security," *Yonhap News Agency Agency: Vantage Point* 36, no. 4 (April 2013).

279   Ibid. and author's interviews in Seoul, April 2013. In addition, many Pyongyang-watchers in Seoul suggested that the regime wanted to show a formal process of Kim Jong-un meeting with a "national security council-like body." This could be a decision-making structure that Kim would like to put into place instead of the current one. Others contend that the meeting may have been an abbreviated version of Kim Jong-un's Friday national security meetings, which are discussed later.

Image 13: National Security meeting reportedly held on January 25, 2013. From Kim Jong-un's left are: Kim Kye-gwan, Kim Yong-il, General Kim Won-hong, General Choe Ryong-hae, General Hyon Yong-chol, Hong Sung-mu, and Pak To-chun. (Source: KCNA)

On February 3, 2013, North Korean media reported that Kim Jong-un chaired an expanded meeting of the KWP CMC,[280] which was attended by the staff of the KPA Supreme Command, commanding officers of KPA large combined units (*dae-yeon-hap bu-dae*), senior commanders of the KPA Navy, KPA Air and Anti-Air Forces, and the KPA SRF Command. Characterized as an "enlarged meeting of the CMC," this was the first time North Korean media published photographs of an important military gathering. The purpose of the meeting was to discuss "the issue of bringing about a great turn in bolstering up the military capability, true to the ['Military First'] *Songun* revolutionary leadership of the KWP, and an organizational issue."[281] At the meeting, Kim Jong-un delivered a speech "which serves as guidelines for further strengthening of the KPA into a matchless revolutionary army of Mt. Paektu and defending the security and sovereignty of the country as required by the Party and the developing revolution."[282] Many Pyongyang-watchers believed that this was part of the authorization process for a nuclear test.[283]

280   *Nodong Sinmun*, February 3, 2013.

281   "Enlarged Meeting of Central Military Commission of WPK Held under Guidance of Kim Jong Un" *KCNA.* February 3, 2013.

282   Michael Madden, "Kim Jong Un Chairs Meeting of Party Central Military Commission and KPA Senior Command," *North Korea Leadership Watch*, February 3, 2013.

283   Ibid. The "CMC is one body [the NDC being the other in joint coordination] which authorizes and has oversight of military industry production, research and development."

Image 14: An enlarged meeting of the KWP CMC, which reportedly took place in February 2013.
(Source: KCNA)

During the period of rising tensions and shortly after U.S. B-52s sortied over South Korea, *Nodong Sinmun* revealed a series of photographs on March 29, 2013 of Kim Jong-un receiving a military briefing from Kim Rak-gyom, Commander of the SRF; Ri Yong-gil, Director of the GSD Operations Bureau;[284] Hyon Yong-chol, Chief of the GSD; and Kim Yong-chol, Director of the RGB. According to the report, Marshal Kim Jong-un, in his capacity as Supreme Commander, convened the operational meeting in the early morning hours at the Supreme Command headquarters "to discuss the KPA SRF's performance of duty for firepower strike." After receiving a report from Lieutenant General Kim Rak-gyom on the technical conditions of the strategic strike capabilities of the KPA, the report noted Kim Jong-un "made an important decision…[and] signed the plan on technical preparations of strategic rockets of the KPA, ordering them to be on standby for fire so that they may strike any time the U.S. mainland, its military bases in the operational theaters in the Pacific, including Hawaii and Guam, and those in South Korea."[285] This was a not-so-subtle effort to portray Kim Jong-un as a military leader and decision maker. Surrounding him and his advisors were maps showing the SRF's "Plan for Striking the U.S. Mainland and an Order of Battle of North Korean Forces." This came days after Kim had issued an order through the Supreme Command to place the armed forces on "Combat Duty Posture 1," the highest level of readiness. North Korean media had not shown the Supreme Leader in such a martial setting since the days of Kim Il-sung.

---

284   *Nodong Sinmun*, March 29, 2013. It was this report that revealed Ri Yong-gil's new position as Director of the GSD Operations Bureau.

285   *Nodong Sinmun*, March 29, 2013.

Image 15: A March 13, 2013 military briefing for Kim Jong-un. Standing behind Kim Jong-un are, from left to right: Lieutenant General Kim Rak-gyom, Commander of the KPA SRF Command; Colonel General Ri Yong-gil, Chief of the KPA GSD Operations Bureau; General Hyon Yong-chol, Chief of the KPA GSD; and General Kim Yong-chol, Chief of the RGB and Vice Chief of the KPA GSD. (Source: Nodong Sinmun)

Two years later, in August 2015, North Korea found itself again embroiled in a crisis on the Korean peninsula following the explosion of a number of landmines along the DMZ, which critically wounded two South Korean soliders. Seoul responded by reactivating the loudspeakers on its side of the border and tensions grew between the two Koreas. In the midst of this crisis, North Korean media took measures to show that Kim Jong-un was in control of the decision-making process. In particular were a series of still photographs displayed on television showing a nighttime meeting convened to discuss the crisis.

Image 16: A screenshot of Kim Jong-un convening an emergency meeting of the KWP CMC on the night of August 20, 2015. (Source: KCTV)

While there is debate within the Pyongyang-watching community over whether these photographs and reports are a reflection of actual meetings or staged events for the purpose of building Kim Jong-un's legitimacy as the Supreme Leader, there is a general consensus that much of the decision-making process is hidden from sight. Recently, information that has emerged through defector channels suggests that a decision-making process was put in place shortly after Kim Jong-il's death. This framework provides Kim Jong-un with the situational awareness he needs as the final decision-making authority. It also creates an environment in which he can develop the relationships he will ultimately need in order to consolidate power. The sections below discuss this process, but readers should approach this information with caution. It has not been vetted and may at best illustrate a process by which a totalitarian regime educates a young and untested leader.

b. Kim Jong-un's Role as Decision Maker

The Supreme Leader's role as decision maker consists of two levels: strategic and operational. At the strategic level, he is the sole decision maker responsible for setting the overarching guidance that frames the entire policymaking process. At the operational level, the Supreme Leader acts as the Control Tower, making day-to-day decisions that fit within this overarching guidance.

For Kim Jong-un, this linkage between the Supreme Leader and the Control Tower was separated, presumably on Kim Jong-il's orders. As mentioned earlier, Jang Song-taek acted as the Control Tower during the first two years of the Kim Jong-un era. Jang worked with Kim to manage the day-to-day affairs of the regime. If changes were necessary on the strategic level, Kim Jong-un most likely met with one or more of his regents. They could provide context and make him aware of the consequences of various courses of action.

Since Jang's downfall, the role of Control Tower has presumably been restored to the Supreme Leader. If so, Kim Jong-un would have to play a greater micro-managerial role. This restores the natural order to the regime's chain of command, but raises questions about how Kim has positioned himself to assume this operational role. The answer most likely lies in a combination of the expansion of his personal leadership apparatus and the infrastructure that was put in place to educate him on the policy process.

One of the questions that frequently arises when discussing the transfer of power to Kim Jong-un is how he was trained to step into the shoes of the Supreme Leader. Since his formal designation as heir apparent in September 2010, North Korean media began to report on Kim Jong-un's guidance inspections with his father, something that apparently began even before he became the designated successor. Is this the only method by which he learned about the situation throughout the regime and how policies are affecting various groups and the lives of ordinary people? Recent defector reporting suggests that this is not the case. There is an institutional process that has been designed to both inform Kim Jong-un and prepare him for the significant responsibilities of a job that demands micro-management.

According to one well-informed source with contacts inside North Korea, immediately following Kim Jong-il's death, Kim Jong-un began to hold weekly meetings on Tuesday and Friday afternoons. These meetings were attended by top officials from across the regime, including the Party, government, and military.[286]

---

286   Author's interview in Seoul, April 2013. See also Cheong Seong-Chang, "Process for Policymaking Regarding National Security," op. cit. These meetings appear to be a modified continuation

Reportedly including between twenty and thirty people on average, and sometimes restricted to fewer than ten, these meetings appear to serve two functions. First, they give Kim Jong-un situational awareness on issues of importance across the regime. He has a chance to discuss policy with the individuals directly responsible for policy execution. Second, the meetings allow Kim to develop the face-to-face relationships that will be critical to consolidating power. Before each meeting, the agenda is set by Kim's Personal Secretariat in consultation with his closest advisors. Before his aunt's illness and his uncle's execution, this meeting most likely included Kim Kyong-hui, Jang Song-taek, and Choe Yong-rim or Pak Pong-ju. A combination of these individuals would meet with Kim Jong-un to discuss issues and decide the agenda. The Personal Secretariat then circulated the agenda to the participants. After each meeting, there would be a dinner that allowed for a more relaxed setting for continued conversation and relationship-building.[287] It should be stressed that these were not decision-making meetings and Kim Jong-un made decisions outside of this context.[288]

The Tuesday meetings focus on domestic and social issues. Early on, Choe Yong-rim was responsible for organizing these meetings in consultation with Kim Jong-un's Personal Secretariat. This role presumably moved to Pak Pong-ju when he became Premier in 2013. Both Choe and Pak have carried out ongoing inspections of entities in the economic sector. The Premier now appears to be actively engaged in information gathering for the leadership and, as such, would be one of the Supreme Leader's closest advisors on domestic matters. This was unheard of in the Kim Jong-il era. Presumably, the Tuesday meetings include individuals with relevant and critical portfolios inside the Party and government. From the Party, regular invitees likely include: the KWP Secretaries for Light Industry, Education, Pyongyang Affairs, Propaganda and Agitation, General Affairs, Personnel, and Finance, as well as relevant KWP department directors and provincial secretaries. From the Cabinet and wider government, regular invitees likely include: the Premier, vice premiers, relevant ministers, relevant members of the SPA leadership, and the head of the State Planning Commission (SPC).[289]

---

of Kim Jong-il's decision-making process before his stroke, when he held large, regime-wide meetings on Thursdays. These meetings dealt with issues across the policy spectrum. They were followed up by Saturday evening drinking parties at one of Kim's residences, where discussions critical to decision-making were held.

287   Author's interviews in Seoul, April 2013. Allegedly, the Friday dinner parties include participants from both the Tuesday and Friday meetings.

288   Ibid.

289   Ibid.

The Friday meetings focus on military and security matters, as well as particularly sensitive foreign policy issues, such as inter-Korean relations and North Korea's ties with China and the United States. Kim Kyong-hui, in her role as guarantor of the Kim family equities, was responsible for organizing these meetings. She also reportedly took the lead in preparing her nephew in a private meeting beforehand that possibly included Jang Song-taek and Kim Kyok-sik. Presumably, the Friday meetings include top officials from the CMC, NDC, and Cabinet. Friday meetings, more so than the Tuesday meetings, also likely take place in a much smaller setting, depending on the sensitivity of the issues being discussed. The January 25, 2013 "national security council" meeting suggested that this may not have been an uncommon occurrence.[290]

Image 17: Kim Jong-un receives a briefing at a defense industry consultative meeting.
(Source: KCTV)

While Jang Song-taek may have been involved in the preparatory meetings before the Tuesday, and possibly the Friday, meetings, defector sources agree that he was not actually part of either meeting.[291] This would suggest that Kim Jong-un used

290   Ibid. See also Cheong Seong-Chang, "Process for Policymaking Regarding National Security," op. cit. According to one source, this National Security Council meeting was similar to the Tuesday and Friday meetings, but was probably convened for a special reason. It reportedly took place around midnight.
291   "North Korea Embarks on Full-Scale Economic Development with the State Economic Development Committee (Headed by Jang Song-taek) Taking the Lead," *NK Intellectuals Solidarity*, October 31, 2013. A meeting of Party, Cabinet, and senior local officials in the economic sector was reportedly held behind closed doors on Tuesday, October 8, 2013. It was attended by Kim Jong-un. The meeting

these meetings as an alternative source of information to the Control Tower channel. They could also have served as a useful venue for Kim to discuss existing policies and receive advice beyond what he received from his regents. Such step-by-step education would be vital for Kim to develop the broad knowledge he would need to understand the policy-making process and the levers of influence at his disposal to affect that process.

Since Jang Song-taek's downfall, these meetings most likely serve as an informational channel for the Control Tower, now Kim Jong-un, to stay informed on policy matters. It is not clear whether these meetings have replaced the policy task groups or act as a venue to ensure that Kim does not issue contradictory policy guidance.[292]

4. Role of Formal Leadership Bodies

The role of formal leadership bodies in North Korea is still being debated by the Pyongyang-watching community. Under Kim Jong-il, the formal leadership structure weakened, giving way to informal lines of authority and communication. Toward the end of his life, Kim tried to revive this structure, especially within the Party, in order to give his heir an apparatus to base his rule upon. Kim Jong-un has utilized the formal leadership bodies in both the Party and state apparatus to facilitate decision-making. They give his decisions, as well as his status as Supreme Leader, a sense of legitimacy within the wider North Korean leadership. Each leadership body plays a special role that may or may not continue once Kim consolidates his power. The main leadership bodies include the Politburo, NDC, and CMC.

The Politburo of the KWP, officially known as the Political Bureau of the Central Committee of the KWP, is the highest body of the KWP. Article 25 of the Party Charter stipulates: "The Political Bureau of the Party Central Committee

---

was supposedly called at the request of Jang Song-taek to discuss basic ideas and plans for the outward reform of North Korea's economic development. At this meeting, Jang Song-taek reportedly chaired a plenary session of officials in the economic sector nationwide. It was interpreted by North Korean cadres as a sign that Jang, with Kim's endorsement, was starting to assume command over state economic development. Since this meeting was held during a period in which Jang was allegedly under investigation, the accuracy of the report remains in question.

292   According to one Pyongyang-watcher who has closely followed the photographs tied to these Tuesday and Friday meetings, the North Korean media quit publishing photographs of Kim Jong-un taking part in informal meetings soon after the purge of Jang Song-taek. He is now only photographed chairing meetings of formal bodies, such as the CMC. This might suggest that the Tuesday and Friday meetings no longer take place and their function has now been subsumed in the Control Tower apparatus within Kim's Personal Secretariat.

and its Presidium organize and direct all party work on behalf of the Party Central Committee between plenary meetings. The Political Bureau of the Party Central Committee shall meet at least once every month."[293] The Politburo is responsible for managing and coordinating the Party's political activities, as well as deliberating on current events and policies between Central Committee plenums, which are supposed to be held every six months. According to the Party bylaws, the Politburo is required to meet once a month.[294]

A number of Politburo directives have appeared in North Korean media,[295] but there is little evidence on how many times the body has actually met—although some sources suggest it has met a few times since Kim Jong-un took power.[296] An examination of North Korean media and reports by defectors suggests that the Politburo currently performs various roles. It is involved in personnel management and announces Central Committee meetings. It is also the mouthpiece through which official decisions are announced. However, the Politburo is not a decision-making body. Rather, its deliberations provide information for Kim Jong-un to use to make decisions.[297] The Politburo also gives legitimacy to Kim Jong-un's rule by creating a venue for the regime to demonstrate standardized procedures. Finally, it is a body composed of a number of vested interests throughout the regime. As such, it is also a venue whereby shifts in policy and politics can be made clear to the wider leadership and even the general public—as was the case with the purge of Jang Song-taek and the rumored purge of Ri Yong-ho.[298]

The second main leadership body is the NDC, which became the leading state body under Kim Jong-il. The 1998 constitution defined the NDC as "the

---

293   Korean Workers' Party (KWP) Charter (*Jo-seon Ro-dong-dang Gyu-yak*), as published in *North Korea Tech*, January 22, 2011.

294   As with other Communist regimes, North Korea uses the Party apparatus to give legitimacy to what is otherwise a regime built on secretive, closed decision-making.

295   It was the Politburo that announced the appointment of Kim Jong-un as the Supreme Commander of the KPA on December 30, 2011 after an apparent meeting. It also adopted a "decision paper" on future policy that explicitly announced the regime's continued pursuit of the "Military First" (*Songun*) policy. It went on to proclaim as special breaking news in January 2012 that North Korea would preserve the body of Kim Jong-il "exactly as it is in a glass coffin in Kumsusan Memorial Palace." On November 4, 2012, the Politburo announced its decision to create the SPCSGC, headed by Jang Song-taek.

296   "Top NK General Ousted For Debating Economic Reform," *Dong-A Ilbo*, July 31, 2012. The only account of a Politburo meeting to date is the one that allegedly took place on Sunday, July 15, 2012 where Ri Yong-ho was purged. There is no additional evidence to suggest that the Politburo meets regularly on any particular day.

297   Assuming, of course, the Politburo meets on a regular basis, which is not clear.

298   Ri Yong-ho was allegedly purged in the middle of a Politburo meeting when he argued against the June Economic Measures, which called for transferring many of the hard-currency operations from the military to the Cabinet. His removal, within the context of a Politburo meeting, was likely the first clear indication that the Military First policy was no longer in ascendance.

highest guiding organ of the military and the managing organ of military matters." Following Kim Jong-il's stroke in 2008, an enhanced bureaucratic structure was created to support NDC operations, including a policy office and formal secretariat. While it apparently did not meet as a body, Kim Jong-il sought information from individuals on particular issues to inform his decisions. He allegedly tasked members with responsibilities and oversight of specific policies. Therefore, the NDC was used more for policy execution than decision-making. Article 109 of the constitution outlines the NDC's responsibilities:

- Establish important policies of the state for carrying out the "Military First" (*Songun*) revolutionary line
- Guide the overall armed forces and defense-building work of the state
- Supervise the status of executing the orders of the Chairman of the DPRK NDC and the decisions and directives of the NDC, and establish relevant measures
- Rescind the decisions and directives of state organs that run counter to the orders of the Chairman of the NDC and to the decisions and directives of the NDC
- Establish or abolish central organs of the national defense sector
- Institute military titles and confer military titles above the general-grade officer rank.

Since Kim Jong-un has taken over as the First Chairman of the NDC, this organization seems to have faded into the background. It is a mouthpiece on certain issues, especially on inter-Korean relations, and is the source for announcements regarding tests of critical defense systems.[299] There have been no reported meetings of the NDC thus far.

As the final main leadership body, the KWP CMC has played a special role in the transfer of power to Kim Jong-un. At the Third Party Conference in 2010, the only leadership post Kim Jong-un received was Vice Chairman of the CMC. According to the Party Charter, the CMC directs Party activity in the KPA and is chaired by the Party's General Secretary.[300] According to Section 27 of the

---

299   "DPRK National Defense Commission Proposes 'High-Level Talks' with US," *KCNA*, June 16, 2013. The NDC released a statement in advance of the February 2013 nuclear test. For the nuclear tests of 2006 and 2009, the Ministry of Foreign Affairs was responsible for the release of such statements. In June 2013, the NDC took the lead in reasserting North Korea's nuclear status as part of an offer for high-level talks with the United States with the expressed purpose of creating a world free of nuclear weapons.
300   When Kim Jong-un became First Secretary following Kim Jong-il's death, he assumed the roles and responsibilities once reserved for the General Secretary.

KWP Charter, the CMC "discusses and decides" on the Party's military policy and methods of its execution, organizes work to strengthen military industries, the people's militia, and all armed forces, and directs the military establishment of the country. According to a *KCNA* report, during an August 25, 2013 meeting, the CMC "discussed and decided upon practical issues of bolstering up the combat capability of the revolutionary armed forces and increasing the defense capability of the country in every way as required by prevailing situation and the present conditions of the People's Army."[301]

Image 18: Kim Jong-un chairs an expanded meeting of the KWP CMC in August 2013. According to the report that accompanied the photograph, Kim "made an important concluding speech which would serve as guidelines for firmly protecting the sovereignty and security of the country and promoting the cause of the songun revolution of the Party."
(Source: Nodong Sinmun, August 26, 2013)

According to some reporting, CMC and NDC decision-making is done at the same time in order to ensure that the "military follows the Party's lead."[302] If this is the case, decision-making most likely does not take place within the CMC. Instead, the CMC coordinates and facilitates decisions made higher up the chain of command. It is composed of critical military and security leaders, which ensures that orders from the CMC have maximum support across the country's national

---

301   "Kim Jong Un Guides Meeting of WPK Central Military Commission," *KCNA*, August 25, 2013.
302   Author's interviews in Seoul, April 2013.

security establishment.[303] Like the NDC, it is not clear that the CMC meets on a regular basis. The only evidence of meetings to reach the outside world was the handful of photographs in North Korean media of expanded meetings in February 2013, August 2013, April 2014, and February 2015, all of which were chaired by Kim Jong-un.[304]

5. KIM JONG-UN'S LEADERSHIP STYLE

Decision-making is not just about setting agendas and convening meetings. In North Korea's leader-centered system, the Supreme Leader's personality, demeanor, and leadership style impacts how decisions are made. It is a system that makes it difficult for regents and advisors to keep a leader focused on a set of issues or priorities. Policies can be made at the Supreme Leader's whim; he can sidestep any formal processes that are in place to guide and inform his decision-making. In addition, since the regime depends on the Supreme Leader's input in order to function, his work ethic and attention to detail have a dramatic impact on the efficiency of the policymaking process.

A well-worn refrain from Pyongyang-watchers and government officials is that the international community had developed a certain understanding of how Kim Jong-il operated. No matter how serious the crisis seemed on the surface, there was a sense that a pragmatic and calculating decision maker was operating behind the scenes in Pyongyang. From what has been reported about Kim Jong-il's leadership style, this may have been the case on some occasions, but the reality is more complex. He was an introverted, solitary decision maker. He relied on his own reading of official reports, the foreign press, and even the Internet to inform his worldview.[305] He would hone these views through discussions with close advisors

---

303   The CMC relies on a number of organizations to carry out its mandate, including the KPA GPB, the KWP Military Department, and the KWP MID. The CMC also uses the KWP Civil Defense Department to transmit guidance and indoctrination to North Korea's reserve military training units.
304   Photographs of the February 2013 meeting did not appear at the time. On March 5, 2013, North Korean state media released a documentary film that focused on Kim Jong-un's interactions with the armed forces. Loosely translated as *Unleashing a New Heyday of the Formidable Forces of Mt. Paektu*, the eighty-minute film consists mainly of footage that had previously appeared in short documentaries about Kim Jong-un's activities. Tacked on to these activities was footage of the CMC meeting of February 3, 2013. For a more detailed discussion of the meeting, see Michael Madden, "CMC Meetings Shown in DPRK Documentary on Kim Jong Un's Military Activities," *North Korea Leadership Watch*, March 18, 2013. As for the Sunday, August 25, 2013 meeting, *Nodong Sinmun* carried photographs of the event. See *Nodong Sinmun*, August 26, 2013.
305   Ken E. Gause, "The North Korean Leadership: System Dynamics and Fault Lines," In *North Korean Policy Elites*. Alexandria, VA: Institute for Defense Analysis Paper P-3903, June 2004.

and by reaching out to key nodes within the regime. He was a micro-manager and obsessive about controlling information to ensure that his knowledge on issues extended beyond that of anyone else's within the leadership.[306] Kim preferred to run the regime through fear and competition. In this way, he kept other leaders off-balance and beholden to him. He often used bribery, humiliation, and threats of punishment to keep the leadership in line. Defectors have also characterized Kim Jong-il as self-centered with no enduring commitment to principles other than his own self-interest.[307] He would entertain the creative ideas of others as long as they did not clash with his opinions or threaten his position as Supreme Leader. In other words, Kim Jong-il was a leader who was very comfortable operating in a loose and informal system, as opposed to a formal bureaucratic structure. The consequences of this leadership style were:

- Self-assured decision-making, even if he was subject to misinterpreting the situation
- Delays in policymaking
- Extreme caution when it came to major departures from the established policy line
- Occasional conflicting and contradictory policies because the Supreme Leader did not realize he had signed off on both.

Kim Jong-il's Leadership Style

Laid over a web of close aides was a leadership style and set of processes that Kim used in order to run the regime on a day-to-day basis. Kim's leadership style, often described as "hub-and-spoke," operated on two levels. Within the formal bureaucracy, he held the key positions that gave him both authority and situational awareness. His positions of General Secretary of the KWP and Supreme Commander of the Armed Forces gave him control over the two most powerful elements of the regime. They also provided him the legitimacy he needed to rule without obvious challenge. It was also generally assumed that he

---

306   This need for control stretched back to the 1970s, when he set up the "Three Revolution Teams" concept to give him unparalleled control and sources of information independent of those used by Kim Il-sung.

307   Merrily Baird, "Kim Chong-il's Erratic Decision-making and North Korea's Strategic Culture" in Barry R. Schneider and Jerrold M. Post, eds., *Know Thy Enemy: Profiles of Adversary Leaders and Their Strategic Cultures* (Maxwell Air Force Base, AL: USAF Counterproliferation Center, 2003).

occupied the posts of Director of the KWP OGD and Director of the SSD, two institutions that allowed him to quickly identify and destroy any potential threat.

But even these formal trappings of power were not enough. Kim created an informal system that circumvented direct chains of command in order to give him alternate reservoirs of information. This allowed him to access information that might otherwise have been denied through formal channels. It also allowed him to keep tabs on the senior leadership. He did this by forming alliances with trusted individuals within key ministries and commands. This kept other senior leaders off-balance and prevented them from using their bureaucracies as breeding grounds for anti-regime cabals and plots.

While he has only been in power for less than four years, some information, albeit highly speculative, is beginning to emerge about Kim Jong-un's leadership style. The most obvious departure from the way his father operated is Kim Jong-un's open persona. He conveys an impression of an outgoing, people-friendly, and ambitious leader, markedly different from Kim Jong-il's isolationist, solitary, and secretive image. Kim Jong-un appears to be comfortable giving speeches and interacting with large groups of ordinary citizens, whereas his father only gave one publicly recorded speech that lasted twelve seconds. This aspect of Kim Jong-un's leadership style harkens back to his grandfather, Kim Il-sung.[308] Defector reporting also paints a picture of a young and impetuous Supreme Leader who is sometimes quick to make decisions without seeking advice.[309] He apparently understands the tremendous power of the position he holds, but also understands that there are constraints established by his father and grandfather that the system imposes.[310]

---

308   The similarities between Kim Jong-un's and Kim Il-sung's public personae are so striking that many have suggested that Kim Jong-un is deliberately patterning his mannerisms after his grandfather in order to build rapport with the people who look on the original *Suryong* with great fondness.

309   This could possibly explain his decision to have the KPA conduct the Masikryong Speed Battle, a land reclamation project in Gangwon Province centered on the construction of a ski resort. This venture, allegedly designed to attract tourism, appears to be the result of an impetuous and self-indulgent decision by Kim Jong-un. After all, North Korea is facing international sanctions and its relations with the international community, including China, are at a low point. Some, however, have suggested that in the aftermath of the May 2013 reshuffle of the high command, such a "Speed Battle" was designed to show that the military is acting as a leading edge in support of Kim's shifting focus to the economy. According to defector reports, this was the first time that a personal appeal to workers from Kim Jong-un had been made public.

310   This observation is based on a series of interviews the author conducted with Pyong-yang-watchers in Seoul in April 2013. There were some who hold the opposite view that Kim Jong-un lacks an understanding of boundaries and is enamored with the power his position affords him.

How eager he is to challenge some of these constraints remains unclear.[311] His decision to reveal the failure of the Unha-3 missile test in April 2012 may have been his own decision or could have resulted from the fact that he listened to advisors who advocated for transparency, given the unprecedented openness leading up to the launch.[312] Other reports describe Kim as a spontaneous decision maker who is quick to anger. The story of Ri Yong-ho's removal during a Politburo meeting fits this personality profile.

Image 19: Kim Jong-un delivers his first public address in Kim Il-sung Square on the 100th anniversary of his grandfather's birth. (Source: KCTV)

311   "Is Kim Jong-un Throttling Back Personality Cult?," *The Chosun Ilbo*, July 8, 2013. There is some debate within Pyongyang-watching circles over whether Kim Jong-un's cult of personality has begun inside North Korea. Some media reports said that Kim Jong-un badges were spotted in Pyongyang in May 2013, worn by members of the elite. Later reports suggested that this may not be the case. Sources at the border village of Panmunjom alleged that Kim Jong-un prohibited the production of such badges. The South Korean delegation to the inter-Korean talks in July 2013 did not spot them on their North Korean counterparts. Instead, according to North Korean sources, the delegation wore pins featuring Kim Il-sung or both Kim Il-sung and Kim Jong-il, but no badges with only Kim Jong-un's face on them. In 2015, South Korean media reported that the North was manufacturing badges showing the faces of Kim Il-sung, Kim Jong-il, and Kim Jong-un together to mark the 70th anniversary of the Workers' Party on October 10, 2015. "N. Koreans To Wear New Kim Jong Un Badges," *The Korea Times*, July 8, 2015.

312   Ahn Jong-Sik, "Time to Take a Step Back on North Korea," *Daily NK*, February 8, 2014. According to Ahn, decision-making in the Kim Jong-un era has been characterized by an air of improvisation and immaturity. In April 2012, at the time of the long-range missile launch, Pyongyang invited foreign reporters to view the launch site and watch the rocket launch, but prevented them from viewing the event on the day of. Then, having raised tensions in March and April 2013, Kim completely reversed direction in May and began an over-the-top diplomatic charm offensive. These, and other events, such as the sporadic family reunions, have led many in Washington and Seoul to conclude that Kim and the North Korean leadership lack a strategic plan and are driven by short-term tactical considerations primarily tied to internal pressures.

Early in his tenure as leader, there was an ongoing debate within Pyongyang-watching circles over the extent to which Kim Jong-un controlled his own public appearances. While many speculated that he was stage-managed, given his obvious mannerisms that appear to be patterned after his grandfather, a photograph that appeared in June 2013 suggested that he may write some of his own speeches. *Nodong Sinmun* published a photograph of Kim delivering a speech at an event in Jagang Province.[313] The notes that Kim spoke from were written in blue ink and contained a number of amendments and deletions, which suggested that this was not an officially generated speech, but one written by Kim himself.[314] The fact that *Nodong Sinmun* did not reproduce the speech in its entirety, even though it was described as historic, led some to believe that it may have been lacking in propaganda elements precisely because Kim Jong-un wrote it. Conversely, others pointed out that it was impossible to say whether Kim really wrote it. They suggested that *Nodong Sinmun* was ordered to publicize an image showing the hand-written notes because it showed that Kim is a caring leader who strives to better connect with his people.[315]

Image 20: Kim Jong-un delivers a speech in Jagang Province. (Source: Nodong Sinmun)

---

313   According to the article that accompanied the photograph, he delivered a "historic" speech after reviewing a performance by the Moran Hill Orchestra (Moranbong Band).

314   The KWP PAD and the Central Committee secretary in charge of events involving the Supreme Leader (No. 1 events) have traditionally drafted the leader's speeches and then submitted them to him for approval. The speeches are usually typed. The fact that the Jagang speech is both handwritten and contains amendments implies that Kim wrote it personally. Only the Supreme Leader would be able to make amendments to a No. 1 event speech.

315   Lee Sang-Yong, "Kim's Hand-written Speech Sparks Debate," *Daily NK*, June 24, 2013.

Fully assuming the role of Supreme Leader requires more than just acting on one's own initiative and making decisions. It also requires the leader to interact with the wider leadership. Recent defector reports suggest that Kim Jong-un is becoming increasingly comfortable in his role as Supreme Leader. He is dealing not only with his closest advisors but also with powerful institutions, such as the high command.[316] Furthermore, he appears to be keenly aware of the protocols that need to be observed and seems to understand the boundaries within which he must operate to safeguard his position and maintain regime stability. However, his policies indicate a bolder approach to dealing with the issues facing the regime, both internal and external.[317] Some have suggested that his April 15, 2012 speech, in which he promised the North Korean people that they would "no longer have to tighten their belts," reflected his willingness to move away from the *Songun* politics that characterized the regime under Kim Jong-il. Others point to the March/April crisis on the Korean peninsula in 2013 as evidence of a desire by Kim Jong-un and North Korea to push the limits on the international front. Additionally, the unconditional abrogation of the armistice went much further than any similar moves his father made.

As Kim Jong-un grows into his leadership role, it will likely become harder for his advisors to control him from behind the scenes. This could result in a very different leadership style than is evident today, which is firmly tied to Kim's legitimacy-building campaign. Once he is able to fully step into the shoes of the Supreme Leader, his decision-making process may change and the character and direction of his policies may become less opaque. Whether and how far he will depart from his father's legacy remains to be seen.

---

316   Author's interviews in Seoul, April 2013.
317   See "The Rise of Moderate and Hardline Factions in North Korea," *Sankei Shimbun*, op. cit. According to one theory reportedly emerging from sources inside North Korea, Kim Jong-un is at the mercy of surrounding factions. He "is merely an avatar of his grandfather, Kim Il-sung, with no close associates of his own or real authority." Policymaking depends on which faction comes out on top in the struggle to interpret Kim Jong-il's legacy.

Image 21: Unlike his father, Kim Jong-un does not appear to be shy around strangers. Here, he leads a tour of the renovated Victorious Fatherland Liberation War Museum in Pyongyang in July 2013. (Source: Nodong Sinmun)

No ruler governs exactly like his predecessor. Age, experience, legitimacy, and relationships affect a leader's characteristics and help determine the amount of power and authority he possesses. But these factors do not completely determine a leader's position. In regimes like North Korea, political culture plays a fundamental role in how a leader comes to power and is treated by the wider leadership. The North Korean regime is subservient to a *Suryong*-based doctrine that is not easily undone. Regardless of Kim Jong-un's qualifications, he was chosen by his father, the Supreme Leader, and is of the Kim bloodline. Unlike his father, he went through the "proper" channels to receive his titles of power. In his early thirties, he is the legitimate ruler, the Supreme Leader.

What Kim Jong-un does not possess is the unquestioned, absolute, and enduring loyalty of the leadership and the population. Although political culture may guide the succession, the new leader's ability to deliver on his policy agenda affects his ability to consolidate his power. Kim Jong-un is two hereditary transitions away from Kim Il-sung's revolutionary credentials. His claim to legitimacy is thus weaker, and his policy decisions will play a greater role in maintaining legitimacy in the eyes of the country's elite.

As the guidance in Kim Jong-il's last will and testament gradually becomes less relevant to the issues confronting the regime, these policy decisions will likely grow in number. Once Kim Jong-un has consolidated his power, he will be able to make his own decisions. In the meantime, Kim will have to rely on his closest advisors, working with his Personal Secretariat to set the agenda, present policy options, and ensure that his decisions are implemented.

The following chapters will describe Kim Jong-un's personal apparatus, which is likely to grow now that he has assumed the role of Control Tower. The Personal Secretariat and Royal Economy emerged in the 1970s with Kim Jong-il's rise to power and have become institutionalized as part of the leadership apparatus dedicated to ensuring the authority of the Supreme Leader. Both of these parts of the leadership apparatus are tied to the internal security apparatus. Together, these three pieces of the apparatus provide the foundation of the *Suryong* system.

CHAPTER FIVE: THE SUPREME LEADER'S PERSONAL SECRETARIAT

A poorly understood aspect of totalitarian regimes is the role and importance of the leader's personal apparatus. In these regimes, top-down control is zealously enforced. A leader's situational awareness and penchant for micro-management are essential to running the regime, and the need for a network of loyal and devoted aides and advisors is paramount.

Under Kim Jong-il, the role and function of the Personal Secretariat came to light through defector reports and books published by senior members of the leadership who made their way to South Korea. When Kim Jong-il died, theories about the fate of this institution emerged. Some believed that it was passed down to his successor, Kim Jong-un. Others believed that the new leader may have leaned on his father's apparatus in the first few months of his reign but slowly created his own smaller Personal Secretariat that answers only to him. As one well-informed South Korean Pyongyang-watcher noted:

Anyone who says they know anything about Kim Jong-un's Personal Secretariat will probably be proven wrong. This subject is too sensitive and no information about it is known for sure—just rumors and speculation.[318]

Readers must keep this in mind while reading the following description of the role and function of the Personal Secretariat. It is based on information that came out during the Kim Jong-il era. It is further augmented with the latest information about its existence today under Kim Jong-un emerging from defector networks in Seoul.

Following a brief overview of the history of this powerful, yet obscure apparatus, this chapter will examine the role and function of Kim Jong-un's Personal Secretariat. Its organizational structure and key figures will be given special consideration, as well as its ties to the larger leadership structure, especially the NDC.

---

318   Author's interview in Seoul, April 2013.

1. The Personal Secretariat under Kim Jong-il

In the 1970s, as Kim Jong-il was engineering the second hereditary succession, he began to establish his own personal apparatus with the blessing of Kim Il-sung. Although he had a personal office since the 1960s when he entered the Central Committee, the Personal Secretariat that Kim Jong-il established in 1974 was geared towards assisting him with the succession. During this period, the office was often referred to as the Secretarial Office of the KWP OGD. This was part of Kim's strategy to develop a unified guidance system to solidify his father's role as the unassailable leader of the country. It also ensured that opposition to his role as heir apparent was identified and eliminated.

Kim Jong-il looked to the Party apparatus to nest his Personal Secretariat, leveraging the KWP OGD, the part of the Central Committee bureaucracy that already served as his base of power within the leadership. His Personal Secretariat had a direct tie to the OGD Secretariat, although it was a separate entity.[319] His new office was staffed by OGD personnel who became known as "secretariat members."

The original role of Kim Jong-il's Personal Secretariat was to assist the new heir apparent in carving out his position within the wider regime. Shortly after being designated heir apparent in 1974, Kim Jong-il established a reporting system throughout the regime. According to one source:

Information is power. Kim Jong-il was well aware of this. In order to establish the unified guidance system, he set up a detailed reporting-notification system, in which, every large and small matter that arose in all sectors and units in all of North Korea, would be quickly reported to him in detail.[320]

To maximize situational awareness, Kim authorized his Personal Secretariat, working through the OGD, to establish the "three-line, three-day reporting notification system" and the "direct reporting system." The "three-line, three-day reporting notification system" referred to the Party organization channel, the administrative channel, and the SSD channel. Based on this system, within three

---

319 Kim Jong-il's Personal Secretariat was often referred to within the leadership as the Secretarial Office of the KWP OGD. Although the Secretariat and the OGD were located on the same floor of the Third Main Party Building in Pyongyang's Central District and worked closely in processing information to and from Kim's office, they were distinct organizations.

320 Chong Chang-Hyon, *Gyeoteso Bon Kim Jong-il* [The Kim Jong-il that I saw] (Seoul: Kimyongsa, 2000). This book is based on interviews with Sin Kyong-Wan, former Deputy Director of the KWP PAD.

days these organizations were obligated to separately report and notify the OGD of issues that had arisen throughout North Korea. Through the "direct reporting system," Kim Jong-il was notified immediately by means of communication such as telephone or telegraph. This was used when an emergency situation or accident occurred, when there was loss of life, or when there was a violation of the unified thought system or unified guidance system. In the military, the "three-line, three-day reporting notification system" referred to the Party organization channel, the GSD channel, and the MSC channel.

Image 22: A young Kim Jong-il at his desk. (Source: Osamu Eya, Great Illustrated Book of Kim Chong-il. (Tokyo: Shogakukan, 1994))

Throughout the 1980s and early 1990s, Kim Jong-il's Personal Secretariat existed alongside Kim Il-sung's Presidential Secretariat. But unlike his father's office, Kim Jong-il's office expanded as he took on more responsibilities for running the day-to-day operations of the regime. Following Kim's appointment to the Politburo at the Sixth Party Congress in 1980, his office, which became a formal bureaucratic entity called the Secretarial Office of the Central Committee (SOCC), began to expand its power and reach. Its organizational structure included sections that ensured communications throughout the regime, including with Central Committee departments, the SPA, NDC, Cabinet, military, and SSD. At the time of Kim's death in 2011, it is rumored that his Personal Secretariat had a staff of nearly 300, including a director, vice directors, department heads, guidance officials, clerks, and secretaries.

Kim Jong-il's Personal Secretariat had several directors since its creation. However, only those since his formal designation as heir apparent in 1980 have been made public. They are:

- **Ri Myong-je (unknown–1992)** was a cadre within the KWP PAD. His relationship with Kim Jong-il most likely began in the 1960s, when Kim joined the PAD, and continued into the 1970s, when Kim became KWP Secretary for the PAD. While Ri's formal designation as Director of Kim Jong-il's Secretarial Office did not occur until 1982, it is possible that his tenure started in the early 1970s with the creation of the office. In 1992, he stepped down due to illness and took up a post as a Party secretary to the North Korean mission in France, where he received medical treatment. He retired in the 1990s and died in 2007.
- **Ri Song-bok (1992–2001)** also came out of the KWP PAD, where he was on the editorial staff of *Nodong Sinmun*. He reportedly formed a close relationship with Kim Jong-il and took up the post of Director of the SOCC in 1992. He served in this position until his death from lung cancer in May 2001.[321]
- **Kim Jang-son (2001–2002)** began his career as a Party cadre in the MPAF External Affairs Bureau, which is responsible for interactions between the KPA and foreign militaries. After serving as a Deputy Military Attaché at the North Korean Embassy in Moscow in the early 1970s, he returned in 1980 to eventually head the MPAF External Affairs Bureau. In 1984, he moved into the Central Committee apparatus, becoming a Vice Director of the KWP Administrative Department. He moved up to become Director, holding the post until the department was merged into the KWP OGD in 1992. He joined Kim Jong-il's Personal Secretariat in the early 1990s, assuming the role of Chief of Secretaries after Ri Song-bok's death.[322] For unknown reasons, Kim was relieved from his post and banished from Pyongyang sometime between

---

321   "Kim Jong-il Sends Wreath to Bier of Late Ri Song-bok," *KCNA*, May 21, 2001.
322   Kim Chang-son's ties to the ruling Kim family came through his wife, Ryu Chun-ok. She was the daughter of Ryu Kyong-su, the former Commander of the 105th Tank Brigade and Hwang Sun-hui, the Director of the Korean Revolution Museum, both of whom were partisan comrades of Kim Il-sung. Ryu Chun-ok was also a close friend of Kim Kyong-hui, Kim Jong-il's sister.

2001 and 2002. He served as the Organizational Secretary on the Anju City KWP Committee until 2009 when, with the assistance of Jang Song-taek and Kim Kyong-hui, he returned to Pyongyang to work in the NDC. In 2010, he appeared in public as a close aide to Kim Jong-un.[323]

- **Kang Sang-chun (2002–2011)** had a relationship with Kim Jong-il dating back to when they were classmates in the Political Economy Department at Kim Il-sung University. After university, Kang entered the GC, eventually being assigned to the Second Bureau, which was responsible for the protection of the heir apparent. He began service in Kim Jong-il's Personal Secretariat in the early 1980s as a division chief in charge of Kim's protocol and protection. He later became the Director of the Secretariat's Building Management Section, which was responsible for managing Kim's overseas slush fund and procuring items for the Kim family. In 2002, Kang Sang-chun became Director of the SOCC.[324] In 2006, Kang was reportedly arrested for money laundering in Macau by Chinese police.[325] The affair was resolved quietly and Kang returned to North Korea and continued in his position as head of the SOCC. According to several defectors, he has continued in this post under Kim Jong-un.

The source of much speculation by Pyongyang-watchers, Kim Jong-il's Personal Secretariat was where the formal and informal systems of power came together. Wielding influence by virtue of its gate-keeping function, this office was often compared to the royal order system that operated during the Chosun Dynasty (1392–1910). Kim Jong-il's Personal Secretariat apparently had no official sanction and was never mentioned in North Korean media. It received, classified, and facilitated documents addressed to the Chairman, Kim Jong-il, and then issued instructions.[326] It also administered Kim's schedule, itineraries, protocol, and logistics, and liaised with the GC to ensure his security. Because Kim Jong-il's

---

323   This biography is based in large part on information from *North Korea Leadership Watch*.
324   "Kang Sang-chun, New Director of the Secretariat for General Secretary Kim Jong-il," *Yonhap News Agency*, April 25, 2002.
325   Min Dong-Yong, "Kang Sang-chun Rumored to Have Been Arrested in China is Kim Jong-il's Butler—Manager of Slush Funds," *Dong-A Ilbo*, January 28, 2006. A frequent visitor to Macau on business related to the Kim family funds, Kang was reportedly detained during the period when Kim Jong-il was making an unofficial visit to China in January 2006.
326   Lee Gyo-Gwan, "Kim Jong-il Secretariat, at the Center of Power although not Listed as an Official Organization," *The Chosun Ilbo*, April 15, 2001. For a detailed discussion of Kim's Personal Secretariat, including a list of presumed personnel, see Ken E. Gause, *North Korea Under Kim Chong-il: Power, Politics, and Prospects for Change*, op. cit.

Personal Secretariat was not an official organization, its senior cadre worked externally as members of the KWP OGD.[327]

Closely associated with Kim Jong-il's Personal Secretariat, even overlapping at times, was an entity known as the Third Floor.[328] This element of Kim Jong-il's personal staff assisted him in conducting numerous special operations, both inside and outside the country. The members of the Third Floor cadre normally had long political careers. Paek In-su, former head of Office 39, worked for the apparatus for twenty-eight years, and Kwon Yong-rok and Ri Su-yong (Ri Chol) did so for more than twenty years.[329] While it would have been difficult to replace them, as they were in charge of secret affairs, their long hold on their positions was also related to Kim Jong-il's personality. These behind-the-scene members of the leadership were critical to the maintenance of the regime.[330]

---

327   Ibid.

328   The name comes from the location of this office, which was on the third floor of Office Complex Number 1, where Kim Jong-il's offices were located.

329   "3 DPRK Men who Procured Luxury, Military Items for Kim Jong-il," *Uin Hatsu "Konfidensharu,"* March 10, 2010. Kwon Yong-rok is tied to Office 39. According to some sources, he was a Deputy Director, a position he may still hold. He has been based in Vienna, Austria since the early 1980s when he held the post of the now defunct Kumsong Bank, North Korea's only bank operating in Europe until it was forced to close at the end of June 2004. He was officially an auditor, but in actuality, he was the bank head. A fluent German speaker, Kwon was one of the primary procurers of luxury items for the Kim family. Other Third Floor operatives in Europe included Yun Ho-chin and Kim Chong-ryul. Yun Ho-chin is a specialist in nuclear programs. He was a diplomat who served for a long time as a senior North Korean representative at the International Atomic Energy Agency (IAEA). Using Vienna as his base, Yun roamed all over Germany and the rest of Europe looking to purchase equipment and devices needed for North Korea's nuclear development. Yun later became the Director of the Namchonkang Trading Corporation, a subsidiary of North Korea's General Bureau of Atomic Energy that is tasked with procuring nuclear-related equipment. He had tried to secretly import from a German company aluminum tubes for centrifuges used in uranium enrichment facilities, but this plan ended in failure when it was uncovered. Yun is one of the five individuals targeted by UN sanctions imposed on North Korea in July 2009. Kim Chong-ryul is a former KPA Colonel. Based in Austria and Germany, he procured luxury items for the Kim family and weapons-related equipment. But when Kim Il-sung died in 1994, Kim Chong-ryul decided to defect, and he went into hiding in Austria. In 2010, he published his autobiography recounting his secret past.

330   These special operations marked a significant departure from the role of the Personal Secretariat as it existed under Kim Il-sung. For example, the concept of a slush fund, which was managed by Kim Jong-il's staff, did not exist before he took power. Instead, Kim Il-sung's needs were paid for by "presidential bonds," which were created by taking three percent of the budget. They were akin to the resources reserved in preparation for war. The slush funds were used as Kim Jong-il's personal money to buy whatever he thought necessary, including daily necessities from foreign countries or presents for his subordinates. Many contend that the operation of this nefarious activity by a key component of the regime undermined Kim Jong-il's legitimacy.

2. The Personal Secretariat under Kim Jong-un

As noted above, before Kim Jong-il died, he took great measures to revive the Party apparatus in order to create a formal leadership environment for his son. The Party gives legitimacy to Kim Jong-un's status as Supreme Leader. It also provides formal mechanisms through which Kim can steer and execute policy. What Kim Jong-il allegedly left to his son to accomplish was the construction of his own Personal Secretariat. Because of the sensitive nature of this institution, the Supreme Leader must be directly responsible for choosing its members. Loyalty and long-standing relationships are critical to its mode of operation.

According to some Pyongyang-watchers and senior-level defectors, Kim Jong-un began to construct his Personal Secretariat soon after he became heir apparent in 2009.[331] For the next few years, his apparatus was closely tied to the SOCC.[332] This makes sense because Kim Jong-un would increasingly be given access to the reports coming and going from Kim Jong-il's office. After Kim Jong-un became the official heir apparent in the wake of the Third Party Conference in 2010, he was given more situational awareness and allowed to receive reports as they made their way to his father. Some Pyongyang-watchers have speculated that Kim Jong-un not only received these reports, but also was allowed to make comments as they were processed so that his father would understand his point of view on matters of state.[333] Kim Jong-un's Personal Secretariat most likely played an important role in assisting the heir apparent in understanding the reports and putting them in context.[334]

Sometime shortly before or after Kim Jong-il's death in December 2011, Kim Jong-un's Personal Secretariat began to separate from his father's apparatus. Descriptions of this new office are quite different from ones of his father's Personal Secretariat. While Kim Jong-il's Personal Secretariat has been described as huge, numbering nearly 300 members at one point, Kim Jong-un's office has recently been described as more intimate, numbering fewer than fifty core members.[335] Its

---

331   Author's discussions with senior-level defectors in Seoul, 2009 and 2010.

332   Ibid.

333   There is some debate among Pyongyang-watchers in Seoul over what types of reports Kim Jong-un was allowed to see. Some contend that his access did not extend to reports pertaining to the military or foreign affairs, but he was allowed to access these reports later.

334   Author's interviews with numerous senior North Korean defectors in Seoul, 2002 to 2010. This picture of how Kim Jong-un's Personal Secretariat functioned early on stands in stark contrast to defector reports of how Kim Jong-il used his Personal Secretariat. By the late 1980s and early 1990s, Kim Jong-il's apparatus was reportedly bugging Kim Il-sung's offices and determining which reports the *Suryong* would see. In this way, Kim Jong-il was increasingly responsible for running the regime while limiting Kim Il-sung's situational awareness.

335   Author's interview with a defector who has ties with the regime, April 2013.

role, function, and manner of operation, however, appear to be similar to those of Kim Jong-il's personal office, absent the broader administrative structure of the SOCC. Just as his father's Personal Secretariat, Kim Jong-un's office receives, classifies, and facilitates documents addressed to the Supreme Leader and then issues instructions. It also administers Kim's schedule, itineraries, protocol and logistics, and, presumably, liaisons with the GC to ensure his security.

According to recent reports, the separation between Kim Jong-un's and Kim Jong-il's personal offices ended with the purge of Jang Song-taek. Before the purge, Kim Jong-un's Personal Secretariat had ties to the regents, especially Kim Kyong-hui and Jang Song-taek, in terms of coordinating meetings and processing incoming reports.[336] This would not be surprising because ever since Kim Jong-il's stroke in 2008,[337] the Kim family clan has formed the first line of defense around Kim Jong-un. In addition, Jang served as Control Tower, which necessitated his direct liaison with the SOCC, the large apparatus that was closely tied to Kim Jong-il's Personal Secretariat. As the Control Tower role has moved to the Supreme Leader, this apparatus has apparently now become tied to Kim Jong-un's Personal Secretariat.

3. Organization and Function

The Supreme Leader's apparatus is composed of two parts: his Personal Secretariat and the SOCC, which is presumably tied to his position as General Secretary of the KWP. The Personal Secretariat has direct responsibilities for the Leader's schedule, communications, and protection. It also reportedly has direct control of the Kim family finances. It works directly with the Third Floor apparatus, such as Offices 38 and 39, to procure goods and services for the Kim family. In terms of situational awareness across the regime, as well as Control Tower policy coordination, the Supreme Leader works through the SOCC. Under Kim Jong-il, both of these offices reported up to Kang Sang-chun. Kim Kang-chol acted as the Supreme Leader's personal secretary and oversaw the day-to-day operations of his private office. Kim Jung-il, the son of Kim Yong-nam and a close personal advisor on foreign policy issues, oversaw the day-to-day operations of the SOCC through his position as Director of the Main Office of Secretaries.

---

336   Ibid.
337   Following Kim Jong-il's stroke, the part of his personal apparatus that handled his daily affairs and enabled his decision-making shrank. Kim Ok, Kim Kyong-hui, and Jang Song-taek were critical to ensuring the continuation of governance. After Kim Jong-il died, it made sense that Kim Kyong-hui and Jang Song-taek would maintain ties to Kim Jong-un's Personal Secretariat, as his two principal regents.

Under Kim Jong-un, the relationship between these two parts of the Supreme Leader's apparatus is reportedly not as close. This is largely due to the fact that the Control Tower role was, until recently, not included in the Supreme Leader's portfolio. Kim Jong-il allowed his son full latitude to develop his own Personnel Secretariat, which is composed of individuals close to the young leader, such as Kim family members and cadre hand-chosen by Kim Jong-un. The makeup of the SOCC, on the other hand, is populated by officials from the Kim Jong-il era.

Chart 1: Supreme Leader's Personal Apparatus

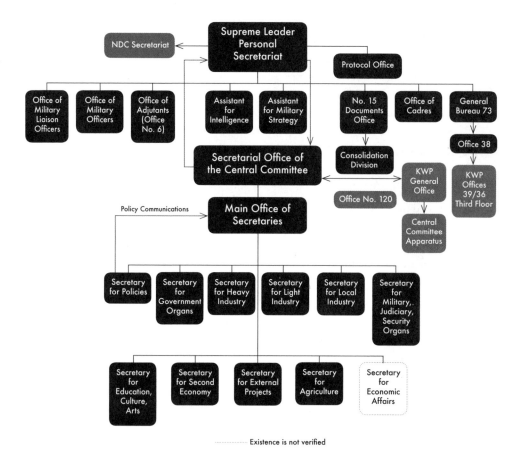

a. Personal Secretariat Personnel and Structure

According to several sources, Kim Sol-song, Kim Jong-un's half-sister, leads his Personal Secretariat.[338, 339] By many accounts, Kim Sol-song was Kim Jong-il's favorite child. She was the first of two daughters born to Kim Jong-il and his second wife, Kim Yong-suk, and the only grandchild apparently recognized by Kim Il-sung. Kim Jong-il mentioned Kim Sol-song in his last will and testament, noting that she "should be supported as a caretaker of Jong-un."[340]

Kim Sol-song, at age 41, has extensive experience working inside the Party and state apparatus. She was born in 1974 and began work in Kim Il-sung's Presidential Office in her teens. She moved to the KWP PAD, where she worked with one of her father's closest associates, Kim Ki-nam. In the late 1990s, she moved into her father's Personal Secretariat as a department head and the Chief of Office 99,[341] which had responsibility for some of the more sensitive financial accounts and the acquisition and proliferation of technology.[342] In the 2000s, reports began to surface that Kim Sol-song had become one of her father's closest aides. A multilingual speaker, she served as her father's interpreter on several of his trips, including his 2002 trip to Russia. She is also rumored to be an officer in the GC and most likely had liaison responsibilities with this body in coordinating her father's security. She allegedly is very close to her aunt, Kim Kyong-hui, as well as Kim Ok,[343] with whom she worked closely in Kim Jong-il's Personal Secretariat.

---

338   Author's interviews in Seoul, April 2013. According to one defector, Kim Sol-song is not the first Director of Kim Jong-un's Personal Secretariat. There have been several directors as the institution has evolved.

339   Jeong Yong-Soo and Kim Hee-Jin, "Pyongyang Did China Business As It Purged Jang," *Korea JoongAng Daily*, December 12, 2013; Michael Madden, "Biographies: Kim Chang-son," *North Korea Leadership Watch*, May 14, 2013. According to one source, Kim Jong-un's original Chief of Staff was Kim Chang-son. In January 2012, he formally replaced Jon Hui-jong, Director of the NDC Foreign Affairs Bureau, as the Supreme Leader's Chief Protocol Officer and Kang Sang-chun as Director of the Personal Secretariat. This essentially created the firewall between the Personal Secretariat and SOCC, which were intertwined during Kang's tenure as Kim Jong-il's senior aide.

340   Kim Hee-Jin, "Before His Death, Kim Jong Il Wrote Instructions," *Korea JoongAng Daily*, April 14, 2012.

341   Ken E. Gause, *North Korea Under Kim Chong-il: Power, Politics, and Prospects for Change*, op. cit.

342   "North Korea Creates New Front Company to Supply Iran With Nuclear Technology," *Moscow Times*, April 27, 2010; "DPRK's Office 99 Said to Have Played Central Role in Syrian Nuclear Project," *NHK General Television*, April 25, 2008; Nicolas Levi, "A Big Day for the Elite Clans," *Daily NK*, April 10, 2012. In more recent reports, Kim Sol-song was identified as a high-level bureaucrat in the KWP MID.

343   "Kim Jong-il's Widow 'Purged'," *The Chosun Ilbo*, July 3, 2013. According to recent South Korean reporting, Kim Ok and her father Kim Hyo, a Deputy Director of the KWP FAD, have been dismissed from all their posts. It is not clear whether this was a purge or is tied to their health. Kim Hyo is in his 90s and his daughter allegedly tried to commit suicide following Kim Jong-il's death. Kim Ok appeared at various leadership events during the mourning period and then disappeared from public view.

Not only is Kim Sol-song a seasoned facilitator and experienced political operative within the North Korean regime, but she is also rumored to be as calculating as her aunt in wielding power. Therefore, it makes sense that she would be closely tied to Kim Jong-un and play an important role in his personal office. As Kim Kyong-hui's illness weakens her ability to advise and coach her nephew, and to support his efforts to consolidate power, it seems natural that Kim Sol-song would step into this role.[344]

Another family member who may also be tied to Kim's Personal Secretariat is his younger sister, Kim Yo-jong. She has apparently been trained in the nuances of the country's political affairs by both Kim Kyong-hui and Jang Song-taek at least since 2009, when she began working in the Party Central Committee. She also has close ties with Kim Ok, Kim Jong-il's technical secretary and last wife. Kim Yo-Jong's central role in the regime was hinted at during the funeral ceremonies for her father. She assumed a role similar to the one that her aunt played during Kim Il-sung's funeral ceremonies in 1994; she stood behind her brother as Kim Jong-un received foreign dignitaries. She lined up with members of the leadership when they paid their respects at Kim Jong-il's casket and led core members of the North Korean leadership to the bier for viewing.

Image 23: Kim Yo-jong voting in an SPA election of delegates in 2014. (Source: KCBS)

344   Lee Young-Jong and Ser Myo-Ja, "Kim Yo-jong Grows In Clout As Brother Relapses," *Korea JoongAng Daily*, December 10, 2014. It should be stressed that there is much debate within Pyongyang-watching circles about the role of Kim Sol-song. Her role is often emphasized by North Korean defectors. South Korean officials have been silent on the topic, although some have stated off-the-record that claims that she plays a prominent role within the regime are "groundless."

In 2013, South Korean media reports placed Kim Yo-jong either in the NDC or the KWP OGD.[345] At the end of 2014, some reports placed her in the KWP PAD after she was identified as a vice director of a Central Committee department on the occasion of her brother's guidance inspection of the April 26 Cartoon Film Studio.[346] She has also been identified as a Protocol Secretary for Kim Jong-un and the person responsible for handling his travel appointments. She was responsible for organizing his attendance at ceremonies. According to one North Korean source, "It's widely whispered in the Party that you have to get on Kim Yo-jong's good side if you want to invite Kim Jong-un to your ceremony."[347]

Following the purge of Jang Song-taek, Kim Yo-jong's status began to rise. She has allegedly been given responsibility for several of the hard currency lines of operation tied to Department 54, which is no longer operating.[348] According to some sources, she has also been appointed Chief Secretary,[349] handling the delivery of reports from the Party, Cabinet, and NDC to Kim Jong-un.[350] It is not clear whether her responsibilities extend beyond Kim Jong-un's Personal Secretariat and into the SOCC.

In addition to the Kim family members within the Personal Secretariat, there are a number of other offices and aides that support Kim Jong-un's daily affairs:

- The **Protocol Office** is responsible for controlling Kim Jong-un's schedule and movements. Although some reports from 2013 identified Kim Yo-jong as the Chief of Protocol,[351] recent reporting claims that this role is now filled by Kim Chang-son, who also oversees the NDC

345   Michael Madden, "KJI Youngest Daughter Working as Events Manager for KJU?" *North Korea Leadership Watch*, July 22, 2013; "Kim Jong-un's Sister 'Given Key Party Post'," *The Chosun Ilbo*, July 22, 2013.

346   "Kim Jong Un Gives Guidance at April 26 Cartoon Film Studio," *KCNA*, November 26, 2014. Her father Kim Jong-il did not reach the position of Vice Director until he was 32 while being trained to become leader and her aunt, Kim Kyong-hui, was appointed Vice Director at the age of 30.

347   North Korean official's interview with *Radio Free Asia*, as quoted in "Kim Jong-un's Sister 'Given Key Party Post'," *The Chosun Ilbo*, op. cit.

348   "Kim Jong-un's Sister Put in Charge of Regime's Coffers," *The Chosun Ilbo*, January 13, 2014.

349   Jeong Yong-Soo, "Son of Kim Jong-un's Chief Secretary Undergoes Ideological Training After Stepping Down from His Position," *Korea JoongAng Daily*, February 24, 2014. This post was reportedly held by Kim Chang-son. According to South Korean reporting, Kim's son, Kim Ki-sik (Chairman of the State Development Committee), was sent to a "revolutionization course for ideological training" in the aftermath of the Jang Song-taek purge and a month before reports that Kim Yo-jong assumed the role of Chief Secretary. Kim Jang-son was reportedly appointed Chief of Protocol. "N.K. Leader's Sister Serving As Chief Of Staff," *Yonhap News Agency*, March 30, 2014.

350   "N.K. Leader's Sister Serving as Chief of Staff," ibid.

351   Ibid. According to South Korean sources, acting under the assumed name Kim Ye-jong, Kim Yo-jong oversaw the invitation of former NBA player Dennis Rodman to North Korea.

Secretariat.[352] Kim Chang-son has been a constant presence around Kim Jong-un since the latter took power.[353]

- The **Office of Adjutants (Office 6)** coordinates the protection of the Supreme Leader. It presumably liaises with the GC and other elements of the internal security apparatus. Adjutants from this office accompany Kim Jong-un on his guidance inspections. According to one source, the adjutants form the inner circle of security around the Supreme Leader and are the only people allowed to carry guns in his presence. Under Kim Jong-il, this office had approximately 1,200 officers and soldiers, the size of a KPA battalion. The current chief of the Office of Adjutants is unknown. Under Kim Jong-il, Choe Pyong-yul held this post.[354] Recent reporting suggests that under Kim Jong-un, Colonel General Ko Su-il, an uncle on his mother's side, may be in charge of Kim Jong-un's personal security.[355]

- The **Office of the Assistant for Intelligence** coordinates foreign intelligence for the Supreme Leader. Under Kim Jong-il, this office was composed of two divisions: Division 25 and Division 31. These divisions had separate geographic responsibilities, gathering and monitoring intelligence and working closely with the SSD, RGB, Office 35, and North Korean embassies. Pak Yong-jin was in charge of Division 25 and Kim Hyon-chol headed Division 31.[356] It was from this office that the plans for the kidnapping of Japanese citizens were developed. Today, the office is presumably tied to the North Korean investigation into what happened to those Japanese citizens.

- The **Office of the Assistant for Military Strategy** is a large office with eight divisions, numbering over 100 officers spread across various parts of the KPA. It is responsible for coordinating military information from around the world and devising a coherent set of operational plans.

---

352   Michael Madden, "Biographies: Kim Chang-son," op. cit. Kim Chang-son was instrumental in establishing an executive office for Kim Jong-un in the NDC, modeled after Kim Jong-il's Personal Secretariat.

353   During Kim Jong-il's funeral, Kim Chang-son escorted Kim Yo-jong and a group of close Kim family aides in paying their respects. As funeral events unfolded, he routinely appeared at Kim Jong-un's side.

354   Interview with a North Korean defector in Seoul, May 2013. See also "DPRK Defector on Kim Jong-il's Family and Close Aides," *Gendai Weekly*, August 2003. A graduate of Kim Il-sung Military University, Choe Pyong-yul was handpicked by Kim Jong-il, who recognized his sharpshooting skills.

355   Choe Seon-Yeong and Jang Yong-Hun, "Kim Jong-un's Uncle Reported to be in Charge of Kim's Personal Security," *Yonhap News Agency*, September 22, 2013.

356   Pak Yong-jin is the son of Kim Po-pae, who served as a housekeeper for Kim Il-sung throughout her life. Recent reporting suggests that Pak may now be the Director of the Daesong Guidance Bureau.

These plans inform the larger strategy that is facilitated through the Supreme Command apparatus to the GSD for implementation. This office is also home to the Supreme Leader's senior military advisors. According to several senior-level defectors, Kim Kyok-sik, until his death in May 2015, was Chief of this office.[357]

- The **Office of Military Officers** is responsible for coordinating counter-intelligence on the armed forces. It is a small office with approximately twenty agents who work closely with the GPB and the MSC. Under Kim Jong-il, Kim Du-nam, the younger brother of Kim Yong-nam, oversaw this office. Since Kim Du-nam's death in 2009, a new head of this office has not been identified.

- The **Office of Military Liaison Officers** is the direct link between Kim Jong-un's Personal Secretariat and the Supreme Command. It is responsible for issuing orders from Kim in his capacity as Supreme Commander of the Armed Forces. Under Kim Jong-il, this office was led by two senior liaison officers, An Yong-chol and Nam Yong-chol, both of whom come from military families with ties to Kim Il-sung.[358] It is likely that they have been replaced by officers closer to Kim Jong-un.

- The **Documents Office 15** is the office primarily responsible for routing documents to and from Kim Jong-un's Personal Secretariat. Critical to this function is its link to the KWP General Affairs Office, which is responsible for facilitating communications throughout the Party apparatus. Documents Office 15's Consolidation Division coordinates paperwork with the KWP General Affairs' Office

---

357   Interview with North Korean defectors, 2013 and 2014. Kim Kyok-sik's career, while it predated Kim Jong-un's appointment as heir apparent, was tied to the succession. After apparently being demoted in February 2009 (one month after Kim Jong-un's status was announced within North Korean leadership circles) from Chief of the GSD to Commander of the Fourth Corps, Kim oversaw the operations tied to the heir apparent's rise to power. From his position as commander of the western front, Kim Kyok-sik may have played a role in both the sinking of *Cheonan* and the shelling of Yeonpyeong Island—the first event was critical to the succession, and the second was designed to bolster Kim Jong-un's credentials as a military leader. He was made an alternate member of the KWP Central Committee at the Third Party Conference. In November 2011, he returned to the GSD as a Vice Chief and, according to defector sources, following Kim Jong-il's death, he moved into Kim Jong-un's Personal Secretariat as a military advisor, a position he held until taking over the MPAF. At the Central Committee Plenum and SPA in 2013, he was made an alternate member of the Politburo and a member of the NDC. After leaving these posts, he presumably returned to Kim's Personal Secretariat as the senior military advisor. On May 11, 2015, *Nodong Sinmun* reported that Kim Kyok-sik had died of cancer. See "Obituary on the Death of Comrade Kim Kyok-sik," *Nodong Sinmun*, May 11, 2015.
358   An Yong-chol is a son of anti-Japan partisan fighter General An Kil, and Nam Yong-chol is a son of General Nam Il who served as North Korea's representative to the armistice talks during the Korean War.

120. This is how agendas are coordinated for senior Party meetings involving the Politburo, Secretariat, and the CMC. Documents Office 15 is also responsible for translating the Supreme Leader's instructions into foreign languages and ensuring the classification of all messages originating from the Personal Secretariat. Under Kim Jong-il, this office was directed by Ri Pyong-chan. Ho Myong-ok, sister of former foreign minister Huh Dam, was head of the Consolidation Division.[359]

- The **General Bureau 73** is the source of much speculation within the Pyongyang-watching community. It is responsible for procuring gifts for the Supreme Leader to facilitate loyalty and ensure stability within his patronage system and the wider leadership.[360] Recent speculation is that this body controls the Kim family funds. It does so through Office 38, which it directly oversees.[361] According to one source, Kim Sol-song has responsibility for General Bureau 73, having assumed this responsibility once Kim Kyong-hui withdrew from politics. She manages the office with the acquiescence of Kim Jong-un and in coordination with Kim Yo-jong, who plays a key role in the operations of Office 38.[362]

- There are a number of **administrative offices** likely contained within Kim Jong-un's Personal Secretariat. These offices are responsible for the internal operations within the Personal Secretariat, as well as looking after the Supreme Leader. They likely include those dedicated to cadre affairs and facilities. Cadre affairs would be responsible for the recruiting and vetting of new personnel entering the Personal Secretariat. Reportedly, the 5th Section of the Cadres Office recruits, trains, and staffs ensembles of female singers, musicians, and dancers, such as the Moranbong Art Troupe, who entertain the North Korean leadership. A facilities office would be dedicated to the upkeep of the Kim family estates, as well as overseeing the staff associated with the residences.[363]

---

359   "DPRK Defector on Kim Jong-il's Family and Close Aides," *Gendai Weekly*, op. cit.

360   This is one of the oldest offices in the Supreme Leader's Personal Secretariat. It was created under Kim Il-sung and was responsible for ensuring all aspects of the Supreme Leader's life, including the Longevity Research Institute. Since the 1990s, it has been downsized and now focuses primarily on securing the funds necessary for the Supreme Leader.

361   Office 38 has a complex history. It exists in the Central Committee apparatus. At one time, it was incorporated into Office 39. With Kim Yo-jong now being responsible for Kim family finances, some defector sources believe that Office 38 has been brought into Kim Jong-un's Personal Secretariat as a banking and facilitating body.

362   Interview with senior-level North Korean defector in Seoul, May 2014.

363   Michael Madden, "The Personal Secretariat," *North Korea Leadership Watch*.

b. Secretarial Office of the Central Committee Personnel and Structure

The purge of Jang Song-taek most likely had a dramatic impact on the day-to-day operations of the regime in terms of both policy formulation and implementation. Where both of these functions came together was in the role of the Control Tower. As noted earlier, a large part of the policy process occurred as a result of the Control Tower's meetings with various issue groups dedicated to generating policy recommendations. This process provides information to and from the Supreme Leader's apparatus. The facilitating agent for this paperwork is the Main Office of Secretaries, which is part of the SOCC.[364]

Chart 2: Regime Communications with the Supreme Leader's Apparatus

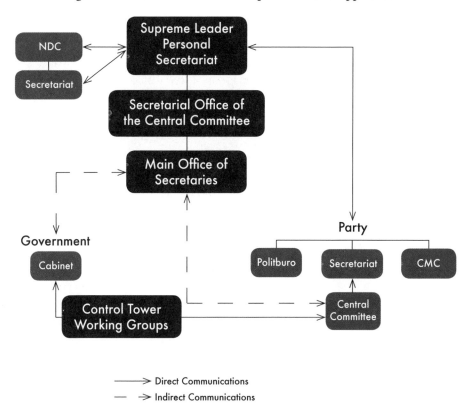

---

364   Author's interview with Hwang Jang-yop in Seoul, 2009. Under Kim Jong-il, the SOCC did not serve a policy function. According to Hwang Jang-yop, Kim Jong-il once noted that he did "not need policy secretaries [in his personal office] since there is the KWP Secretariat in the Party Central Committee."

Under Kim Jong-il, the SOCC was led by a group of five permanent members: a director and four vice directors. All five also served as vice directors within the KWP OGD. This was because the SOCC was created during a period when Kim Jong-il was the Director of the KWP OGD and his Personal Secretariat originally drew from its staff. In addition, the SOCC relied on the KWP OGD to monitor the Supreme Leader's orders and policies to ensure that they were carried out in the manner in which he intended.

According to several sources, Kang Sang-chun has retained his position as Director of the SOCC.[365] The last known head of the Main Office of Secretaries was Kim Jung-il. This office oversees the activities of several secretarial offices, which operate in a similar fashion to the Central Committee departments. They are issue-specific, but instead of simply monitoring the operations of government ministries and departments, as is the mandate of the Central Committee departments, they are also responsible for the operations of the party bodies. More importantly, they are responsible for receiving and classifying the briefing documents and reports for the Supreme Leader across the policy spectrum. As Kim Jong-un assumes the role of Control Tower, this apparatus will become more active and vital to his day-to-day operations. The SOCC is made up of several offices:

- The **Office of the Secretary for Policies** is responsible for facilitating documents to and from the other secretary offices. It ensures that the documents are properly classified. It is also responsible for collating the work from the other secretarial offices to forward to the Supreme Leader's Personal Secretariat for his review. It works closely with the KWP OGD to monitor whether policies are implemented.
- The **Office of the Secretary for Government Organs** is responsible for monitoring the affairs of core state institutions, including the NDC, Cabinet, and SPA. It works with the secretariats of each of these bodies to generate meeting agendas and facilitate the transmission of decisions. According to some sources, this office has been divided into several offices to oversee the operations of each of these core institutions.
- The **Office of the Secretary for Military Affairs** is responsible for the collation and processing of information on the armed forces. Reports

---

365   "N.K. Leader's Sister Serving as Chief of Staff," *Yonhap News Agency*, op. cit. In early 2014, Kim Jong-un's sister, Kim Yo-jong, was identified as Chief Secretary. Given her youth, it is highly unlikely that she has assumed all, if any, responsibilities of running the SOCC. However, she is a liaison from her brother's Personal Secretariat to the SOCC. Later in 2014, she was identified as a vice director of a Central Committee department, raising questions about her exact position within the regime.

from the field commands, as well as counterintelligence assessments of loyalty from the GPB and MSC, are probably routed through this office for the Supreme Leader's review. It has a close relationship with the Central Committee's Military Affairs and Civil Defense departments and most likely is involved in setting the agenda for CMC meetings. Under Kim Jong-il, this office was led by Paek Kun-son.

- The **Office of the Secretary for Judiciary and Security Organs** is responsible for keeping the Supreme Leader informed on the activities of the legal and internal security apparatus. Before the purge of Jang Song-taek, this office relied heavily on the KWP Administrative Department. Now, its primary Party link is most likely with the KWP OGD. It also has ties to the NDC, through which Kim Jong-un now has direct oversight of the SSD, MPS, and MSC. It would also have ties to the Prosecutor General's Office and the Central Court.

- The **Office of the Secretary for Second Economy** is responsible for processing the information related to the defense industry. It maintains close ties with the KWP Secretary for Defense Industry, as well as the KWP MID, SEC, and Second Academy of Natural Sciences. Kim Jong-un makes decisions regarding the nuclear and missile programs based on the information he receives through this channel. Decisions to test weapon systems would likely be issued through this office.

- The **Office of the Secretary for External Affairs** is responsible for coordinating information related to the regime's interactions with the international community. It is unclear whether this office is subdivided into special sections on China, South Korea, and the United States. The office has ties to the Ministry of Foreign Affairs and the Central Committee's UFD and International Department.

- The **Office of the Secretary for Heavy Industry** is responsible for providing information on the conventional industrial sectors, such as those devoted to manufacturing, metal production, mining, coal, and logging. It most likely produces reports on key industries, including the Anju District coal mining complex or the metal producing factories in Dancheon, Nampo, Haeju, and Munpyeong. This office is closely tied to the Cabinet, which contains several ministries related to heavy industry.

- The **Office of the Secretary for Light Industry** is an office that is likely growing in importance with the increased emphasis on the light industry sector. Since coming to power, Kim Jong-un has repeatedly referenced the need for progress in this sector and has appeared at numerous events involving light industry. It is probable that this was one of the offices through which Kim Kyong-hui coordinated her activities with the Personal Secretariat when she was the Director of the KWP LID and later KWP Secretary for Light Industry. Since her disappearance from the political scene, the office most likely continues to liaise with the relevant Central Committee bodies, as well as the Ministry for Light Industry.

- The **Office of the Secretary for Education, Culture, and Arts** is an office that has its origins in Kim Jong-il's passion for the arts.[366] It has ties to Choe Tae-bok, the KWP Secretary for Education, as well as the KWP Science and Education Department. Kim Jong-un has made a number of statements on education, including advocating that compulsory education be expanded from eleven to twelve years in 2012. Presumably, the office generates reports on educational issues. As for the arts, it is unclear whether Kim Jong-un shares his father's passion.

- The **Office of the Secretary for Economic Affairs** did not exist under Kim Jong-il, but may now exist under Kim Jong-un. According to defector testimony, it has been one of the more forward-leaning offices in his Personal Secretariat. It not only facilitates communications with the Cabinet and technocrats throughout the regime, but also devises long-term economic strategy. Presumably, this is where Kim Jong-un's key economic advisors sit.

- The **Office of the Secretary for Agriculture** is an office that did not exist within the Main Office of Secretaries in the Kim Jong-il era. However, the emphasis that Kim Jong-un has placed on agriculture as part of the June 2012 reforms would suggest that a relevant line of communication now exists for this sector.

4. ROLE IN THE SUPREME LEADER'S DECISION-MAKING

Every leader has a unique process through which he makes decisions. This is informed by his leadership style and relationship to the apparatus that serves him. In North Korea, this has certainly been the case. Kim Il-sung, who was a powerful leader with revolutionary credentials, preferred to utilize the formal leadership apparatus to inform his decision-making. His personal office was small and purely

---

366   There are numerous stories of Kim Jong-il making comments and notes in margins of opera and movie scripts. Presumably, this office would have coordinated this correspondence.

administrative. Kim Jong-il, a more reclusive leader, relied much more on his personal apparatus, while marginalizing many of the formal leadership bodies. The decision-making model under Kim Jong-un has evolved. It began as something that very much mimicked the Kim Il-sung model with a powerful regent structure attached for guidance and direction. Since the purge of Jang Song-taek, it appears that Kim Jong-un may begin to adopt a model closer to his father's, which was firmly rooted in informal networks and personal lines of communication. As such, an understanding of the Kim Jong-il model will probably provide insights into the future of Kim Jong-un's decision-making process.

As noted above, the process most likely began in meetings with close aides or during field guidance inspections. It was during these times that Kim Jong-il set the broad parameters for policy, both domestic and foreign. Once the broad outlines were set, policymaking was usually initiated by a direct request from Kim in the form of an instruction. Sometimes this instruction went to a particular department or even a particular individual.[367] On other occasions, the instruction was distributed to several relevant departments. Typically, more than one department was involved, and, in these cases, the instruction was managed through issue-related task forces that were organized to reach consensus.[368] In all circumstances, the KWP OGD made a note of Kim's request so it could be tracked through the policymaking process.

After sufficient consultation by relevant departments, a counselor or a task force of counselors would draft policy that addressed Kim Jong-il's instruction.[369] It was then sent to Kim's Personal Secretariat either as a document report (*mun-geon bo-go*) or a fax report (*mo-sa bo-go*). Reports submitted in document form included items less urgent, but still important for policy, such as proposals, direction of

367   For example, Kim Jong-il's instructions given to the Ministry of Foreign Affairs were mostly in the form of "remarks addressed to the First Vice Foreign Minister." In the past, Kang Sok-ju occupied this post. Now Kang is a Vice Premier, and it is unclear whether the current Foreign Minister Ri Su-yong or First Vice Foreign Minister, Kim Kye-gwan, plays this role.
368   Author's interviews in Seoul, April 2013. Issue-related task forces were set up for a range of policy areas, such as inter-Korean relations and the economy.
369   Author's discussion with senior North Korean defectors residing in Seoul, April 2009. Every ministry and department throughout the government and Party has counselors. Under Kim Jong-il, these were usually people with close ties to Kim or his Personal Secretariat who had a clear understanding of his policy intentions. It was their job to draft correspondence between their ministry or department and the Kim apparatus.

activities, and situation materials.[370] Kim's Personal Secretariat prioritized the reports and submitted them for his comment and approval.[371]

According to elite defector accounts, Kim Jong-il used a series of formulaic handwritten notations to convey his approval or disapproval of proposals and reports. There were three main categories:

- **Signed instructions** (*chin-pil ji-si*) included a signature, a date, and occasionally a written opinion. Such a document was referred to as a handwritten instruction. By signing and dating the document, the Leader signified that the contents of report documents should be regarded as his intentions and instructions to be implemented as written. The Leader would personally take responsibility for their results. Such documents carried the weight of verbal instructions and were implemented unconditionally.

- **Signed documents** (*chin-pil mun-geon*) included the date of review without Kim's signature or comment. Such a document was referred to as a handwritten document. By merely dating the document, the Leader signified that he agreed with the contents of the report but would not be responsible for the results. However, like a handwritten instruction, it was considered sanctioned policy and must be implemented to the letter.[372]

- **Documents returned unsigned or dated** signified that the Leader either did not agree with or did not understand the document report. It also probably meant that the counselor and his chain of command did not accurately judge the Leader's intentions, something that likely resulted in criticism and punishment.[373]

Once a document was ratified by Kim it became policy. Upon receipt of the policy guidance from Kim's Personal Secretariat, the originating institution of the document report was responsible for its implementation. The person charged with

---

370   Hyon Song-il, *North Korea's National Strategy and Power Elite*, op. cit. These reports are registered at the KWP's Confidential Documents Bureau after the final approval of the department or ministry's leadership is received. They were then sent to Kim Jong-il's Personal Secretariat, where they were prepared for his approval.

371   Ibid. Kim Jong-il's Personal Secretariat was not authorized to reject any document without first receiving his approval.

372   Ibid. A distinction was made between a handwritten instruction and a handwritten document in the early 1990s as the volume of guidance from Kim Jong-il's office increased dramatically, leading to careless interpretation during the implementation process.

373   Ibid.

overseeing the implementation of the policy then registered it with the institution's records office and drew up a policy implementation plan. This plan laid out the method of, relevant departments and ministries responsible for, and timeline for implementation. The policy could then be monitored by the institution's organization department, which submitted progress reports to the KWP OGD.[374]

5. THE FUTURE OF THE PERSONAL SECRETARIAT

Just as leadership dynamics are evolving in the post-Jang Song-taek era, the purge has likely had an impact on North Korean decision-making and policy formulation. If the speculation about Jang being the Control Tower is accurate, from a policy perspective, his downfall probably created a huge void in the day-to-day operations of the regime. According to some defector reporting, Jang served a facilitating role by working with various government and Party issue groups dedicated to generating policy options. In addition to enforcing consensus around policy options, Jang, as a senior policy advisor, was responsible for explaining the options to Kim Jong-un. By having Jang serve as the Control Tower, Kim was able to focus his attention more on the power consolidation process.[375] With Jang gone, Kim Jong-un will likely assume the role of Control Tower.

There was speculation in 2012 that Kim Jong-un's Personal Secretariat had begun to assume some of the administrative responsibilities of the Control Tower. Reports surfaced that his Secretariat Office for Economic Affairs was developing a roadmap that would best position the regime for securing its goal of becoming a strong and prosperous nation by 2020. This included completing a study that began under Kim Jong-il to examine the implications of China's economic revolution. The Military Office was focused on designing a strategy for enhancing training in the most cost-efficient manner. The External Affairs Office was tasked with writing a report on a negotiating strategy to elicit South Korean economic support.[376]

The little information available on the Personal Secretariat's role during this period suggests that it was working in parallel to Jang's Control Tower responsibilities, focusing more on long-term policy in addition to its day-to-day operations. As such, it is plausible that with Jang's downfall, Kim's apparatus may bolster its policy

---

374   Ibid.

375   Policy consistency will be an early indicator of the success in this shift in the role of Control Tower. The tension caused throughout the regime by Jang's purge could lead to bureaucratic self-protection, which could cause policy reversal or stagnation.

376   Hann Sung-Kwan, "North Korea, Getting Ready for Total Revolution and Opening in 2019, What's the Behind Story?," *NKSIS*, June 7, 2012.

coordination position in order to support the return of the Control Tower role to the Supreme Leader. If this occurs, decision-making in the regime will likely revert to something akin to the "hub-and-spoke" model that existed under Kim Jong-il. The Supreme Leader acts as the micromanager and is solely responsible for signing off on all policies, relying on the Personal Secretariat, which will likely expand, to set the agenda and coordinate the decision-making process. Depending on how prepared Kim Jong-un is to assume this role, policymaking could become erratic in the absence of family guardians, such as Kim Kyong-hui, or a regent structure like that of Jang Song-taek, to provide checks and balances on the young leader's sporadic leadership style.

C. CHAPTER SIX: THE ROYAL ECONOMY— CONTROLLING THE KIM FAMILY FINANCES

Over the years, there have been a number of articles devoted to the Royal Economy in North Korea, which is the part of the economy that is devoted to keeping the Kim family in power. Most of these articles discuss the number of illicit programs the regime has put in place to raise hard currency across the world. A 2014 report by the Committee for Human Rights in North Korea entitled *Illicit: North Korea's Evolving Operations to Earn Hard Currency* reveals an underworld where North Korean financiers, money launderers, counterfeiters, and scam artists conduct their business all while seeking to circumvent the sanctions and surveillance of the international community.[377]

This chapter will briefly discuss the overseas aspects of the Royal Economy. It will mainly focus, however, on the apparatus and key individuals inside the regime that generate and control the funds that Kim Jong-un relies on to maintain and consolidate power. It will also look at some of the critical funding streams that feed the Kim family's coffers.

1. ORIGINS OF THE ROYAL ECONOMY

The creation of the Royal Economy dates back to the 1970s and is tied to the politics of succession. In many respects, the 1970s was a watershed decade in North Korean history. During this period, Kim Il-sung fully consolidated his power, as spelled out in the 1972 constitution. Kim Il-sung also attempted to institute a direct hereditary transition of power to his son, Kim Jong-il. Finally, the regime began to feel the ire of the international community, which began to freeze North Korea out of the capital markets. Pyongyang had defaulted on its loans after incorrectly predicting the value of its raw materials, leaving the country scrambling to secure hard currency.[378]

---

377   Sheena Chestnut Greitens, *Illicit: North Korea's Evolving Operations to Earn Hard Currency* (Washington, D.C.: Committee for Human Rights in North Korea, 2014).
378   Bruce Cumings, *Korea's Place in the Sun: A Modern History* (New York: W. W. Norton & Co., 1998). In the 1970s, the expansion of North Korea's economy, with an accompanying rise in living standards, came to an end and began to contract a few decades later. Compounding this was a decision to borrow foreign capital and invest heavily in military industries. North Korea's desire to lessen its dependence on aid from China and the Soviet Union prompted the expansion of its military power, which began in the second half of the 1960s. The government believed such expenditures could be covered by foreign borrowing and increased sales of its mineral resources in the international market. North Korea invested heavily in its mining industries and purchased a large quantity of mineral extraction infrastructure from abroad. However, soon after making such investments, international prices for many of North

Before this time, the Royal Economy had been centered on a tax on the People's Economy, which was generated by economic activities controlled by the Cabinet. This three percent tax funded the operations of Kim Il-sung's Presidential Office.[379] Facing increasing stagnation in the 1970s, Kim Il-sung came to the conclusion that if Kim family control of the regime was to survive, the economic model nested in the command economy would have to change. Critical funds necessary for maintaining the defense-industrial complex would have to be generated and controlled through separate channels. This was done by removing the munitions industry from Cabinet control and placing it under the newly created SEC.

Chart 3: Royal Economy Under Kim Il-sung

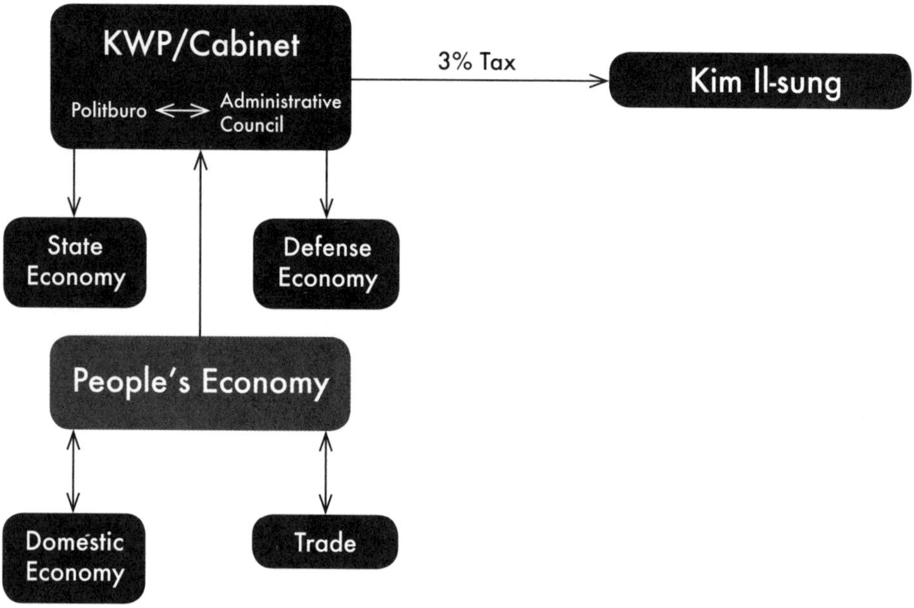

In addition to securing national security, Kim Il-sung was also faced with what to do about the future of the Kim family regime. The North Korean leadership had just emerged from a decade of internal struggles that led to widespread purges

---

Korea's minerals fell, leaving the country with a large amount of debt. Pyongyang was unable to pay off these debts while still providing a high level of social welfare to its people. To further exacerbate this situation, the centrally planned economy, which emphasized heavy industry, had reached the limits of its productive potential in North Korea.

379   Discussion with North Korean defectors familiar with administration during the Kim Il-sung era, 2010.

for Kim Il-sung's own consolidation of power. For him to pass the mantle of power to Kim Jong-il, he still needed to purge or co-opt more officials. With the depletion of the regime's coffers, a separate line of funding became necessary. Following the anointment of his son as the heir apparent in 1974, Kim Il-sung gave Kim Jong-il the authority to create a Royal Economy to ensure a smooth transition of power.

> Under Kim Il-sung's People's Economy, state funds completely provided for the people and the leadership. Under Kim Jong-il, the economy became personalized in order to allow the heir apparent to consolidate his power.
>
> - Anonymous senior-level North Korean defector

The Royal Economy was developed along two lines. The first line was dedicated to a daunting task Kim Jong-il faced upon becoming heir apparent. He needed to appease the rent-seeking class of the North Korean economy. These were the members of the elite whose loyalty he would need to secure in order to rule the regime. They included Party, military, and technical cadres and their families, numbering close to 20,000 individuals.[380] The second line was dedicated to the Kim family. The creation of the heir apparent essentially doubled the costs within the Kim family. Kim Jong-il now had assets and an apparatus of his own that would need to be managed.

2. Constructing the Royal Economy

In order to create what has become known as North Korea's secret economy, Kim Jong-il turned to the blueprint used by his father to secure financing for the defense-industrial complex. It consisted of four principles:

1. Establishing an economic sector that is not under the administration of the Cabinet
2. Planning for this economic sector would not fall under the National Planning Committee

---

380   When expanded beyond those who received special gifts to members of the trusted sector of the North Korean population, the figure rises to nearly three million individuals who received gifts on special holidays.

3. Control of this economic sector ultimately resides with the Kim family through the Party apparatus

4. Hard currency for this economic sector would be managed by a dedicated bank, not the Foreign Trade Bank, which oversees the hard currency generated for the People's Economy.[381]

Under the pretext of procuring funds to manage the Party and supporting the regime's strategy of revolutionizing South Korea, Kim Jong-il carved out a section of the Central Committee FAD to create Office 39. The rationale, as communicated to the wider leadership, was that the Party economy was growing so fast that the FAD was incapable of managing it on its own. Income generated by Office 39 would complement funds from the FAD, but would be dedicated to providing the living expenses of senior Central Committee cadre; galvanizing the idolization of the Kim family, an effort led by Kim Jong-il; and creating a treasure chest for Kim Jong-il's personal use. The office was presumably led by Kim Jong-il himself until 1990, when he appointed Choe Pong-man, a close associate director. Choe was replaced by Kim Tong-un in 1993.

Chart 4: Command and Control of Office 39

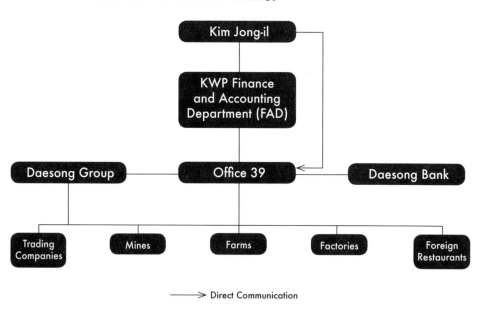

Following the creation of Office 39, Kim Jong-il quickly expanded its apparatus. In May 1974, he removed the Daesong Guidance Bureau from the Ministry of Trade and placed it under the new Party body,[382] a small outfit dedicated to procuring building material for the Kim Il-sung idolization campaign, as well as goods for the Kim family's own consumption and to use as gifts for loyalists.[383] The Daesong Guidance Bureau soon became the largest trading company in North Korea. It generated an annual net revenue in the tens of millions of dollars.[384]

By the late 1970s, the foreign currency coming into the regime through this channel had grown to such an extent that Office 39 required its own bank. In November 1978, Kim Jong-il turned to the Ministry of Trade once again, removing a small department that until that time had managed his personal funds. This department was then placed under Office 39 and renamed the Korea Daesong Bank. In addition to handling the funding streams of the various entities under Office 39, it also conducted foreign exchange transactions.[385] It managed funds in the tens of millions of dollars.

Chart 5: Foreign Transactions via the Korea Daesong Bank

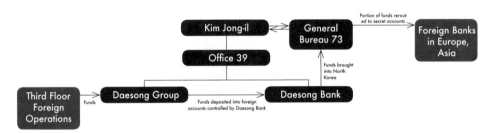

---

382 Andrei Lankov, "The Shadowy World of North Korea's Palace Economy," *Al Jazeera*, September 3, 2014. *Daesong* means "great prosperity." Since the late 1970s, the Daesong Group has become the face of Office 39. As such, the group enjoys a number of significant privileges, such as monopoly rights on gold mining and export.

383 Kim Kwang-jin. Goods and services for the Kim family are normally preceded in the North Korean lexicon by the designation "No. 1." According to one defector source, domestically produced goods are sometimes preceded by the designation "No. 8" or "No. 9." Foreign imports sometimes carry the designation "No. 88."

384 Ibid.

385 Ibid. The Korea Daesong Bank was the first Party-operated foreign exchange bank independent of Cabinet control. Until other similar Party banks were established, the Korea Daesong Bank was responsible for the banking services tied to the various entities of Kim Jong-il's apparatus, including the Guard Command.

In the late 1980s, Office 39 underwent reorganization in order to accommodate the growing markets with ties to North Korea's domestic resources. This led to the creation of three new bureaus:

1. The **Kumgang Guidance Bureau** emerged as an independent agency carved out of the Daesong General Trading Corporation. It handled Office 39's precious metals trade and external operations. In addition, it oversaw the regime's two major refineries: Munpyeong Refinery and September 21 Refinery, both located in Gangwon Province. Over the years, it has engaged in sales worth hundreds of millions of dollars.

2. The **Daehung Guidance Bureau** also emerged out of the Daesong General Trading Corporation. It was placed in charge of trading agricultural, seafood, and local products. Its focus has largely been on exporting mushrooms and medicinal herbs, while procuring gas and fuel.

3. The **Kyonghung Guidance Bureau** was created in 1987 to oversee the operation of a number of foreign currency shops and restaurants inside North Korea. It engaged in the trade of a variety of food products, such as sugar. Its network was mainly centered in Asia with specific ties to China, especially Macau.[386]

By the beginning of the 1990s, the Royal Economy apparatus was well established and connected to a vast procurement and export network throughout Asia, if not worldwide. However, exploitation of the available markets on the Korean peninsula paled in comparison. South Korea was, in many respects, a harder target to penetrate. In addition, it was a more politically sensitive target and, as such, was already the focus of a number of intelligence organizations within the North Korean regime. But, as power and responsibility for running the day-to-day operations of the regime increasingly shifted to Kim Jong-il, his need for additional lines of funding increased. As a consequence, on March 8, 1991, he reportedly signed the instruction to create Office 38.[387]

---

386   "Kim Jong Un's Sister Put In Charge Of Regime's Coffers," op. cit. An additional guidance bureau, the Rakwon Guidance Bureau, was presumably established during this period. Like the Kyonghung Guidance Bureau, it oversaw restaurants and foreign exchange shops. By the 2000s, both guidance bureaus were controlled by Kim Kyong-hui.
387   Kim Kwang-jin.

The Early European Connection

In the 1970s and 1980s, a large part of the Kim family's slush fund was tied to Europe. The Ambassador to Sweden, Kil Chae-kyong, a Third Floor operative and reputed personal secretary in charge of Kim Jong-il's personal funds, oversaw the operations of the major North Korean embassies of Europe. He also handled procurements for the Kim family, including automobiles, liquor, cigarettes, electrical appliances, and so on without paying customs duties by exercising diplomatic privilege. Diplomats would secretly sell the goods to private companies in the countries where they were posted, regularly earning large amounts of foreign currency. They stashed these funds in the Foreign Ministry's "loyalty funds" account in a bank in Bern, Switzerland.

These secret money-making operations were referred to as the "movement to earn foreign currency for ensuring loyalty." It began in the early 1980s at the prompting of Kim Jong-il. At first, then Foreign Minister Huh Dam, a confidante to Kim Il-sung, had overall responsibility for the operations. However, as power passed to Kim Jong-il in the latter half of the 1980s, Ri Chol, a member of Kim Jong-il's inner circle and future North Korean Ambassador to Switzerland, took over that role. In 1998, Kil Chae-kyong was arrested by Russian police for trying to sell $30,000 in counterfeit U.S. currency.[388]

At its inception, Office 38 was dedicated to creating a hub for securing South Korean aid and investment into North Korea. Previously, South Korean funds had come into North Korea through a variety of channels controlled by a number of state and Party entities. Some of these supply channels belonged to Office 39 through the Finance and Supply Department (FSD). Others were tied to Kim Il-sung's Presidential Supply Department, as well as the Party apparatus and state bodies.

This created a problem for Kim Jong-il. First, his ability to account for these funds and tap into them for his personal use was complicated by many competing interests within the leadership. Second, and more importantly, hard

---

388   "Tracing the Whereabouts of Kim Jong-il's 'Secret Funds' –Kim Jong-un Inherits Huge Amount of Money Together with the Transfer of Power," *Bessatsu Takarajima*, Issue No. 1984 (April 25, 2013).

currency brought power. Access to foreign currency funding streams brought influence and independence. Allowing these funds to come into the regime unchecked created a potential problem for Kim's ability to consolidate power. Therefore, by creating Office 38 to oversee and coordinate these various funding streams, Kim Jong-il exerted his control over a source of revenue that would become increasingly important at a time when support from North Korea's traditional patrons, such as the Soviet Union, and other sources was declining.

To create Office 38, Kim Jong-il used some of the infrastructure belonging to the KWP FSD. The centerpiece of the office's apparatus was the Kwangmyongsong ("bright star") General Corporation. This trade organization was the face of Office 38 and was responsible for deals ranging from food and raw materials to high-tech areas, such as information technology (IT) and biotechnology (BT).[389] As the Director of the Kwangmyongsong General Corporation and the Director of Office 38, Rim Sang-chong was able to travel incognito around the world, including to critical markets in the West.[390] The Koryo Bank was established to conduct the banking for Office 38 operations.

Early on, Office 38 became responsible for procuring the daily necessities from foreign countries for Kim Jong-il and his family. In contrast to Office 39, where funds were primarily earmarked for Kim Jong-il's power consolidation and *giftpolitik*, Kim treated the earnings generated by Office 38 as his own personal funds. Office 38 also became a channel for tapping into hostile western economies through their connections to South Korean businesses. As such, the office maintained a close working relationship with the intelligence bodies dedicated to operations against the South, namely Office 35.

As Kim Jong-il became the Supreme Leader, the Party economy began to dwarf the state economy, surpassing it in terms of production, exports, and imports.[391] The infrastructure of Office 38 and 39 grew substantially, adding

---

389   Jang Yong-Hoon, "What Kind of an Organization Is North Korea's Kwangmyongsong Guidance Bureau?" *Yonhap News Agency*, December 3, 2002. The Kwangmyongsong General Corporation steadily grew in importance as South Korean administrations eased restrictions on North Korea. In 1996, South Korea secretly sent approximately 3,400 tons of flour (worth $986,000) to North Korea. This was a quiet deal arranged by South Korea's Presidential Secretariat, despite the government's policy at the time to suspend food aid to North Korea. An additional $4 million worth of food aid was given to Pyongyang later in 1996 with the financial support of several big business groups. Hyundai Group financed the first shipment, which was delivered to the Kwangmyongsong General Corporation.
390   Ibid. By the early 2000s, the Kwangmyongsong General Corporation was identified as existing under the Ministry of Trade. It is unclear whether it had been removed from Office 38 by this time.
391   Author's interviews with several Pyongyang-watchers in Seoul with special knowledge of the North Korean economic system. Under Kim Jong-il, the Royal Economy accounted for nearly sixty percent of the economy by the late 1990s and 2000s.

numerous subordinate trade and foreign currency-earning entities, as well as finance, commerce, distribution, and service companies with overseas branches throughout Europe, China, and Southeast Asia.[392] Much of the modern industrial and reve-nue-generating infrastructure throughout the country was shifted from the state economy to the Party economy, including factories, trade units, and department stores. The funds they generated went into the Party coffers, which Kim Jong-il used to maintain the system.[393]

Chart 6: Royal Economy Apparatus under Kim Jong-il

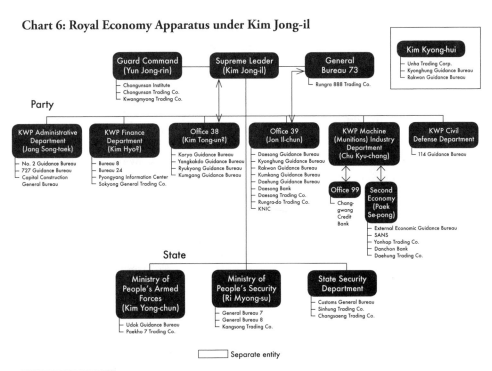

---

392   Hyon Song-il, *North Korea's National Strategy and Power Elite* (Seoul: So'nin Publications, 2007).

393   Hong Sung-Ki, "South Korea Needs New Policy on North Korea in Kim Jong Un Era," *Daily NK*, September 2, 2015, http://www.dailynk.com/english/read.php?catId=nk03600&num=13439. A recent article by Hong Sung-ki, a professor at Ajou University, lays out a number of sources of funding that came into the North Korean regime since the end of the Kim Il-sung era and over the course of the Kim Jong-il era (1991-2012), a portion of which ended up in the Royal Economy. The total amount of this funding was approximately $20 billion, including: $5.1 billion from international aid and "denucle-arization payoffs;" $4.8 billion from oil and coal trade with China; $4 billion in trade with South Korea (including profits from the Kaesong Industrial Complex and the Mt. Kumgang tourism); $3.9 billion from the North Korean service sector (including profits from Chinese tourism, foreign remittances, and shipping charges); $1.3 billion from overseas restaurants and other projects (outsourcing manual labor for overseas logging and mining companies); and $2.8 billion from profits from illicit operations (weapon sales and other illicit goods and services). This is an approximation, and the reader should not treat these individual numbers as ground truth. Other sources, for example, contend that the regime's illicit operations netted much larger returns.

Ken E. Gause

a. Gift-giving

At the heart of Kim Jong-il's power consolidation strategy was the notion of gift-giving. This practice began in the 1970s when Kim Jong-il became heir apparent. Lacking his father's inherent legitimacy, Kim Jong-il had to buy the loyalty of the North Korean elite. Gift-giving became a major undertaking, growing as a proportion of the overall Party economy throughout the 1980s and 1990s, eventually reaching a staggering figure of nearly $300 million per year.

Table 6: Examples of Kim Jong-il's Gifts to Maintain Loyalty

Housing	As part of the Pyongyang remodeling campaign, Kim Jong-il provided specially funded housing on Changgwang Streets 1 and 2 for Party and government officials.
Medical Facilities	Bonghwa Medical Center, located in Potonggang District of Pyongyang, is for the Kim family and most senior Party officials above the vice director level. Namsan Medical Center, located in the Taedonggang District of Pyongyang, is for officials just below the vice director level, as well as two-star generals and above. In 1992, the Eo-eun Hospital was built to take care of members of the high command.
Monetary Gifts	Party secretaries, the Premier, and vice premiers received foreign exchange coupons worth between $1,000 and $2,000.
National Holiday Gifts	The following are some examples of national holiday gifts given by Kim Jong-il: • Automobiles: Mercedes Benz, Japanese SUVs • Accessories: Swiss Omega gold watches • Appliances: Japanese color televisions, refrigerators, VCRs, CD players • Alcohol: Johnnie Walker scotch whiskey • Food: Danish hams and candy, fruit boxes • Clothing: Japanese underwear, suits, socks
Privileged Distribution System	Vice ministers and above received regular deliveries twice a week. Deliveries included rice, sugar, meat, fish, liquor, beer, cigarettes, vegetables, eggs, soy beans, and soap. They also received end-of-year special gifts.

According to a former diplomat who defected from North Korea in the 1990s, the privileged classes in North Korea number in the tens of thousands, including: the leaders from the Central Committee of the KWP and above, cabinet vice ministers and above, and KPA regimental commanders and above. From time to time, Kim Jong-il would bestow these people with foreign goods or imported foodstuffs to "buy their hearts and minds."

"For example, deluxe condominiums have been constructed among the trees here and there along Munsu Street in Pyongyang, where a number of establishments for entertaining [guest houses] are lined up. These are five-story buildings, with each floor having an area of 100 square meters. High-ranking officials from the Foreign Ministry, the Party, and the military are given one floor each. Refrigerated trucks make the rounds, distributing fresh foodstuffs. Wives are given $2,000 a month in spending money."

–Former North Korean Diplomat

According to South Korean reports in the early 2000s, Kim Jong-il delivered gifts to some 20,000 individuals who formed the core leadership of the regime.[394] This included leading members of the Party, military, and state apparatuses, as well as specially chosen individuals who had made contributions to the regime. Of this number, approximately 6,000 individuals received gifts in the name of Kim Jong-il on all major holidays, including New Year's Day and the birthdays of Kim Il-sung (April 15) and Kim Jong-il (February 16). The value of these gifts to the core leadership averaged $20,000 per person.[395]

---

394   Lee Gyo-Gwan, "20,000 Receive Gifts from Kim Jong-il Every Year," *NKChosun.com*, January 12, 2002.

395   Ibid. Included in this number were 1,000 leading Party officials, including secretaries, department heads, deputy department heads, and section chiefs; nearly 1,000 members of the high command, including regimental commanders and above; cabinet members, including the premier, vice premiers, ministers, and vice ministers; and more than 300 retired veterans, anti-Japanese partisans, or bereaved families of "revolutionary combatants." Vice Directors of the KWP OGD, Commander of the GC, Vice Directors of the SSD, and Minister and Vice Ministers of the People's Armed Forces received gifts on par with Party secretaries and the premier.

Chart 7: Securing Gifts for Kim Jong-il

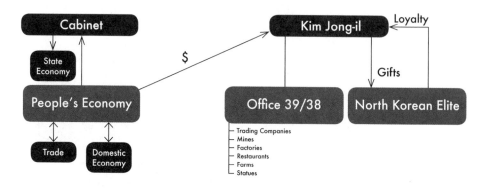

As with all operations, gift-giving gave rise to an extensive infrastructure. The regime established collection hubs around the world, close to where major gifts were purchased, namely: Vienna, Austria; Australia; and Canton and Macau, China. These hubs were usually operated by North Korean embassies or by special offices set up by Office 39. The operatives who worked in these offices were skilled in strategies for working around local customs, regulations, and law enforcement. In addition, Kim Jong-il relied on a collection of special agents, also known as Third Floor operatives,[396] dedicated to procuring items both for Kim's personal use, as well as gifts to satisfy the rising consumer expectations of the North Korean elite. These operatives worked out of General Bureau 73 of Kim Jong-il's Personal Secretariat.

Life of a Third Floor Operative

"Trieste is a port city in northeastern Italy. Among the shipping companies that have their base in Trieste are companies that began as large merchant fleets in the 19th century. One of those companies was used as a cover for the activities of the man in charge of procuring Kim Jong-il's luxury goods.

The man's name is O Myong-kun. From 1988, he worked at the North Korean embassy in Yugoslavia, and from 1992, O was posted

---

396   Michael Madden, "Third Floor," *North Korea Leadership Watch*, October 18, 2012. "The term refers to the original location of these offices on the third floor of Kim Jong-il's office building in the KWP Central Committee Office Complex in the Central District of Pyongyang. The Third Floor is technically subordinate to the Party Central Committee. However, it is directly tied to the Kim Family."

to Italy as an embassy counselor. An official from South Korea's National Intelligence Service (NIS) said, "At the same time as he was posted to Italy, O Myong-kun was likely also a member of the Secretarial Office," Kim Jong-il's closest executive office. He was officially attached to North Korea's embassy in Italy, but he took orders from the Secretarial Office or from North Korea's Ambassador to Switzerland at that time, Ri Chol, and not from the ambassador in Italy.

O rented office space on the premises of a shipping company in Trieste, and he worked hard to earn foreign currency in the cargo business using a cargo ship registered as North Korean. At the same time, he used the office as his base for his 'real business.'

O Myong-kun's assignment was to procure all of the items Kim Jong-il needed. Based on the requests he received from the home office, he screened and purchased all of the items needed for the events Kim Jong-il participated in. He bought everything from the foodstuffs, daily necessities, pets, and sports equipment for Kim Jong-il and his family to the equipment for Kim Jong-il's bodyguards and the presents Kim gave to his underlings.

According to intelligence received by the NIS, O succumbed to his chronic illnesses and has already died, but his son, O Yong-hwan, took over as his successor."[397]

---

397   "Tracing the Whereabouts of Kim Jong-il's 'Secret Funds' –Kim Jong-un Inherits Huge Amount of Money Together with the Transfer of Power," *Bessatsu Takarajima*, op. cit.

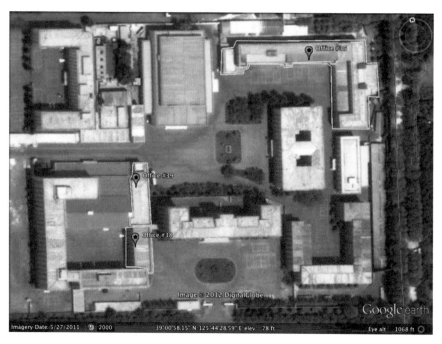

Image 24: The Third Floor's office buildings in the KWP Central Committee's #1 Office Complex. (Source: North Korea Leadership Watch)

These Third Floor operatives were recruited from trusted families throughout North Korea. They were trained on par with the diplomatic corps and intelligence service. Following the training, they were dispatched to one of over twenty countries around the world with instructions to develop networks. They spent years abroad, occasionally returning to North Korea for special assignments. Throughout the year, they received lists of items to be procured, primarily from Office 39, but also from Office 38. If they were not able to procure an item, it was perceived by officials in Pyongyang that the operatives opposed the order. This was particularly the case with any No. 1 order, those orders to be received by the Kim family. Thus, Third Floor operatives went to extraordinary lengths to fulfill Pyongyang's wish list.

Once an item was procured and delivered to Pyongyang, it went to either Office 39 or Office 38 for processing. The items that were to be given by Kim Jong-il as gifts were transferred to his Personal Secretariat. This was presumably through General Bureau 73, which, in turn, oversaw their distribution to the wider leadership and North Korean elites.[398] Most North Korean citizens received

---

398   Lee Gyo-Gwan, "20,000 Receive Gifts from Kim Jong-il Every Year," op. cit. According to some sources, the organization responsible for delivering the special presents under the name of Kim Jong-il was called the Kumsusan Assembly Hall Accounting Department. On the eve of national holidays,

Committee for Human Rights in North Korea

188

gifts through their place of employment. Every North Korean organization had a department dedicated to gift-giving. On New Year's Day and key birthdays, these departments would receive gifts from Kim Jong-il's Personal Secretariat for distribution to its workforce. Presumably, instructions accompanied the gifts indicating to whom they were to be given. The branch office of the OGD made note of who received what gift and reported back up the chain of command.

b. Weapons Sales

As noted earlier, Kim Il-sung removed the defense sector from the state economy in the early 1970s. But instead of becoming a fully independent part of the North Korean economy, it was integrated into the Party economy under the KWP MID and the SEC. This apparatus, which runs sales and acquisitions through a number of companies and trade firms, was tied to the Royal Economy via strong connections to Offices 38 and 39. As such, a portion of the defense industry's foreign currency earnings was redirected to the coffers that supported Kim Jong-il's "revolutionary funds."

Open source reporting suggests that North Korean defense sales fall largely under the purview of the Second Economic Committee (SEC), which is largely responsible for the manufacturing side of the defense-industrial complex. Founded in the early 1970s, the SEC has operated trading companies to represent state interests in weapons transactions with foreign countries. These organizations, managed by the External Economic General Bureau, were assigned geographic responsibilities, such as the Yongaksan Trading Corporation and the Puhung Trading Corporation, both believed to specialize in the former Soviet Union.[399] Similarly, the Korean Mining Development Trading Corporation (KOMID) and its many affiliates were responsible for South Asia and the Middle East.[400] These were the more well-known parts of the proliferation apparatus that North Korea used to conduct its weapons sales. This was also the part of the apparatus that the United

---

guidance officers from this department distributed these gifts throughout the country at special loyalty-pledging ceremonies. The gifts were paid for from a special department account funded by one percent of the state budget and foreign exchange earnings from over fifty companies managed by the department. It is highly likely that the Kumsusan Assembly Hall Accounting Department and General Bureau 73 are different names for the same organization.

399   Yim Ui-Chul, "DPRK Missile Industry, Technology Examined," *Tongil Kyongje*, August 1999.
400   KOMID fell under U.S. government sanctions following the discovery of a shipment of Hwasong-6 missiles to Yemen in 2003.

States targeted with vigorous sanctions, which led to a fundamental restructuring of many of the entities tied to this network in the early 2000s.[401]

A critical part of this apparatus was Office 99, which was responsible for executing the Central Committee's weapons acquisition and trade initiatives.[402] This office was established in 1981 at the direction of Kim Il-sung and placed under Division 5 of the KWP MID. It was divided into at least four sub-bureaus: production and planning, transportation, facilities, and commerce and banking. Defector testimony suggests that it coordinated closely with the SEC to facilitate exports. Indeed, Kim Min-su, who worked in Office 99, claimed that the bureau's leadership was also part of the SEC, at least through the early 1990s, when the top officer in the bureau concurrently held the post of Deputy Chief of the SEC.

Office 99 also had strong ties to Kim Jong-il's Personal Secretariat. His daughter, Kim Sol-song, was reportedly a prominent figure in Office 99 in the 1980s and 1990s.[403] In addition, Office 38 was the parent organization of Office 99's primary bank, the Changgwang Credit Bank. As weapons sales and acquisitions became increasingly lucrative and important in the 1980s and 1990s, Kim Jong-il authorized a channel of communication between Office 99 and Offices 38 and 39 in order to tie this part of the defense-industrial complex to the Royal Economy.

On the sales side, Office 39 took the lead. In the hubs where it facilitated its other activities, Office 39's agents established offices dedicated to the front end of defense sales.[404] According to sources in the region, one of the more active offices operated out of Macau with responsibility for sales in Southeast Asia, the Middle East, South Asia, and Africa.[405] Initial meetings were held between the agents and potential buyers. Once a general agreement was reached, the agents would connect the buyers to Pyongyang through an established channel that existed between Office 39 and Office 99. This would then lead to meetings in Pyongyang where potential buyers would be allowed to view the merchandise and a final price would be agreed on. Once the sale was completed, a portion of the proceeds would be channeled

---

401   Lee Beom-Jin, "Torpedo that Attacked *Cheonan* was Export Weapon of North Korea's Green Pine Association," *Weekly Chosun*, 17 August 2010. In the 2007 to 2009 timeframe, the architecture supporting weapons sales was changed due to the sanctions regime. The "Green Pine Association" was created as a weapons export company to replace KOMID and was placed under the RGB in 2009. By 2010, it was handling over fifty percent of the total volume of North Korean weapons sales overseas. A percentage of each sale was transferred from the RGB into Kim Jong-il's "revolutionary fund."
402   "Iran-DPRK Missile Cooperation, Role of Office No. 99" (Tokyo: Japan Policy Institute, February 7, 2008).
403   Interview with senior North Korean defector, 2013 and 2014.
404   Interview with Pyongyang-watchers in South Korea and Japan who focus on North Korea's illicit networks.
405   Ibid.

back to Office 39 and into the Royal Economy. Depending on how the sale was handled, Office 99 could task Office 39 to facilitate the transfer of the weapons through its operations in China.

Chart 8: The Royal Economy and Foreign Weapons Sales and Acquisitions

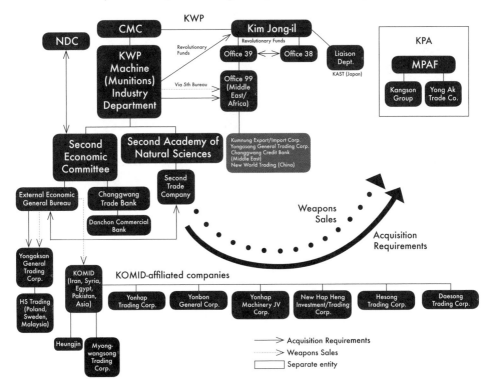

The institutions responsible for weapons acquisition were very similar in structure to those responsible for proliferation. The SEC's structure was nearly identical to that of many of its trade organizations that handled both sales and acquisitions. The major point of divergence was in how the Central Committee and the Royal Economy apparatus were involved in the acquisitions process. This was largely tied to special relationships that existed between Central Committee organizations and organizations in Japan, which played a critical role in North Korea's defense technology development. Pyongyang leveraged its networks in Japan, such as Chosen Soren and the Association of Korean Scientists and Technicians in Japan (AKST), to procure technology necessary for its defense programs. Office 99 set the requirements, which were then reportedly passed to Offices 38 and 39 for acquisition. Normally, these requirements were tied to technology and human capital that could be procured through the private sector, allowing Offices 38 and 39 to leverage their numerous ties to the quasi-legal Chosen Soren business operations throughout Japan.[406] It is unclear whether Offices 38 and 39 conducted similar acquisition operations in other countries, although this is unlikely. The operations in Japan appear to have been tied to special circumstances.

At its high point in the late 1990s and early 2000s, illicit weapons sales accounted for nearly $1 billion in the Royal Economy.[407, 408, 409] But as the international community began to clamp down on proliferation operations through enhanced sanctions and monitoring of smuggling routes, the ties between the Royal Economy and the sales and acquisitions part of the defense-industrial complex began to weaken. The freezing of North Korean accounts in Banco Delta Asia in 2005 reportedly led Kim Jong-il to the realization that these ties threatened his own funding streams. In response, he ordered that firewalls be erected to essentially remove the Royal Economy from direct involvement in weapons proliferation. From that point on, the Royal Economy could provide funds to critical defense programs but not utilize its apparatus in support of them procurement or sales. As a consequence, the parts of the Royal Economy closely tied to defense sales and acquisition were removed. Control of the Changgwang Credit Bank, for example, was transferred from Office

---

406   Acquisition agencies tied to the SEC also operated in Japan and were likely responsible for procuring more sensitive technologies that could not be secured through commercial channels.

407   This figure is only an approximation of the amount of hard currency that the Royal Economy siphoned off of weapons sale proceeds. The time period for this estimate is not clear, somewhere between 1995 and 2005. It is based on interviews with sources who study North Korea's illicit arms trade.

408   Lee Beom-Jin, "Torpedo that Attacked *Cheonan* was Export Weapon of North Korea's Green Pine Association," op. cit. In 2010, U.S. and international authorities estimated that North Korea's illegal weapons transactions totaled between $100-500 million. Following the institution of the U.S.-led Proliferation Security Initiative, which became operational in 2003, North Korean profits plummeted, reaching a low of $49.6 million in 2007. By 2009, North Korea's profits reached $150 million. The annual profit clearly falls far short of what it was in the early 2000s. Stephan Haggard and Marcus Noland argue that the slump may have begun much earlier. They note that the U.S. State Department's publication *World Military Expenditures and Arms Transfers* and the Stockholm International Peace Research Institute (SIPRI) show steadily declining North Korean sales over time. These sources suggest that the upper-end estimates that are sometimes reported—such as the statement by a U.S. official that North Korea earned $560 million from missile sales in 2001—are probably exaggerated. See Stephan Haggard and Marcus Noland, "Follow the Money: North Korea's External Resources and Constraints," *2008 Korea's Economy*, Korea Economic Institute (2008).

409   In the 1980s, during the Iran-Iraq War, the Defense Intelligence Agency estimates that North Korea earned an estimated $4 billion from arms sales with Iran. How much of that $4 billion was paid into the Royal Economy coffers is not known. *North Korea: The Foundations for Military Strength*. Defense Intelligence Agency (October 1991).

38 to Office 99 in 2005. According to recent reports, the Office 39 hub in Macau dedicated to defense sales has been shut down.[410]

Chart 9: Restructured Apparatus for Foreign Weapons Sales and Acquisition

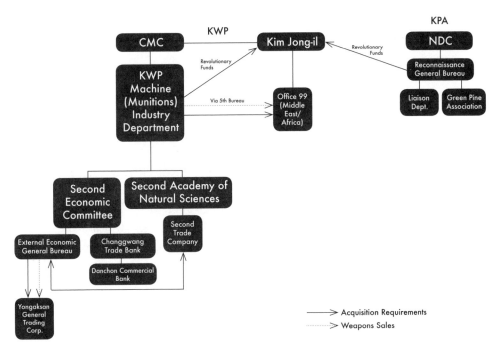

However, the Royal Economy's funding ties to the defense-industrial complex did not disappear. In fact, five years earlier in 2000, a funding channel was established that would have implications well into the Kim Jong-un era.

c. Tapping into the Royal Economy: Jang Song-taek's Network

The KWP OGD had played a central role at the heart of power since the beginning of the regime. It was the apparatus that Kim Jong-il used to consolidate

---

410   NHK special on North Korean illicit business operations, which aired in 2014. According to reporting out of Japan, the Office 39 operations in Macau shifted to precious metals after weapons sales dried up. This decision was largely driven by the fallout from the Banco Delta Asia incident. North Korean agents looked for transactions that could be completed with very little, if any, paper trail. The sale of gold and other metals by Office 39's businesses are done on a cash only basis in order to avoid tracking. This shift also takes advantage of the fact that North Korea is a leading producer of many precious metals, such as gold, a distinct advantage it did not have in the sale of weapons and defense technology.

his power as heir apparent. In the early 1990s, the power of this Central Committee department increased significantly when it absorbed the KWP Administration Department, which was responsibile for Party surveillance of the judicial and internal security apparatus.[411] In 1995, Kim Jong-il brought Jang Song-taek into the KWP OGD as a First Vice Director to run the new Administrative Section.

Jang's appointment occurred at a critical period in Kim Jong-il's power consolidation process. Kim Il-sung had died the year before and the People's Economy had begun to falter. For Kim Jong-il to move forward, he needed to accelerate the idolization of the Leader and firmly manage his close aides. As a consequence, those close to Kim began to expand the Party's encroachment on the national economy. Most likely with Kim's blessing, Jang Song-taek followed suit and the OGD moved from being just a surveillance and enforcement mechanism to being one of the main revenue-generating entities of the Kim family.[412]

As the 1990s progressed, the Administrative Section grew in importance and size under Jang's guidance, eventually taking up an entire section of the Central Committee office building. This was largely due to its growing responsibilities for a number of hard currency operations, most of which were directly tied to the Royal Economy.[413] Jang expanded his network of revenue generation along two lines:

1. *Using the institutional authority that came with his new posting.* For example, the Administrative Section secured access to significant funds by using customs control rights, which fell under its oversight, to grant clearance on state organs' export items earning fees or service charges in the process.[414]

2. *Co-opting hard currency operations from powerful entities across the regime by leveraging his Kim family ties.* For example, soon after his appointment as First Vice Director of the OGD, Jang engineered the transfer of the Korea National Insurance Corporation (KNIC) from the Daesong

---

411   The dissolution of the KWP Administration Department followed a turf battle with the KWP OGD over who would manage the internal security portfolio. Kim Si-hak, the Director of the KWP Administration Department, had been a close associate of Kim Jong-il, but lost favor as a result of the power struggle. The department was dissolved in the early 1990s, and its responsibilities transferred to the newly created OGD Administrative Department.

412   Kim Kwang-jin. Before coming to the KWP OGD, Jang Song-taek had been engaged in economic affairs. He had overseen the capital construction campaign in preparation for the 13th World Youth and Student Festival, which had brought him into contact with a number of hard currency generating operations throughout North Korea. By the late 1980s, he had become one of the key members within the Kim family with access to a number of revenue streams.

413   Kim Kwang-jin.

414   Hyon Song-il, *North Korea's National Strategy and Power Elite*, op. cit.

General Trading Corporation, then affiliated with the Ministry of Finance, to the Administrative Section.

In the lead up to the first inter-Korean summit in 2000, the KWP OGD was embedded even deeper in the Royal Economy when Kim Jong-il began to employ it to manage part of the "revolutionary funds." This practice reportedly began with a bribe of roughly $500 million that Kim Jong-il received from the Kim Dae-Jung administration through the Hyundai Corporation in order to secure the inter-Korean summit.[415,] [416] This money was allegedly turned over to Jang Song-taek for distribution. Of the $500 million, $100 million was used to repair the economy and over $400 million was allocated to the military—$200 million of which was earmarked for the munitions industry.[417] From this decision, the OGD established a relationship with the North East Asia Bank (NEAB) in order to manage a number of special "revolutionary funds" accounts, also known as NEAB 611 accounts.[418] As the decade progressed, these accounts, as well as other Royal Economy funding streams, became vital to ensuring the viability of critical North Korean defense systems, such as the nuclear and missile programs. They were used to top off or supplement the already substantial funding coming into the regime through weapons sales by the KWP MID channels.[419]

Jang's power, and that of the Administrative Section of the KWP OGD, continued to grow in the early 2000s, largely drawing on the revenue from the Royal Economy. This access to resources and funds allowed Jang to not only successfully engage in politics with other elements of the regime, but it also afforded him the opportunity to push back against his rivals within the OGD, namely First Vice Directors Ri Yong-chol and Ri Je-gang.

Just as Jang was firmly establishing himself among the close aides around Kim Jong-il, he overreached. Soon after becoming Premier in 2003, Pak Pong-ju tapped into Jang Song-taek's patronage network to appoint Sin Il-nam, a Vice Minister of People's Security, as Vice Premier and Chairman of the Capital Construction Committee. Sin Il-nam very likely saw this as a demotion, given the lack of status surrounding the Cabinet. He maintained his close ties to Jang and ignored orders from the Premier. When he refused Pak Pong-ju's order to deliver

---

415   Kim Kwang-jin.
416   Sung-Yoon Lee, "Engaging North Korea: The Clouded Legacy of South Korea's Sunshine Policy," *American Enterprise Institute*, April 19, 2010.
417   Kim Kwang-jin.
418   Ibid.
419   Ibid. According to Kim Kwang-jin, a single missile test could cost nearly $340 million, while a single nuclear test costs close to $400 million.

materials in connection with efforts to modernize Pyongyang,[420] which followed Kim Jong-il's directive to make the capital a world-class city, Jang's opponents took the opportunity to move against him.

For Ri Yong-chol and Ri Je-gang, who were supporting Ko Yong-hui's efforts to push for the designation of one of her sons as heir apparent against the objections of Jang Song-taek and Kim Kyong-hui, the timing could not have been better. They reportedly provided the Premier with information that allowed him to construct a dossier for Kim Jong-il. This dossier outlined cases where the KWP OGD infringed upon the state economy in the name of earning foreign currency, as well as the arbitrary actions of state entities in the economic sector.[421] Kim responded by supporting Pak, granting him executive authority over the economy. He also ordered the return of all state enterprises to the Cabinet and mandated against external interference.[422] Within a few months, he sent Jang Song-taek into exile. In 2005, several other revenue-generating bodies under the now defunct Administrative Section were moved to other parts of the Royal Economy.[423]

d. Jang Song-taek's Return

Soon after the OGD had been stripped of many of its ties to the Royal Economy, the regime suffered an enormous blow to its finances, especially Kim Jong-il's personal funding streams. In September 2005, the U.S. Treasury designated Banco Delta Asia, a Macau-based bank, as a primary money laundering concern due to its role in assisting North Korean companies to launder money from counterfeiting and drug smuggling. Under Section 311 of the USA PATRIOT Act, Washington banned all U.S. banks from dealing with Banco Delta Asia. Macau banking authorities froze fifty North Korean accounts worth $24 million. The U.S. action had a chilling effect on foreign businesses and banks, primarily in Europe,

---

420   Sin Il-nam claimed that Pak's orders interfered with prior tasking of the Capital Construction Committee by the KWP OGD.

421   Hyon Song-il, *North Korea's National Strategy and Power Elite*, op. cit.

422   It is important to note that Kim Jong-il's decision came at a time of economic reform inside the regime. His decision might have stemmed from the concern that raising the cost of maintaining the regime was threatening the regime by ruining the state economy. Pak Pong-ju made the argument that the state economy had become impoverished to the extent that there was no longer any room for further infringement by the Party economy. Unlike during the period after Kim Il-sung's death, Kim Jong-il may have felt that he could begin to reverse some of the funding flows within the regime in order to take care of the overall state economy. But in the interest of the "Military First" (*Songun*) policy, this thinking only went so far. Kim also ordered that production and trade units that belonged to the Cabinet in the past, but had been transferred to the munitions economy, be left alone and that state assistance to the munitions industry be further strengthened.

423   Kim Kwang-jin.

Hong Kong, and Singapore. These businesses and banks became unwilling to engage with North Korea even on legal business ventures for fear of being designated complicit in North Korea's illegal activities.[424]

Since Banco Delta Asia served as a hub for funneling money from international banks into the regime, closing this channel essentially "closed Kim Jong-il's wallet" in the words of one North Korean defector. The funding streams that had been carefully constructed over decades to keep the Royal Economy alive were now under threat. Any existing support for economic reform dried up. Kim Jong-il's thinking returned to what it had been in the 1990s. He needed to protect the "Party Center" (*Dang Jung-ang*). Over the next few years, the Royal Economy became increasingly removed from channels that can be tracked through bank accounts. As noted above, Office 39 moved away from supporting weapons sales and into less detectable sectors, such as the precious metals market, only relying on cash for all transactions. Reliance on diplomatic couriers to move gold and other metals out of the country and hard currency into the country became common practice.[425]

In 2006, Kim Jong-il brought Jang Song-taek back into the center of politics. While this move was in part due to Kim Kyong-hui's pleas, he also needed someone with the skills to balance the regime's need for international aid while also containing internal dissent, which had begun to grow with the proliferation of the markets. Jang had been tied to a number of attempts to secure foreign aid in the past and had overseen the internal security apparatus in his role as First Vice Director of the OGD. In addition, he was a member of the Kim family, albeit a "side branch." Despite the purge just years before, Kim Jong-il gave Jang Song-taek the portfolios for China, the economy, and internal security. The Administrative Section was removed from the OGD and remade a fully independent Central Committee department. In October 2007, Jang was made Director of the new Administrative Department.

Almost immediately upon Jang's return, the leadership was plunged into crisis as the KWP OGD and the Administrative Department launched widespread investigations of corruption. It is unclear whether this was the result of a power struggle between the two Central Committee departments or an outright power grab. Regardless, the subsequent arrests and purges created the space for Jang to re-establish his ties to the Royal Economy and hard currency networks.

The purge was ostensibly aimed at officials responsible for relations with South Korea and other foreign countries. The KWP UFD was the most obvious target, and the KWP OGD oversaw the investigation. KWP UFD Vice Director

---

424   Bruce Klingner, "WebMemo #1389: Banco Delta Asia Ruling Complicates North Korean Nuclear Deal," *The Heritage Foundation*, March 15, 2007.
425   Author's interviews in Seoul with North Korean defectors, 2013 and 2014.

Choe Sung-chol, who managed the 2007 summit with President Roh Moo-Hyun, was relieved of his official duties. However, it was the less publicized investigation into Office 39, presumably led by the KWP Administrative Department, that had the greatest implications for the Royal Economy.

While evidence is lacking, some sources suggest that this purge was part of a move by Jang Song-taek to not only re-establish his ties to valuable hard currency channels, but to also put in motion a plan to increasingly exert control over parts of the Royal Economy. Following the investigation, Kim Jong-il dismissed several officials handling secret funds deposited in Macau and economic projects involving cooperation with South Korean officials:[426]

- The President of the Daesong Trading Company,[427] operating under the supervision of KWP Office 39, was fired for embezzling $1.4 million.
- National Economic Cooperation Council President, Chong Un-op, who provided overall supervision of economic cooperation projects with South Korea in the private sector, was accused of embezzling funds and arrested.
- Chongsaeng General Trading Company President, Kim Chol, was arrested for illegally selling pig iron to South Korea and reportedly died while in custody.[428]

These purges increased surveillance of the officials involved in hard currency operations, especially those who worked directly in service of the Royal Economy. It may have convinced Kim Jong-il of the need for greater supervision of these sources of revenue vital to the stability of the regime and his leadership.

If these rumors are to be believed, Jang did not gain access to the control levers of the Royal Economy until 2008, following Kim Jong-il's stroke in August. While key members of the NDC, such as Jo Myong-rok and Kim Yong-chun, as well as SPA Presidium President, Kim Yong-nam, were the faces of the regime at major Party and military functions, behind the scenes, Kim Kyong-hui, Jang Song-taek, and Kim Ok,

426   "North Korea Purging Senior Officials Dealing With ROK?," *NK Focus*, February 16, 2008.
427   Kim Ah-Young, "Targeting Pyongyang's drug trade addiction," *Asia Times*, June 18, 2003. According to a 2003 article, the Daesong Trading Company coordinated opium trafficking through its trading corporation, *Daesong Sangsa*, which had twenty overseas branches at the time. North Korea reportedly produced more than forty tons of opium a year. Estimates of revenue earned ranged from a low of $48 million to as much as $1 billion annually, if all illegal drugs, such as heroin, cocaine, and methamphetamines were included. The other major trade organization dealing in opium was the Aesung Trading Company. Both companies were part of the Office 39 apparatus.
428   The Chongsaeng General Trading Company was located at the Kim Chaek Steel Plant in Chongjin City, North Hamgyong Province. It sold pig iron, hot-rolled steel, and scrap iron. Its ties to the Royal Economy are unclear.

Kim Jong-il's private secretary and mistress, jointly ran Kim Jong-il's office. While Kim Kyong-hui was responsible for overseeing the Kim family's assets, which included the Royal Economy, Jang was reportedly given wide latitude for ensuring the day-to-day operations of the government, including the economic sector. This continued after Kim Jong-il recovered and reached out to Jang to support the upcoming succession of Kim Jong-un.

In 2009, Kim Kyong-hui returned to public life after a six-year hiatus. It was presumed that Kim Jong-il was relying on his family to pave the way for the succession. Overlapping with this reinvigoration of Kim family participation in politics was a series of moves tied to the Royal Economy:

- In January 2010, the European Union identified the Director of Office 39, Kim Tong-un, as one of thirteen North Korean officials targeted for sanctions related to the regime's nuclear activities.
- In February 2010, reports surfaced that suggested Office 38 had been merged with Office 39 some time in 2009.[429] In addition, Jon Il-chun was identified as the Director of Office 39, replacing Kim Tong-un.[430]
- In early 2010, Kim Hyo was reportedly named Director of the KWP FAD.[431] The post had previously been vacant. According to South Korean government sources, Kim was believed to be the father of Kim Ok.
- In March 2010, reports surfaced that Ri Kwang-gun, who had fallen out of favor in 2004, had been appointed Vice Director of Office 39 in 2009. Ri had previously run a trading company and served as an economic counselor at the North Korean mission in Germany. His purge and subsequent return to politics suggested that he was part of Jang Song-taek's network.
- In March 2010, Ri Chol, the Ambassador to Switzerland and the caretaker of Kim Jong-il's secret funds, left office after thirty years to return to Pyongyang.[432] He was succeeded by So Se-pyong, North Korea's former Ambassador to Iran and onetime aide to Ri Chol. The

---

429   Kim So-Hyun, "DPRK Scraps Panel on Security Law," *The Korea Herald*, February 18, 2010.
430   Jon Il-chun is also the Director of the Daesong Group, the business arm of Office 39. In his long career, Jon has served in various roles in the State External Economic Affairs Commission and the KWP FAD, as well as a five-year tenure as Vice Chairman of the North Korea-Rwanda Friendship Association.
431   Ro Myong-kun, who used to work as a carpenter for Kim Il-sung, served as Director of the FAD from 1983 to 2001. His successor, Ri Pong-su, was reportedly dismissed shortly after the death of Ko Yong-hui, Kim Jong-il's wife, in 2004. After Ri Pong-su was removed, the position of FAD Director remained vacant.
432   "N. Korean Ambassador to Geneva Expected to Leave Office," *Yonhap News Agency*, March 10, 2010.

speculation was that Ri moved into Kim Jong-un's Personal Secretariat as an advisor on the Royal Economy.[433]

The most prominent change in this period of restructuring was Jang Song-taek's appointment as Vice Chairman of the NDC in June 2010. According to North Korean allegations tied to his investigation and execution, this was when Jang Song-taek began to move with impunity within the regime. By this point, he was vital to Kim Jong-il's control of the regime. He ran operations with China on the economic front. He also held the portfolio for the domestic economy. As Vice Chairman of the NDC, he had access to military-based hard currency operations and the power to reorient them to the KWP Administrative Department through Department 54. In addition, he controlled the internal security apparatus, which allowed him to limit the situational awareness across the regime of his own actions, as long as it did not interfere with Kim's own control of the regime.

Kim Jong-il's worsening health problems and the demands of succession politics may have contributed to the lack of pushback against the growing power of the Jang Song-taek network, which was based in the KWP Administrative Department. Reports of Jang's growing presence in the Royal Economy surfaced in early 2010, when he took on the currency operations of his rival O Kuk-ryol through the creation of a trading firm called the Korea Daepung Group.[434] Throughout 2010 and into 2011, control of trading companies and other lucrative hard currency operations was moved from a range of regime institutions, including Office 39, to the Administrative Department.

---

433   Kim Young-Gyo, "Return of N. Korean envoy in Geneva enhances Jong-un's succession," *Yonhap News Agency*, April 1, 2010. According to some sources, before his departure, Ri transferred Kim Jong-il's secret funds, estimated at $4 billion, from Swiss banks to banks in Luxembourg and other European countries.

434   Lee Young-Jong, "O Kuk Ryol, Who Returned Around the Time of Jang Song Taek's Downfall," op. cit. According to South Korean intelligence sources, the power struggle between O Kuk-ryol and Jang Song-taek began in full force in 2009 after O's appointment as Vice Chairman of the NDC. Within five months of entering the NDC, O Kuk-ryol created the Korea International Company, a trading company which was sanctioned by the SPA. Jang Song-taek, fearing that this organization would inhibit his ability to expand his hard currency operations, launched the Korea Daepung Group in January 2010 and appointed Pak Chol-su, a Korean-Chinese businessman in China, as President. According to defector sources, Jang had the state-run media run a report that the activities of the Daepung Group were ordered by NDC Chairman Kim Jong-il. As the politics of succession unfolded, O Kuk-ryol faded into the background.

Jang's Channel to China

The Korea Daepung International Investment Group was reportedly established in January 2010 in order to attract foreign investment. At the heart of its operations was an agreement with a Chinese bank to create a fund worth $10 billion, a figure many international monetary experts dispute. Two months later in March 2010, the Korea State Development Bank was established to oversee the Daepung Group and its assets. Jon Il-chun, the head of Office 39, was appointed Director General of the State Development Bank.

Foreign monetary officials continued to be highly doubtful about the amount of investment. Instead, they argued that, based on the timing, North Korea was feigning this investment from China. In actuality, North Korea was laundering their secret funds in China to return them to North Korea. Although Daepung is registered in Hong Kong as a corporation, it is actually no more than a paper company. Ever since financial sanctions were imposed by the United States in August 2010, Hong Kong authorities closely watched the movements of Daepung and related funds.[435]

In 2013, the South Korean Ministry of Unification announced that North Korea had dissolved Daepung Group due to its unsatisfactory performance. In hindsight, this may have been an early indication of Jang Song-taek's fall from power.

The evolving processes that allowed Jang to use his network to task other parts of the Royal Economy leaked out as part of a 2010 Japanese investigation into illegal exports to North Korea.[436] The investigation focused on Om Kwang-chol, a

---

435   "Tracing the Whereabouts of Kim Jong-il's 'Secret Funds' –Kim Jong-un Inherits Huge Amount of Money Together with the Transfer of Power," *Bessatsu Takarajima*, op. cit.
436   "Austrian convicted for yacht sale to North Korean leader," *Reuters*, December 7, 2010. See also "Wirepuller Kwon Yong-rok Behind Purchase of Luxury Yachts for Kim Jong-il," *Uin Hatsu "Konfidensharu,"* July 28, 2009. North Korean acquisition operations in Europe reportedly continued to rely heavily on Third Floor operatives via the Jang Song-taek network. According to Austrian court documents tied to a failed business transaction involving a local businessman, a North Korean operative made the initial approach to the Austrian company with instructions to purchase two yachts and eight Mercedes Benz automobiles. This operative was reportedly Kwon Yong-rok, a Deputy Director of Office 39. Then, a Chinese front company made the down payment, which led to suspicion and investigation by the authorities. The items were believed to be birthday presents for Kim Jong-il.

North Korean trade official who was a Vice Director of the SSD, which formally reported up to the KWP Administrative Department.[437] Om, in his other position as President of the Sinhung Trading Company, allegedly received letters of consignment from Kim Jong-il's office via Rungra 888, a trading company tied to General Bureau 73. These letters allowed Om to assign tasks to other parts of the Royal Economy, such as Office 39 and the military, through their own trading companies.[438] Kim Jong-il may have allowed this kind of network to develop because much of the legal and illicit deals were deeply tied to Dalian Global, a trading company located in China that was a critical hub for regional goods and services to be funneled into North Korea.[439] Because of its long-standing on-the-ground presence in China, the SSD would have been uniquely suited to run these sensitive operations.

---

437   "Detour Route to China, South Korea Used for Illegal Exports to DPRK, Senior DPRK Official Directs Trade," *Sankei Shimbun*, February 3, 2010.

438   Ibid. These letters of consignment were mainly for luxury goods. In one case, Om ordered cosmetics and foodstuffs through a trading company called Suruusu Ltd, based in Osaka, under the pretense of exporting the goods to Dalian. In fact, the goods were diverted to North Korea. In another case, Om tasked the Office 39 apparatus to work through Dalian Global to secure illegally exported Mercedes-Benz luxury cars and pianos from Japan to North Korea. In a non-luxury item case, Tadao Morita Co., Ltd., a company dealing in used cars located in Maizuru City (Kyoto Prefecture) was caught trying to export large tanker trucks that could be converted for military use to North Korea by pretending to export them to South Korea.

439   In the late 2000s, a lucrative channel for luxury goods and dual-use items was Japan, where several companies, because of financial problems, were willing to overlook export controls. Of note were the following: Meisho Yoko, which did business with HELM Pyongyang (controlled by Rungra 888); Toko Boeki, which did business with New East International Trading Ltd. (controlled by the SEC); Tadao Morita Company, which did business with Paekho 7 Trading (run by the KPA); Meishin, which did business with Korea Daesong No. 3 Trading Corporation (controlled by Office 39); and Keinan Trading, which did business with Sinhung Trading (controlled by the SSD).

Chart 10: Jang's Channel into the Royal Economy

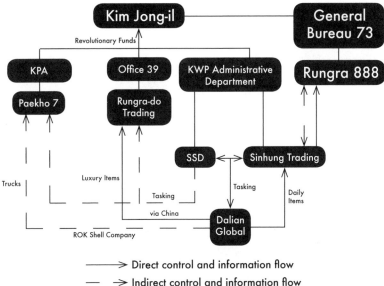

Direct control and information flow

Indirect control and information flow

By allowing this manner of business to go forward, Kim Jong-il gave Jang Song-taek authority inside an infrastructure that, up until that point, had answered exclusively to the Supreme Leader. At the time, it most likely fit with Kim's strategy for pushing forward the succession. Jang was vital to this strategy and Kim Kyong-hui was well-positioned to ensure that his ambitions did not get out of hand. In addition, the KWP Administrative Department continued to pay into Kim's "revolutionary funds," a sign of loyalty and trust throughout the regime.

Chart 11: Movement of "Revolutionary Funds" Within the Regime

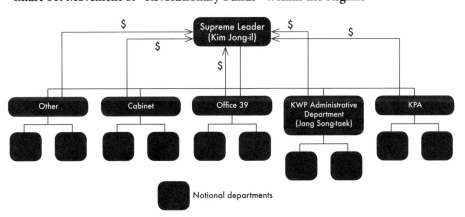

Command and control over the Royal Economy was the subject of speculation in the months leading up to Kim Jong-il's death. In February 2011, rumors surfaced that Office 38 had been reconstituted as an independent body in May 2010 after having allegedly been incorporated into Office 39 in 2009.[440] The veracity of these rumors regarding Office 38's supposed closure and reinstatement was open to question. What was particularly intriguing was the accompanying rumor that the office was now headed by Kim Tong-un, the former head of Office 39. The day before Kim Jong-il's death, on December 17, 2011, North Korean state television showed Jon Il-chun, Director of Office 39, standing closer to Kim than the heir apparent, Kim Jong-un, on an inspection tour of a supermarket in Pyongyang.[441] Whether this was a deliberate signal of the Kim family's control over the "revolutionary funds" is not clear. However, Jon Il-chun had not been seen in public for five months, making his reappearance particularly notable.

Image 25: Kim Jong-il conducts an inspection of Kwangbok Region Supermarket. (Source: KCBS)

3. THE ROYAL ECONOMY UNDER KIM JONG-UN

Kim Jong-il's last will and testament makes clear that his heir, Kim Jong-un, is the sole proprietor of the funds controlled by the Kim family and, by extension,

---

440   "Kim Tong-un Named Kim Jong-il's Fund Manager," *Yonhap News Agency*, February 20, 2011. The South Korean government speculated that Kim Jong-il had separated Office 38 and 39 to once again open up two revenue streams into the Kim family coffers to cover the increasing cost of the succession. 441   "Kim Jong-il Visits Kwangbok Region Supermarket," *KCBS*, December 15, 2014. The night after this report, North Korean television carried photographs of the event.

the Royal Economy. In the summer of 2010, Kim Jong-il reportedly began to shift control of the funds in several banks, primarily in Europe, to Kim Jong-un. When Kim Jong-il died, decision-making responsibilities with regards to the Royal Economy fell to Kim Jong-un, with guidance from both Kim Kyong-hui, who had helped her brother manage the Kim family funds for years, and Kim Sol-song, who was a key figure, possibly the Director, of General Bureau 73.[442] Jang Song-taek may have been involved in some of the conversations about how to secure funds from outside the regime, namely China, but was likely kept out of the conversations on how to utilize the funds inside the regime to build power around Kim Jong-un.[443]

Circumstantial evidence suggests that the Kim family was increasingly desperate because of depleted family coffers. Expenditures ballooned during Kim Jong-il's later years as he sought to solidify the succession process. In addition, there were huge costs associated with the events commemorating the centennial of late President Kim Il-sung's birth in April 2012. Finally, in the absence of any accomplishments and leadership charisma, Kim Jong-un was forced to embark on an idolization and gift-giving campaign that dwarfed that of his father. This anxiety existed amidst an ongoing struggle within the regime as power-brokers fought over control of lucrative sources of hard currency inside and outside North Korea. This has resulted in many rumors that have obscured assessments of the Royal Economy.

What follows is a highly speculative examination of the Royal Economy under Kim Jong-un. It is based on a close reading of regional media, as well as a number of interviews in 2013 and 2014 with defectors and Pyongyang-watchers in Asia and Europe. The reader should be careful in placing too much faith in any one story or the specific amounts of money tied to various parts of the Royal Economy. Instead, the narrative should be taken as a whole to represent one theory of the money trail under Kim Jong-un.

a. Struggles to Maintain the Royal Economy

Even before becoming Supreme Leader, Kim Jong-un was faced with a fundamental challenge to his ability to consolidate power: the lack of funds. In the past, Kim Jong-il had given Mercedes Benzes, high-end watches, and other luxury

---

442   "Economic Reforms Stalled, Controls on Economy Tightened One Year After Death of Kim Jong-il," *Sankei Shimbun*, November 29, 2012. When Kim Jong-il died, foreign currency operations were reportedly halted temporarily as they were consolidated under Kim Jong-un's control. When these operations resumed, some sources contended that a new Department 81 was established under the NDC to manage these funds. The department is supposedly tied to Kim Jong-un's NDC Secretariat, which is headed by Kim Chang-son.

443   Author's interviews in Seoul with senior defectors and Pyongyang-watchers, 2013 and 2014.

items to high-ranking officials at celebrations, banquets, and parties in order to secure their loyalty. But as early as 2009, stories emerged from inside the regime about the sharp decline in the number and value of gifts that the Kim family was giving to senior officials. This decline accelerated in 2010 following the sinking of the *Cheonan*. While events were still being held, officials were receiving less. On the occasion of Kim Jong-il's birthday on February 16, 2010, the shortage of gifts was quite apparent. The situation became such a source of conversation within the regime that outsiders hearing this chatter began to wonder whether Kim Jong-il's power had begun to wane.[444]

Upon assuming power, Kim Jong-un initially tried to enhance the level of gift-giving beyond what his father had done in the late 2000s. According to some sources, he nearly doubled the amount of spending on gifts to nearly $650 million.[445] A large portion of this money, reportedly $330 million, was used for idolization projects throughout the country.[446] Kim Jong-un approved the building of more bronze statues of the late President Kim Il-sung and the remaking of images of Kim Il-sung and Kim Jong-il. The square in front of the Kumsusan Palace of the Sun in Pyongyang, where the bodies of his father and grandfather are laid to rest, began to transform into a park modeled on a European palace. This was important because Kim Jong-un lacked the patronage system his father had when he came to power and the legitimacy his grandfather possessed.

Office 39's Africa Venture

North Korea has made idolization of leaders a source of income for the regime. Since the early 2000s, North Korean companies, such as the Mansudae Overseas Development Group and the Mansudae Art Institute, have received contracts from a number of African countries to build statues and other sculptures. According to a 2010 report, the profits from this venture tallied close to $160 million. Both organizations have ties to Office 39, which manages the funds coming back into the regime. Reportedly half of revenue generated by these

---

444   "Sharp Decreases in Gifts to Senior Officials Suggests Kim Jong-il's Influence May be in Danger of Waning," *Tokyo Shimbun*, April 2, 2010.
445   "NK Leader Spends $650 mil. on Luxury Goods," *The Korea Times*, March 11, 2014.
446   "Economic Reforms Stalled, Controls on Economy Tightened One Year After Death of Kim Jong Il," *Sankei Shimbun*, op. cit.

projects ends up in the Royal Economy as either Supreme Leader governing funds or in secret bank accounts.[447]

The Mansudae Art Institute was founded in 1959 to support the idolization campaign surrounding the Kim family through a wide variety of projects from designing lapel pins to the 164-foot tall Monument to the Founding of the KWP. Its place within the regime was made clear in 2013 by the SPA: "44.8 percent of the total state budgetary expenditure for the economic development and improvement of people's living standard was used for funding the building of edifices to be presented to the 100th birth anniversary of President Kim Il-sung."[448]

In the 1970s, the institute began to expand its operations outside of North Korea, launching an international branch called Mansudae Overseas Project Group. Since then, it has earned millions of dollars on projects built for countries including Algeria, Angola, Botswana, Benin, Cambodia, Chad, the Democratic Republic of the Congo, Egypt, Equatorial Guinea, Ethiopia, Malaysia, Mozambique, Madagascar, Namibia, Senegal, Syria, Togo, and Zimbabwe. In recent years, it has been commissioned by European governments to restore statues using technical skills that have long since been lost in the West.[449]

According to a source quoted by *Daily NK*, the Mansudae operations in Africa are substantial.[450]

---

447   "Foreign Currency Earning Constructions in Africa," *Daily NK*, June 21, 2010.
448   Caroline Winter, "Mansudae Art Studio, North Korea's Colossal Monument Factory," *Bloomberg*, June 6, 2013.
449   Ibid.
450   "Foreign Currency Earning Constructions in Africa," *Daily NK*, op. cit.

Table 7: North Korea's Projects in Africa[451]

Country	Total Amount	Projects
Namibia	$66.03 million	• Presidential Palace: $49 million • Cemetery of National Heroes: $5.23 million • A military museum: $1.8 million • Independence Hall: $10 million
Angola	$54.5 million	• António Agostinho Neto Culture Center: $40 million • Cabinda Park: $13 million • Peace Monument: $1.5 million
Senegal	$25 million	• Monument to the African Renaissance
Congo	$19.2 million	• Basketball stadium: $14.4 million • Academic center for athletes: $4.8 million
Equatorial Guinea	$12.54 million	• Presidential vacation resort: $800,000 • Government office building: $1.5 million • Luba Stadium: $6.74 million • Conference halls: $3.5 million

One significant departure from his father was that Kim Jong-un, while continuing to give personal gifts on special occasions, began the practice of defining major construction projects as "gifts" from either the Supreme Leader or the Party to the people of North Korea. Presumably, this allows Kim to maximize the impact of funding from the Royal Economy on his power consolidation. He would be able to not only pay for critical infrastructure, but also tie these tangible examples of progress to his "wise leadership." The chart in Appendix B provides numerous examples where North Korean media mentions the term "gift" or reveals the act of Kim Jong-un presenting gifts to members of the North Korean elite.

As the regime scrambled to access Kim family funds from foreign banks to offset the disappearance of lucrative sources, such as weapons sales and drug trafficking, the Royal Economy began to stall, making it impossible for Kim Jong-un to maintain the pace of gift-giving. According to a defector who has examined recent

---

451 Ibid. The cost of the Senegal project was updated to reflect recent work on the monument.

leadership dynamics inside North Korea, gift-giving presentations during guidance inspections precipitously declined towards the end of 2012 and throughout 2013, increasingly replaced by verbal expressions of gratitude by Kim Jong-un.[452] While the Royal Economy continues to make up nearly sixty percent of the overall North Korean economy, it is becoming increasingly questionable whether, in an era of declining foreign funds, Kim Jong-un can effectively conduct the politics of consolidation.

b. Sources of Funding

The Royal Economy sits on a web of different funding streams coming from both inside and outside the regime to the offices of the Supreme Leader. In other words, Kim Jong-un draws not only on money that comes from overseas through the elaborate mechanisms outlined above, but also through internal funds siphoned from various parts of the regime. According to numerous sources, the broad contours of this architecture have not changed much since the 1970s.

At the heart of Kim Jong-un's finances are the "revolutionary funds" that were left to him in Kim Jong-il's last will and testament. The total amount is unknown but is rumored to be around $4-5 billion. The fund is supplemented on a yearly basis through a variety of collection schemes. These procurement schemes can be broken down into three parts: Revolutionary Funds; Loyalty Funds; and the People's Economy.[453]

"Revolutionary funds" are those funds directly controlled and managed by the Supreme Leader's offices, including revenue generated by Office 38. The annual amount of funds generated is not known but is rumored to be roughly several hundred million dollars.[454]

- **Samcheolli Depository**, mentioned in Kim Jong-il's will, refers to funds generated from North Korean labor and social organizations. The memberships of these organizations, which number in the millions, pay annual dues, a portion of which goes to the "revolutionary funds." This Depository is located in Kim Jong-un's Personal Secretariat and is rumored to be managed by Kim Jeong.

---

452   Interviews in Seoul in 2014. Also see Kim Sun-chol's comments for a NHK special on the DPRK's Secret Fund, which aired in April 2014.

453   The description of these funding streams and the amounts associated with them are highly speculative and based on interviews with several sources during the author's trips to Seoul in 2013 and 2014.

454   According to some sources, the Revolutionary Funds could account for $1-2 billion.

- **2.16 Fund**, also mentioned in Kim Jong-il's will, refers to both the Party and secret funds. The Party funds are generated from Party membership dues. According to the last public figures, the membership of the KWP was approximately 3 million. A portion of the annual dues goes to the 2.16 Fund managed by Ri Cheol-ho, a member of Kim Jong-un's Personal Secretariat.
- **Party organization and administrative unit taxes** also contribute to funds. Each Party and state body pays a three to five percent tax to the 2.16 Fund. This reportedly accounts for approximately $100-200 million per year.
- **Revenue, interest, and earnings** generated from illegal transactions on the funds managed by General Bureau 73 and Office 38 result in approximately $200-300 million per year for the 2.16 Fund.
- **Foreign investments** generate approximately $200-400 million per year for the 2.16 Fund.
- **Bank transactions**, including those from the Foreign Trade Bank, generate approximately $100-200 million per year for the 2.16 Fund.
- Mandatory **embassy tributes** account for approximately $50-100 million per year for the 2.16 Fund.
- **Second Economic Committee** and associated defense industry funds transferred to the 2.16 Fund total approximately $100-200 million per year.

Each of the components of the regime involved in the generation of hard currency is responsible for meeting a mandated target of revenue to be turned over to the offices of the Supreme Leader through General Bureau 73.[455] These are considered loyalty funds. Most of this money comes from the operations of front companies tied to these regime organizations. Failure to meet the mandated targets can result in institutional and individual punishments.

- The **KWP FAD** has a target of $20 million per year.
- **Office 39** has a target of $20 million per year.

---

455   Author's discussion in 2014 with sources in Seoul with knowledge of North Korean hard currency operations. Under Kim Jong-il, his style of leadership fomented competition among leadership units, which played out in hard currency operations. Because the pressure was fierce to show loyalty through funds given over to Kim, there was little coordination and delineation between units. This inevitably led to turf wars, which continued to grow under Kim Jong-un.

- The **KWP Administrative Department** <u>had</u> a target of $20 million per year.[456]
- The **KWP OGD** is tied to the Supreme Leader's personal apparatus. It is not clear if it has a mandated target.[457]
- The **GC** is tied to the Supreme Leader's personal apparatus. It is not clear if it has a mandated target.
- The **KPA GPB** has a target of $10 million per year.
- The **KPA GSD** has a target of $10 million per year.
- The **MPAF** has a target of $10 million per year.
- The **MSC** has a target of $10 million per year.
- The **RGB** has a target of $10 million per year.[458,459]
- The **SSD** has a target of $10 million per year.
- The **MPS** has a target of $10 million per year.
- **Other Party and administrative offices** (such as KWP LID and Pyongyang City Administration) have targets of $2 million per year.

The final source of revenue for the Supreme Leader comes from a one percent tax on the People's Economy.[460, 461] The total amount that goes into a governing

---

456   Since the dissolution of the KWP Administration Department, its hard currency operations (and accompanying loyalty funds) have dispersed to several other organizations within the regime.

457   If the stories of Choe Ryong-hae assuming the position of KWP Secretary for the OGD are true, this would be the first time the OGD has fallen under the control of someone other than a Kim family member. This could result in the OGD being given a mandated target for loyalty payments.

458   "Dangers in a Cutthroat World," *Daily NK*, September 2, 2011. According to some sources, soon after its creation in 2009, the RGB advanced its hard currency operations into China, sending more than 100 operatives there under the cover of monitoring Sino-South Korean relations. This move apparently caused problems for other China-based hard currency operations run by the Ministry of Foreign Trade, the SSD's General Security Bureau, the MPS, and the MPAF.

459   "North Korea Requiring Diplomats to Raise Millions in U.S. Currency," *UPI*, September 29, 2015. In the lead up to the celebration of the 70th anniversary of the founding of the Party in October 2015, reports surfaced in the international media that North Korean RGB agents in the field were required to deliver $200,000 in "kickback" money to the regime or face penalties. According to Japanese reporting, this led many spies to turn away from their normal duties to focus on generating foreign currency.

460   The GDP of North Korea is estimated to be $40 billion according to the International Trade Office of Korea. The domestic economy has either contracted or grown at one percent in recent years, according to South Korean government estimates based on limited data, with annual exports of about $3 billion, falling well short of the total amount of imports.

461   "Pyongyang Imposes Duty on Diplomats To Obtain Foreign Currency To Raise Funds To Celebrate 10 October 70th Anniversary of Founding of Workers' Party of Korea," *Sankei Shimbun*, September 29, 2015. In an indication of the Royal Economy's declining condition, Kim Jong-un placed increasing pressure on the North Korean diplomatic corps in the summer of 2015 to raise funds ahead of the Party's 70th anniversary in October. Each embassy staff member was responsible for raising $1 million in U.S. currency to be passed to the regime. Average North Korean citizens were also asked to contribute $6 per household (twice the monthly salary of the average North Korean worker) to offset the celebration expenses. The

fund for the Supreme Leader is estimated by some sources to be approximately $100 million per year.[462] There are rumors that the Supreme Leader also receives a tax on the underground economy, which results from trade in the markets, but information on this source of funding is extremely opaque.

- **North Korean official trade** is estimated at approximately $6 billion, almost exclusively with China.[463, 464] Each transaction is accompanied by a kickback to the Supreme Leader's office.

- **Foreign currency of $10,000 or more** coming across the border into North Korea is monitored by the regime and is subject to a tax that goes into the coffers of the Supreme Leader.[465]

- There are some **50,000-100,000 North Koreans working overseas**. They send approximately $300 million a year back to the home country, some of which is siphoned off by the state.[466] In addition, these projects generate between $2-3 billion in hard currency for the regime, much of it presumably going into the coffers of the Royal Economy.

regime also requested that the General Association of Korean Residents in Japan, (Chosen Soren or Chongryon), to attend a ceremony marking the 70th anniversary of the Party's founding. Each official would be required to pay about $2,500 (300,000 yen) in participation fee and other expenses, such as transit fees. As a result, Ho Chong-man, the head of Chongryon, decided not to attend the ceremony.

462   The governing budget for the Cabinet is approximately $200 million per year. Author discussions in Seoul with sources familiar with the North Korean budget, 2013 and 2014.

463   Scott Snyder, "China-North Korea Trade in 2013: Business as Usual," *Forbes Asia*, March 27, 2014. China's 2013 trade with North Korea grew by over ten percent from that recorded in 2012 to $6.5 billion. This steady growth in Sino-North Korean trade relations occurred despite rising political risks resulting from North Korea's political succession in 2011 and 2012, and Pyongyang's nuclear and long-range missile tests in 2012 and 2013. It also weathered the shock of Jang Song-taek's execution, but the long-term implications of this incident remain to be seen. In 2012, trade with South Korea, which the Bank of Korea excludes from North Korea's trade statistics, was worth $1.97 billion dollars, up fifteen percent from 2011. Almost all of that trade came from the Kaesong Industrial Complex, which was shut down during the 2013 crisis.

464   Alastair Gale, "Cash Crunch Hits North Korea's Elite," *Wall Street Journal*, October 8, 2015. China absorbs as much as 90 percent of North Korea's exports, compared to around 50 percent in the early 2000s. According to Chinese customs data, North Korean exports to China in 2014 totalled $2.9 billion. This is compared to $10 million in North Korean exports to Russia in 2014. Over the last year (mid-2014 to mid-2015), according to Chinese data, the value of North Korean exports to China has fallen by 9.8 percent. In addition, Beijing's attempts to scale back its bloated steel industry, as well as the steep decline in coal prices, is having a dramatic impact on North Korea's ability to generate foreign currency.

465   According to data from the Korea Trade Investment Promotion Agency [KOTRA], North Korea brings in about $230 million in foreign currency per year. The Korea Development Institute [KDI] puts that number at $440 million per year.

466   "After Three Years of Kim Jong-un, Skyscrapers Popping Up on Pyongyang's Skyline," *Hankyoreh*, December 29, 2014.

- **Tourism** represents a growing source of hard currency. An estimated 300,000 tourists from China and other countries visit North Korea on an annual basis.[467]
- **Foreign investment** in North Korea is difficult to track. North Korean authorities claim to have secured $1.44 billion in investment from 306 foreign companies. The actual figure of foreign investment, according to outside sources, is closer to $400 million, with all of this in the Rason Special Economic Zone (SEZ).[468]
- **Sale of cell phones** is a growth market for the regime. The meteoric increase in cell phone availability has provided a steady funding stream from the population. The registration fee is $140 and the minimum price for a new phone in 2012 was an average of $300. From 2008-2012, nearly two million people signed up for cell service, netting the regime a profit of approximately $720 million ($280 million in registration fees and $440 million in phone sales).[469]

c. Jang's Interference in the Kim Family Business

Just as his father had done before his death, Kim Jong-un turned to Jang Song-taek as a guarantor of the Royal Economy's viability soon after coming to power. It was expected that Jang would be able to leverage his relations with the senior Chinese leadership to bring a substantial amount of hard currency into the regime, which would reinvigorate the People's Economy as well as the Royal Economy.

In the last months of Kim Jong-il's life, Jang Song-taek had been engaged in frequent talks with China, which came to fruition at the end of 2011 with the agreement to jointly develop the Rajin-Sonbong SEZ in the northeastern corner of the isolated country.[470] According to reports at the time, China planned to invest $3 billion to build infrastructure in the SEZ, such as railroads, power plants, and other facilities by 2020.[471] North Korea would provide cheap labor.[472]

---

467   Ibid.
468   Ibid.
469   Hong Sung-Ki, "South Korea Needs New Policy on North Korea in Kim Jong Un Era," op. cit.
470   The zone is seven times larger than the Kaesong Industrial Complex (65.7 square kilometers), the site of inter-Korean economic cooperation. The agreement entitled China to develop three new piers and granted them the right to use the piers for fifty years.
471   These estimates proved to be "wildly optimistic" and ultimately unrealizable.
472   Choi Yoo-Sik, "China To Invest $3 Billion in DPRK Special Economic Zone," *The Chosun Ilbo*, February 16, 2012.

The success of this venture seemed to solidify Jang's position within Kim Jong-un's inner circle, which began to evolve. The powerful Chief of the GSD, Ri Yong-ho, who had risen significantly in influence at the Third Party Conference, now appeared to be in an increasingly precarious position. Choe Ryong-hae and Jang Song-taek appeared to be the beneficiaries of Ri's downfall. Choe benefited politically and Jang benefited in terms of the economy. Following Ri Yong-ho's purge in June 2012, rumors emerged that at the source of his power struggle with Jang Song-taek was the latter's schemes to transfer control over several hard currency operations from the military to the KWP Administrative Department. After Ri's fall, Jang secured control over Department 54, the GSD unit responsible for supplies and necessities for the armed forces. Within a year, Department 54 became the centerpiece of Jang's network, commanding twenty-four coal mines and other foreign currency operations across the country.[473]

An investigation after Kim Kyong-hui's stroke in the fall of 2012 allegedly revealed that Jang controlled multiple funding streams into the Royal Economy to an extent that the Kim family had not anticipated. Not only had he used his position as Vice Chairman of the NDC and Department 54 to siphon off funds from military-run operations, he had also used his growing power within the leadership to engineer the transfer of administrative control over lucrative operations, such as trade companies and mines, to the KWP Administrative Department, including some operations belonging to Office 39.[474] This not only made it easier for Jang's faction to pay its loyalty tax, it also made it more difficult for other critical parts of the regime to demonstrate their worth to the Leader.[475]

---

473   Kim Min-Seo. "When Its Investment is Defrauded by the North, China Says that It Can No Longer Put Up With North Korea," *Segye Ilbo*, February 16, 2015. Department 54 managed North Korean coal sales to China, an especially lucrative hard currency operation. Between 2004 and 2013, China tried to advance into North Korea by investing in twenty-one mines, which resulted in making investment in equipment or acquiring mining concessions through joint ventures with six of the mines. These were not just coal mines, but mines involved in the extraction of other critical minerals such as iron and copper.

474   "N. Korea Abolishes Secret Fund Organ for Kim Jong-il," *Kyodo World Service*, October 18 2012. In October 2012, rumors began to emerge that Kim Jong-un had eliminated large parts of the Royal Economy apparatus, shifting their roles and missions to the Cabinet. He allegedly abolished Office 39 because of its close ties to the military, which had been forged during the "Military First" (*Songun*) era and were now suspect in the aftermath of Ri Yong-ho's purge. According to regional media, Kim was eager to weaken the military's vested interests and shift more resources and investment toward economic development. These reports also contended that Kim's efforts to streamline the economy had led to the elimination of Office 38 with many of its responsibilities being transferred to the Cabinet's "Moranbong Bureau." It is most likely that these stories were false. The rumors were likely sparked by Jang's activities, which may have raised questions inside the regime about the stability of the Royal Economy apparatus.

475   According to some sources, despite the profits from these operations that were accruing to Jang's apparatus, he was taking an increasingly larger cut of the loyalty tax for himself.

Chart 12: Jang's Tapping into Military Funds

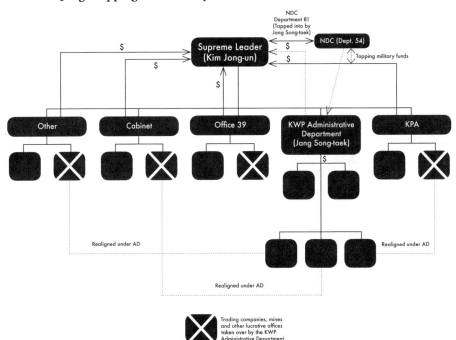

After Jang Song-taek's execution, an additional theory emerged about his interference in the Royal Economy. South Korean sources suggested that his greatest transgression was the embezzlement of Kim family funds in banks in Asia and Europe.[476] The amount of these funds is estimated to be in the hundreds of millions, if not billions, of dollars. Many of the individuals responsible for managing them had ties to Jang Song-taek.[477] While there is no tangible proof that he was skimming from foreign accounts, there is circumstantial evidence that he might have had access to these accounts. As noted earlier, his August 2012 visit to China may have been a secret mission to secure Kim family funds from a number of Chinese banks.

There are numerous theories about how Jang Song-taek planned to use the funds he was drawing from the Royal Economy. Some have suggested he was building a "war chest" in order to exercise even greater power within the regime by forcing a collapse of the Royal Economy, thus making the Supreme Leader a dependent puppet. Others believe he was working with China to position North Korea for meaningful economic reforms and the funds would be critical to this

476 "N. Korean Purge All About The Money," *The Chosun Ilbo*, December 12, 2013.
477 This most likely accounts for the rumors that emerged in early 2014 of Ri Yong-su's execution before he emerged with his appointment as Foreign Minister.

endeavor. Regardless of Jang's motives, Kim Jong-un most likely viewed his uncle's actions as dangerous to his own control of the regime.[478]

d. Restructuring the Royal Economy

The removal of Jang Song-taek from the leadership was the first move in what appears to be a major revamping of the command and control structure of the Royal Economy. The new structure is still unclear and assessments of who controls what are based on rumors emerging from various defector networks.[479]

In the days after Jang's execution, Kim Jong-un reportedly issued orders on the reorganization of the regime's foreign currency earning apparatus. Notably, the parts of the apparatus that were tied to the KWP Administrative Department were dissolved and reintegrated into the KWP OGD.

- **Department 54**, which had been at the center of Jang's growing "empire," was placed under Office 39.
- **Office 39** was removed from the KWP FAD and transferred to the KWP OGD.
- **Daesong Bank** was separated from Office 39.
- **Department 44**, which oversees the military's foreign currency earnings, was reportedly moved from the GSD to the GPB.[480]
- Approximately **thirty trade companies**, which had been moved to the Cabinet by Jang Song-taek, were returned to the military.[481]

---

478   As a final indignity in November 2013, soon after Jang Song-taek's arrest, Kim Jong-un was informed of a debt of $38 million that Department 54 had incurred in China as a result of several agreements with Chinese trade organizations and companies that were allegedly tied to Chinese security organizations. According to sources in Seoul and Beijing familiar with the issue, Kim Jong-un tasked Office 39 with repaying the debt.

479   "Kim Jong-un Orders Agents Overseas to Return Home to Achieve Generational Change," *Sankei Shimbun*, December 22, 2014. According to recent regional reporting, Kim Jong-un has issued orders calling for the return to North Korea of agents, smugglers, and other officials assigned to long-term overseas duties. Some suggest that this could be tied to a generational turnover. It, however, could undermine some of the on-going hard currency operations since it would interfere with transaction networks based on personal connections with those in local underground communities necessary for foreign currency trading.

480   Choe Ryong-hae, who was the Director of the GPB at the time, allegedly tried to persuade Kim Jong-un to put Department 54 under the GPB.

481   "Kim Jong Un Reorganizes North Korea's Foreign Currency Earning System; Kim Yo-jong to Oversee Party's Foreign Currency Earnings," *NK Intellectuals Solidarity*, January 10, 2014.

In addition to these reforms, Kim Jong-un placed his younger sister, Kim Yo-jong, in charge of the more critical foreign currency funding streams in an apparent effort to exert greater control over the Royal Economy. According to one defector group, she has authority over the Party's foreign currency earning bodies, including Office 38 and Office 39, as well as direct oversight of the international financial transaction organs, such as Daesong Bank. In addition, she has taken over the substantial portfolio that her aunt, Kim Kyong-hui, used to control, including the Kyonghung and Rakwon guidance bureaus.[482] At the end of October 2014, South Korean media reported that Kim Yo-jong had married a senior official in Office 39.[483]

Chart 13: Royal Economy Lines of Control under Kim Jong-un

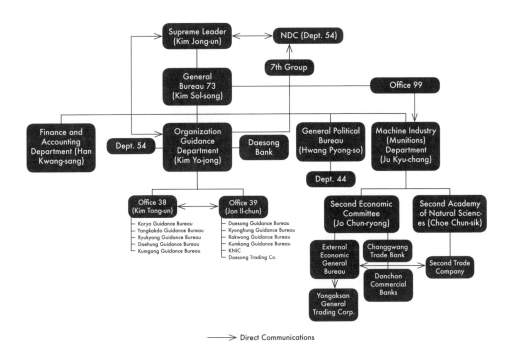

---

482   Ibid.

483   Kim Myeong-Seong, "Kim Jong-un's Sister 'Married' Senior Party Official Managing Slush Funds," *The Chosun Ilbo*, October 29, 2014. In January 2015, the South Korean media reported that Kim had married one of Choe Ryong-hae's sons. Speculation was that it was his second son, Choe Song. "NK leader's sister weds son of Choe Ryong-hae," *Yonhap News Agency*, January 2, 2015.

While the reporting on this restructuring is highly speculative, it is consistent with the North Korean media's treatment of Kim Yo-jong as the "reincarnation" of her aunt in the Kim Jong-un era. The question is whether Kim Yo-jong is simply a figurehead or an actual manager. More than likely, she is being groomed to assume the role of the Kim family financier. Actual day-to-day Kim family management of the Royal Economy probably resides in the hands of senior advisors to Kim Jong-un, such as his half-sister Kim Sol-song. Many Pyongyang-watchers believe that the transition of this oversight responsibility to Kim Yo-jong will occur in concert with Kim Jong-un's full consolidation of power.

4. The Future of the Royal Economy

Created in the 1970s to support the first hereditary transition of power from Kim Il-sung to Kim Jong-il, the Royal Economy has steadily grown to become the regime's primary source of revenue. The very stability of the regime, to say nothing of the survival of the Supreme Leader, is based on this highly secretive part of the economy.[484]

The Royal Economy has evolved over the last four decades, shifting its dependence between various sources of funding. Much of the funding comes from mundane commercial activities, such as the sale of seafood, gold, coal, iron ore, and the export of labor. However, as has been made abundantly clear to the outside world, there is an illegal side to many of North Korea's revenue-generating activities. In the 1990s and 2000s, much of this funding was tied to illegal weapons sales, drugs, and counterfeiting. This has since become the legacy of covert yet bureaucratic-sounding entities, such as Office 38 and Office 39. But in recent years, many of these illicit sources of funding have been severely curtailed by the efforts of the international community. Programs, such as the Proliferation Security Initiative (PSI), and enhanced measures to track North Korea's finances through the banking system have severely constrained the regime. This has forced North Korea to look elsewhere, such as building statues for other dictators and trading gold and other precious metals, where transactions are exclusively cash-based, leaving no paper trails.

---

484   A very interesting series of articles by Jonathan Corrado of Georgetown University and *Daily NK* collectively entitled, "Economic Incentives Make Good Bait for Reform," suggests that the long term pathway for North Korea is dependent on the eventual extinction of Fearpolitik and gift politics, the later initimately tied to the Royal Economy. See Jonathan Corrado, "Part I: A New Approach," *Daily NK*, June 25, 2015; ———— , "Part II: The Path to Healthy Cash & Market Receptivity," *Daily NK*, July 6, 2015; and ———— , "Part III: Helping North Korea find a better self interest," *Daily NK*, July 17, 2015.

Despite the regime's efforts to shift to other money-making ventures, the Royal Economy has not recovered the same scale of foreign currency generation that it had in the early 2000s. During this time, weapon sales, drugs, and counterfeiting alone brought nearly $2 billion into the regime's coffers. At the same time, the Supreme Leader's needs are growing. In addition to keeping up a lavish lifestyle of palaces and yachts, Kim Jong-un faces an uphill battle to consolidate his power, which will take at least two years to complete. In 2012, his gift-giving reportedly reached record levels of over $600 million, twice the highest level his father spent to secure the leadership's loyalty. In the absence of progress in the People's Economy, Kim Jong-un will remain constrained in his ability to show his credentials as a leader that the nation must follow. Thus, he will have to continue to lean heavily on the Royal Economy to sustain the regime.

If the stories about Kim Yo-jong becoming a critical player inside the Royal Economy are true, it suggests that the Kim family has learned a lesson from the Jang Song-taek affair and is strengthening its grip on many critical funds inside the regime. However, this hoarding of hard currency assets will only work so long as Kim Jong-un is respected and feared as the Supreme Leader. If the situation persists, it could exacerbate the already fierce power struggles at the second and third echelons over continuously decreasing shares of control of hard currency operations. Even more threatening to Kim's own power is that the Royal Economy could become the center of future power struggles within the Kim family. As Kim Jong-un consolidates his power, he will have to continue to purge potential rivals and sources of opposition, even within his own family. If the Royal Economy begins to contribute to the escalation of such struggles, it will further deplete the funding Kim needs to secure the loyalty of the wider leadership. The result could be a gradual breakdown of control.

D. CHAPTER SEVEN: THE INTERNAL SECURITY APPARATUS— PROTECTING THE SUPREME LEADER

In 2012, HRNK published a book by this author entitled *Coercion, Control, Surveillance, and Punishment: An Examination of the North Korean Police State*, which examines the institutions and processes surrounding how the regime deals with crime and punishment. This chapter will not only update this work, but will also expand the analysis to include other relevant bodies, the KWP OGD and the GC, two bodies dedicated to the protection of the Supreme Leader and the implementation of his orders.

Any study of the Supreme Leader's apparatus of power is incomplete without an examination of the Praetorian Guard. This is the part of the leadership that keeps eyes and ears on the regime, and provides the physical protection that prevents any individual or faction from wresting power from the center. It conducts night raids of people's houses to look for illicit videos and contraband. Members of the Praetorian Guard undergo arduous training to ensure that they can protect the Supreme Leader. According to some defector sources, they are the real power behind the regime.

As suggested in previous chapters, the internal security apparatus is closely tied to Kim Jong-un's personal apparatus. These are the institutions and individuals that Kim and his retinue deal with on a daily basis. They are the foundation of the regime. If they were to weaken or become corrupt, the Kim family regime would face peril, crumble, and possibly collapse. Ironically, it is also the one part of the regime that the Supreme Leader must be the most wary of.

1. EVOLUTION OF THE PRAETORIAN GUARD UNDER KIM JONG-UN

It is often assumed that in authoritarian and totalitarian regimes, the Praetorian Guard is part of the inner sanctum. By virtue of its trusted status, it is also assumed that turnover and evolution among these institutions is rare or impossible. History shows that this is not the case. The death of Caligula clearly demonstrates what can happen when a leader places too much trust in or turns a blind eye to the Praetorian Guard. Stalin frequently purged those closest to him, but in the end, his Chief of Police, Laverenti Beria, may have been plotting Stalin's downfall when he died. Hitler moved quickly to destroy one part of his guard in order to consolidate his power when he went after Ernst Röhm in the

Night of the Long Knives. Saddam Hussein, like Stalin, also frequently reshuffled elements within his personal apparatus, including the Republican Guard and the Special Republican Guard. Kim Jong-il, taking a page from Adolf Hitler's leadership style, was fond of setting up rivalries throughout his apparatus of power to keep the Praetorian Guard more focused on each other and subservient to himself. There is no reason to expect that Kim Jong-un will be any different. In his first three years in power, the Praetorian Guard has stayed out of the public eye. There have been some personnel changes and it has been the subject of many rumors. While Jang Song-taek's purge has reconfigured part of the apparatus, there are some indications that major changes could be impending.

a. Last Days of the Kim Jong-il Era

As with the other parts of Kim Jong-un's apparatus, the Praetorian Guard began to come into focus at the Third Party Conference in 2010. In April, Kim Jong-il issued Supreme Commander's Order No. 0046, promoting two officers to senior ranks within the armed forces: Yun Jong-rin was promoted to General and Kim Song-tok was promoted to Colonel General.[485] While the promotions went largely unnoticed by the international press, a cursory reading of the promotion order highlighted the importance of the event.

While we firmly believe that the commanding officers of Unit 963, who grew up in the bosom of the party and the leader [Suryong], to hereafter faithfully uphold the party's leadership; to firmly guard, with gun barrel, the juche revolutionary cause; and to fulfill its honorable mission and duty as the main force of the revolution in the construction of a powerful socialist state...[486]

The GC is designated as Unit 963. In this promotion cycle, Kim Jong-il was ensuring that the part of the Praetorian Guard most responsible for his and his heir apparent's lives was properly recognized. Yun Jong-rin had occupied the post of Commander of the unit since 2004 and Kim Song-tok was its Chief Political Officer.

---

485   "Comrade Kim Jong Un, Supreme Commander of the Korean People's Army [KPA], Inspected the Artillery Company Under KPA Unit 963," *Nodong Sinmun*, December 2, 2014. Yun Jong-rin disappeared from public view until December 2014. When he reappeared, he had been demoted to Colonel General. Kim Song-tok retained his rank.

486   "The Korean People's Army [KPA] Supreme Commander's Order No 0046," *KCBS*, April 22, 2010.

Five months later, at the Third Party Conference, Yun Jong-rin was made a member of the KWP CMC,[487] thus solidifying him as a key advisor and protégé of Kim Jong-un, who was appointed to his one and only post as CMC Vice Chairman.[488]

In addition to Yun Jong-rin, several other members of the internal security apparatus received appointments to key Party bodies. Ju Sang-song, Minister of People's Security, was appointed a member of the Politburo. U Tong-chuk, First Vice Director of the SSD, and Kim Chang-sop, Director of the SSD Political Bureau, were appointed alternate members of the Politburo.[489] U Tong-chuk, Kim Won-hong, Commander of the MSC, and Kim Kyong-ok, First Vice Director of the KWP OGD, were appointed members of the KWP CMC. Essentially, the five parts that make up the Praetorian Guard apparatus (GC, MPS, SSD, OGD, and MSC) were included in the promotions associated with the very beginnings of the Kim Jong-un era.

At this point in its development, Kim Jong-un's apparatus was not completely independent. It was tied to his father's apparatus of power, as well as that of Jang Song-taek's KWP Administrative Department, which had formal oversight of the SSD and MPS. As the chart below reveals, the foundation for a dual system of internal security was well established before Kim Jong-il's death.

Chart 14: Command and Control of the Internal Security Apparatus

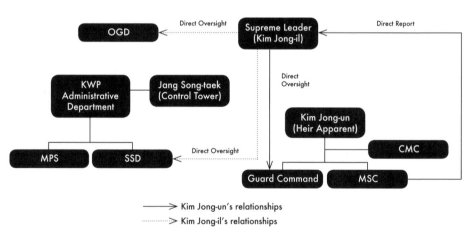

487   "Members, Alternate Members of Central Committee, WPK," *KCNA*, September 28, 2010. Yun Jong-rin and Kim Song-tok were made members of the KWP Central Committee at the Third Party Conference.
488   "Central Military Commission of WPK Organized," *KCNA*, September 28, 2010.
489   Kim Pyong-hae, a former official in the OGD, was appointed an alternate member of the Politburo, Secretary for Personnel Affairs, and Director of the KWP Cadre Affairs Department.

In the months following the Party conference, Kim Jong-il began to focus on ensuring the long-term survival of his heir. Since Kim Jong-il's stroke in 2008, it was widely speculated that any collective leadership that was built around Kim Jong-un would be unstable at best and most likely would relegate the heir apparent to a figurehead. To ensure that this could not happen, Kim Jong-il began to realign the loyalties within the internal security apparatus to make it more difficult for any other member of the senior North Korean leadership to assume more power than his own chosen successor.

The first step of this strategy took place in January 2011 with the dismissal and alleged execution of Ryu Kyong, the SSD's Vice Director and Chief of Bureau 2 (Counter-espionage Bureau). Ryu oversaw approximately 50,000 counterintelligence agents dedicated to identifying spies and dissidents within the regime. His close ties to Kim Jong-il and his growing power were reflected in his promotion to Colonel General on the eve of the Third Party Conference. His rising status, however, made him a natural rival of both Jang Song-taek and U Tong-chuk. In addition, his pervasive presence within the secret police apparatus reportedly made it difficult to carve out a role for Kim Jong-un, who became increasingly tied to the organization.

According to sources inside North Korea, Ryu was summoned to one of Kim Jong-il's residences, where he was arrested by the GC. He was later interrogated and secretly executed.[490] His removal was followed by the purge of over 100 SSD personnel. While some sources suggested that Ryu was removed for "being a double agent," the more likely cause was probably tied to succession politics. Senior defector sources in South Korea suggest that Ryu's sacrifice might have been tied to Kim Jong-il and Kim Jong-un's efforts to secure U Tong-chuk's loyalty and support.[491] If this speculation is true, it contradicted the general consensus at the time among Pyongyang-watchers that U Tong-chuk belonged to Jang Song-taek's patronage network.[492] While he no doubt reported up to Jang in the formal chain of command, U was also in a position to serve as a counterweight to Jang's power within the security apparatus or, at the very least, to provide the heir apparent with situational awareness of his uncle's activities.

In 2011, both Kim Jong-un and U Tong-chuk were featured prominently in SSD-related events profiled in North Korean media. On April 15, 2011, Kim

---

490   "Exclusive: DPRK Security Head Ryu Kyong Purged," *NKChosun.com*, May 20, 2011.
491   Author's discussions in Seoul in May 2011. According to defector sources, while the GC carried out the arrest, U Tong-chuk oversaw the operation. These same sources contend that U had "recently shifted his complete support to Kim Jong-un."
492   Many South Korean and Chinese Pyongyang-watchers placed U Tong-chuk in Jang Song-taek's patronage network as late as 2010. They based this assessment on defector accounts and U's rise in prominence after Jang's return from exile in 2007.

Jong-un was listed as one of his father's cohorts at a performance of the Art Squad of KPA Unit 10215, which is reportedly tied to the SSD.[493] The next month, U Tong-chuk took part in a high-profile meeting between Kim Jong-il and a delegation led by M.Y. Fradkov, the Director of Russia's External Intelligence Bureau.[494]

The restructuring continued in March 2011 with the dismissal of Ju Sang-song from his post as Minister of People's Security due to illness.[495] This move was surprising not only because of Chu's rising profile, but also because it was highly abnormal for a member of the KWP Political Bureau and the MPS to be relieved from his post for the ambiguous reason of "illness."[496] Outside speculation about the reasons for his dismissal ranged from fallout due to Chinese protests over border security to a mysterious "Mangyongdae Incident" involving a protest near Kim Il-sung's birth home.[497, 498]

Regardless of the reason, the appointment of Ju's replacement, Ri Myong-su, appeared to have significant implications for the succession. Unlike Ju, who lacked a significant power base and whose allegiance to Jang Song-taek was ambiguous, Ri was a powerful figure in his own right with strong, enduring ties to Kim Jong-il. Before assuming administrative duties within the NDC, Ri was the Director of the GSD Operations Bureau, an organization that Kim Jong-il relied on to provide direction for the armed forces. According to some sources, Ri Myong-su was also one of the first members of the high command to support Kim Jong-un.[499]

493   Michael Madden, "Jong Un Attends Guidance of SSD (MSS) Unit," *North Korea Leadership Watch*, October 26, 2010. Some sources go so far as to suggest that this unit designation actually refers to the SSD. This assessment is based on previous Kim Jong-il inspections, including one in October 2010 shortly after the Third Party Conference, which included Kim Jong-un, U Tong-chuk, and Kim Chang-sop.
494   According to several sources, Kim Jong-un met Fradkov and other officials. If true, U most likely served as the heir apparent's main escort.
495   "DPRK National Defense Commission Decision No. 8," *KCBS*, March 16, 2011. The position remained vacant until April 2011, when Ri Myong-su was appointed Ju's successor at the fourth session of the 12th SPA.
496   "NDC Decision on Dismissing People's Security Minister Ju Sang Song," *KCBS*, March 16, 2011. Interestingly, Ju was not publicly retired from his posts in the Politburo or the NDC.
497   "South Korean Government Confirms Top North Korean Security Official Dismissed for Mishandling China, North Korea Border Control," *Yomiuri Shimbun*, April 9, 2011.
498   Kang Cheol-hwan, "Story of 'Mangyongdae Incident' That Led to Sacking of North's People's Security Minister," *The Chosun Ilbo*, April 9, 2011.
499   As a former Chief of Staff of the Third Corps and head of the GSD Operations Bureau, Ri Myong-su had a unique understanding of the command and control nodes in and around Pyongyang. This knowledge, combined with his control of the MPS, made him an important player in any future succession scenario.

According to South Korean sources, he became one of Kim Jong-un's mentors soon after his designation as heir apparent in 2009.[500]

As for the MSC, its profile continued to grow. Kim Won-hong was increasingly seen on guidance inspections and in the presence of Kim Jong-un. While the link between the heir apparent and the MSC was not made public and was not even the subject of speculation, the fact that the regime was increasingly tying the Party Center, Kim Jong-un, with "Military First" (*Songun*) politics suggested that the MSC would likely continue its vaunted status within the security apparatus.

Rumors and speculation regarding the KWP OGD and the GC were generally lacking in 2011. However, there were reports of GC tank movements as part of an exercise in the Taedong River area of eastern Pyongyang in February 2011.[501] The next month, additional reporting described an additional fifty GC tanks being deployed to the Pyongyang area in response to the Jasmine Revolution in North Africa and the Middle East.[502] Finally, Kim Jong-il and Kim Jong-un apparently paid a visit to Unit 985 of the GC in the immediate aftermath of Muammar Qaddafi's death.[503] All three of these events suggest that while the GC did not suffer the turnover that impacted other parts of the internal security apparatus, its loyalty and operational status were not far from the Supreme Leader's thoughts.

b. Early Kim Jong-un Era

In the early days of the Kim Jong-un era, the Praetorian Guard was on prominent display. On the Funeral Committee, several members of the internal security apparatus were listed among the first 125 members of a 232-member list.

500   An Yong-Hyeon, "Kim Jong-il's Son Effectively Controls Security Forces," *The Chosun Ilbo*, April 13, 2011. According to this source, Kim Jong-un was groomed as the successor in the NDC Administrative Bureau.

501   Yun Il-Geon, "Tanks Ready to be Used Against Uprising in Pyongyang," *The Chosun Ilbo*, February 16, 2011.

502   An Yong-Hyeon, "More Tanks in the Streets of Pyongyang," *The Chosun Ilbo*, March 7, 2011.

503   Cho Sung-Ho, "NK Leader Rushes to Defense Command After Gadhafi's Death," *Dong-A Ilbo*, October 26, 2011.

Table 8: Members of the Internal Security Apparatus on Kim Jong-il's Funeral Committee List

Name	Position	Ranking
Jang Song-taek	Director, KWP Administrative Department	19
U Tong-chuk	First Vice Director, SSD	25
Kim Chang-sop	Director, SSD Political Department	26
Ri Ul-sol	Former Commander, GC	31
Kim Kyong-ok	First Vice Director, KWP OGD	56
Kim Won-hong	Commander, MSC	58
Yun Jong-rin	Commander, GC	64
Ri Myong-su	Minister of the People's Armed Forces	74
Ri Pyong-sam	Political Director, Korean People's Internal Security Forces (KPISF)	83
Kim In-sik	Commander, KPISF	86
Hwang Pyong-so	Vice Director, KWP OGD	124

At the funeral procession on December 28, 2011, Jang Song-taek and U Tong-chuk accompanied Kim Jong-un as he walked beside the car carrying his father's casket. Kim Won-hong was a constant presence in the new Leader's first guidance inspections of military units across the country.

Image 26: Kim Jong-il's Funeral Procession. Jang Song-taek is on the left side of the hearse behind Kim Jong-un. U Tong-chuk is at the rear right bumper of the hearse behind Ri Yong-ho, Kim Yong-chun, and Kim Jong-gak. (Source: KCTV, December 28, 2011)

In April 2012, the regime made a number of personnel appointments at the Fourth Party Conference and the Fifth Session of the 12th SPA. Jang Song-taek was elevated to full Politburo member status. Jo Yon-jun, First Vice Director of the KWP OGD, was appointed an alternate member of the Politburo. Kim Won-hong was appointed as the Director of the SSD, the first publicly identified director since the death of Ri Chin-su in the early 1980s. Kim was also appointed a full member of the Politburo, a member of the CMC, and a member of the NDC. Kim replaced U Tong-chuk, who was removed from the NDC.[504] Ri Myong-su was also appointed as a member of the Politburo, CMC, and NDC, replacing Ju Sang-song in the NDC. Ri Pyong-sam, the Director of the KPISF Political Bureau, was made an alternate member of the Politburo. Finally, the successor to Kim Won-hong as head of the MSC was not made public. According to South Korean reports, Jo Kyong-chol assumed that position.

Days after these meetings, a surprising rumor emerged in the South Korean press claiming that Jang Song-taek had taken control of the GC. This claim was based on the fact that Jang had appeared wearing a military uniform of the GC in the days after Kim Jong-il's death.[505] The report went further to suggest that Yun Jong-rin had been relieved of his command and replaced with an unnamed Jang protégé. The fact that Yun remained out of sight for two months lent some credence to this report. However, Yun reappeared on the leadership rostrum in June 2012,[506] thus putting an end to speculation that Kim Jong-un had turned over responsibility for his personal safety to his uncle.

In January 2013, Ri Myong-su disappeared from sight. Three months later, at the Central Committee Plenum, North Korean media announced that he had been replaced by Choe Pu-il,[507] a First Vice Chief of the GSD. Choe, who is considered to be close to Kim Jong-un and was already a member of the

504   "N. Korea Purged Senior Intelligence Official: source," *Yonhap News Agency*, April 17, 2012. Some South Korean reports suggested that U Tong-chuk might have been purged or suffered a stroke.

505   Lee Yong-Su, "Exclusive: Jang Song-taek Gains Control of Kim Jong-un Guard Unit," *The Chosun Ilbo*, April 30, 2012.

506   "Central report meeting held to commemorate the 48th anniversary of Kim Jong-il starting work at the Party Central Committee," *KCTV*, June 18, 2012.

507   Indications are that Choe assumed the position as early as February 2013. On the anniversary of Kim Jong-il's birth (February 16), Kim Jong-un visited the Kumsusan Palace of the Sun with key members of his security apparatus. It was yet another opportunity for the Pyongyang-watching community to confirm the members of the Praetorian Guard. In addition to Jang Song-taek and Kim Kyong-hui, the delegation included (in order of mention): Kim Won-hong (SSD), Kim Kyong-ok (OGD), Yun Jong-rin (GC), Choe Pu-il (MPS), and Jo Kyong-chol (MSC). Ri Myong-su last appeared in state media as Minister of People's Security on January 5, 2013, when Pyongyang radio reported his attendance at an intra-ministry meeting to implement the tasks outlined in Kim Jong-un's New Year's address.

KWP CMC,[508] was appointed to the Politburo as an alternate member.[509] Shortly thereafter, at the Seventh Session of the 12th SPA, Choe was appointed to the NDC. In June 2013, he was also promoted to the rank of General.[510] While Ri Myong-su continued to appear in public, he was a political non-entity. In March 2014, he was not even elected as a deputy to the SPA, suggesting that he had also lost all of his Party posts.[511]

Chart 15: Internal Security Apparatus in 2013

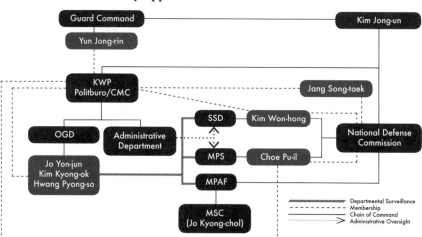

Later in the month, Kim Won-hong was featured prominently as the only member of the internal security apparatus to be at a meeting of Kim Jong-un's "National Security Council."[512] At the meeting, the decision to conduct a third nuclear test was reportedly reached. While very little information on the meeting was provided in the media other than a few photographs, Kim Won-hong was presumably present because of the SSD's responsibilities tied to the test and the nuclear weapons stockpile.

508   According to Pyongyang-watchers in Seoul, Choe Pu-il, unlike his predecessor, was not close to Jang Song-taek. Choe's appointment could have been designed to give Kim Jong-un more direct control over the internal security apparatus.

509   "Comrade Choe Pu-il: Alternate Member of the Political Bureau," *Nodong Sinmun*, April 1, 2013. According to North Korean media, which provided a biographic profile of Choe on his appointment to the Politburo, he assumed command of the MPS in February 2013.

510   "Kim Jong Un Orders to Confer Rank of General Upon Minister of People's Security," *KCNA*, June 11, 2013.

511   Park Byong-Su, "N. Korea To Shuffle Senior Defense Figures Next Month," *Hankyoreh*, March 21, 2014.

512   "Photos of Kim Jong Un With State Security, Foreign Affairs Officials," *KCTV*, January 27, 2013.

Image 27: The attending officials seen clockwise from the left of Kim Jong-un are Kim Kye-gwan, First Vice Minister of Foreign Affairs; Kim Yong-il, KWP Secretary for International Affairs; Kim Won-hong, Minister of State Security; Choe Ryong-hae, Director of the GPB of the KPA; Hyon Yong-chol, Chief of the GSD of the KPA; Hong Sung-mu, Vice Director of the KWP Munitions Department; and Pak To-chun, KWP Secretary for Defense Industry. (Source: KCTV)

The internal security apparatus became a frequent fixture in North Korean media over the course of 2013. Many of these events were tied to the idolization of the Kim family, such as the unveiling of giant statues of Kim Il-sung and Kim Jong-il. In most cases, one or two members from the security apparatus were featured. On some occasions, even more were featured. In July 2013, at the Kim Jong-il University of People's Security, several representatives showed up, including Jang Song-taek, Jo Yon-jun from the OGD, Kim Won-hong and Kim Chang-sop from the SSD, Choe Pu-il from the MPS, and Ri Pyong-sam from the KPISF.[513] The KPISF was the primary beneficiary of the education provided at the university. At this time, the KPISF was on the rise primarily because of its ties to Jang Song-taek. It was later revealed that Jang was under investigation by the KWP OGD and the SSD during this period.

---

513   "Kim Jong Il's Statue Erected At Kim Jong Il University Of People's Security," *KCNA*, July 19, 2013.

Statue Unveiling at the Ministry of People's Security

Choe Pu-il

Jang Song-taek

Jo Yon-jun

Ri Pyong-sam, Kim Chang-sop, Kim Won-hong

Image 28: Choe Pu-il speaking at the unveiling of statues of Kim Il-sung and Kim Jong-il at the Ministry of People's Security in April 2013. (Source: KCTV, 15 April 2013)

As the commotion surrounding Jang Song-taek intensified behind the scenes, curious meetings were convened that brought together members of the security apparatus. Many of them were highly unusual. Kim Jong-un, in his capacity as Supreme Commander, oversaw meetings of the KPA company commanders and instructors from October 22 to 23, 2013, and of KPA security personnel in November 2013. The first meeting was attended by several members of the internal security leadership, including Kim Won-hong, Yun Jong-rin, and Choe Pu-il. The latter meeting was only the second of its kind in the history of the regime; the first such meeting was held by Kim Jong-il in October 1993. While the subject of the meeting was not revealed, it was one of the first meetings where Jo Kyong-chol, the Commander of the secretive MSC, played a prominent role.[514] He and Choe Ryong-hae, Director of the KPA GPB, delivered speeches, suggesting that the

---

514   "Second Meeting of Security Personnel of KPA Held," op. cit.

focus of the meeting was tied to loyalty and security within the armed forces. Kim Won-hong and Hwang Pyong-so were also present at the meeting.

Image 29: On October 25, 2013, Nodong Sinmun carried a panoramic picture of military officers who sat at the leadership rostrum at the fourth meeting of the company commanders and political instructors of the KPA.

Image 30: On November 21, Nodong Sinmun carried photos of Kim Jong-un's guiding the second meeting of security personnel of the KPA at the April 25 House of Culture.

Image 31: Jo Kyong-chol making a speech at the second meeting of security personnel of the KPA.

Image 32: Kim Jong-un at the second meeting of security personnel of the KPA.
He is accompanied by Jo Kyong-chol (1), Kim Won-hong (2), and Hwang Pyong-so (3).

On December 9, 2013, North Korean media revealed the purge that captured the world's attention.[515] *KCTV* ran footage of the special meeting of the Politburo in which Jang Song-taek was removed from all of his posts. As Kim Jong-un and other members of the leadership watched, two members of the GC escorted Jang from

---

515   Yi Ji-Seon, "Kim Jong Un's 'Samjiyon Aides' In The Spotlight As The Rising Stars In North Korean Politics," *The Kyunghyang Shinmun*, December 12, 2013. The final decision regarding Jang Song-taek's fate was reportedly made during Kim Jong-un's visit in early December 2013 to Samjiyeon, which overlooks Paektu Mountain. He was accompanied on the visit by a number of key leaders within the regime, including Kim Won-hong and Hwang Pyong-so. These aides have since been referred to as the "Samjiyeon aides."

the hall. Two seats removed from Kim Jong-un on the leadership rostrum sat Kim Won-hong, and immediately behind him sat Kim Kyong-ok. They were two of the key architects of Jang's downfall.

Image 33: KCTV footage of the December 8 Politburo meeting. Seated on the leadership rostrum are Kim Won-hong (1) and Kim Kyong-ok (2).

Image 34: KCTV footage of the December 8 Politburo meeting. Jang Song-taek being removed from the meeting by members of the GC.

c. The Aftermath of the Purge of Jang Song-taek

The purge and execution of Jang Song-taek on December 12, 2013 was not just a simple matter of removing an individual from the leadership. It had profound implications for the internal security apparatus. Structural changes and subsequent purges to eliminate Jang's protégés have been highlighted by regional media and have given rise to theories about how the regime operates. The KWP OGD has gained its share of notoriety as its cadre have become central to North Korea's political narrative in 2014. This has taken place within the context of an increasingly brutal crackdown inside North Korea that has led some to speculate that the regime's internal power structures may be breaking down. Whether or not this is true, it raises questions about the stability of the regime and the continued viability of the internal security apparatus.

i. Dismantling Jang's Empire

In the days after Jang Song-taek's execution, reports began to surface about purges in the provinces throughout North Korea. The Pyongyang-watching community initially assumed that these purges were tied solely to the eradication of Jang Song-taek's patronage system, but they were later found to fit within a fairly coherent institutional narrative. In essence, it was a return to the state of affairs that existed before Jang's return from exile six years earlier.

Since 1990, when the KWP Administrative Department was merged into the KWP OGD, the local Party organizational departments were in charge of the public security institutions and had authority over personnel management. With Jang Song-taek's appointment as Director of the KWP Administrative Department in 2007, however, administrative departments were established even in the lowest counties to oversee local public security.

By 2013, only two of the more than thirty Central Committee departments had sub-structures that reached the lowest levels of administration—the KWP Administrative Department and OGD. The result of this development was an evolving struggle for power and resources. The majority of cadres in local Party administrative departments had personal connections to Jang Song-taek's network and expanded their authority in each region. In the process, the local Party administrative departments constantly clashed with the organizational departments that formed the core of the local Party.

Following Jang's removal, Kim Jong-un took steps to rearrange the organizational structure and lines of authority tied to the internal security apparatus as it related to the KWP Administrative Department. On December 22, 2013, he reportedly issued an order for all administrative departments at the provincial, city, and county levels to cease their work pending an investigation.[516] This was followed by the purge of those individuals directly tied to Jang Song-taek and his two key lieutenants, Ri Ryong-ha and Jang Su-gil. In the following months, nearly all officials tied to the KWP Administrative Department apparatus were demoted, excluded from future appointments, and reassigned throughout the Party apparatus.[517] In January 2014, Mun Kyong-tok, who was the head of the Pyongyang apparatus, an alternate member of the Politburo, and had once served in the KWP Administrative Department,[518] disappeared from public functions.[519] It was reported that the KWP Administrative Department was unceremoniously disbanded in February 2014. Most of its functions were returned to the KWP OGD.

Command and control of the internal security apparatus was not placed under the KWP OGD, except for the authority to vet senior appointments, which had never left the OGD. [520] Instead, direct oversight for the MPS and the SSD rests with Kim Jong-un in his capacity as the First Chairman of the NDC. In other words, the chain of command that ran up through the KWP Administrative Department to the Vice Chairman of the NDC has been severed.[521] The chart below shows the realignment of authority within the internal security apparatus.

516   "Source Says Purge Spreads to DPRK's Regional Areas After Jang's Execution," *Yonhap News Agency*, December 22, 2013.

517   Ishimaru Jiro, "North Korean Authorities Distribute Jang Song-thaek 'Purge List' to Local Officials," *AsiaPress International*, January 28, 2014. The executions and purges that accompanied these demotions appear to have been widespread, but the stories are largely apocryphal. According to one report, some 3,000 people regarded to be affiliated with "Jang's faction" were displaced from Pyongyang to Ryanggang Province.

518   Mun was a Kim Il-sung Youth League cadre under Jang Song-taek when the latter was Director. In addition, in the late 2000s, he assisted Jang in the KWP Administrative Department. Due to these ties, he was quickly promoted to KWP Secretary for Pyongyang Affairs in 2010.

519   "'Jang's Confidant' Mun Kyong Tok Disappears From the North's Official Events…Has He Been Purged?" *Yonhap News Agency*, February 18, 2014.

520   However, according to defector reporting in late 2015, the OGD established the "7th Group" to assume many of the tasks that the Administrtive Department had once been responsible for. The 7th Group is reportedly an independent agency, but they get comprehensive guidance from the OGD. See Lee Sang-Yong, "Organization, Guidance Department '7th Group' Rises in Power," *Daily NK*, October 1, 2015.

521   Author's interviews with Pyongyang-watchers in Seoul, May 2014.

Chart 16: Command and Control of the Internal Security Apparatus After Jang's Purge

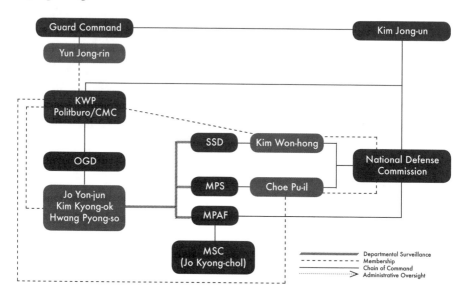

Throughout 2014, reports continued to surface about residual operations tied to Jang's purge. Some of these operations were directly tied to dismantling Jang's network, while others were using the purge as an excuse to institute crackdowns. In January 2014, sources began to discuss how the regime had begun to reach beyond its borders in pursuit of regional traders.[522] These traders are a select group of individuals from every province who are allowed to travel to and from China for cross-border trading purposes. In the past, these traders had mutually beneficial ties with the SSD and MPS, which allowed easy passage to and from China in return for kickbacks and bribes.[523] Following Jang's purge, the necessary visas and permissions were moved from the provincial level to the local level,[524] where more strict surveillance on the family of the regional traders could be easily linked to their travel. In other words,

---

522   Oh Se-Hyeok, "Jang Triggers Trials For Regional Traders," *Daily NK*, January 23, 2014.

523   The system requires applicants to renew their visas, which are normally valid for six months, twice a year. They must apply six months in advance for this process, which requires a trip to Pyongyang. Bribes are an essential element. For instance, it is common practice for traders to pay for sixtieth birthday celebrations for the parents of "gatekeeper" Party and security cadres as a precursor to receiving a valid visa. For the traders, the new measures only add to the burden imposed by the corrupt North Korean system.

524   According to one foreign currency-earner in Pyongsong, if traders want to get a visa issued, they have to obtain the written consent of the head of security assigned to their local "People's Unit" (*In-min-ban*).

it became more difficult for traders to exploit loopholes in the system and gaps in communication within the internal security apparatus.

The Kim Jong-un regime went beyond enforcing stricter surveillance, launching investigations, and carrying out purges. Central to the allegations against Jang Song-taek was that he and the KWP Administrative Department were guilty of "empire-building." As a consequence, part of the remedy was to reallocate the resources and the sources of hard currency throughout the regime. The military was a prime beneficiary of fund-generating bodies that once belonged to Jang's "empire." In August 2014, South Korean media highlighted the example of the Taedonggang Tile Plant, which had once been subordinate to the KWP Administrative Department and run directly by Jang's right-hand man, Jang Su-gil. When Kim Jong-un visited the plant in August 2014, he not only shifted the responsibility of operating the plant to the military, but he also changed its name to the Chollima Tile Plant, thus elminating any ties to its tarnished past.[525]

ii. Rise of the KWP Organization and Guidance Department

As Jang Song-taek's empire dissolved, many within the Pyongyang-watching community began to look for who had gained and who had lost from these developments. Numerous sources contend that the KWP OGD had come out on top after a nearly decade-long battle with Jang Song-taek. Some of these sources went even further to claim that the OGD was now the powerful "puppeteer" behind the young Leader, pulling the strings and even dictating policy. While the argument can certainly be made that the OGD's profile has risen even in North Korean media, the extent of its power relative to the Supreme Leader's is still a matter of speculation.

The first indication of the OGD's rise was visible on the second anniversary of Kim Jong-il's death, when Jo Yon-jun, First Vice Director of the KWP OGD, appeared in the front row for the first time as a part of the memorial service. This was a departure from the first memorial service and, thus, an indication of Jo's rising status within the leadership. That he had played a central role in organizing Jang's purge indicates that Kim's decision to highlight Jo was not just an individual accolade, but also an institutional one.[526]

This was followed in April 2014 by an even more significant change in leadership dynamics that brought the OGD to the center of attention. Hwang

---

525   "North's Kim Jong-un has Changed Everything at a Plant Related to Jang Song-taek," *Yonhap News Agency*, August 4, 2014.

526   "Kim Jong Un Marks Father's Death By Promoting Key Aides," *The Asahi Shimbun*, December 18, 2013.

Pyong-so, another First Vice Director of the KWP OGD, was promoted to the rank of vice marshal.[527] This raised speculation that he might replace Choe Ryong-hae, whose public profile as the top political officer in the armed forces had been waning. In May 2014, this speculation was proven true as Hwang was appointed Director of the GPB.[528] Four months later, Hwang replaced Choe Ryong-hae as Vice Chairman of the NDC, a post he had assumed in April 2014. Over the course of his dramatic rise, Hwang surpassed Choe in the formal ranking, becoming the de facto number-two man in the regime. For many Pyongyang-watchers, this confirmed that the OGD was on the rise and that its influence was spreading throughout the regime.

This speculation was further supported by an examination of the North Korean leadership, which shows that a fraternity of current and past OGD vice directors now holds key positions throughout the regime. A study by South Korean media shows that at the very senior levels of power, both in Pyongyang and in the provinces, the KWP OGD bolsters its institutional ties through command and control responsibilities. Some of these positions, such as Hwang Pyong-so's position as head of the GPB, are held by current members of the OGD. In addition, many more positions are held by former OGD members. It is speculated that the bond between these individuals remains strong, given that the OGD has enhanced influence throughout the regime. The table below includes individuals with current and past ties to the OGD.

Table 9: Regime Members with Ties to the OGD

Name	Post	Relationship to the OGD
Kim Kyong-ok	CMC Member	First Vice Director, OGD[529]
Hwang Pyong-so	GPB Director, Vice Chairman, NDC	First Vice Director, OGD[530]
Jo Yon-jun	Politburo Alternate Member	First Vice Director, OGD
Kim In-kol		Vice Director, OGD

---

527   "Decision on Conferring Title of Vice Marshal of Korean People's Army on Hwang Pyong-so," *KCNA*, April 28, 2014.

528   "May Day Banquet for Workers Given," *KCNA*, May 1, 2014. At this event, Hwang was identified as the Director of the KPA GPB.

529   According to recent rumors in the summer of 2015, Kim Kyong-ok may have retired from his official posts for "health reasons." "How Kim Jong Un Gets Rid Of Threats To His Power," *The Chosun Ilbo*, May 18, 2015.

530   There is debate within the Pyongyang-watching community over whether Hwang remains a First Vice Director of the OGD since assuming his post in the GPB.

Name	Post	Relationship to the OGD
Min Pyong-chol		Vice Director, OGD
Ri Su-yong	Minister of Foreign Affairs	Former official in the OGD
Kim Pyong-hae	Politburo Member, KWP Secretary for Cadre Affairs	Former official in the OGD
Jong Myong-hak	First Vice Chairman, KWP Inspection Committee	Former official in the OGD
Ri Jae-il	First Vice Director, KWP PAD	Former official in the OGD
Choe-hwi	First Vice Director, KWP PAD	Former official in the OGD
Kang Pil-hun	Director of the Political Department, MPS	Former official in the OGD
Jang Pyong-kyu	Prosecutor General	Former official in the OGD
Pak Tae-song	Chief Secretary, South Pyongan Provincial Party Committee	Former Vice Director, KWP OGD[531]
Ri Man-kon	Chief Secretary, North Pyongan Provincial Party Committee	Former Vice Director, KWP OGD
Ri Son-won	Chief Secretary, Ryanggang Provincial Party Committee	Former Vice Director, KWP OGD
Pak Jong-nam	Chief Secretary, Gangwon Provincial Party Committee	Former Vice Director, KWP OGD[532]

The enhanced influence of the OGD was tied not only to its apparent hegemony throughout the leadership system, but also to its evolving relationship with the Kim family. Reports centered on the vacuum left behind by Kim Kyong-hui's decision to remove herself from politics. Both Kim Yo-jong and Kim Sol-song, who were tied to the OGD, were seen by Pyongyang-watchers and senior defectors as increasing their power and responsibility to fill this vacuum.[533] Kim Yo-jong's ties to the OGD have been largely institutional. She has been identified as both a vice

---

531   According to one defector, he also has ties to Kim Jong-un's Personal Secretariat.

532   Yun Wan-Jun, "KWP OGD Making a Clean Sweep of Key Posts in the Party, Military, and Provinces…Even Leading South Korea Policy in Reality," *Dong-A Ilbo*, June 26, 2014.

533   Author's interviews in Seoul, 2014. According to one senior defector interviewed by the author, the KWP OGD is not a homogenous body with a unified point of view and sense of loyalty. In fact, it is made up of at least two groups tied to the Kim family. Many of the OGD officials tied to Kim Jong-un's Personal Secretariat (Kim Kyong-ok, Pak Tae-song, Ri Su-yong, Seo Sang-gi, and Kim Su-yong) have long-standing ties to Kim Sol-song. On the other hand, officials such as Hwang Pyong-so, Jo Yon-jun, and Min Pyong-chul are much closer to Kim Jong-un.

director and a "key official."[534] As for Kim Sol-song, her institutional links to the OGD are not as robust as her half-sister's, but she is married to Kim Kyong-ok according to some rumors.[535]

Whether by design or coincidence, the fortunes of the OGD appeared to diminish later in 2014. Kim Kyong-ok disappeared from public view for several months and was rumored to have been executed. As Choe Ryong-hae returned to prominence in the fall following a brief hiatus, his status once again eclipsed that of Hwang Pyong-so. According to some Pyongyang-watchers, Choe may have even been appointed Director of the OGD.[536] Although the reasoning for this speculation is somewhat suspect and based almost entirely on interpretations of public appearances, it does suggest the possibility that Kim Jong-un may have grown weary of the rumors centered on his role as Supreme Leader, especially after having disappeared from public view for several weeks in the fall of 2014. By circulating rumors of OGD ties to the Kim family and former regents, Kim Jong-un may have taken steps to rein in the OGD.

iii. Jo Kyong-chol's Public Profile Begins to Rise

If it is true that Kim Jong-un has taken the next step in power politics inside the regime to include institutional manipulation, an example of this appears to be the changing profile of the MSC. Jo Kyong-chol, the Commander of the MSC, had been one of the most obscure members of the internal security apparatus. This changed in February 2014.

At a ceremonial gathering at the Kumsusan Palace of the Sun on February 16th, Kim Jong-il's birthday, Jo Kyong-chol was shown standing in the row of military commanders just behind First Chairman of the NDC Kim Jong-un. This was the first time that Jo was shown side-by-side with the head of the GPB, Choe Ryong-hae, and GSD, Ri Yong-gil. In previous gatherings, he had stood in the second or third rows in the company of KPA commanders. Two days later, Jo appeared in *Nodong Sinmun* seated three seats away from Kim Jong-un and Ri Sol-ju during a concert by the Merited State Choir in celebration of the "Day of the Shining Star."[537]

---

534   In 2015, Kim Yo-jong has mainly been identified as working with the KWP PAD. References to her work with the OGD have for the most part disappeared.
535   Ibid.
536   Recent speculation is that Choe Ryong-hae is the KWP Secretary for Working Organization, a significant demotion from his past positions a Secretary for Military Affairs and Director of the GPB. No one has yet been identified as the Director of the KWP OGD.
537   Yun Il-Geon, "Change in Seating of North's Security Commander Jo Kyong-chol…Has His Status Risen?" *Yonhap News Agency*, February 19, 2014.

His elevation in North Korean media suggested that his public profile began to reflect the influence he reportedly exercised behind the scenes for quite some time.

Jo continued to be a constant presence at Kim Jong-un's public appearances. On May 14, 2014, he appeared on page two of *Nodong Sinmun* as part of Kim's inspection of Unit 447 of the Air and Anti-Air Force carrying a firearm on his hip.[538] This photograph further highlighted Jo's growing status. In North Korea, when accompanying the Supreme Leader, the protocol is that nobody is permitted to carry weapons with the exception of his close-contact bodyguards and the person in charge of escorting him.[539] Even field commanders, who often carry personal weapons, as well as the Director of the GPB, Chief of the GSD, Minister of the People's Armed Forces, and other top ranking cadres of the military need to turn over their weapons to the team of bodyguards before greeting the Supreme Leader on a visit to a military unit.[540]

Image 35: Jo Kyong-chol with a side arm at Kim Jong-un's guidance inspection
(Source: Nodong Sinmun)

The MSC continues to be one of the most secretive parts of the internal security apparatus. However, Jo's rise in stature suggests that it is rising in

---

538   An analysis of photographs in early 2014 suggests that Jo Kyong-chol was promoted to General at the expanded meeting of the KWP CMC on April 26, 2014.

539   That Jo Kyong-chol was carrying a pistol in such close proximity to Kim Jong-un led to speculation that Jo is now the Commander of the GC. This rumor was dispelled when Yun Jong-rin appeared accompanying Kim Jong-un on an inspection of Unit 963 (Guard Command) in December 2014.

540   "North's Security Command Commander Jo Kyong-chol Drawing Attention by Carrying a Revolver While Accompanying Kim Jong Un," *Yonhap News Agency*, May 14, 2014.

power. The fact that Jo was one of the first cadres to accompany Kim Jong-un after his return to the public eye following a reported foot surgery in October 2014 reinforces the notion that the Supreme Leader sees the MSC as a critical support mechanism in periods of uncertainty within the regime. Jo Kyong-chol was promoted to Colonel General in February 2015.[541]

iv. The Guard Command's Leadership Becomes Unclear

Yun Jong-rin's profile rapidly declined in the months following Jang Song-taek's execution. He appeared at the Central Memorial Meeting for Kim Jong-il on December 17, 2013. Two weeks later, he again appeared on the rostrum of a report meeting on Kim Jong-un's Supreme Commandership. Then, he disappeared until April 2014, when he turned up as part of a group of leaders accompanying Kim Jong-un to a women's soccer match. He disappeared again and reappeared in December 2014 as part of Kim Jong-un's guidance inspection of Unit 963, although he had been demoted to Colonel General.

v. Profiles of the State Security Department and Ministry of People's Security Appear to be Diverging

Before Jang Song-taek's removal from power and in the months following, the SSD and MPS remained in the public eye. The SSD was attached directly to Jang's downfall.[542] Although Jang had ties to the KPISF, the MPS did not appear to suffer in terms of influence.[543] Kim Won-hong was a constant presence at Kim Jong-un's public appearances and Choe Pu-il's public persona did not significantly change.

In April 2014 at the First Session of the 13th SPA, both Kim Won-hong and Choe Pu-il were reappointed as members of the NDC.[544] This move slightly altered the command and control structure of the SSD and MPS. Instead of Kim Jong-un having formal oversight of these institutions in his capacity as First Chairman of the

---

541   "Kim Jong-un's Order Number 0078 to Promote KPA Commanding Officer Ranks," *Nodong Sinmun*, February 16, 2015.

542   Lee Young-Jong and Ser Myo-Ja, "Ripples Still Felt From Jang Killing," *Korea JoongAng Daily*, November 17, 2014. According to this source, Kim Won-hong's status dramatically increased inside the circles of power in Pyongyang for his "effective" handling of Jang's arrest, investigation, trial, and execution.

543   Gang Byeong-Han, "Jang Song-thaek was Purged Because of Conflicts Surrounding Coal Mining Rights," *The Kyunghyang Shinmun*, December 24, 2013. According to this source, Choe Pu-il underwent investigation in the aftermath of Jang's purge. However, it did not appear to impact his standing within the leadership.

544   Kim Won-hong had initially been appointed to the NDC in 2012 and Choe Pu-il assumed the seat left vacant by Ri Myong-su in 2013.

NDC, he was now able to directly command their leaders. As members of the NDC, Kim Won-hong and Choe Pu-il carried more institutional power in terms of policy implementation outside of their direct chains of command.

Chart 17: Command and Control of the SSD and MPS

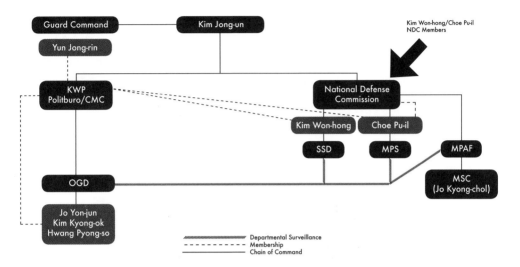

In May 2014, the fortunes of the two internal security bodies began to diverge. Kim Won-hong and the SSD continued to play a prominent role.[545] Kim remained a frequent cohort of the Supreme Leader. His public profile as a leader was highlighted in November 2014, when he led the ceremonies unveiling the statues of Kim Il-sung and Kim Jong-il at the Security University of the DPRK.[546] He was also the senior leader chosen by Kim Jong-un to meet with James Clapper, the U.S. Director of National Intelligence, when he arrived in Pyongyang to secure the release of the American citizens Kenneth Bae and Todd Miller.[547]

---

545   "Exclusive: Elite purges ahead, fracturing among N. Korea's power circles," *New Focus International*, September 1, 2014. There were very few rumors that painted Kim Won-hong in a negative light. In September 2014, however, stories surfaced that Kim Chol, Kim Won-hong's son, was under investigation by the MSC for improprieties tied to his foreign currency dealings. It was suggested that the investigation was linked to a long-standing power struggle between Kim and Hwang Pyong-so, the new Director of the GPB, which dates back to the 1980s, when both served in the GPB. Kim Won-hong led surveillance operations and executions that brought him into frequent conflict with Hwang Pyong-so, who was then serving as the GPB Vice Director for military cadre affairs. The most recent dispute between the two emerged when Kim advocated that responsibility for protecting Kim Jong-un should move from the GC to the SSD. Hwang Pyong-so countered that this responsibility should reside with the MSC.
546   "Statues of Kim Il Sung, Kim Jong Il Erected at Security University," *KCNA*, November 18, 2014.
547   "Release Of U.S. Prisoners Baffles N. Korea Watchers," *The Chosun Ilbo*, November 11, 2014.

Conversely, Choe Pu-il's public profile appears to have declined in the second half of 2014. In May, Choe was given the responsibility to make the public apology following the collapse of the apartment building in Pyongchon District, Pyongyang. The construction unit tasked with building the apartment belonged to the MPS. In his statement, Choe said that the responsibility for the accident rested with him, as he failed "to uphold well the KWP's policy of love for the people." He reprimanded himself, saying that he failed to identify factors that "could put at risk the lives and properties of the people and to take thorough-going measures, thereby causing an unimaginable accident."[548] From that point on, Choe's profile began to decline. He disappeared from the public eye after appearing on the leadership rostrum as part of a meeting to mark the sixty-first anniversary of the "war victory anniversary." He did not appear at the SPA meeting that was held in September 2014, raising speculation that his political fortunes may have suffered.[549] He finally reappeared in December 2014 as part of a delegation accompanying Kim Jong-un to Kumsusan Palace on the third anniversary of Kim Jong-il's death.

Image 36: Choe Pu-il expressing apology for collapse of apartment building
(Source: Nodong Sinmun, May 18, 2014)

2. Overview of the Internal Security Agencies

As of 2015, the internal security apparatus inside North Korea appears to be evolving in the aftermath of Jang Song-taek's purge. Outside observers' assessments of the connections between the larger regime, the Supreme Leader, and these institutions are frequently shifting as individual leaders and organizations within the regime rise and fall. In particular, changes regarding the police agencies following the elimination

---

548   "People's Security Minister Expresses 'Apology' for 13 May 'Serious Accident' in Pyongyang," *KCNA*, May 17, 2014.
549   "2nd Session of 13th Supreme People's Assembly of DPRK Held," *KCNA*, September 25, 2014.

of the KWP Administrative Department have drawn great attention.

In his book on the North Korean police state published in 2012, *Coercion, Control, Surveillance, and Punishment: An Examination of the North Korean Police State*, the author laid out the organizational structure of the police agencies in detail. This analysis will be updated and expanded below to include an examination of the KWP OGD and the GC. These two organizations, along with the SSD, MPS, and MSC, make up North Korea's internal security apparatus, which is dedicated to the preservation of the regime and the continuation of Kim family rule.

a. KWP Organization and Guidance Department

The Central Committee of the KWP is made up of more than thirty departments that conduct its day-to-day operations. The most important of these departments, considered by many Pyongyang-watchers to be the Supreme Leader's most critical lever of power, is the KWP OGD (*Jo-jik Ji-do-bu*). Initially a division within the KWP General Affairs Department, it was made an independent "Organization Committee" at the Third Plenary Session of the Second Central Committee in 1946, which was chaired by Kim Il-sung. It was transformed into the KWP Organization Department in 1952 under Pak Yong-bin, who held the position until 1959, when it was transferred to Kim Yong-ju, Kim Il-sung's younger brother, and became the KWP Organization and Guidance Department (OGD). In 1974, Kim Jong-il replaced his uncle as Director of the OGD. Since then, no director has been publicly identified.

The KWP OGD serves various roles and missions. First and foremost, it is responsible for upholding the "Ten Principles for Establishment of the Party's Monolithic Ideological System" laid down by Kim Jong-il, which essentially guarantees the Supreme Leader's absolute control.[550] As part of this system, Kim Jong-il created a daily reporting system whereby relevant sections of the OGD, at all levels of administration, provide reports up the chain of command. The headquarters of the OGD in Pyongyang then passes these reports to the Supreme Leader's office overnight. These reports give the Leader daily situational awareness throughout the regime, as well as information about the current opinions of key cadres and generals.

---

550   At his father's instructions, Kim Jong-il introduced the "Ten Principles for Establishment of the Party's Monolithic Ideological System" in 1974. This reporting system enabled him to successfully lead the "revolution" launched by Kim Il-sung. These ten Party tenets obligated people to report even the most trivial activities of all organizations via the KWP OGD, thus creating the internal Party conditions favorable for closely monitoring the evolving opinions of all cadres and generals.

In addition to acting as the Supreme Leader's reporting system throughout the regime, the KWP OGD controls senior-level appointments across the regime. It "appoints, demotes, dismisses, promotes and has personnel control over: KWP Central Committee personnel who hold the rank Bureau Chief, office director, or deputy department director; the membership and secretaries of the thirteen (13) KWP Provincial/Municipal Committees; all DPRK Cabinet Vice Ministers; general-grade officers and deputy directors (civilian and military) directly subordinate to the National Defense Commission [NDC] and the Ministry of People's Armed Forces [MPAF]."[551]

A core function of the OGD, throughout its entire structure, is to ensure that Party organizations operate effectively and to supervise the "Party life" of all KWP members. Although the OGD defines its mandate in terms of the Party, it does not confine itself strictly to the Party and intervenes extensively in the administrative affairs of all government and social organizations.

Finally, the OGD is a surveillance organization. It is the only organization allowed to carry out investigations of senior Party officials.[552] On occasion, it conducts investigations on matters deemed too sensitive or immune to investigation by lower organs of government. Such investigations can involve corruption or anti-Party acts.

Image 37: This is reportedly a photograph of the KWP Organization Guidance Department (Source: Google Earth as published on North Korean Economy Watch)

---

551   Michael Madden, "The Organization Guidance Department," *North Korea Leadership Watch*, https://nkleadershipwatch.files.wordpress.com/2009/10/kwpcentralcommitteeorganizationandguidancedepartment.pdf.

552   Ken E. Gause, *Coercion, Control, Surveillance, and Punishment: An Examination of the North Korean Police State* (Washington, D.C.: Committee for Human Rights in North Korea, 2012).

i. Structure

The headquarters of the OGD is located within the Central Committee Office 1 Complex in Haebangsan-dong, Central District, Pyongyang. It is composed of around 300 staff members. Traditionally, the department exists under a chain of command that begins with a KWP Secretary for Organizational Affairs, who also holds the post of Department Director. Since Kim Jong-il's death, no official holding these positions has been identified. It was speculated that for some time, Kim Kyong-hui may have had at least part of the portfolio for organizational affairs. Other speculation has suggested that Choe Ryong-hae may have assumed the portfolio as part of his role as one of Kim Jong-un's lead advisors on Party issues.[553] Of course, there is the very real possibility that Kim Jong-un has assumed this portfolio in its entirety in his capacity as First Secretary of the Party.

Beneath the director, there have traditionally been four first vice directors who hold the portfolios for central Party affairs, national Party affairs, military personnel, and administrative affairs.[554] Each of these first vice directors oversees a number of bureaus dedicated to Party life guidance, reporting, and inspection. Together they are responsible for surveillance and control of the critical aspects of the regime, including:

- **Central Party Affairs.** This portfolio belongs to First Vice Director Jo Yon-jun. He oversees the Party life of the nearly 3,500 members of the central Party apparatus. He also has the authority to investigate senior Party leadership. This has only occured a few times in the history of the Party. Such investigations are the purview of the OGD alone.
- **National Party Affairs.** This portfolio covers the rest of the Party's organizational life below the central level. This First Vice Director manages all the Party organizations of the regional Party and state organizational sections, as well as Party organizations of social organizations. It is not clear whether anyone holds this portfolio. Kim Hee-taek, who was a First Vice Director from 2001 to 2009, was the last known person to directly manage national Party affairs for the OGD.

---

553   Although not confirmed, most Pyongyang-watchers believe that Choe Ryong-hae is the KWP Secretary for Working Organizations, not Organization Affairs.

554   At present, there are reportedly two to three first vice directors: Kim Kyong-ok; Jo Yon-jun; and possibly Hwang Pyong-so. It is not clear whether Hwang formally severed his ties with the OGD when he became Director of the GPB. Kim Kyong-ok has not been seen in public since December 2014 and may have retired or been removed from the OGD.

- **Military Affairs.** This portfolio monitors the Party life within the armed forces, including those organizations controlled by the MPAF and the GPB. It ensures that the Kim Il-sung and the Kim Jong-il philosophies are adhered to in military political guidance. Party committees and the GPB must coordinate with the OGD's Life Guidance Bureau 13 for their training of the troops. The OGD's Personnel Management Bureau 4 first vets all senior-level appointments that are tied to Supreme Commander appointments and promotions. The portfolio for military affairs belonged to First Vice Director Hwang Pyong-so, however, it is not clear whether he still holds this post since he became the Director of the GPB.

- **Administrative Affairs.** The first vice director for this portfolio manages offices that have the authority to submit letters of suggestion directly to the first secretary. It also vets all senior appointments to the SSD, MPS, Public Procurator's Office, Court of Justice, and Ministry of State Inspection. From the early 1990s until 2007, the internal security affairs portfolio was tied to the first vice director for administrative affairs.[555] This changed with the creation of the KWP Administrative Department under Jang Song-taek. Only the responsibility for vetting personnel remained with the OGD. Since Jang's purge and the dismantling of the KWP Administrative Department, the surveillance function presumably has returned to the OGD, although this has not been verified. The portfolio currently belongs to First Vice Director Kim Kyong-ok.

The leadership of the OGD also includes a number of vice directors, some of whom have responsibilities inside the OGD apparatus and others who operate in other parts of the regime.[556] Not all the OGD vice directors "need be actively involved in the department because the title affords them a special status."[557] Several members of the KWP Central Committee Secretariat, the Supreme Leader's Personal Secretariat, and diplomatic corps are vice directors.[558] They are neither bound by North Korea's criminal statutes nor KWP protocols.

---

555   Jang Song-taek held this portfolio within the OGD until his execution in 2004.
556   Kim In-kol and Min Pyong-chol are the only publicly identified vice directors.
557   Michael Madden, "The Organization Guidance Department," *North Korea Leadership Watch*, op. cit. "In the 1980's, Kim Jong-il reportedly circulated a memorandum that put a veil of confidentiality around relations among OGD deputy [vice] directors. They are prohibited from taking any intra-OGD disputes outside of the department and any sanctions against OGD deputy directors are kept confidential."
558   Ibid.

Chart 18: Organizational Chart of the KWP OGD[559]

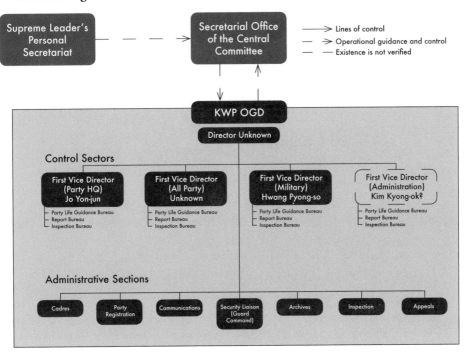

The OGD vice directors oversee a number of administrative sections. Although the exact number and identification of these sections has never been made public, some of the more notable include the Inspection Section and the Party Registration Section. The Inspection Section is responsible for inspecting any anti-Party, non-Party, undisciplined, or unreasonable activities that develop within the regime or leadership of the Party. It reports directly to the Supreme Leader. It is strictly separated from other sections and is feared by all North Korean Party members and officials.

ii. Role in the Regime

In 2015, the OGD is the source of much controversy within the Pyongang-watching community. It is believed by some to be the power behind the throne, using the death of Jang Song-taek to claw back influence it had lost in the last years of the Kim Jong-il era.[560] A close reading of the shifts and turns of the leadership

559   This chart is based on the author's interviews.
560   This is the view most closely associated with *New Focus International* and perpetuated by Jang Jin-sung in his book *Dear Leader: Poet, Spy, Escapee—A Look Inside North Korea* (New York: Atria

since 2014 would suggest that this view is likely flawed. While it is true that some leaders with ties to the OGD, such as Hwang Pyong-so, have flourished, others, such as Kim Kyong-ok, have disappeared and their fates are unknown. As such, the argument that the OGD continues to play a central role in surveilling and protecting the regime is likely true, but the view that it is a unified force driven by a Machiavellian grand plan is likely an overstatement. The contention that it acts outside of the purview and interest of the Supreme Leader is almost certainly false.

b. Guard Command

The GC (*Ho-wi Sa-ryeong-bu*), which is also referred to as the Bodyguard Command, is responsible for the safety and welfare of Kim Jong-un, his family, and senior North Korean officials.[561] Its origins date to 1946, when elements of the 90th Training Command were made responsible for providing security for North Korea's emerging leadership. It has since been restructured several times.[562] Since the 1990s, it has been growing in importance as the center of the regime's Praetorian Guard.[563]

The GC numbers close to 100,000 personnel dispersed across the country in a number of battalions, regiments, and brigades.[564] In addition to providing for the personal security of Kim Jong-un and other high-ranking officials, it conducts surveillance on high-ranking political and military officials. It also shares responsibility for the defense of the capital with the Pyongyang Defense Command and the Pyongyang Anti-Aircraft Artillery Command. Located in Puksae-dong, Moranbong District, Pyongyang, the corps-sized GC is equipped with tanks, artillery, and

---

Books, 2014).

561   The GC has also been referred to over its history as the General Guard Command and the General Guard Bureau.

562   The origin of the GC was the Bodyguard Regiment, which was organized to protect Kim Il-sung, who entered Pyongyang with the Soviet Union's military forces right after the 1945 liberation of Korea. The regiment was mainly composed of anti-Japanese partisans, and its Commander was Senior Colonel Kang Sang-ho. After the Korean War, the guard regiment protecting Kim Il-sung became the Bodyguard Office. Its first Director was O Paek-ryong. In 1965, the office was redesignated the General Guard Bureau, with Colonel General O Paek-ryong remaining as the Bureau Chief. Three years later, in conjunction with Kim Il-sung's purge of the military, O Paek-ryong retired and was replaced by Colonel General Chon Mun-sop. In the late 1970s, the General Guard Bureau was redesignated as the Guard Command. Marshal Ri Ul-sol was appointed Commander in 1984 and remained in the post until 2004, when he was succeeded by Yun Jong-rin.

563   According to some sources, Kim Jong-il began to place more emphasis on the GC following the execution of Romanian President Ceausescu in 1989.

564   The members of the Guard Command are chosen by Bureau 5 of the KWP OGD, where they go through a rigorous background check that extends to six levels of their family tree. Once chosen, the member is separated from society and his activities outside the GC are highly restricted. Officers in the GC are educated in a three-year program provided by a branch campus of Kim Il-sung Higher Party School.

missiles. It has several combat brigades stationed at the Kim family's residences and other critical facilities throughout the country.

Image 38: GC Headquarters, Pyongyang
(Source: Google Earth as published on North Korea Leadership Watch)

i. Structure

Although formally subordinate to the MPAF, the GC reports directly to the Supreme Leader in his capacity as head of the Party.[565] Its Commander, since 2004, has been Colonel General Yun Jong-rin, who is a member of the Party Central Committee and CMC.[566] His standing within the leadership has been a source of speculation since he disappeared from the public eye between April and December 2014. When he returned, he had been demoted to Colonel General. The other GC officer frequently featured in North Korean media is Colonel General Kim Song-tok, who is the GC's Political Officer.

---

565   Security for Kim Jong-il was originally handled by the State Defense Department. However, beginning in 1976, this activity was taken over by the General Guard Bureau.
566   Yun Jong-rin was promoted to General in April 2010 by Supreme Commander's Order No. 0046.

Image 39: Yun Jong-rin and Kim Jong-un during inspection of Unit 963 in December 2014
(Source: KCTV, 02 December 2014)

Below the commander is a chief of staff and at least two vice commanders, who oversee the bureaus responsible for security and administration. The First Bureau is responsible for the security and protection of the Supreme Leader, his relatives, and senior Party officials and infrastructure. This bureau is closely tied to Office 6 of the Supreme Leader's Personal Secretariat, which oversees the inner circle of protection around the Leader. It is also closely linked to a separate Capital Security Bureau and a Rapid Response Unit. The Second Bureau is in charge of logistics and carries out the administrative functions tied to transportation, construction, and maintenance of the Supreme Leader's properties.[567]

The **First Bureau** is made up of three guard departments, a rear area logistics department, and several protection units at the battalion, regiment, and brigade levels:

- The **First Guard Department** was originally responsible for the protection of Kim Il-sung.[568] Since his death, this department has assumed responsibility for the protection of the Kumsusan Memorial

---

567   The information for this section is based on numerous interviews with Pyongyang-watchers specializing in internal security affairs, as well as some senior defectors with unique access to information on the GC. Additional information is based on Ho Hye-il's book, *Bukan Yojigyeong* [Kaleidoscope of North Korea] (Seoul: Malgeun Sori Publishing, 2006). He is an alleged former bodyguard and trade official who defected from North Korea in 2004.

568   During Kim Il-sung's life, this command was also responsible for the protection of his wife, Kim Song-ae. It is not clear whether the First Guard Department still has this responsibility.

Palace of the Sun, which holds the remains of Kim Il-sung and Kim Jong-il. It reportedly numbers between 500 and 1,000 personnel.

- The **Second Guard Department** was originally responsible for the protection of Kim Jong-il. Upon his death, this department allegedly shifted its focus to the protection of Kim Jong-un.[569] Its forces are deployed around his Party headquarters and residences. It works closely with Office 6 (Kim's personal bodyguards) in coordinating his personal security both inside Pyongyang and when he travels. It reportedly numbers between 1,500 and 2,000 personnel.

- The **Third Guard Department** is responsible for the protection of Party and national infrastructure, as well as the residences of other senior leaders. It reportedly numbers between 500 and 1,000 personnel.

- The **Rear Area Department** is responsible for procuring supplies and providing logistical support throughout the GC. It reportedly numbers close to 3,000 personnel.

- The **Capital Security Bureau** provides security on the access routes into Pyongyang. A unit of nearly 2,000 troops, it is responsible for securing and vetting access to the city for both individuals and vehicles. It accomplishes this through a number of checkpoints. The bureau likely coordinates its activities with the Pyongyang Defense Command and the Third Corps, the two primary KPA units dedicated to defense of the capital city.

- The **Rapid Response Unit** is an anti-coup force. It consists of approximately 1,500 troops deployed throughout Pyongyang who are able to respond in overwhelming force at a moment's notice. Presumably, their mission is to secure critical command and control nodes throughout the city, as well as provide additional protection to the Supreme Leader. This unit is reportedly outfitted with tanks and armed personnel carriers.

The **Second Bureau** is the main logistical and administrative center of the GC. It is responsible for command operations across North Korea, including maintenance of the Supreme Leader's residences and guest houses. Its staff numbers between 15,000 and 20,000. The Bureau is also responsible for procuring goods for the Kim family, most likely in coordination with the Personal Secretariat. It is also responsible for running farms and a food factory called the Ninth Factory, which

---

569   In addition to protecting Ri Sol-ju, the Second Guard Department is also most likely responsible for protecting Kim Kyong-hui. Some defectors, however, claim that Kim's protection falls within the purview of the Third Guard Department.

is dedicated to raising and processing particular foodstuffs, and coordinating Kim Jong-un's events. Lastly, the Second Bureau is responsible for guarding the train used by the Supreme Leader to travel around the country.

Attached to the Second Bureau is a **Special Medical Team** dedicated to the health and well being of the Supreme Leader. In 2008, this Team was reportedly responsible for providing care to Kim Jong-il during his stroke and making the determination to summon doctors from France to provide guidance on further treatment. This Team is also responsible for research designed to prolong the life of the Supreme Leader.[570]

Chart 19: Organizational Chart of the Guard Command (GC)[571]

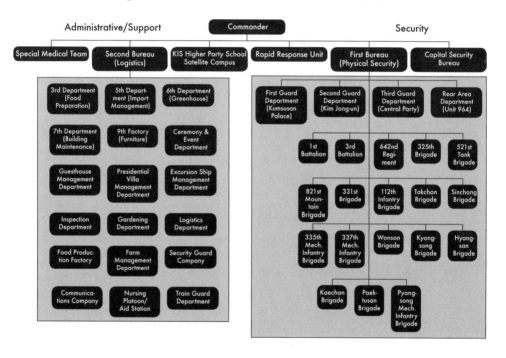

570   Kim Hye-Rim, "Kim Jong-il Receives Medical Examination by French Doctors," *Open Radio for North Korea*, August 25, 2010.
571   This chart is based on interviews and a number of sources, including Atsushi Shimizu, *An Overview of the North Korean Intelligence System: The Reality of the Enormous Apparatus that Supports the Dictatorship* (Tokyo: Kojin-sha, 2004).

ii. Cordon of Security: Relationship with Office 6 of the Personal Secretariat

In 1980, the existence of Kim Jong-il's personal security detail, known as Office 6, or the Office of Adjutants, was revealed. It is a unit of approximately 1,200 officers and soldiers led by individuals with twenty-five to thirty years of previous experience in the GC. Presumably, this unit remains intact under Kim Jong-un in similar numbers.

Chart 20: Organizational Chart of Office 6[572]

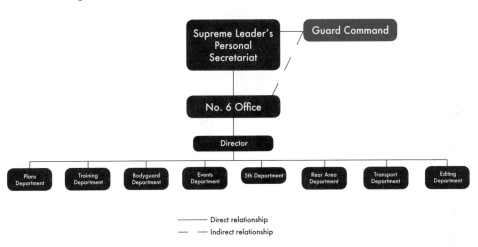

According to some reports, the Director of Office 6 is Colonel General Ko Su-il, the brother of Ko Yong-hui, Kim Jong-un's mother.[573] Ko was ranked 134th on Kim Jong-il's Funeral Committee list. He was appointed an alternate member of the Central Committee in 2010 and was one of the first recipients of the Order of Kim Jong-il in February 2012. Under Kim Jong-il, Ko Su-il was a member of the GC responsible for guarding the Supreme Leader's residences. He began to appear

---

572   This chart is based on interviews and a number of sources, including Joseph S. Bermudez, Jr., *Shield of the Great Leader* (St. Leonards, Australia: Allen and Unwin, 2001), and Atsushi Shimizu, *An Overview of the North Korean Intelligence System: The Reality of the Enormous Apparatus that Supports the Dictatorship*, op. cit.

573   Choe Seon-Yeong and Jang Yong-Hun, "Kim Jong-un's Uncle Reported to be in Charge of Kim's Personal Security," *Yonhap News Agency*, September 22, 2013.

in North Korean media in 2009, the year that Kim Jong-un was made heir apparent, when he was promoted to Colonel General.[574]

Office 6, which reports directly to Kim Jong-un's Personal Secretariat through the GC, takes the lead in all of Kim Jong-un's public appearances. It is responsible for the protection of the Supreme Leader at the closest range. As such, it provides security inside the first two layers of security in a seven-layer cordon every time the Supreme Leader travels outside of his Party headquarters or one of his residences.[575]

Table 10: Security Cordons for Supreme Leader's Public Events

Layer of Protection	Responsibility	Comments
Layer 1	Office 6, Bodyguard Department	5-6 bodyguards
Layer 2	Office 6, Bodyguard Department	200-300 troops stationed 100 meters from the Supreme Leader, coordinated with Second Guard Department
Layer 3	SSD, Events Bureau	1 kilometer from the second layer, with Office 6 personnel dispersed throughout this layer depending on the situation
Layer 4	SSD	1.5-2 kilometers from the third layer
Layer 5	SSD and MPS	Distance depends on the situation
Layer 6	Local SSD	Distance depends on the situation
Layer 7	Local MPS	Distance depends on the situation

In addition to providing physical security, which is the responsibility of the Bodyguard Department, Office 6 has a number of other functions. The Plans Department coordinates the Supreme Leader's events in terms of the list of participants and the operational aspects of the protection plan. An editorial bureau attached to Office 6 is responsible for how the images and news of the Supreme Leader are crafted by North Korean media.

---

574   "Korean People's Army Supreme Commander's Order No 0029: On Promoting the Military Ranks of KPA Commanding Officers," *KCBS*, April 14, 2009.
575   Kim Jeong-Eun, "Strengthening Close Guard on North's Kim Jong-un?" *Yonhap News Agency*, June 18, 2013. As of 2013, photographs of Kim Jong-un's guidance inspections reveal that his inner cordon of security is composed of general-grade officers. Particular individuals wearing the rank of lieutenant general and armed with pistols and carrying walkie-talkies are often pictured following behind the Supreme Leader. During the Kim Il-sung and Kim Jong-il eras, bodyguards were often dressed in civilian clothing.

iii. Role in the Regime

It is assumed by most Pyongyang-watchers that the Guard Command continues to occupy a central role in the regime of Kim Jong-un. It is vested with the protection of the Supreme Leader and members of the senior leadership, after all. However, in 2014 and 2015, subtle indications in the North Korean media suggest that the Guard Command may have lost some influence in the politics around the senior leader to other security agencies, namely the MSC. Stories appeared in South Korean media, reportedly based on North Korean sources, that the GC had been placed under Jang Song-taek. This was followed by stories of the MSC's meteoric rise and photographs of its commander with a side arm in close proximity to Kim Jong-un. Finally, Yun Jong-rin disappeared from public view for several months in 2014 and 2015. Taken separately, none of these pieces of evidence proves anything. But taken together, they suggest a possible diminution of power and influence of the GC.

c. State Security Department

The SSD (*Guk-ga An-jeon Bo-wi-bu*) is one of the most obscure institutions in the North Korean regime. Although its existence was known for years, it was not until 1987, at the time of SSD Director Ri Chin-su's funeral, that North Korean media officially acknowledged the SSD's existence.[576] The SSD is often referred to by foreign media as the Ministry of State Security or the State Political Security Department.[577] Its military cover designation is allegedly KPA Unit 10215.[578]

The SSD's personnel numbers approximately 50,000.[579] Its headquarters is in Pyongyang,[580] but it also has offices at the provincial, city, and local levels. The

---

576   In September 2007, the central media unveiled this opaque institution in a television broadcast devoted to a SSD news conference warning the public against the smuggling and use of contraband media and communication devices. The following year, in December 2008, the central media again mentioned the SSD in a story that accused South Korea of plotting to assassinate Kim Jong-il.

577   Also called the "State Security Agency" in the *White Paper on Human Rights in North Korea* (Seoul: Korean Institute for National Unification, 2007, 2008, and 2009) and "National Security Agency" in David Hawk, *The Hidden Gulag*, 2nd ed. (Washington, D.C.: Committee for Human Rights in North Korea, 2012).

578   Kim Jong-un's second public on-site inspection after becoming heir apparent in September 2010 was at KPA Unit 10215.

579   "Real Power of the State Security Department," *Economisuto*, October 1, 2008. According to this Japanese source, the SSD has approximately 70,000 personnel.

580   Choe Seon-Yeong and Jang Yong-Hun, "Competition Between North's Power Organs To Show Loyalty to Kim Jong-un Intensifies," *Yonhap News Agency*, May 31, 2009. This article identifies Amisan, Daesong District, Pyongyang as the location of the SSD headquarters.

SSD carries out a wide range of counterintelligence and internal security functions normally associated with the secret police. It is responsible for finding anti-state criminals—those accused of anti-government and dissident activities, economic crimes, and disloyalty to the political leadership. In addition, it runs political prisons and has counter-intelligence and intelligence collection responsibilities. It monitors political attitudes and maintains surveillance on people who have returned from foreign countries. Department personnel escort high-ranking officials, guard national borders, and monitor international entry points.[581] The degree of fear it instills in the political security bureaus of the KPA, which have representatives at all levels of command, is uncertain. However, it occasionally takes actions against members of the elite.

Image 40: SSD Main Complex in Pyongyang
(Source: Google Earth as published on North Korea Economy Watch)

In the past, SSD agents were assigned to military units and placed under the control of the unit's Party committee. Since the elevation of the MSC in the 1990s, this no longer seems to be the case.[582] North Korea's unique internal security system has layers of competing and conflicting responsibilities. SSD agents sometimes

581   "Who Is in Charge of N.Korea's Nuclear Weapons?" *The Chosun Ilbo*, December 26, 2011. According to South Korean reports, the SSD and MSC are also responsible for security at sensitive defense facilities, such as the Yongbyon uranium enrichment facility.
582   Lee Seok-Young, "Officer Families Just Like the Rest," *Daily NK*, December 2, 2011. It should be noted, however, that the SSD occasionally takes part in cases involving the military. For example, according to a source in Ryanggang Province, a number of wives of army officers from the Tenth Corps reservist training base in Bocheon County were intending to smuggle some metals out of the country to buy food. When they were caught, officials at the base turned to the SSD in an effort to quietly handle the matter. However, friction between the SSD and the MSC led to a turf battle that generated a "No. 1 Report" that went directly to Kim Jong-il's office. Kim decided to let the MSC resolve the matter.

assume the role of political officers and ordinary soldiers, focusing their monitoring on company-grade officers. They also indirectly supervise the work of the Security Guidance Bureau (SGB), which also runs a covert monitoring network within the armed forces. Like the SSD, the SGB reports directly to the NDC.[583] In effect, internal spies monitor other internal spies.

i. Structure

The SSD's chain of command is composed of one director, one first deputy director, and several deputy directors.[584] Since Ri Chin-su's death in the late 1980s, the position of director had been officially unoccupied. For years, the duties of this position were presumed to belong to Kim Jong-il. Following the Fourth Party Conference in 2012,[585] KCNA announced that General Kim Won-hong had assumed the position.[586] The importance of the SSD under Kim Jong-un was revealed when he accompanied his father on visits to SSD facilities throughout 2009 and 2010, including one to the SSD headquarters in October 2010.[587]

Until Jang Song-taek's purge, the KWP Administrative Department was responsible for Party oversight of the SSD. According to several sources, one of Jang's deputies was responsible for monitoring SSD activities. In early 2012, this oversight was reportedly strengthened with the removal of U Tong-chuk, the SSD First Vice Director. Over the next year, Kim Won-hong expanded his control and reportedly began to communicate directly with Kim Jong-un, circumventing the

---

583   Seiichi Ino, *Kim Jong-Il's Will* (Tokyo: Asahi Shimbun Publications, Inc., 2009).

584   "N. Korea Purges Deputy Spy Chief," *The Chosun Ilbo*, May 20, 2011. See also "Ryu Kyong Had Actual Grip on North Korean Intelligence and Armed Forces," *NKChosun.com*, May 20, 2011. Some sources identify Ryu Kyong as a powerful Deputy Director, who "has received numerous medals for uncovering alleged U.S. and Japanese spy rings within North Korea." However, South Korean sources contend that Ryu was removed as part of a purge in May 2011 to lay the foundation for Kim Jong-un's succession. According to reports, Ryu was arrested by the GC, interrogated, and executed. Speculation was that he was becoming too powerful, even eclipsing U Tong-chuk within the SSD. This purge is similar to the one in the early 1980s, when Kim Pyong-ha was removed as head of the SSD and forced to commit suicide.

585   At the Fourth Party Conference in April 2012, Kim Won-hong was made a full member of the Politburo and a member of the CMC. At the Fifth Session of the 12th SPA, he was appointed to the NDC.

586   "Brief History of Member of Presidium, Members and Alternate Members of the Political Bureau of C.C., WPK Elected to Fill Vacancies," *KCNA*, April 11, 2012.

587   Christine Kim and Lee Young-jong, "Kim Jong-un in charge of intelligence: Source," *Korea JoongAng Daily*, April 21, 2011. In April 2011, the NIS allegedly informed the South Korean National Assembly's Intelligence Committee that Kim Jong-un had assumed the post as Director of the SSD. NIS sources contend that Kim's association with the SSD dates back to April 2009, when he ordered a sting on the vacation home frequented by his older brother, Kim Jong-nam. Several of Jong-nam's associates were arrested by the SSD in an apparent purge of "side branches" within the Kim family.

chain of command. Since the death of Jang Song-taek and the elimination of the KWP Administrative Department, the SSD now directly reports to Kim Jong-un in his capacity as the First Chairman of the NDC. Kim Won-hong's elevation to membership in the NDC has solidified this channel of communication.

Below Kim Won-hong are six vice directors for organization, propaganda, personnel,[588] inspection, rear logistics services, and security.[589] They oversee more than twenty bureaus, which in turn operate local SSD offices in each province (*do*), city (*si*), county (*gun*), and village (*ri*), as well as organizations and enterprises. Of these bureaus, the First (General Guidance), Second (Counterespionage), Fourth (Counterintelligence), Seventh (Prisons), Eighth (Border Security), Tenth (Investigation), and Eleventh (Prosecution) are the most involved in ensuring the internal security of the regime.[590] Kim Chang-sop, who was elevated to alternate member status in the KWP Politburo at the Third Party Conference, is the Director of the Political Bureau.

- The **First Bureau (General Guidance Bureau)** is responsible for the dissemination of Kim Jong-un's guidance and instructions. It also serves a number of housekeeping functions, including gathering and analyzing domestic intelligence from all SSD bureaus and preparing comprehensive, overarching SSD reports for Kim Jong-un.

- The **Second Bureau (Counterespionage Bureau)** monitors, investigates, and arrests those involved in spying for foreign countries. It also monitors foreign activity within North Korea's borders and conducts immigration functions, such as issuing passports and visas.

- The **Fourth Bureau (Counterintelligence Bureau)** is responsible for rooting out anti-regime and anti-Kim elements within the North Korean government. It deploys its personnel within the Party, government, and military, as well as at universities, enterprises, and factories.

- The **Seventh Bureau (Prisons Bureau)**, also known as the Farm Bureau, is responsible for the management and control of political prisoners and political prisoner confinement facilities throughout the country.

---

588   To work for the SSD, background checks include investigation out to an applicant's third cousins, because workers at this agency handle many classified materials.

589   Seo Jae-Jin and Kim Kap-Sik. *A Study of the North Korean Ministry of People's Security* (Seoul: Korea Institute for National Unification, 2008). According to this source, Kim Sang-kwon, Yun To-sun, and Hong Pong-sik are vice directors in the SSD.

590   According to some defectors, the SSD's Eleventh Bureau is responsible for surveillance, while the Thirteenth Bureau is dedicated to prosecutorial affairs.

- The **Eighth Bureau (Border Security Bureau)** monitors foreign activity on the border, such as foreign nationals who might try to enter North Korea, and locates and captures North Korean escapees close to the border. It works closely with the MPAF Border Guard Command and also operates in China, where it checks the identification of North Korean citizens to determine whether they are escapees. It has arrest authority for high-profile defectors, but only identifies ordinary escapees for arrest by other sections of the SSD.[591]

- The **Tenth Bureau (Investigation Bureau)**, also known as the **Preliminary Investigation Bureau**, investigates and arrests those suspected of anti-regime activities. This Bureau is particularly feared by the public for the arbitrary manner in which it carries out executions. Bureau personnel have reportedly assassinated political prisoners for their own personal or career advancement. In recent years, this Bureau has devoted much of its time to investigating incidents involving graffiti and leaflets opposing Kim Il-sung and Kim Jong-il, and the destruction and damage of their portraits. The Investigation Bureau allegedly keeps files on the handwriting of every North Korean resident over the age of 17 in order to help it identify disobedient individuals.

- The **Eleventh Bureau (Prosecution Bureau)** is the primary point of contact with the Procurator General and the court system. This Bureau oversees cases and determines how to proceed with adjudication. Presumably, it is also involved in SSD decisions on whether an individual should be handled as a political criminal or transferred to the MPS.

- The **Central 109 Combined Inspection Command** was identified by defector sources in 2014 as a result of an emergency meeting of senior functionaries of the agencies responsible for internal security. At this meeting in June 2014, Kim Jong-un discussed how this agency is leading the crackdown on the leakage of state secrets and the spread of foreign trends inside the regime. Headed directly by Kim Won-hong, the Command is in charge of the "109 Combined Inspection Groups" across the country, which are responsible for inspecting and confiscating

---

591   Kim Kwang-Jin and Choi Song-Min, "Border Security Goes Back to NSA," *Daily NK*, April 22, 2012. According to some sources, in April 2012, Kim Jong-un gave the SSD sole authority over border security. Before this move, the SSD and MPAF had shared responsibility—the MPAF had the mission of protecting the border and preventing defections, while the SSD carried out arrests and repatriations. Now, the SSD allegedly is responsible for both roles.

digital devices and information from foreign sources, which is spreading throughout North Korea.[592]

Other bureaus directly involved in the SSD's internal security function include the Communications Interception Bureau,[593] which may be North Korea's primary signals intelligence agency, responsible for a system of listening posts throughout the country. It monitors internal, foreign, civilian, and military transmissions. Other SSD bureaus are responsible for external intelligence (Third Bureau), protection of Kim Jong-un and other senior officials, as well as a number of management and protection services. According to a former SSD officer who defected in the late 1990s, the SSD frequently changes the designations of its bureaus.[594]

---

592   "Kim Jong-un Declares War on Spread of Foreign Trends via Cell Phones, Computers," *NK Intellectuals Solidarity*, June 30, 2014.

593   "No. 27 Bureau of the State Security Department Leads Crackdown on Cell Phone Use in North Korea," *NK Focus*, February 21, 2008. According to this source, communications interception is the responsibility of the Bureau 16. Another source notes that the Bureau 27 is responsible for developing technology for jamming and monitoring radio waves. Bureau 27 is reportedly responsible for cracking down on illegal cell phone use.

594   During the research for this study, the author came across different number designations for the same bureau. In all likelihood, bureaus change designations over the years.

Chart 21: Organizational Chart of the State Security Department[595]

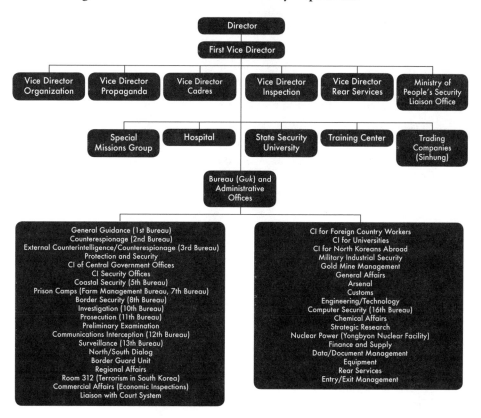

Each bureau of the SSD is under the direction of a chief and under him are an array of positions including managers (*bu-jang*), section chiefs (*gwa-jang*), and guidance members (*ji-do-won*). Of these positions, section chiefs are particularly important because they control SSD agents in the field. Each of North Korea's nine provinces has a SSD office, which more or less replicates the structure of the headquarters in Pyongyang.[596] The provincial SSD (*An-jeon Bo-wi-bu*) office is

595   This chart is based on interviews and several sources, including Kang Cheol-Hwan and Lee Gyo-Gwan, "NK Report: State Security Department…Stops Even a Running Train," *The Chosun Ilbo*, March 12, 2002; Yun Tae-il, *The Inside Story of the SSD* (Seoul: Chosun Monthly, 1998); Joseph S. Bermudez, Jr., *Shield of the Great Leader*, op. cit.; and Atsushi Shimizu, *An Overview of the North Korean Intelligence System: The Reality of the Enormous Apparatus that Supports the Dictatorship*, op. cit.
596   Concurrent with the creation of the SSD in the 1970s, provincial SSD offices were created and assumed the missions of the provincial public security sections (*an-jeon-gwa*) of the provincial public security departments (*an-jeon-guk*). In the 1980s, these offices were redesignated provincial SSD (*An-jeon Bo-wi-bu*).

headed by a chief and deputy chief who oversee a number of section chiefs and guidance members.[597] Each provincial SSD headquarters has approximately 200 to 300 personnel.[598]

In addition to the functional bureaus, the SSD apparatus also includes a hospital, several colleges, a training center, several trading companies,[599] and a Special Mission Group. The Special Mission Group allegedly reported directly to Kim Jong-il, although its current chain of command is unclear. It is charged with conducting surveillance and ideological investigations of high-ranking officials within the KWP, SSD, Cabinet, and MPAF. It is supposedly composed of fifteen members who were hand-selected by Kim Jong-il. Its role and function under Kim Jong-un is unclear.

ii. Role in the Regime

The SSD has enjoyed a privileged place in the political space around Kim Jong-un since he became the heir apparent in 2010. In the first official photograph of Kim, the future head of the SSD, Kim Won-hong, was seated next to the future Leader at the Third Party Conference. Soon after the death of Kim Jong-il and the advent of the Kim Jong-un era, Kim Won-hong took over the directorship of the SSD, a position presumably occupied by the recently deceased Supreme Leader. In the years since, Kim Won-hong's influence continued to grow to the point that he is now considered by many Pyongyang-watchers to occupy a seat in the inner circle of advisors around Kim Jong-un. In 2015, rumors have begun to spread about Kim Won-hong's appetite for power, spurred on by stories of power struggles with Hwang Pyong-so (GPB) and Jo Kyong-chol (MSC). How the relationships between these powerful figures play out will have an impact on the future dynamics inside the police state.

---

597   Author's interview with a North Korean defector, Seoul. Within the provincial SSD, the chief normally oversees the Tourist Surveillance Department and the Finance Department. Counterintelligence and investigative affairs (including the tasks of the Prosecution Office) fall under the deputy chief.

598   Although not precise, the number of SSD personnel at the provincial level is based on a ratio of one agent per 1000 people. The SSD at the county (*gun*) level normally has seventy to eighty personnel. At the district (*gu*) level, the SSD normally has six to ten personnel.

599   A number of offices attached to these trading companies are rumored to be involved in drug smuggling.

d. Ministry of People's Security

The MPS (*In-min Bo-an-bu*)[600] functions primarily as the national police in North Korea. According to the Public Security Regulation Law, adopted by the SPA in 1992 and modified in 1999, the MPS is tasked with defending the sovereignty and the socialist system of North Korea, as well as protecting the constitutional rights, lives, and assets of the people.[601] Within this broad mandate, the Ministry's usual police missions range from maintaining law and order, investigating common criminal cases, and controlling traffic to overseeing the country's non-political prison system. It also maintains organizations responsible for protecting the country's railroads; key government facilities and officials; as well as resident registration (birth, death, marriage, change of address); the preservation and management of secret documents; and the construction and security of sensitive and national infrastructure projects. Like the SSD, the MPS is also responsible for conducting political surveillance, though political suspects are remanded to the SSD. In 2009, the KWP Administration Department expanded the Ministry's criminal jurisdiction to include the investigation of offenses committed by the military, SSD, public prosecutors, and cadres of courts in every area except anti-regime crimes.[602]

The MPS maintains a large organization of approximately 210,000 personnel extending down to the provincial, county, district, city, and village levels.[603] MPS police officers are the most visible face of the North Korean public security apparatus, routinely conducting checks on travelers to ensure they possess appropriate travel documents, maintaining checkpoints to inspect buses, trucks, and trains, and performing regular police patrols.

---

600   Some defectors use the short hand *An-jeon-bu* to refer to the regular police. See David Hawk, *The Hidden Gulag*, 2nd ed., op. cit.

601   The Public Security Regulation was adopted as the 22nd Decision of the SPA Standing Committee on December 28, 1992 and modified as the 540th Decree of the SPA Standing Committee on March 24, 1999.

602   This includes the ability to search the homes of suspects from these organizations.

603   Seo Jae-Jean and Kim Kap-Sik, *A Study of the North Korean Ministry of People's Security*, op. cit. An additional 100,000 civilian staff are attached to the Ministry, bringing its total size to 310,000.

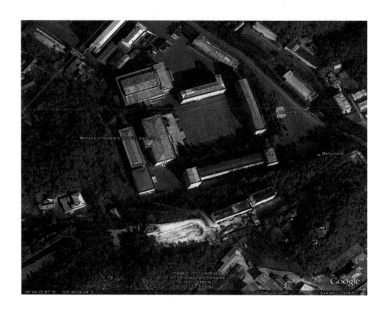

Image 41: MPS Headquarters in Pyongyang
(Source: Google Earth as published on North Korea Economy Watch)

i. Structure

The MPS has its headquarters in Pyongyang. The Minister of People's Security is General Choe Pu-il. Although not publicly announced, Choe took over the MPS in February 2013, replacing Ri Myong-su, who was assigned to other duties.[604] At the Central Committee Plenum in April 2013, Choe was elevated to the Politburo as an alternate member.[605] Shortly thereafter, at the Seventh Session of the 12th SPA, he was appointed a member of the NDC, replacing Ri Myong-su. Before his appointment, Choe was the First Vice Chief of the GSD and Director of the GSD Operations Bureau.[606] At the Third Party Conference in 2010 he was appointed to the KWP CMC.

The MPS has several vice ministers and a chief of staff who oversee several divisions and bureaus.[607] The Political Bureau exists outside of the Chief of Staff's

---

604   "Comrade Choe Pu-il, Alternate Member of the Political Bureau," *Nodong Sinmun*, April 1, 2013.
605   While it was not announced in North Korean media, it is presumed that Ri Myong-su was removed from the Politburo as part of this reshuffle.
606   Choe's predecessor, Ri Myong-su, had served as Director of the GSD Operations Bureau.
607   *North Korea Directory* (Japan: Radio Press, Inc., 2004). See also *KCBS*, December 19, 2009, as cited in Open Source Center (KPP20091219032006). Some of the Vice Ministers include: Kim Sung-pom, Han Nam-chol, Ho Yong-ho, Pak Chung-gun, Paek Pong-man, Ri Yong-il, Choe Jung-hwa, Kang Yong-ho, Won Hwa-sop, Kim Chang-byok, Kim Po-kyong, Han Chon-ho, Kim Chol-ung, So Chun-

chain of command and is responsible for various Party-related functions. It reports directly to the Minister, as does the MPS Security Department.

- **Chief of Staff Apparatus**. The position of the chief of staff, which is subordinate to the first vice minister, was created in 1994, following an order from Kim Jong-il to place the Ministry on a wartime footing.[608] The chief of staff is the minister's senior aide and primary conduit to the headquarters apparatus.

The apparatus contains approximately forty bureaus and offices. Some of the more important include: Inspection Bureau; Investigation Bureau; Resident Registration Bureau; and Preliminary Examination Bureau.

- ○ The **Inspection Bureau** supervises the circulation of proclamations and directives and ensures that they are implemented. It also conducts routine inspections of provincial and local public security bureaus.
- ○ The **Investigation Bureau's** duties include criminal (general and economic) investigations and arrests, forensic analysis, and guidance and supervision of scientific investigation activities of provincial and local public security bureaus.
- ○ The **Resident Registration Bureau** guides and supervises the tracking of North Korean citizens throughout the country. It keeps track of citizens' resident classification and movement documents using the so-called "Resident Registration Dossier." It also oversees the census.
- ○ The **Preliminary Examination Bureau** oversees the initial investigation of criminal cases and determines how to handle them under what jurisdiction. If cases are determined to be political in nature, they are transferred to the SSD.
- ○ The **Operations Bureau** manages the operational affairs of the provincial security bureaus. It also directs civil defense at the

---

bong, Sin Il-nam, Paek Yong-chol, and Yu Yong-chol. Over the years, the number of vice ministers has varied between three and ten. Pak Chung-gun, who, as of 2004, was described as the First Vice Minister, allegedly handles the administrative departments within the Ministry, as well as the Foreign Trade Bureau. The other vice ministers oversee other critical bureaus within the Ministry. During Ju Sang-song's 2009 trip to China, North Korean media identified Kim Po-kyong as a vice minister and Ri Pyong-sam as the Director of the Ministry's Political Bureau.

608   DPRK National Defense Commission Order No. 7 (1994).

provincial level. This includes providing shelters for the public in case of an enemy air attack, evacuating factories and enterprises, and overseeing civil defense training for the general public.

- The **Railway Security Bureau** is responsible for the security of North Korea's railroad tunnels, bridges, rail lines, rail facilities, military supplies at rail depots, and freight and passenger trains.
- The **People's Security Political College**, also referred to as the University of Politics, is responsible for the education of senior cadre. In addition to the college, the Ministry has a Cadre Training School, a General Training School, and an Engineering College.[609]

- **Political Bureau.** The Political Bureau is responsible for monitoring the lives and activities of Party members. The Bureau consists of approximately ten departments, led by the organization, propaganda, and cadre departments.[610] While the Political Bureau exists within the Ministry's chain of command, it is also under the control and guidance of the KWP OGD.[611]

- **Security Department.** This Department is located within the MPS, but reports to the SSD. Its stated purpose is to guarantee the safety of the Ministry, its affiliated organizations, and personnel. However, its more important mission is to monitor the Ministry for anti-revolutionary elements, spies, and opponents to the regime. This Department also allegedly contains the Penal Affairs Bureau, which oversees systems of both prisons and detention camps. These traditional prisons, sometimes referred to as "Indoctrination Houses," are for persons convicted of common crimes.

- **Anti-Socialist Inspection Team.** Soon after the execution of Jang Song-taek, the MPS issued new judicial instructions aimed at bolstering internal security. Provincial MPS bureaus and offices received four guidelines related to transgressions that carry particularly

---

609   The last publicly identified President of the University was So Chun-bong. The Rector is Kim Jang-kil. In October 2012, the University was renamed the Kim Jong-il People's Security University.

610   Lee Keum-Soon et al., *White Paper on Human Rights in North Korea 2008* (Seoul: Korea Institute for National Unification, 2008). To work for the MPS, applicants must undergo a very thorough background check, extending to six degrees of family relationships. No relatives up to and including one's second cousins can have served time, even in a correctional center. According to one defector, background checks within the Ministry have become significantly less strict in recent years, but people who have personal or family backgrounds tied to South Korea are not able to get positions in the Party.

611   The Political Bureau is headed by Ri Pyong-sam. The Vice Director is Paek Kye-ryong.

severe punishment: slander of Kim Jong-un; "superstitious behavior," including of a religious nature like Christianity; production, sale, or consumption of illicit substances; and viewing or distributing illicit recordings.[612] Following the promulgation of these new guidelines, North Korean authorities formed new inspection teams to address border security concerns. The teams were "created out of the graduating class of a university of politics under the Ministry of People's Security in Pyongyang...[and] border security was tightened."[613, 614]

ii. Korean People's Interior Security Forces

The MPS also has authority over the KPISF, a national guard-like entity dedicated to quelling social unrest and suppressing domestic rebellions.[615] The KPISF is headed by General Kim In-sik.[616] In April 2012, Kim was appointed Vice Premier at the Fifth Session of the 12th SPA, while Ri Pyong-sam, the Director of the KPISF Political Bureau, was made an alternate member of the Politburo at the Fourth Party Conference.

Image 42:
General Kim In-sik
Commander, KPISF

Image 43:
Colonel General Ri
Thae-chol
Led KPISF delegation to
China in 2011

Image 44:
Ri Pyong-sam
Director, KPISF
Political Bureau

---

612   Kang Mi-Jin, "New MPS Guidelines Portend Hard Times," *Daily NK*, January 7, 2014.
613   Kang Mi-Jin, "Regime Pushing To Stem Defection Tide," *Daily NK*, January 15, 2014.
614   At the same time, the SSD began to collaborate with smugglers to track potential defectors.
615   The KPISF assumed its current name in early 2010. Before that, it was known as the Korean People's Security Force. The new name (*Nae-mu-gun*) means "a force to maintain internal order and stability," in contrast to its previous name (*Gyeong-bi-dae*), which means "guard units."
616   An alternate member of the KWP Central Committee, Kim In-sik was a member of both Kim Jong-il's and Jo Myong-rok's Funeral Committee lists.

Image 45: Minister of People's Security General Ri Myong-su gives the keynote speech at a rally of MPS and KPISF personnel in April 2012. Seen behind him is Colonel General Ri Pyong-sam, head of the MPS/KPISF Political Bureau (Source: KCNA)

Image 46: Kim Jong-un with commanding officers of the MPS and the KPISF on May Day 2013.
(Source: Nodong Sinmun, May 2, 2013)

Chart 22: Organizational Chart of the MPS[617]

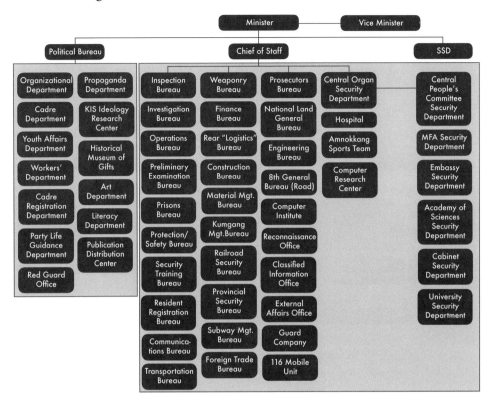

North Korea is divided into nine provinces (*do*), two municipal cities, one special city (*teuk-byeol-si*), twenty-four cities (*gun*), twenty-seven districts (*gu-yeok*), 148 counties, two wards (*gu*), two zones (*ji-gu*), and 3,230 villages (*ri*). The MPS is represented at all levels. People's Security departments exist in municipal cities, special cities, and provinces.[618] In May 2010, the Ministry revealed the existence of provincial Special Mobile Police Squads composed of 300 officers, each under

617   This chart is based on interviews and a number of sources, including: Seo Jae-Jin and Kim Kap-Sik, *A Study of the North Korean Ministry of People's Security*, op. cit.; Joseph S. Bermudez, Jr., *Shield of the Great Leader*, op. cit.; and Atsushi Shimizu, *An Overview of the North Korean Intelligence System: The Reality of the Enormous Apparatus that Supports the Dictatorship*, op. cit.

618   At the provincial level, the People's Security department is overseen by a department chief. Underneath him are a security guidance officer and political officer. The political officer oversees the organization and propaganda offices, each headed by a secretary. The third official reporting to the chief of the People's Security department is the chief of staff, who oversees a number of functional deputies (safety, security, citizen registration, national lands, air defense, and railway police). Of these deputies, the deputy for safety oversees the day-to-day operations of the police force, including investigations and pre-trial examinations. The chief of staff also has liaison offices for county and district people's security offices.

the authority of the provincial People's Security departments. The mission of these squads is to seek out and neutralize foreign sources of negative information about the regime.

Chart 23: Organizational Structure of the People's Security Departments – the Local Offices of the MPS

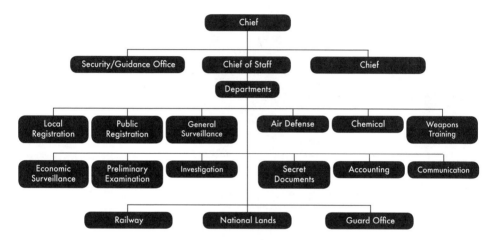

People's Security departments are the backbone of the Ministry's local organization. Approximately 200 of these departments exist in cities, counties, and districts. Security offices also exist at the village level. These bureaus are headed by either a senior colonel or a lieutenant colonel of police, depending on the size of the population. People's Security bureaus at each city or county and smaller substations throughout the country are staffed with about 100 personnel each.[619] The Ministry's Railroad Security Bureau also maintains work and management offices at the city and provincial levels.

iii. Role in the Regime

The MPS has had mixed fortunes under Kim Jong-un. At the beginning of Kim's reign, the MPS was closely tied to Jang Song-taek and was staffed by officers whose fortunes seemed tied more to the Kim Jong-il era than the Kim Jong-un era. With the promotion of Choe Pu-il, a long-time Kim family associate, these

---

619   These bureaus play an especially important role in maintaining security in the border areas. Attached to each bureau is a patrol team made up of twenty to fifty agents dedicated to capturing North Korean escapees and conducting surprise inspections.

fortunes began to change. The Ministry became closely tied to the new Supreme Leader, while the KPISF remained linked to Jang Song-taek. With the purge of Jang Song-taek and the collapse of the apartment building in Pyongyang, for which Choe Pu-il had to apologize, the MPS's influence seemed to plummet. Choe Pu-il disappeared from public view and was rumored to have been purged. In mid-2015, however, the MPS has undergone a resurgence, at least in profile. Choe Pu-il returned to the public eye and was even featured in photographs of a CMC meeting in which Kim Jong-un was dealing with the inter-Korean crisis following the landmine explosions on the DMZ. While the MPS is no longer at the center of a power vacuum within the internal security apparatus, its political influence within this apparatus continues to pale in comparison to the other security-based institutions.

e. Military Security Command

The MSC (*Bo-wi Sa-ryeong-bu*) is the counterintelligence and counterespionage organization within the North Korean military, responsible for internal security within the KPA. It actively seeks out elements that are corrupt, disloyal, or present a potential coup threat by conducting investigations, surveillance, and wiretapping of high-ranking general officers in their offices and homes.[620] In addition, it has the authority to make arrests on evidence of criminal activity or political unreliability.

North Korea's police agencies cannot report to the government offices they report on. The MSC, which reports officially to the MPAF up to the NDC, reported directly to Kim Jong-il in the past. This practice presumably continues under Kim Jong-un. It regularly produces reports on the ideological trends, friendships, and daily activities of general officers. The Minister of the People's Armed Forces takes these reports, together with similar reports from the GPB, and forwards them to the Leader's Personal Secretariat. These reports often provide the evidence upon which periodic purges of the armed forces are launched. On occasion, the MSC is tasked with special purpose, non-military investigations.

Aside from its police function, the MSC's mandate also extends to providing security for the Leader during his visits to military units, handling residential registration for military officers and their families, and monitoring military and civilian movements along North Korea's borders. Despite its broad mission and ubiquitous presence, the MSC is small compared to the SSD and the MPS, with less than 10,000 personnel.

---

620   Atsushi Shimizu, *An Overview of the North Korean Intelligence System: The Reality of the Enormous Apparatus that Supports the Dictatorship*, op. cit. According to this source, for officers with the rank of major general or above, either their driver or senior deputy reports to the MSC.

Image 47: According to some North Korean exiles, this is a picture of MSC headquarters. This has not been confirmed and may be an auxiliary MSC base. The complex used to house Kim Il-sung's presidential security detail. (Soruce: Google Earth with information provided by North Korean Leadership Watch.)

i. Structure

The MSC has its headquarters in Pyongyang. Its Commander is Jo Kyong-chol.[621] Not much is known about General Jo. He is a former Political Commissar of the KPA Air Force.[622] According to South Korean reports, he assumed command of the MSC in 2009 soon after Kim Jong-un was appointed heir apparent. He replaced Kim Won-hong, who is now the Director of the SSD. Since Kim Jong-il's death, Jo has appeared in North Korean media as part of Kim Jong-un's guidance inspections, most notably in March 2012, when the Supreme Commander visited Panmunjom. In 2014, following Jang Song-taek's death, his profile began to rise and he was apparently promoted to the rank of General in April.

The structure of the MSC is fairly streamlined, especially compared to the organizational structures of the SSD and MPS. The day-to-day affairs of the Command fall to four deputy commanders. The Command has three overarching offices: the Cadre Department, the Political Department, and the Chief of Staff. The Cadre Department appears to have a typical human resources function, overseeing recruitment and personnel affairs. The Political Department ensures ideological

621   Jo Kyong-chol's appearance in close proximity to Kim Jong-un at guidance inspections led some Pyongyang-watchers to speculate that he was the Commander of the GC. However, this speculation came to an end when Yun Jong-rin reappeared in North Korean media.
622   Hisashi Hirai, *Kitachosen no Shidotaisei to Kokei* (Tokyo: Iwanami Shoten, 2011).

loyalty and conducts a variety of indoctrination activities. However, the bulk of the apparatus falls under Jo's Chief of Staff.[623] This apparatus includes an Inspection Department, which conducts routine inspections of military units,[624] as well as a guard unit dedicated to providing security during the Leader's visits to military units. The organizational structure also includes a university for training agents and senior personnel within the Command.[625]

Much of the MSC's work is centered on its counterintelligence departments. The number of departments varies based on sources. Some of the more important departments include the following:

- The **Investigation Department**, the most visible part of the MSC, is in charge of conducting investigations into anti-regime activity.[626]
- The **Interrogation Department** takes over the case once suspects have been identified by the Investigation Department.
- The **General Incident Department** is a senior agency within the MSC that provides oversight and monitoring of the casework of the other investigative departments.

A number of other departments provide technical and administrative support to these police-related departments. The Technical Department, for example, provides wiretapping and surveillance support to the Investigation Department.

---

623   "Extensive Analysis of the Supreme Nerve Center of the Korean People's Army," *Shindong-A*, May-1 June 2006.
624   According to defector sources, the MSC, until recently, was in charge of conducting inspections of border units. This mission was carried out by MSC agents stationed at each brigade, squadron, and company. However, rumors of cronyism between the MSC and the border troops led to significant changes in border security. After responsibility for border security was transferred from the MPAF to the SSD in April 2012, it is not clear if the MSC continues in this role. Presumably, this mission has been transferred to the SSD.
625   Yun Tae-il, *The Inside Story of the SSD*, op. cit. Intelligence officers in the MSC graduate from the Security University under the management of the MPAF. Until around 1983, the education of military intelligence officers mostly took place at the SSD's Political University located in Kangso District of Nampo City. However, in 1984, the MPAF Security University was established in Mangyongdae District in Pyongyang, where it implements specialized education. The curriculum consists of specialized subjects, such as investigations, intelligence, and tactics, as well as vehicle driving and taekwondo.
626   According to one defector, this department also has the authority to conduct investigations abroad, presumably in China, pursuant to its larger mission.

Chart 24: Organizational Chart of the MSC[627]

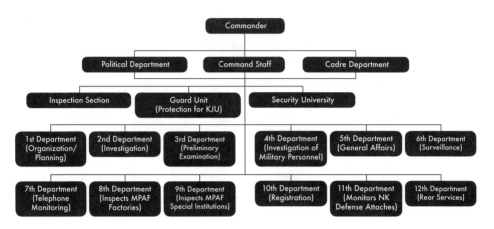

The MSC maintains agents within all critical KPA entities, including the GSD and the GPB.[628] Within the KPA itself, the MSC maintains elements down to the battalion level. Each battalion has a security guidance officer. Each regiment has a senior security guidance officer and two or three security guidance officers. Each division has the departments necessary for carrying out MSC tasks. Security guidance officers employ informants from among the soldiers, who report on spies that have infiltrated the units, rumors about the Kim family, and individual soldiers' behavior. About six or seven informants exist in any given company, which consists of about 120 soldiers.[629] In the 1990s, Kim Jong-il allowed the MSC to establish offices at the provincial and city levels, thus enhancing its ability to support non-military investigations.

---

627   This chart is based on interviews and a number of sources, including Joseph S. Bermudez, Jr., *Shield of the Great Leader*, op. cit, and Atsushi Shimizu, *An Overview of the North Korean Intelligence System: The Reality of the Enormous Apparatus that Supports the Dictatorship*, op. cit.

628   Defector reports have recently highlighted a new unit of "elite guards" who are tasked with covert surveillance against potential threats at the leadership level against Kim Jong-un's rule. Allegedly falling under the control of the MSC, this unit's mandate extends beyond just monitoring military officials to include authority figures in general. Information gathered by this unit is reportedly forwarded directly to Kim Jong-un. In many respects, this unit's mandate overlaps with that of the Guard Command. Lee Sang-Yong, "Elite Guards Form to Quash Anti-Kim Activity," *Daily NK*, April 24, 2015.

629   Yun Tae-il, *The Inside Story of the SSD*, op. cit.

Jo Kyong-chol seated at the far left watching a performance by the Merited State Choir.
(Source: Nodong Sinmun, 18 February 2014)

ii. Role in the Regime

The MSC has steadily risen in stature under Kim Jong-un. In 2014 and 2015, Jo Kyong-chol began to appear at critical military/security meetings and accompany Kim Jong-un on military-related guidance inspections. In August 2015, he appeared in the photographs of a CMC meeting dealing with the crisis on the Korean Peninsula following the landmine explosions on the DMZ. Traditionally, the role and influence of the MSC has risen in times of uncertainty within the leadership. Kim Jong-un seems to have adopted this model as he works to consolidate his power. The question is whether this will have an impact on the balance of power and influence within the internal security apparatus, especially as it relates to the SSD and the GPB. In other words, the fortunes of the MSC are a bellwether for stability. Its ascendance is likely to continue as the young Supreme Leader works to secure his future as the unbridled center of authority of the North Korean regime.

3. The Future of the Internal Security Apparatus

In 2015, the North Korean regime finds itself faced with many threats to internal stability. Kim Jong-un moves along the path of power consolidation, having frozen the leadership in place with the purge and execution of his uncle, Jang Song-taek, and other senior leaders, such as Hyon Yong-chol. In a hedging strategy against the potential thaw in this freeze, he has bolstered the internal security apparatus, placing increased power in the hands of the KWP OGD and the SSD. The MSC also appears to have grown in influence, while the GC and MPS have reportedly suffered setbacks, as reflected in the public profiles of their leadership. Regardless of the politics of the moment, all of these organizations continue to play a vital role in ensuring the regime's control over society, as well as the protection of the Supreme Leader himself. And, more importantly, any suggestion that these organizations have become independent sources of power separate from the Supreme Leader seems to be a flawed representation of the dynamics currently in play inside the North Korean regime.

Looking towards the future, many North Korea-watchers have already begun to speculate about the eventual collapse of the Hermit Kingdom. How could it continue to defy gravity? The Soviet Union has collapsed and Mao's China has evolved. The Kim family dynasty surely cannot continue living in the dark ages, refusing to join the community of nations—or can it?

For sixty years, the internal security apparatus has ensured the survival of the Kim family dictatorship. Whether North Korea collapses, evolves, or continues to muddle through will depend greatly on the viability of this all-pervasive apparatus. In recent years, rumors have begun to seep out through the defector community that cracks may have begun to appear in this repressive system. Security personnel are becoming more susceptible to bribes, discipline among provincial-level police is waning, and even the public is taking retribution against members of the police force. That said, there are no obvious indications that the security apparatus has broken ranks with the raison d'être of the North Korean regime—protection of the center, especially the Supreme Leader, from all threats, foreign and domestic. Whether erosion through corruption will eventually take a political toll on the regime's ability to control the population is a question for the future. But for now, scholars and intelligence analysts can only observe and attempt to piece together the puzzle while sure of only one thing: as long as the regime continues to adhere to the tactics of a police state to hold onto power, human rights will continue to be violated in North Korea as the unfortunate citizens of the country continue to live in the shadows.

XI. CONCLUSION

To commemorate the 19th anniversary of Kim Il-sung's death on July 8, 2013, a leadership procession led by Kim Jong-un made its way to the Kumsusan Palace of the Sun, where the founder of the regime lies. In the commemorative photograph that appeared in *Nodong Sinmun*, Kim Jong-un was seen walking two steps ahead of a group of North Korean leaders dressed in military uniform, with the exception of Premier Pak Pong-ju. Kim and his "companions" entered the main hall of the palace and bowed in respect to the statues of Kim Il-sung and Kim Jong-il. They then visited the chamber containing Kim Il-sung's preserved remains and bowed to him "in humblest reverence," according to *KCNA*.[630] This scene was meant to portray a stable leadership that is steeped in history and unified behind its Supreme Leader.

This ceremony tried to convey the message that the transition of power from Kim Jong-il to Kim Jong-un had gone smoothly. Kim Jong-un had received the titles of authority. He was, in all likelihood, the ultimate decision maker. Despite this official portrayal, many Pyongyang-watchers at the time argued that he had not consolidated his power. This would most likely take at least another year or two as he "learned the ropes" and developed the relationships he would need to rule. Until then, he would have to rely on a close-knit group of regents and advisors. The protective inner circle around Kim Jong-un appeared stable, although a struggle for influence between Jang Song-taek and Choe Ryong-hae may have emerged. This struggle appeared benign and unlikely to upset the delicate balance that was needed for the consolidation process to proceed. While there were struggles for power and influence going on at the second and third echelons of the regime, they did not directly involve the young leader and he was largely immune.

Five months later, as the second year of Kim Jong-un's rule came to a close, the execution of Jang Song-taek sent the Pyongyang-watching community scrambling for explanations. They were left wondering what this would mean for the future of the regime. What could be said with some certainty in the months after this shocking incident was that a watershed event had taken place. The regent structure, which was fundamental to governance in the first year and a half, now lay in ruins. Kim Jong-un had broken the protective inner circle in which he previously operated. While Kim had consolidated his position within the regime as the Supreme Leader, the extent of his power was unclear. The answer to that question depended on the motivation behind Jang Song-taek's violent and very public purge, which is still being debated.

630　"Senior Party, State Officials Visit Kumsusan Palace of Sun," *KCNA*, July 8, 2013.

If Kim Jong-un was behind his uncle's purge, it suggests that his political skills have developed to the point that he may be able to run the regime on his own, most likely through the "hub-and-spoke" leadership style of his father. At the very least, he was able to successfully eliminate his uncle, who was believed to be the second most powerful individual in the regime, without throwing the entire regime into chaos. At present, the wider leadership appears frozen in place, which bodes well for near-term stability. If Kim Jong-un has assumed the role of the Control Tower within the regime, the long-term prognosis of stability will still depend on his ability to rule effectively.

However, if Jang Song-taek's purge was the result of a power struggle that forced Kim Jong-un to act, the implications for near-term stability are much less certain. If Jang could be brought down without the Supreme Leader's direct involvement, this suggests that a coalition of powerful forces had been forged, possibly without Kim's full knowledge. Some have suggested that the purge was the result of a natural coalescing of forces of the KWP OGD, military, and internal security apparatus. If this is true, these influential institutions have agendas that Kim will have to pay attention to, if not follow. The existence of several centers of power would impair near-term stability now that the unifying force, Jang Song-taek, has been removed. Kim Jong-un's ability to keep these powerful forces in check will be critical for regime cohesion in the future.

This book has argued that the answer to Jang's purge likely lies in a decision largely driven by the Kim family. Jang Song-taek had become a liability. He could not be trusted to uphold the best interests of the Kim family above all else. However, power struggles at the second echelon of power between Jang and other powerful interest groups undoubtedly accelerated his downfall and may have even contributed to his final fate.

The story behind Jang's purge still remains unclear. Possible motives, potential oversteps, and miscalculations figure prominently in any discussion of the decision-making process leading up to December 12, 2013. What also remains a source of contention among Pyongyang-watchers is the nature and stability of the regime under Kim Jong-un. Some see tentative steps, especially in the economic realm, toward reform and away from how the regime has been ruled in the past. They point to Kim Jong-un's unprecedented promise of "no more belt tightening" in his April 15, 2012 speech. They talk about the "May 30 Measures" issued by the Cabinet in 2014. They argue that the ongoing diplomatic charm offensive is evidence of a regime desperate to reach out to the international community for its long-term survival.

Others see a ruthless regime that is doubling down on security measures that harken back to the 1950s and 1970s when the leadership went through periods of consolidation, first under Kim Il-sung and later under Kim Jong-il. They point to ongoing executions tied to the purge of Jang's network. They contend that there are various classes of people under investigation. They range from "Class A" subjects, who had direct family and business ties to Jang, to "Class B," "Class C," and "Class D" subjects, which include distant relatives and those who have "guilt-by-association" (*yeon-jwa-je*). According to some figures, this investigation and purge may extend to thousands of people. The purge of other leaders, such as Hyon Yong-chol, has also raised questions of support for the young leader within the wider regime. There have been enhanced SSD operations designed to not only clamp down on defections, but also to set traps for brokers who facilitate escapes. Some Pyongyang-watchers contend that this activity is being driven by increased paranoia at the center by Kim Jong-un and his cohorts.

What this book has tried to show is that these two views of North Korea need not be mutually exclusive. The regime is going through a transition not just of the Supreme Leader, but also of the wider apparatus of power that supports him. While Kim Jong-un is most likely the ultimate decision maker, these decisions are based on diverse processes supported by a large personal apparatus of power, as well as a larger leadership structure. For now, it appears that the young Leader has seized the reins of power and managed to build a network that is loyal to him. However, the leadership system as a whole is made up of many critical nodes where the messages up to Kim Jong-un and down the chain of command can be manipulated for personal gain. Recognition of this systemic flaw may prompt Kim's constant reshuffling of the leadership, as well as draconian punishments for violating his instructions. As Kim Jong-un and the regime wrestle with the continuing reverberations of the transition of power, it should not come as a surprise that there are seemingly contradictory narratives about the nature of North Korea. If and when Kim consolidates his power, the narrative may become more focused and coherent.

The major question facing this regime in the next two to five years is whether it can ensure the continued survival of the "Leader" (*Suryong*) based system and Kim family rule. In this period, Kim Jong-un must consolidate his power or face systemic challenges, both economic and political, that he most likely cannot overcome. As a third-generation leader, Kim cannot rely on the inherent legitimacy of his grandfather. He cannot bend the system to his will, as his father did, because he lacks the web of connections that fosters loyalty secured through battles fought inside the system for decades. Instead, he must slowly build his own system of rule, while implementing successful policies at the same time. If he fails, he may survive as the Supreme Leader, but his ability to dictate the course of the regime will be compromised. He will have to negotiate with other powerful elements in the regime. The notion of Kim family rule will become a ruse used to justify the regime, not the driving force behind the regime.

Section Two of this book has focused on the parts of Kim Jong-un's apparatus that are most critical to his success or failure as a third-generation Supreme Leader: the Leader's Personal Secretariat, the Royal Economy, and the internal security apparatus. They were highlighted not only because of their inherent importance to the North Korean regime and how it operates, but also because they are important to the success of any totalitarian regime. These three elements are intertwined. If any one of these elements fails, it will place increasing strain on the others. If any one of these elements becomes corrupt and goes beyond the control of the Leader, it will severely compromise his ability to rule.

At the beginning of Kim Jong-un's rule, his apparatus of power was weak and unstructured. Some parts of it were tied to him, but many parts were tied to his father and other individuals within the system. His Personal Secretariat was, and is, still being formed as some of his critical aides moved over from Kim Jong-il's own apparatus. The Royal Economy had been passed to Kim Jong-un in his father's will, but various assets and hard currency operations were beyond his control. The internal security apparatus lacked any handpicked leaders by the new Supreme Leader, and its formal chains of command largely passed through the hands of Jang Song-taek. Even Kim Jong-un's ability to make decisions was a highly scripted process controlled by a regent network that kept him inside a protective circle isolated from the larger leadership.

The purge of Jang Song-taek can easily be understood in this context. It was, in many respects, a decisive maneuver that allowed Kim Jong-un to take a major step forward. By purging his uncle, Kim removed a nexus of control that was metastasizing across hard currency operations and beginning to constrain the efficacy of the Royal Economy. In turn, this allowed Kim's Personal Secretariat to grow and become firmly established as a control mechanism for distributing largess throughout the regime. It also provided Kim with assets and access to hard currency that allowed him to secure loyalty at the highest levels of power. Unlike the military, which Kim has reshuffled with impunity, the internal security apparatus was not so easily bent to his will. Jang's purge placed him in direct control of this apparatus, and a more streamlined Royal Economy most likely eased this process.

Nevertheless, the purge of Jang Song-taek is only a temporary tactical maneuver. It does not solve the larger systemic problems the regime is facing. While Kim Jong-un's apparatus may be able to maintain regime stability in the near term, it remains to be seen whether this is a system that is capable of making dynamic adjustments to changing economic and social challenges and realities. The Royal Economy is facing an uphill battle. Because of the measures taken by the international community, hard currency operations, both illicit and legal, are filling the Kim family coffers at a much slower rate than in the past. At the same time, Kim Jong-un, because of the inherent challenges he faces as a young third-generation leader, has to expend more funds to retain and build loyalty across the regime. His major construction enterprises, including theme parks, ski resorts, and upgrades to Pyongyang's infrastructure have cost hundreds of millions of dollars. Additionally, the Royal Economy has been drawn on to continue research and development of North Korea's weapons of mass destruction. At some point, the funding brought in by the Royal Economy will fall too far behind the threshold Kim Jong-un needs to freely run the regime. If he has not consolidated his power by then, his position within the regime could become vulnerable.

Even more important than the Royal Economy to Kim Jong-un's near-term survival is the internal security apparatus. Jang's purge has brought this apparatus under Kim's control, but its loyalty is still somewhat in question. Many of the key leaders throughout the apparatus once belonged to Kim Jong-il's and Kim Kyong-hui's patronage networks. This is certainly true of Kim Won-hong, Director of the SSD, Choe Pu-il, Minister of People's Security, and Yun Jong-rin, Commander of the GC. Kim Jong-un appears to be moving very carefully in securing his hold on these institutions. He has apparently fostered competition between them, perhaps emulating his father's strategy in the 1990s. As a result, the MSC has once again risen in stature, while the SSD and KWP OGD have grown in power with the purge of their mutual enemy, Jang Song-taek. Kim Jong-un's ability to control the internal security apparatus in the long term will depend on his ability to satisfy their appetite for hard currency while controlling their inclination toward destructive competition. This will be difficult since many of the more lucrative, independent hard currency operations inside the regime are run by family members tied to the internal security apparatus.

Meanwhile, Kim Jong-un's Personal Secretariat is growing to suit his newly expanded powers as the Control Tower. Many of the functionaries are younger cadres from the fourth generation of leaders. However, a critical component of this personal apparatus, the SOCC, is reportedly still populated with members of Kim Jong-il's Personal Secretariat. Many of these individuals are critical for running the day-to-day operations of the regime and are also important for the Supreme Leader's situational awareness. Until this part of the apparatus has been thoroughly revamped and Kim Jong-un's own cadre have been put in place, his ability to manipulate the levers of power will be tenuous and suspect.

Finally, there is the Kim family itself; Kim Kyong-hui has disappeared. Regardless of her status, it is being kept from the wider North Korean leadership, which suggests that there may be dissent within the ruling family. If this is true, the implications for North Korean stability are profound. While the international media focuses on Kim Yo-jong and her status within the regime, what is going largely unreported is the role of Kim Jong-un's older half-sister, Kim Sol-song. Her role is admittedly opaque and the subject of much debate, but if rumors of her influence are true, Kim Jong-un could be facing a significant challenge. She is the only child of Kim Jong-il who was officially recognized by Kim Il-sung and she allegedly controls a large portion of her aunt's patronage network. If she decides to play politics, she is a player her brother cannot ignore. She cannot be hauled out in front of a firing squad like Jang Song-taek without potentially catastrophic consequences. How Kim Jong-un decides to address this division of power within the Kim family, if it does indeed exist, will be critical to the future of the regime and reflect his abilities as a ruler.

What does this all mean for the North Korean people? What does it say about human rights under this oppressive regime? Leadership dynamics inside North Korea are at the heart of the question of whether the regime can ever change in any meaningful way and respect the rights of its people. It is clear that the answer is currently no. In any country where one individual's control is dominant and pervasive, the needs of the people are disregarded in the near-term calculus. Kim Jong-un will do what he needs to do to stay in power. He will need to improve the economy if he is to consolidate power and this will impact the lives of the people. However, any such decisions will be made out of necessity for the Supreme Leader's power, not the livelihood of his people. If economic improvement runs up against the needs of internal security, the arguments of the technocrats will lose. Unquestionably, economic reforms will not be permitted to infringe upon internal security.

The Kim dynasty may be living on borrowed time. The regime has entered into its third generation, which is unheard of in the annals of recent political history. Totalitarian regimes may be ruthless and draconian, but they are built on weak foundations. They are the result of informal alliances that are forged at a moment in time. As time marches on, these alliances become weaker as they are replaced again and again. North Korea is no exception. The Kim regime lacks the vigorous mandate it once had when Kim Il-sung was the "living embodiment of the Korean people," a fatherly figure. Now, this figure is a man in his early 30s whose existence was not even known to the North Korean people six years ago.

The apparatus of power continues to create the image of a new, great, and powerful leader, all-knowing and omnipresent. However, the message does not carry the same weight as it did for his grandfather and father, which puts Kim Jong-un in a very difficult situation. If he attempts to continue along the same path as his grandfather and father as an unwavering tyrant, the system will eventually falter. If he chooses to pursue reform and tries to reinvent the regime by departing from totalitarianism, the regime could collapse into chaos. Whichever path Kim Jong-un follows, the rights of the majority of the North Korean people are likely to continue to suffer.

XII. APPENDIX A: BIOGRAPHIES OF INNER CIRCLES OF POWER AROUND KIM JONG-UN

A. KEY ADVISORS

The purge of Jang Song-taek and the dissolution of the regent structure have increased the political space around Kim Jong-un, which has been filled by a handful of rising individuals. Best described as key advisors, these leaders often accompany the Supreme Leader. In addition to their formal positions, they most likely enjoy further influence by virtue of their proximity. This influence sometimes manifests when they are ranked above their cohorts on recent funeral committee lists, which Pyongyang-watchers use to identify the formal leadership ranking within the regime.[631]

Ironically, it is at this level where much of the turmoil within the leadership ranks occurred in 2015. In February, the international media claimed that Pyon In-son, Director of the GSD Operations Bureau had been purged, allegedly for disregarding or taking exception to Kim Jong-un's orders.[632, 633] This was not confirmed in the North Korean press, although he was no longer highlighted as being part of Kim Jong-un's retinue during guidance inspections. In May 2015, the NIS claimed that it had intelligence that Hyon Yong-chol, the Minister of the

---

631   The question many Pyongyang-watchers struggle with is whether or not any of these advisors impact policy or doctrine development. In other words, do they matter? In some cases, long-term advisors on critical policy areas, such as Kang Sok-ju, probably play a role in providing context and critical advice. Others, especially powerbrokers in the military and security apparatus, are less relevant to policymaking and, as such, more interchangeable in the balance of power inside the regime.

632   Colonel General Pyon In-son (69) was Director of the GSD Operations Bureau. He was part of the third generation of the military leadership. He was also a member of the KWP Central Committee and deputy to the SPA. He was promoted to Colonel General on July 25, 2003. Pyon's career was spent moving between Pyongyang and the field commands. His early career primarily served in MPAF headquarters before he assumed the command of the Seventh Corps in South Hamgyong Province in the late 1990s. In 2007, he returned to Pyongyang as a Vice Minister of the People's Armed Forces. Four years later, he was returned to the field as the Commander of the Fourth Corps in South Hwanghae Province. Following the March/April crisis, he returned to the center as a Vice Minister of the People's Armed Forces and Director of the GSD Operations Bureau in August 2013. He was ranked 43rd on Jon Pyong-ho's Funeral Committee list.

633   "Unidentified South Korean Government Official Says DPRK Kim Jong Un 'Removed' Two Aides," *NHK*, February 4, 2015. The media also speculated that Ma Won-chun, the Director of NDC Design Department, had been purged. Later speculation said that he had either been executed or died before he could return to Pyongyang. In October 2015, Ma was identified as a member of Kim Jong-un's guidance inspection trip to Rason to examine how the North Korean city was recovering from Typhoon Goni.

People's Armed Forces,[634] had been executed by anti-aircraft fire for treason.[635] In the same timeframe, rumors emerged that Kim Chun-sam, Pyon In-son's successor as Director of the GSD Operations Bureau, and Han Kwang-sang, the head of the KWP FAD, had been purged.[636] The removal of these key advisors, all of whom were presumably handpicked by Kim himself, raised questions about the process of power consolidation. Whether these moves were done out of desperation, malice, or part of a calculated strategy to keep the wider leadership off balance was not clear as this book went to print.

1. Military/Security

- **Vice Marshal Hwang Pyong-so (66)** has been Director of the GPB since 2014, a member of the Politburo Presidium since 2015, and Vice Chairman of the NDC since 2014. Born in 1949, he attended the Mangyongdae Revolutionary Academy and Kim Il-sung University. He came onto the public scene in 2002 when he received the Order of Kim Il-sung for strengthening "single-hearted unity of the entire society"

---

634   Colonel General Hyon Yong-chol (66) was the Minister of People's Armed Forces, an alternate member of the Politburo (since 2013), and a member of the NDC (2014). His rise through the ranks paralleled the period in which Kim Jong-un became the heir apparent, which suggested that there might have been a relationship between the two. For reasons that are still unclear, he was replaced as Chief of the GSD, a month after being raised to the Politburo, in 2013 and appointed the Commander of the Fifth Corps with a reduction in rank from a four-star to a three-star general. Nearly one year later, in June 2014, he was appointed Minister of the People's Armed Forces, replacing Jang Jong-nam. Hyon was re-promoted to four-star General. He was listed sixth on Jon Pyong-ho's Funeral Committee list. At the September 2014 meeting of the SPA, he replaced Jang Jong-nam on the NDC.

635   Yu Shin-Mo, Bak Eun-Gyeong, and Yu Jeong-In, "Kim Jong-un's Reign Of Terror: North Korean Military's Second in Command Purged," *The Kyunghyang Shinmun*, May 14, 2015. An oddity surrounding Hyon's apparent purge is that he continued to appear in the North Korean media days after his apparent execution on April 30, 2015. He appeared in a documentary on Kim Jong-un's military inspections, which aired on May 5, 11, and 12. One explanation for this apparent departure in how the North Korean media handles leaders who have fallen afoul of the Supreme Leader is that the regime did not want to alert the outside world, and maybe the wider leadership, to Hyon's purge. Apparently, Kim Jong-un's ability to lead was challenged in the aftermath of the Ri Yong-ho purge, when the media announced his immediate retirement due to health issues, coded language that suggested he had been purged.

636   Han Kwang-sang (57) was the Director of the KWP FAD. He emerged on the political scene in January 2010 as part of Kim Jong-il's guidance inspection of the Hyangsan Hotel. He was identified as a first vice director of the KWP. In May 2012, his name began to appear before the heads of the first vice directors of the KWP OGD and PAD, something that suggested that he had been promoted to a Director of a Central Committee department. The KWP FAD manages the Party's funds and assets and is responsible for the welfare of cadres and employees working for the central Party apparatus. As such, Han most likely had some access to Kim Jong-un, the extent of which was currently unclear. He was ranked 30th on Jon Pyong-ho's Funeral Committee list.

Ken E. Gause

and contributing to "socialist powerful state construction."[637] Three years later in 2005, he was identified publicly as Vice Director of the KWP Central Committee, presumably as part of the OGD, and began to accompany Kim Jong-il on guidance inspections. In the period between 2007 and 2010, some Pyongyang-watchers believe Hwang began to work with Kim Jong-un to prepare him for elevation to heir apparent.[638] At the Third Party Conference in 2010, he was appointed an alternate member of the Central Committee. He was promoted to a three-star General in 2011 and was ranked 124th on Kim Jong-il's Funeral Committee list. Based on his public appearances with both Kim Jong-il and Kim Jong-un, Hwang Pyong-so's portfolio appears to be tied to the regime's security organizations. He attended a joint Kim Jong-il and Kim Jong-un field inspection of the Guard Command's headquarters at KPA Unit 963 in 2011, and he was prominently seen in state media coverage of Kim Jong-un's inspection of the KPA SRF Command in 2012.[639] He appeared as a First Vice Director of the KWP OGD in March 2014. The next month, he was promoted to a four-star general and appointed to the KWP CMC, preparing the path for his appointment as Director of the GPB on April 28, 2014. At the SPA meeting in September 2014, he was appointed Vice Chairman of the NDC, replacing Choe Ryong-hae. In April 2015, the North Korean media identified him as a member of the Politburo Presidium.[640] He was ranked sixth on Jon Pyong-ho's Funeral Committee list. Hwang Pyong-so's rapid promotion suggests that he has become one of Kim Jong-un's most trusted advisors.[641] His background in security affairs in the OGD has been most useful in his oversight of the military.

---

637   In this period, he assisted Ko Yong-hui in laying the foundation for succession.

638   Michael Madden, "Biography of Hwang Pyong-so," *North Korea Leadership Watch*, September 14, 2012.

639   Ibid.

640   On April 8, 2015, Pyongyang radio and television referred to Hwang Pyong-so as a "member of the Presidium of the Politburo" as part of an event celebrating the 22nd anniversary of Kim Jong-il's election as Chairman of the NDC. This followed Choe Ryong-hae's removal from the Presidium and demotion in status to just a full member of the Politburo in March 2015.

641   This is shown by the fact that he was part of a delegation, with Choe Ryong-hae and Kim Yang-gon, that visited Seoul in October 2014 to try to restart inter-Korean relations. In August 2015, Hwang Pyong-so and Kim Yang-gon participated in three days of tense negotiations with South Korean interlocutors to defuse tensions on the peninsula following the exchange of artillery fire across the DMZ. On August 25, 2015, Hwang made a highly unusual television appearance to explain the outcome of the high-level inter-Korean talks.

- **General Ri Yong-gil (60)** has been the Chief of the GSD since August 2013 and an alternate member of the Politburo since April 2014. His rise has been dramatic. He is a former Commander of the Third and Fifth Corps and a member of the third generation of military officers. At the end of March 2013, he was identified as the Director of the GSD's Operations Bureau during a briefing for Kim Jong-un. The briefing was part of an emergency operations meeting on the KPA SRF's "firepower strike plan."[642] In May 2013, he accompanied Vice Marshal Choe Ryong-hae to China as part of a high-profile visit in the aftermath of the two-month crisis on the Korean peninsula. During the Kim Jong-il era, the director of the GSD Operations Bureau had a direct channel to the Supreme Leader, bypassing the chief of the GSD. Following Ri's appointment to this post, some believed that Kim Jong-un's understanding of military affairs improved. Ri's promotion to Chief of the GSD has likely negated the need for informal channels, as Ri now has a direct and formal channel through which to provide military advice to the Supreme Leader. The importance of this link is underscored by the fact that, unlike the heads of the GPB and the MPAF, the GSD Chief was not overturned in 2014. Ri was ranked fourth and fifth respectively on Kim Kuk-tae's and Jon Pyong-ho's Funeral Committee lists.

- **General Kim Won-hong (70)** has been a member of the Politburo since 2012, the CMC since 2010, and the NDC since 2012. As the Director of the SSD, Kim formally reported to Jang Song-taek, the KWP Director of Administrative Affairs and Vice Chairman of the NDC, before his downfall.[643] This formal reporting chain was augmented by Kim Won-hong's informal channel to Kim Jong-un on issues of a sensitive nature, a channel that has likely become more formalized since Jang's purge. Kim Won-hong's status has been tied to Kim Jong-un more than that of any other member of the North Korean leadership. He publicly appeared in leadership circles in 2010 and has been a frequent member of Kim Jong-un's guidance inspections, where he would have direct access to the Supreme Leader. He is also rumored to have particularly close ties to Kim Kyong-hui, going back to his days

642   "Kim Jong Un Holds Operations Meeting March 29, Ratifies Plan for Firepower Strike," *KCBS*, March 29, 2013.

643   Ken E. Gause, *Coercion, Control, Surveillance, and Punishment: An Examination of the North Korean Police State* (Washington, D.C.: Committee for Human Rights in North Korea, 2012).

as the Director of the MSC and, earlier, in the GPB. He was ranked 15th on Jon Pyong-ho's Funeral Committee list, a rank that understates his real influence.

- **Colonel General Jo Kyong-chol** has not been publicly identified as a member of any leadership body. As head of the MSC, he runs an organization that plays an important role in guaranteeing internal security. Like the GPB, the MSC is responsible for ensuring the loyalty of the armed forces, which it does through surveillance and infiltration. Under Kim Jong-il, the MSC rose in prominence to rival that of the SSD and the MPS. The MSC is formally subordinate to the MPAF and NDC. However, because of its sensitive mission, the commander of the MSC reportedly has a direct line of communication to the Supreme Leader.[644] He was ranked 47th on Jon Pyong-ho's Funeral Committee list. He was also promoted to Colonel General in February 2015.[645]

- **Colonel General Yun Jong-rin (77)** has been a member of the CMC since 2010. As Director of the GC,[646] he is responsible for ensuring Kim Jong-un's protection.[647] Therefore, he not only works with Kim's Personal Secretariat, but also most likely has a direct line of communication to Kim that bypasses any gatekeepers. Yun was a protégé of Jang Song-taek's older brother, Jang Song-u. Some South Korean media suggested that Yun reported directly to Jang Song-taek, but this was unlikely given the sensitive responsibility of the GC and its relationship to the Supreme Leader. There has been no indication that Yun Jong-rin has been removed as part of the Jang Song-taek purge. However, it appears that he was demoted to Colonel General sometime between April and December 2014, a period during which he was not seen in public.

---

644   During Kim Jong-un's inspection of Unit 447 of the KPA Air and Anti-Air Force in May 2014, Jo Kyong-chol was seen carrying a revolver and standing at attention behind First Chairman Kim Jong-un. He was also wearing a general rank insignia for the first time. Presumably, his name was on the official promotion list in April 2014.

645   "Kim Jong-un's Order Number 0078 to Promote KPA Commanding Officer Ranks," *Nodong Sinmun*, February 16, 2015.

646   The Guard Command is also referred to as the General Guard Command, the Bodyguard Command, and the Guard Bureau.

647   He has held this post since 2003, which suggests his close ties to the Kim family. The fact that he was not replaced when Kim Jong-un took power suggests a close relationship between the two.

2. Party

- **Kang Sok-ju (76)** has been a member of the Politburo since 2010 and the KWP Secretary for International Affairs since 2014.[648] Kang has been a major player in North Korean foreign policy since the 1980s, when he was in the Ministry of Foreign Affairs. For nearly two decades, he has been the key advisor to the regime on negotiations and interactions with the United States, including serving as chief nuclear negotiator. He was also often seen at Kim Jong-il's side during summits with regional powers, including China, Russia, and South Korea.[649] His ties to the senior leadership give him additional influence. He is a cousin of Kim Jong-il, as he is related to Kim Il-sung's mother, Kang Pan-sok. His ties to Kim Kyong-hui and Kim Yong-nam go back to the 1970s, when all three served in the KWP International Department. While some of his responsibilities have been shifted to vice ministers of Foreign Affairs, he likely remains an influential strategist in helping Kim Jong-un maneuver within the international arena.[650] His promotion to Party Secretary in 2014 ensures that he has direct talks with Kim Jong-un on a regular basis.
- **Kim Yang-gon (73)** has been an alternate member of the Politburo and the KWP Secretary for South Korean Affairs since 2010, as well as Director of the KWP UFD since 2007. The UFD is the Party's intelligence agency dedicated to South Korean operations. Kim's role in facilitating dialogue between the two Koreas in the past was rarely acknowledged but highly significant. Kim Yang-gon is Kim Jong-il's cousin and was a close confidant. Along with Kim Jong-il, he was responsible for signing off on all media pronouncements related to inter-Korean relations.[651] His influence under Kim Jong-un was not clear until 2014. Because inter-Korean relations have been frozen since the beginning of the Lee Myung-Bak administration, the UFD's

---

648   Kang Sok-ju replaced Kim Yong-il as the KWP Secretary for International Affairs. He also most likely assumed the position of Director of the KWP International Affairs Department.

649   His trip to Cuba in June 2015 in the aftermath of the advent of normalization of relations between the island nation (and traditional North Korean partner) and the United States indicates the trust the regime continues to have in his ability to handle sensitive matters of foreign policy.

650   "Kang Sok Ju Meets European Politicians," *KCNA*, March 6, 2014. In March 2014, Kang Sok-ju traveled to Europe to meet with a number of European politicians as part of North Korea's "charm offensive."

651   Author's interviews in Seoul, November 2012.

mission has been marginalized. In October 2014, however, he was part of a three-person delegation, along with Choe Ryong-hae and Hwang Pyong-so, that visited Seoul in an effort to restart inter-Korean relations. His profile continued to rise in August 2015, when he accompanied Hwang Pyong-so to Panmunjon to conduct negotiations with South Korea following an exchange of artillery fire across the DMZ. He then appeared on North Korean television to discuss the talks.[652] Soon after the talks, North Korean media referred to Kim Yang-gon as a full member of the Politburo.[653] Kim allegedly heads a task force that works on policy towards South Korea. This task force presumably includes representatives from the North Korean committees that make pronouncements on inter-Korean affairs. Examples include: the Committee on the Peaceful Reunification of the Fatherland (CPRF), which is responsible for government-to-government issues; the Democratic Front for the Reunification of the Fatherland (DFRF), which is responsible for Party interests in inter-Korean affairs; and the National Reconciliation Council (NRC), which deals with inter-Korean humanitarian and nongovernmental organization issues. He was ranked 16th on both Kim Kuk-tae's and Jon Pyong-ho's Funeral Committee lists.

- **Jo Yon-jun (76)** has been an alternate member of the Politburo since 2012 and is First Vice Director of the KWP OGD, where he handles political and economic issues. He first appeared in North Korean media in 2003 and received the Order of Kim Jong-il in 2012. In the past, Jo's influence may have come through one of the regents, such as Kim Kyong-hui. He gave a speech at the enlarged meeting of the Politburo when Jang was purged from the Party. His relationship with Kim Jong-un is now likely more direct and he is considered by some Pyongyang-watchers to be one of Kim's key allies within the OGD.[654] He was ranked 24th on Kim Kuk-tae's Funeral Committee list and 22nd on Jon Pyong-ho's Funeral Committee list.

- **Kim Song-nam (62)** is an alternate member of the KWP Central Committee and Vice Director of the KWP International Affairs

---

652   This interview was highly unusual. The North Korean media rarely carries interviews with leaders of Kim Yang-gon's rank.

653   On August 22, 2015, *KCBS* referred to Kim Yang-gon as a member of the Workers' Party of Korea Central Committee Political Bureau. In February 2013, Pyongyang radio had referred to him as an "alternate member of the WPK CC Political Bureau."

654   This relationship is explored in more detail in the chapter on Kim Jong-un's Personal Secretariat.

Department. He is a renowned "China hand" who started working in the KWP International Affairs Department in the 1980s. He accompanied Kim Il-sung and Kim Jong-il many times during their visits to China. He also accompanied Choe Ryong-hae in May 2013 and Jang Song-taek in August 2013 on their visits to China. He appears to be leading the negotiations with Beijing that will eventually pave the way for Kim Jong-un's first trip to China.[655] He is one of Kim Jong-un's primary advisors on China affairs and allegedly has a direct communications channel with the Supreme Leader.

- **Kim Su-gil (76)** has been the Chief Secretary of the Pyongyang Municipal Party Committee since 2014. He replaced Mun Kyong-tok, who was reportedly removed because of his close ties to Jang Song-taek and the former KWP Administrative Department. It is highly likely that he has also replaced Mun as the KWP Secretary for Pyongyang Affairs. Kim Su-gil began to appear on the political scene in 2013, frequently accompanying Kim Jong-un on guidance inspections. North Korean media identified Kim Su-gil in his current post in April 2014. He was the point man for the apology for the collapse of the Pyongyang apartment building in May 2014. He also has a rare background for this position in that he is a Lieutenant General with greater ties to the military than the Party apparatus. He is rumored to be affiliated with the GPB's Organization Department.[656] He was listed 72nd on Jon Pyong-ho's Funeral Committee list.

- **Jon Il-chun (74)** is a Vice Director of the KWP FAD and Managing Director of the State Development Bank. He has also been Director of Office 39 since 2010.[657] As the point man for securing hard currency for the Kim family, he likely has close ties to the Supreme Leader. Chon was reportedly one of Kim Jong-il's closest friends. The two were classmates at Namsan Higher Middle School and Kim Il-sung University. He has been tied to North Korea's foreign trade for more than forty years, having assumed his first significant position as a Director at the Ministry of Foreign Trade in 1973. In 1995, Chon became the First Vice President of the Daeseong Economic Group, one of the corporations linked to Office 39. Three years later, he

655   "DPRK Envoy's Trips to China," *Yazhou Zhoukan Online* 27, No. 29, July 28, 2013.
656   In May 2013, Kim Su-gil accompanied then GPB Director Choe Ryong-hae to China. At the time, South Korean media speculated that Kim was the Vice Director of the GPB's Organization Bureau.
657   Jon Il-chun's role within the regime is discussed in the chapter on the Royal Economy.

moved into the Office 39 apparatus as a Deputy Director. Chon's ties to Kim Jong-un are less clear, as he has been a sporadic presence on guidance inspections. However, his ties to hard currency operations would suggest that he has a direct channel of communication with Kim Jong-un, as well as Kim Yo-jong and Kim Sol-song, who have responsibilities for the Kim family funds. His leadership ranking rose from 41st on Kim Kuk-tae's Funeral Committee list to 35th on Jon Pyong-ho's Funeral Committee list.

3. Government

- **Pak Pong-ju (76)** has been a member of the Politburo since 2013. After being removed as Premier in 2007, following a shift in policy away from the so-called "July 1 Measure" to improve the economy,[658] he re-emerged in 2012 when he was appointed Director of the KWP LID at the Fourth Party Conference. During this period, he was closely tied to Kim Kyong-hui, who gave up the Light Industry position to become KWP Secretary. At the Central Committee Plenum in March 2013 and the SPA in April 2013, Pak moved into the formal leadership of the Party and was re-established as Premier. This was a clear signal to many Pyongyang-watchers that North Korea will, at some point, attempt to resurrect the June Economic Measures of 2012 or even re-embark on the more aggressive economic measures of the early 2000s. Since Jang Song-taek's execution, Pak now most likely interacts directly with Kim Jong-un. According to one defector, Pak has assumed the responsibility from Choe Yong-rim for organizing Kim Jong-un's Tuesday meetings on domestic and social issues.[659] He was listed second and third respectively on Kim Kuk-tae's and Jon Pyong-ho's Funeral Committee lists.

---

658   Ken E. Gause, *North Korea Under Kim Chong-il: Power, Politics, and Prospects for Change*, op. cit. The July 2002 market liberalization reforms undertaken by North Korea were generally associated with four measures. The first was a basic monetization of the economy. The government abolished the coupon system for food rations and relaxed price controls, thereby allowing supply and demand to determine prices. Second, the government abandoned the artificially high value of the North Korean won (KPW), depreciating it from 2.2 KPW: 1 USD to 150 KPW: 1 USD. Third, the government decentralized economic decisions. Fourth, the government pressed forward with special administrative and industrial zones to attract foreign investment. By 2005, political support for these measures began to wane and Pak Pong-ju was replaced at the SPA in 2007, allegedly after tensions with the military over his economic reform plans.

659   Author's interviews in Seoul, April 2013.

- **Ri Su-yong (Ri Chol) (75)** has been the Minister of Foreign Affairs since 2014. Normally a position of little influence, the foreign affairs position will likely take on greater importance under Ri, who has had close ties to the Kim family for decades. In the 1950s, Ri was one of Kim Jong-il's cohorts at Mangyongdae Revolutionary Academy and Namsan Higher Middle School. He was North Korea's Ambassador to Switzerland from the 1980s to 2010. He managed Kim Jong-il's finances in Europe and oversaw the education of Kim Jong-chol, Kim Jong-un, and Kim Yo-jong when they attended school in Bern, Switzerland. He was the Chairman of the JVIC, a government organization under the Cabinet that promotes foreign investment in North Korea and manages cooperative investment projects with foreign investors.[660] He was rumored to have been the driving force behind the deal with Egyptian telecommunications company Orascom that established North Korea's infrastructure for cell phone service.[661] Ri has also been tied to Kim Jong-un's Personal Secretariat and the secret family slush fund, worth billions, that is used to ensure the regime's support among the wider leadership.[662, 663] These ties seem to have increased his influence, as shown in 2014, when he attended the ASEAN Forum and spoke before the UN.

- **Major General Ma Won-chun (59)** is the Director of the NDC Design Department. Ma has been close to the Kim family since 2000,[664] when he was working at the Paektusan Architectural Institute.[665] Kim Jong-il brought him into the Party apparatus as the Vice Director of the KWP FAD's Design Office, which oversees the design of facilities exclusively used by the Kim family and other members of the senior leadership. Kim sent Ma to China in 2001 to learn Chinese

---

660   According to some sources, the JVIC reported to Jang Song-taek in his role as Vice Chairman of the NDC.

661   Sun Yang, "Revealing the Mystery of North Korea's Investment Solicitation Office in Beijing," *Phoenix Weekly*, November 11, 2013.

662   "Kim Jong-un's Secret Billions," *The Chosun Ilbo*, March 12, 2013. After the Sixth Party Congress in October 1980, Ri Chol became a Deputy Director of Kim Jong-il's Personal Secretariat and Deputy Director of the KWP OGD.

663   Michael Madden, "Biography of Ri Chol," *North Korea Leadership Watch*, March 30, 2011.

664   In the late 1990s and early 2000s, state media occasionally referred to an architect named Ma Won-chun who contributed to major state construction projects. According to a 1999 *Nodong Sinmun* article that provided Ma's biographical and career information, he was born in Samchon County, South Hwanghae Province.

665   See "Ma Won-chun: New Face Accompanying Kim Jong-un, 'North's Best Architect'," *Yonhap News Agency*, July 5, 2013.

construction techniques. Ma began accompanying Kim Jong-un on May 9, 2012, when the new leader conducted a guidance inspection of the Mangyongdae Amusement Park in Pyongyang. Within days of the collapse of the Pyongyang apartment building in May 2014, Ma was appointed to his current position and given the rank of Lieutenant General, presumably to authorize him to direct and supervise various kinds of construction work carried out by the MPS, which is responsible for much of the important construction in the capital.[666] In 2015, Ma apparently had a falling out with Kim Jong-un following the latter's displeasure with the renovations to the Pyongyang International Airport. He was purged and reportedly forced to work on a farm in Ryanggang Province with his family. In October 2015, he was featured in North Korean media as part of a delegation accompanying Kim Jong-un to Rason. Photographs of the inspection suggested that Ma had been demoted in rank to Major General.[667]

B. KEY INDIVIDUALS IN THE SECOND ECHELON OF THE LEADERSHIP

In addition to those closest to Kim Jong-un, the wider North Korean leadership is composed of echelons of power where many of the formal elite belong. The second echelon includes officials who hold critical positions within the leadership. They are responsible for relevant policy areas or have control over critical resources and patronage systems. These officials can provide advice and intelligence, but have no decision-making authority. Many have also cultivated a close relationship with Kim Jong-un since 2010, when he became the heir apparent. Some within this echelon may occasionally be able to reach out to him directly bypassing his gatekeepers.[668] As Kim Jong-un consolidates his power, many of these leaders will likely disappear

---

666   It is estimated that the number of soldier-builders mobilized for various kinds of construction sites, which numbered around 100,000 each year during Kim Jong-il's regime, has sharply increased to around 200,000 during the Kim Jong-un regime. See "Why Did the North Appoint Party Vice Department Director Ma Won-chun as Director of National Defense Commission Design Department?" *NoCutNews*, May 19, 2014.

667   "Kim Jong Un Visits Newly Built 'Village' in Rason," *KCNA*, October 7, 2015.

668   This ability to bypass the gatekeepers is likely tied to a person's relationship with Kim Jong-un. Blood relatives of the Kim family and close associates of Kim Jong-il may have a certain amount of access that is denied to others.

from the leadership.[669] As of now, this echelon of the senior leadership includes the following individuals:

1. PARTY

- **Kim Ki-nam (86)** has been the KWP Secretary for Propaganda since the 1990s.[670] He has also been a full member of the Politburo since 2010 and is Director of the PAD. A close associate of the Kim family, Kim Ki-nam is credited for creating the cult of personality around Kim Jong-il and praising Kim Il-sung's historic role as the founder of the regime. His ties to the Kim family date back to the 1930s, when his father was a member of Kim Il-sung's partisan movement.[671] Kim later attended Mangyongdae Revolutionary Academy, where he met Kim Jong-il. Early in his career, Kim Ki-nam served as a Russian translator for Kim Il-sung. He later cultivated a close relationship with Kim Jong-il and was a frequent member of Kim's late night parties where major policy decisions were made.[672] He has had a leading role in the approval or authorship of essays, slogans, and other media in support of the hereditary succession. Kim Ki-nam was given a role in ensuring Kim Jong-un's succession and appointed to the Politburo in September 2010. He was one of only three civilian officials who accompanied Kim

---

669   Nicolas Levi, "Analysis: Old Generation of North Korean Elite Remain Active," *New Focus International*, July 31, 2013. Some Pyongyang-watchers, such as Levi, caution against the belief that the old guard is being forced out. Many still continue to play important roles within the regime despite their age and health.

670   "Ancient N. Korean Propaganda Chief Bows Out," *The Chosun Ilbo*, April 17, 2015. In early 2015, some Pyongyang-watchers began to question whether Kim Ki-nam still holds this post. On April 9, 2015, Kim was sitting in the third pew alongside vice-ministerial officials rather than on the leadership rostrum during the Third Session of the 13th SPA. A few days earlier at the rally marking the 103rd birthday of Kim Il-sung, he was not sitting with the senior leadership. This raised questions about whether Kim Ki-nam had retired and assumed an honorary post. Some speculated that he may have been replaced by Kim Yo-jong, Kim Jong-un's younger sister. In July 2015, however, Kim Ki-nam's profile began to rise, and by October he had begun to be a regular presence at Supreme Leader guidance inspections and made high-profile speeches. According to one defector source, this was due to a series of blunders made by Kim Yo-jong involving the security of her brother in May 2015. Kim Ki-nam returned to the center to reassert stability around the young leader. See "Kim Jong Un's Sister 'Loses Security Job' After Blunders," *The Chosun Ilbo*, October 8, 2015.

671   Author's discussion with Pyongyang-watchers in Seoul, 2013.

672   Kim Jong-il and Kim Ki-nam's relationship dates back to the 1960s when the two allegedly conspired to weaken the Kim Sung-ae faction within the Kim family and position Kim Jong-il to become heir apparent, which he achieved in 1974. Kim Ki-nam was rumored to be one of the authors of the strategy to "cut the side branches," a phrase linked to the purge within the Kim family that took place in the 1970s and 1980s.

Jong-il's coffin during his funeral in December 2011. Since Jang Song-taek's purge, Kim Ki-nam has continued to be active in Party affairs, including speaking at major Party events. He was ranked seventh on Jon Pyong-ho's Funeral Committee list.

- **Choe Tae-bok (85)** has been a member of the Politburo since 2010 and the Chairman of the SPA since 1998. He is also a KWP Secretary. As one of the first graduates of Mangyongdae Revolutionary Academy, he most likely had ties with Kim Jong-il from an early age. He later became one of Kim's closest aides and advisors on international issues. Along with Kim Jong-un and Kim Ki-nam, he was the only other civilian to accompany Kim Jong-il's hearse. Choe is a reported protégé of Yang Hyong-sop, the Vice President of the SPA Presidium, and is tied to Kim Kyong-hui's patronage system.[673] He was ranked eighth on Jon Pyong-ho's Funeral Committee list.

- **Pak To-chun (71)** has been a full member of the Politburo since 2010, the KWP Secretary for Defense Industry until 2015, and a member of the NDC from 2011 to 2015. His career began to rise when he took over the sensitive post of Party Secretary of Jagang Province, which is home to many parts of the defense-industrial complex. In terms of leadership politics, Pak is tied more closely to Kim Jong-un than he was to Kim Jong-il. He was promoted to four-star General in 2012 and was part of the so-called "National Security Committee" that met at the end of January 2013. In the photograph of this meeting that appeared in North Korean media, Pak was seated to Kim Jong-un's immediate right. Given the role that testing of critical defense systems, such as the nuclear and missile programs, has played in the early part of Kim Jong-un's reign, it is highly likely that Pak To-chun has regular access to Kim.[674] He was ranked tenth on Jon Pyong-ho's Funeral Committee list. At the Third Session of the 13th SPA in April 2015, Pak To-chun was removed from the NDC and replaced by Kim Chun-sop. Although North Korean media said that Pak had been recalled due to his transfer to

---

673   Michael Madden, "Choe Thae Bok Biography," *North Korea Leadership Watch*, March 30, 2011.
674   Lee, Sang-Yong, "SPA Session Offers No Substantial Policies," *Daily NK*, April 13, 2015. According to some Pyongyang-watchers, Pak To-chun has been moved into the background, possibly becoming an adviser on defense industrial issues in Kim Jong-un's personal secretariat. This seems to be a possible career progression for leaders with critical knowledge who are generationally linked to the Kim Jong-il, not Kim Jong-un, era.

another post, it is not clear whether he will remain in the pantheon of North Korean leaders.[675]

- **Kim Kyong-ok** has been a member of the CMC since 2010 and is a First Vice Director of the KWP OGD.[676] He began to appear in North Korean media in the months after Kim Jong-il's stroke and his rise has been tied to that of Kim Jong-un.[677] He was promoted to full General on September 28, 2010, as shown on the promotion list, along with Kim Jong-un, Kim Kyong-hui, and Choe Ryong-hae. In July 2011, Kim Kyong-ok was part of a small entourage that accompanied Kim Jong-il and Kim Jong-un on a field inspection of KPA Unit 963 GC headquarters, which provides close protection, security, and logistical services for the Kim family and the central leadership.[678] This is an indication that Kim Kyong-ok has ties to internal security within the regime. He is also rumored to hold the position within the OGD for military and security affairs. His ties to Kim Jong-un reportedly run through Kim Sol-song.[679] He was ranked 32nd on Jon Pyong-ho's Funeral Committee list.

---

675   *KCNA*, April 9, 2015.

676   Nicolas Levi, "Kim Kyong Ok and Ri Pyong-chol are dead?," *Elites et économie de la Corée du Nord*, November 3, 2014. In the fall of 2014, rumors began to appear in defector-run media that Kim Kyong-ok and several of his aides had been arrested and possibly executed. Kim Kyong-ok was last seen in public as part of a documentary on North Korean television in May 2014. His name was mentioned on the Funeral Committee list for Jon Pyong-ho in June 2014. Some of the speculation identified Choe Ryong-hae as leading the purge. NKSIS speculated that Kim Jong-un was eager to eliminate people closely associated to Jang Song-taek's purge. Other Pyongyang-watchers, such as Nicolas Levi, were skeptical of the reporting and urged caution. On October 10, 2014, *Uriminzokkiri*, the state-controlled website providing Korean language news, released a photograph of high-ranking officials visiting the Memorial of the Founding of the KWP. Kim Kyong-ok appeared in the photograph as part of the delegation of officials, which suggests that reports of his purge may have been premature. However, Kim Kyong-ok has not been seen in public since December 2014, and recent rumors are that he retired for "health reasons." See "How Kim Jong Un Gets Rid Of Threats To His Power," *The Chosun Ilbo*, May 18, 2015.

677   However, Kim Kyong-ok's ties to the Kim family mostly ran through Ko Yong-hui, who approached him to help lay the foundation for the succession of one of her sons. When she died, Kim Kyong-ok's ties to Kim Jong-un reportedly began to grow.

678   Interview with a senior defector in Seoul, May 2014.

679   Ibid. According to some rumors, Kim Sol-song is married to Kim Kyong-ok. Other sources contend that she is married to Sin Pok-nam, a senior Party official, who played a central role in purging Jang Song-taek and is now spearheading the reform of the Party.

2. MILITARY

- **General O Kuk-ryol (85)** has been an alternate member of the Politburo since 2012 and Vice Chairman of the NDC since 2009. O's ties to the Kim family date back to the 1930s. He is the nephew of North Korean hero O Jung-hup and son of O Jung-song, a partisan supporter of Kim Il-sung. After the war, O was one of the war orphans looked after by Kim Il-sung and his first wife (Kim Jong-il's mother), Kim Jong-suk. Ever since, the O family has been considered one of the three major families of the North Korean elite and one that the Kim family relies on to ensure that the high command remains loyal to the concept of the "Leader" (*Suryong*) system. For this reason, it is not surprising that O Kuk-ryol returned to prominence in the months after Kim Jong-il's stroke and throughout the succession process for Kim Jong-un. He was featured in the funeral ceremonies for Kim Jong-il and has continued to appear at major leadership events. A former Chief of the GSD and Director of the KWP Operations Department,[680] O sits atop one of the most prominent patronage systems inside the North Korean armed forces. He reportedly has responsibilities within the NDC for intelligence operations abroad as well as for crisis management. In periods of tension on the Korean peninsula, O's influence and access to Kim Jong-un and his advisors may increase.[681] He was ranked 14th on Jon Pyong-ho's Funeral Committee list, which remained unchanged from his ranking in 2013 on Kim Kuk-tae's Funeral Committee list.
- **Vice Marshal Ri Yong-mu (90)** has been a member of the Politburo since 2010 and a Vice Chairman of the NDC since 1998. One of the elderly elite, Ri is related to the Kim family through Kim Jong-il's great-grandmother, Ri Po-ik.[682] He is Kim Jong-un's cousin. Like O Kuk-ryol, Ri Yong-mu oversees one of the major patronage systems inside the military. He fell out of favor with the Kim family in the late

---

680   Prior to 2009, the KWP Operations Department had responsibility for much of North Korea's Special Operations Forces. In 2009, this department was dissolved and merged into the newly established RGB.

681   Author's interviews in Seoul, 2012 and 2013.

682   Ri Yong-mu is also the husband of Kim Jong-sun, Kim Il-sung's cousin.

1970s,[683] but his career was resurrected in the late 1980s. He was a confidant to Kim Jong-il and probably acts as a stabilizing force during Kim Jong-un's transition to power. His access to Kim Jong-un is unclear and most likely not on a regular basis outside of formal channels. It is also rumored that Ri suffers from cancer and therefore limited in his ability to conduct politics. He was ranked 13th on Jon Pyong-ho's Funeral Committee list, which remained unchanged from his ranking in 2013 on Kim Kuk-tae's Funeral Committee list.

- **General Ri Pyong-chol (66)** has been a member of the CMC since 2010, a member of the NDC since 2014, and was Commander of the KPA Air Force until December 2014. Ri has been known to Pyongyang-watchers since 2007, when he became the Commander of the KPA Air Force. Interest in Ri surged in 2011 when he accompanied Kim Jong-il to Russia, presumably to support a request for modern fighter aircraft.[684] His profile continued to rise into the Kim Jong-un era. In addition to being appointed to the CMC, he became a full member of the KWP Central Committee. He has spoken at a number of leadership events and has accompanied Kim Jong-un on a number of military-related guidance inspections. Ri's name has also been associated with the North Korean drone program.[685] With his appointment to the NDC at the meeting of the SPA in September 2014, he most likely gained direct access to Kim Jong-un and no longer has to communicate through the GSD. He ranked 52nd on Jon Pyong-ho's Funeral Committee list. In December 2014, however, he was replaced by Lieutenant General Choe Yong-ho as Commander of the KPA Air and Air Defense Force. After a period in which he was identified as a "responsible worker" of the KWP,[686] in January 2015, Ri was identified as a First Vice Director of a KWP Central Committee department. According to South Korean media, he is attached to the KWP Military Department.

- **Vice Marshal Kim Yong-chun (79)** has been a member of the Politburo and the CMC since 2010.[687] His ties to the Kim family go

---

683   Ri Yong-mu was dismissed as Director of the GPB in the late 1970s because of his relationships with elements within the Kim family that were opposed to Kim Jong-il.
684   "N.Korea Desperately Seeking Cutting-edge Weaponry," *The Chosun Ilbo*, August 29, 2011.
685   "Kim Jong Un Guides Drone Attack, Rocket Drills," *KCBS*, March 20, 2013.
686   "Kim Jong Un Inspects KPA Air, Air Defense Unit 458," *Nodong Sinmun*, December 8, 2014.
687   Since the personnel changes inside the Party leadership have not been made public since 2012, it is possible that Kim Yong-chun has lost both his positions in the Politburo and the CMC.

back to the 1980s, when he was Director of the GSD Operations Bureau.[688] In 1995, he played a key role in preventing an attempted coup d'état by the Sixth Corps, thus cementing his credentials as a loyal supporter of the Kim family. Additionally, he was one of the members who escorted Kim Jong-il's hearse. Even though he lost his position as Minister of the People's Armed Forces in 2012,[689] he holds a critical post within the Party apparatus as the Director of the KWP Civil Defense Department. His degree of access to Kim Jong-un, however, is most likely weakening.[690] He had close ties to Jang Song-taek. Following Kim Jong-il's death, Kim Yong-chun most likely worked closely with Jang on building Kim Jong-un's legitimacy within the high command.[691]

- **General Kim Yong-chol (69)** has been a member of the CMC since 2010, Vice Chief of the GSD since 2013,[692] and Director of the RGB since 2009. His ties to Kim Jong-un allegedly date back to the early 2000s, when he oversaw Kim Jong-un's education at Kim Il-sung Military University. Previously, he was in the GC and served as a bodyguard to Kim Jong-il. The RGB was tied to the succession in 2010 with the sinking of the *Cheonan*. While there has been speculation over the relationship between Kim Yong-chol and Kim Jong-un in recent years, given the former's demotion and re-promotion, he was a lead voice during the tensions of March/April crisis in 2013. In early March, he announced North Korea's abrogation of the armistice. He is also one of the four military officers in the photograph of Kim Jong-un's military briefing on March 29, 2013. Formally, his access to the senior leadership would go through Chief of the GSD, Ri Yong-gil, and

---

688   Kim Yong-chun and O Kuk-ryol were purged in the mid-1980s following a dispute with O Jin-u. However, they were part of an exclusive group within the GSD who enjoyed Kim Jong-il's patronage. It was Kim Jong-il's support that saved them and brought them back to power after O Jin-u's death.
689   Kim Yong-chun was also relieved of his post of Vice Chairman of the NDC in 2014, a post he had held since 2007.
690   In 2015, reports have begun to surface that Kim Yong-chun may have retired in 2013. While his name appeared on Kim Kuk-tae's Funeral Committee list in 2013, it did not appear on the list for Jon Pyong-ho in 2014.
691   There is a range of opinion about Kim Yong-chun's relationships within the high command. While some believe that he has some influence, many believe that he is despised because of his questionable operational credentials. He most likely does not oversee an extensive patronage system.
692   According to the South Korean Ministry of Unification's *Who's Who in Major North Korean Agencies and Organizations in 2013*, the other Vice Chiefs of the GSD are O Kum-chol, Kim Su-hak, Kim Myong-hwan, and Ro Kwang-chol. O Kum-chol (former Commander of the KPA Air Force) and his brother, O Chol-san (member of the KPA Navy's political committee), are sons of O Paek-ryong, former Director of the General Escort Bureau and head of the KWP Military Department.

Vice Chairman of the NDC, O Kuk-ryol. However, Kim Yong-chol's long-time relationship with Kim Jong-un likely provides him with a private channel of communication, especially on issues related to South Korea and in times of crisis. He was ranked 54th on Jon Pyong-ho's Funeral Committee list.

- **General Choe Pu-il (71)** has been an alternate member of the Politburo since 2013, a member of the CMC since 2010, and a member of the NDC since 2013. Although Choe's status has been rising ever since Kim Jong-un became heir apparent, he was catapulted to the senior leadership in 2013. A close associate of the Kim family for years, he is also rumored to be a favorite of Kim Jong-un and was elevated to general in Special Command Order 0036, signed by the Supreme Commander in June.[693, 694] As Minister of People's Security, he reported up to Jang Song-taek and the NDC. This apparently has not hurt his standing within the leadership in the near term, as he remains in his position following Jang's purge. He was ranked 20th on Jon Pyong-ho's Funeral Committee list.

3. GOVERNMENT

- **Kim Yong-nam (87)** has been a member of the Politburo Presidium since 2010. As Chairman of the SPA Presidium, he is considered the de facto head of state of North Korea. His real power, however, comes by virtue of his close ties to the Kim family and relationships throughout the leadership.[695] He was Kim Jong-il's senior at Kim Il-sung University. The two worked closely together in the 1960s to purge the Party of elements that opposed the *Suryong* system and the notion of hereditary succession. He is close to Kim Kyong-hui. His son, Kim Jung-il, was a Vice Director of Kim Jong-il's Personal Secretariat. Kim Yong-nam

---

693   "Korean People's Army Supreme Commander's Order No. 0036," op. cit.

694   Kang Mi-Jin, "Kim 'Repromotes' Choi Bu Il," *Daily NK*, June 11, 2013. In fact, this was a re-promotion. Choe was originally promoted to general alongside Kim Jong-un in September 2010, but was stripped of one rank at some point. His re-elevation appears to now reconfirm his status within the constituency of those who owe their positions to Kim, and who can be expected to remain fiercely loyal to the regime.

695   Nicolas Levi, "A Big Day for the Elite Clans," *Daily NK*, April 10, 2012. Kim Yong-nam's deceased brother, Kim Du-nam, was a member of the CMC under Kim Il-sung and later became President of the Kumsusan Memorial Palace and Chief of the Office of Military Officers in Kim Jong-il's Personal Secretariat. Kim Du-nam and O Kuk-ryol's patronage systems were very closely aligned and served as one of Kim Jong-il's support networks within the North Korean military.

has long played an intermediary role and a stabilizing force within the senior leadership. He most likely has a direct channel to Kim Jong-un. He was ranked second on Jon Pyong-ho's Funeral Committee list.

C. KEY INDIVIDUALS IN THE THIRD ECHELON OF THE LEADERSHIP

The third echelon is composed of bureaucrats, military officers, and technocrats who are responsible for executing operations—many of whom hold positions on senior leadership bodies. They may have decision-making authority over the operations of their institutions, but these decisions are guided by higher-level decisions. They have limited influence or contact with Kim Jong-un other than during guidance inspections and field exercises, although he may reach out to them for subject matter expertise. This is the level at which many of the fourth-generation leaders, who are currently in their 30s and 40s, will appear in the next few years. But for now, the more notable individuals in this echelon include those listed below.

1. PARTY

- **Kwak Pom-gi (76)** has been an alternate member of the Politburo since 2012, KWP Secretary for Finance since 2012, and Director of the KWP FPD since 2012. He is a Kim Il-sung University-educated economic planner and one of the cadre of technocrats who came into the leadership ranks in 2012 and 2013 along with Pak Pong-ju, Ro Tu-chol, and KWP LID Director Paek Kye-ryong. Kwak's career began in the late 1960s, and he moved into the Cabinet as Vice Minister of Machine-Building Industry. But it was his appointment as Chief Secretary of the South Hamgyong Province in 2010 that brought him to prominence. He was tied to the regime campaign celebrating "the flames of Hamnam" and regularly accompanied Kim Jong-il on guidance tours designed to highlight progress made in heavy industry.[696] Kwak Pom-gi's elevation to the senior ranks of the leadership was tied to Kim Kyong-hui and Jang Song-taek with the expectation that he could bring some pragmatism to the decision-making process on the economy. His line of communication to

---

696   Michael Madden, "Biography of Kwak Pom-gi," *North Korea Leadership Watch*, September 25, 2012.

Kim Jong-un likely went through Jang Song-taek. Following Jang's purge, he now most likely works directly with Kim or through Pak Pong-ju. He was ranked 18th on Jon Pyong-ho's Funeral Committee list.

- **Kim Pyong-hae (74)** has been an alternate member of the Politburo, KWP Secretary for Personnel, and Director of the KWP Cadres Department since 2010. He is one of several provincial Party secretaries to be brought to Pyongyang, not only as part of a generational turnover, but also to bring a better technical understanding of regime operations at the regional level into the central leadership. Kim replaced the long serving holder of the personnel position, Kim Kuk-tae,[697] who was moved over to the Central Control Commission. This portfolio will be critical in the coming years as the inevitable turnover of the Party membership takes place.[698] Kim Pyong-hae's relationship to Kim Jong-un is unclear. He allegedly belonged to a group of Party leaders that followed Jang Song-taek.[699] His ties to North Pyongan Province, where he was Party Secretary, suggest this possible link to Jang. In 2002, during the regime's brief brush with economic reform, the Sinuiju Special Administrative Region was set up in the province. In the years since, Jang had ties to the province in terms of economy and political control. That said, Kim Pyong-hae survived Jang's purge and remains in place. He was ranked 18th and 17th respectively on Kim Kuk-tae's and Jon Pyong-ho's Funeral Committee lists.

- **Colonel General O Il-jong (61)** is the Director of the KWP Military Affairs Department.[700] He is the son of O Jin-u, one of Kim Il-sung's closest associates and former Minister of the People's Armed Forces. O Il-jong was appointed to his current post in 2010 at the Third Party Conference, suggesting that his fortunes are closely linked to Kim Jong-un. He was promoted the next year to Colonel General. As the Director of the Military Affairs Department, O supervises reserve

---

697   Kim Kuk-tae still had ties to the leadership by virtue of his role as the head of the KWP Central Control Committee. He was also the son of Kim Chaek, the former Premier and his daughter, Kim Mun-kyong, a Vice Director of the KWP International Department. Kim Mun-kyong worked with Kim Kyong-hui, when the latter served in the International Department in the 1990s.

698   "North Korea Says Certain Party Members Profiting from State Commodities," *Dong-A Ilbo*, August 10, 2013. Reportedly, internal North Korean documents were circulated that express Kim Jong-un's dissatisfaction with Party cadre for irregularities and corruption.

699   Lee Kyo-Duk et al. *Study Series 13-01: Study on the Power Elite of the Kim Jong Un Regime* (Seoul: Korea Institute for National Unification, July 2013).

700   According to some South Korean reporting, O Il-jong is the Director of the KWP Civil Defense Department. If this is true, he replaced Kim Yong-chun most likely in 2013 or 2014.

forces, including the four million-strong Worker-Peasant Red Guards. Pyongyang-watchers believe that O managed to get promoted thanks to his late father's influence, although he was a schoolmate of Kim Jong-il's exiled half-brother, Kim Pyong-il, North Korea's Ambassador to the Czech Republic.[701] His access to senior leadership early in the Kim Jong-un era likely stemmed from Choe Ryong-hae, who was the KWP Secretary for Military Affairs at the time. However, more recently, his ties to Kim Jong-un appear to be more direct, as he is a frequent cohort on Kim's guidance inspections. He was ranked 26th on Jon Pyong-ho's Funeral Committee list, up seven spots from Kim Kuk-tae's Funeral Committee list.

- **Ri Jae-il (80)** is the First Vice Director of the KWP PAD. He came to the public's attention in 2005 when he began to appear on guidance inspections with Kim Jong-il. He was rumored to be close to the Kim family and may have had ties to Kim Jong-il's Personal Secretariat. Ri was one of a group of core elites who laid the foundations for the succession, and he played a major role in constructing the public legitimacy campaign around Kim Jong-un. He was ranked 120th on Kim Jong-il's Funeral Committee list. His position jumped to 38th and then to 33rd on Kim Kuk-tae's and Jon Pyong-ho's Funeral Committee list respectively.

- **O Su-yong (71)** is the KWP Secretary for Light Industry and Chairman of the SPA Budget Committee.[702] A former Party Secretary for North Hamgyong Province, O is a technocrat. Before moving into the Party apparatus, he was Vice Premier and Minister of Electronic Industry. He also worked in the Ministry of Metal Industry and the Ministry of Machine Building Industries. His ties to the Kim family are vague at best, which is surprising since he succeeded Kim Kyong-hui in his current position. His formal rank within the leadership rose dramatically from 47th on Kim Kuk-tae's Funeral Committee list to 19th on Jon Pyong-ho's Funeral Committee list.

701   "N.Korea Promotes Power Elite Ahead of Anniversary," *The Chosun Ilbo*, April 14, 2011. Kim Pyong-il was transferred to the Czech Republic in 2015 after spending seventeen years as Ambassador to Poland. See "Late N.K. Leader's Half Brother Named Ambassador To Czech Republic," *Yonhap News Agency*, January 21, 2015.
702   According to one South Korean source, O Su-yong was appointed an alternate member of the Politburo in April 2014.

- **Ju Kyu-chang (87)** has been an alternate member of the Politburo and a member of the CMC since 2010, and is also the Director of the KWP MID. His ties to senior leadership go back to the early 2000s, when he began accompanying Kim Jong-il on guidance inspections. Because of its responsibility for day-to-day oversight of the development of the regime's critical defense systems, the director of the KWP MID is probably one of the few director-level officials who has regular access to Kim Jong-un. It is interesting to note that in the January 2013 photograph of Kim Jong-un interacting with his national security team, Ju Kyu-chang was not present, and his deputy, Hong sung-mu, handled his role in the meeting. Ju returned to the public eye with the third nuclear test in February 2013. He was, however, dropped from the NDC in 2014, which suggests that his influence may have waned. His formal ranking within the leadership plummeted from 29th on Kim Kuk-tae's Funeral Committee list to 85th on Jon Pyong-ho's Funeral Committee list. Some have suggested that he has been replaced as Director of the KWP MID by Hong Yong-chil.

- **Tae Jong-su (79)** has been an alternate member of the Politburo and KWP Secretary for General Affairs since 2010, as well as the South Hamgyong Provincial Party Secretary since 2012. He was a trusted associate of Kim Jong-il and had strong ties to both Kim Kyong-hui and Jang Song-taek.[703] In 2010, as Kim Jong-il was revitalizing the Party apparatus, he placed Tae in the sensitive post as Director of the KWP General Department, which is in charge of the handling and transmission of Party documents. From this post, Tae would presumably have had direct access to Kim Jong-un, who began receiving reports from various parts of the regime, including the Party. In 2012, Tae Jong-su was sent back to the provinces to take up another sensitive post as Party Secretary of South Hamgyong Province, which is rumored to be a potential source of factionalism within the regime.[704] It is not clear if Tae's ties to Jang Song-taek have hurt his political standing. While he remains within the leadership, his position

---

703   Tae Jong-su is also tied to other leaders within the third echelon. He and Kim Kye-kwan, First Vice Minister of Foreign Affairs are brothers-in-law, both married to daughters of former Vice Premier Jong Il-ryong.

704   "Hamgyong Province: Can there be Factionalism in North Korea?" *New Focus International*, February 27, 2013.

in the formal ranking dropped from 25th on Kim Kuk-tae's Funeral Committee list to 73rd on Jon Pyong-ho's Funeral Committee list.

- **Lieutenant General Choe Chun-sik (60)** is the President of the Second Academy of Natural Sciences.[705] He first appeared in North Korean media standing next to Kim Jong-un in December 2012 as part of the commemoration ceremonies for late leader Kim Jong-il. The Second Academy of Natural Sciences is the research and development wing of the North Korean defense-industrial complex. It exists within the Party apparatus and answers up the chain of command to the KWP MID and Pak To-chun, the Secretary for Defense Industry. In January 2013, Choe was among several scientists to receive the DPRK Hero title, Gold Star Medal, and the Order of National Flag, First Class for his work on the successful launch of the Kwangmyongsong-3 rocket. Several months later, in September 2013, he appeared in public wearing the uniform of a lieutenant general. In addition to guidance inspections where he accompanies Kim Jong-un, Choe most likely has a channel of regular communication with the Supreme Leader on issues of weapons development.[706] But whether that communication is directly with Kim or through the KWP Secretary for Defense Industry is not clear. He ranked 86th on Jon Pyong-ho's Funeral Committee list.

2. MILITARY

- **General O Kum-chol (68)** is a Vice Chief of the KPA GSD. He succeeded Jo Myong-rok as Commander of the KPA Air and Anti-Air Forces in 1995 and served in that position until 2008. His portfolio within the GSD includes military strategy and planning as well as relations with foreign militaries. He also participates in expanded meetings of the KWP CMC and the Politburo. He most likely has an occasional channel to Kim Jong-un. He was ranked 55th on Jon Pyong-ho's Funeral Committee list.

- **General Pak Yong-sik** is the Minister of People's Armed Forces.[707] At the end of April 2015, Hyon Yong-chol was apparently purged and executed.

---

705   According to a defector with ties to the Second National Academy of Sciences, Choe Chun-sik has been in charge of weapons development since the late 1990s.

706   According to one source, in the wake of the rocket launch, Kim Jong-un has increasingly turned to Choe Chun-sik on issues of weapons development.

707   "Reception Given for Lao High-ranking Military Delegation," *KCNA*, July 11, 2015.

In the following months, North Korean media began to highlight General Pak as his successor without naming him. Pak Yong-sik's media profile began in 1999 when he was promoted to Major General. Ten years later, he was promoted to Lieutenant General. In 2013, he was identified as a political functionary with KPA Large Combined Unit 966. In March 2014, he was elected as a deputy to the 13th SPA and in April, he began accompanying Kim Jong-un on guidance inspections as a Colonel General. In April 2015, he was made a Vice Director of the GPB and was promoted to four-star General in May. Rumors began to spread that Pak was the new Minister of the People's Armed Forces in June 2015 when his name appeared second in the cohort list for Kim Jong-un's viewing of a KPA performance after Vice Marshal Hwang Pyong-so (GPB) and before General Ri Yong-gil (GSD).[708] On July 11, 2015, the North Korean media referenced Pak as the Minister of the People's Armed Forces.[709] Although he is a ranking member of the high command, General Pak's ties to and communication channel with Kim Jong-un are unknown.

- **Colonel General Ro Kwang-chol** is First Vice Minister of the People's Armed Forces. He first appeared in North Korean media as a speaker at a rally congratulating the successful satellite launch in December 2012. He next appeared a year later when he was identified as one of the senior officers leading a loyalty pledge to Kim Jong-un. He accompanied Choe Ryong-hae on his trip to Russia in November 2014 and was ranked 58th on Jon Pyong-ho's Funeral Committee list. He began to attend guidance inspections with Kim Jong-un in 2015 and has been a part of several North Korean delegations in military-to-military talks with other countries. Whether he has achieved unfettered access to the Supreme Leader or must still go through the chain of command is currently unclear.

- **Vice Admiral Ri Yong-chu** is the Commander of the KPA Navy. He replaced Kim Myong-sik in April 2015.[710] Before his latest

---

708   A Pak Yong-sik was listed 45th on Jon Pyong-ho's Funeral Committee list. However, that person appears to be tied to the security apparatus, not the military.

709   It took two and a half months between the rumors of Hyon Yong-chol's purge and the confirmation of Pak Yong-sik as the Minister of the People's Armed Forces. This is unusual for the reporting pattern under Kim Jong-un, in which ministers of the MPAF have normally been identified within three weeks of their appointments.

710   "DPRK Media Identify Ri Yong-chu as KPA Navy Commander 4 April," *KCBS*, April 7, 2015. Vice Admiral Ri Yong-chu replaced Colonel General Kim Myong-su. Kim Myong-su had been the

appointment, Ri was a Vice Chief of the GSD. He was also a delegate to the 13th SPA and has been a frequent cohort on Kim Jong-un's guidance inspections of military installations in 2015. He was ranked 61st on Jon Pyong-ho's Funeral Committee list.

- **Colonel General Pak Jong-chon** is a Vice Chief of the KPA GSD and Director of the Firepower Command Bureau (KPA Artillery). He first appeared in an April 2012 photograph Kim Jong-un had with the participants of the parade held to commemorate Kim Il-sung's 100th birthday. He has since accompanied Kim Jong-un on inspections of artillery units. Given that Kim's own military training is in artillery tactics, it is likely that Pak has a special relationship with the Supreme Leader. Pak was promoted to Colonel General in May 2013, and he was ranked 56th on Jon Pyong-ho's Funeral Committee list.

- **Colonel General Ri Pyong-sam (72)** has been an alternate member of the Politburo since 2012. As the Political Director of the KPISF, Ri manages the political indoctrination and Party life of members of the MPS and the KPISF. He has been one of the most ubiquitous figures associated with Kim Jong-un's visits to internal security-related units and facilities. He has served four MPS ministers, giving him a unique perspective on various patronage systems within the internal security apparatus. He was promoted to Lieutenant General in April 1992, and to Colonel General on April 13, 1999. Colonel General Ri was elected to membership on the KWP Central Committee on September 28, 2010. On October 19, 2011, he was bestowed the title of Labor Hero by the SPA Presidium. His line of communication to Kim Jong-un most likely goes through Choe Pu-il, the Minister of People's Security, although he may have an informal channel, given the apparent relationship he has developed with the Supreme Leader over the last two years.[711] That said, the KPISF was closely tied to Jang Song-taek and, if tainted, could limit Ri's access.[712]

KPAN Commander since 2013, but has not been seen in public since January 2015. According to some sources, he was purged.

711   Ken E. Gause, *Coercion, Control, Surveillance, and Punishment: An Examination of the North Korean Police State*, op. cit.

712   "Kim Jong-un's three years in power, and what lies ahead," *New Focus International*, August 17, 2014. Jang expanded the KPISF within the MPS. His rationale for this move was to create a new political surveillance system aimed at coup prevention. According to one source, his real motive was to establish a check on the OGD-SSD alliance. The KPISF arrested Ryu Kyong, the SSD Deputy Director, who was executed by firing squad.

- **Colonel General Choe Kyong-song** has been a member of the CMC since 2010 and is a former commander of the 11th Corps, also known as the "Storm Corps." He first drew attention from the Pyongyang-watching community in April 2010, when he was promoted to Colonel General. These promotions, which came on the eve of Kim Il-sung's birthday, were handed out to "rising stars" of the Kim Jong-un era. The fact that Choe Kyong-song's name was the first called out among the five newly promoted colonel generals suggests his special relationship with Kim Jong-un. Later, at the Third Party Conference in September, he was made a member of the newly invigorated CMC; he was the only field corps commander appointed to the nineteen-member body. Although his direct ties to Kim Jong-un were unclear, he was one of only four commanders to speak at the December 17 loyalty pledge at Kumsusan Palace of Sun—something that earmarked him as having special status with regard to the Supreme Leader.[713] In February, Choe, who had been demoted in 2014 to lieutenant general, was replaced as Commander of the 11th Corps by Lieutenant General Kim Yong-bok. Although it is not clear whether Choe has been transferred to another posting, after his removal from the 11th Corps post, he was again promoted to Colonel General (*Sang-jang*).

- **Colonel General So Hong-chan** is reportedly a member of the KWP CMC, has been the First Vice Minister of the People's Armed Forces since 2013, and Director of the GLD. He first appeared in North Korean media in April 2007 upon promotion to Major General and then suddenly rose as a core military figure of the Kim Jong-un regime by being promoted to Lieutenant General in 2009 and Colonel General in November 2013. He began accompanying Kim Jong-un on guidance inspections in May 2013. He is reportedly the Director of the GLD and was ranked 44th on Jon Pyong-ho's Funeral Committee list. In May 2015, rumors began to surface that So had been purged, presumably because of his links to Hyon Yong-chol, the former Minister of People's Armed Forces. However, he appeared in July 2015 with Kim Jong-un at the Kumsusan Palace of the Sun. He also appeared on the leadership rostrum for the 70th Anniversary of the founding of the Party.

---

713   The other speakers were Ri Yong-gil (Fifth Corps Commander), Jang Jong-nam (First Corps Commander), and Kim Hyong-ryong (Second Corps Commander). Since then, Ri Yong-gil became the Director of the GSD Operations Bureau (and apparently Chief of the GSD), and Jang Jong-nam became the Minister of the People's Armed Forces.

- **Lieutenant General Kim Chun-sam** is First Vice Chief of the GSD and Director of the GSD Operations Bureau. As such, he is responsible for the daily operational management of the armed forces and supervises the formulation and implementation of the KPA's training and contingency planning. He was first announced in this position in January 2015.[714] His predecessor, Colonel General Pyon In-son, has not appeared in North Korean media since November 2014. Not much is known about Kim Chun-sam. He was promoted to Major General in 1992 and Lieutenant General in 2000.[715] According to some sources, before his current appointment, he was the Commander of the Pyongyang Defense Command. He appeared on the Jo Myong-rok's (81), Kim Jong-il's (72), and Jon Pyong-ho's (53) Funeral Committee lists. His name was also mentioned as part of the Fourth KPA Company Commanders and Instructors' Meeting held in October 2014. From his position as Director of the GSD Operations Bureau, Kim Chun-sam most likely has some routine contact with Kim Jong-un, especially as part of the latter's guidance inspections. Whether he has achieved unfettered access or must still go through the chain of command (i.e. Ri Yong-gil) is currently unclear.[716]
- **Lieutenant General Yun Yong-sik** is Director of the GSD Artillery Bureau. He was first identified in this post in January 2015 as part of a Kim Jong-un guidance inspection. This was the first mention of this post in North Korean media and it is not clear whether it replaces the Firepower Command Bureau, which is headed by Colonel General Pak Jong-chon. Yun first appeared in North Korean media on March 7, 2012 in the Cabinet daily *Minju Joson*, which referred to him as a "brigade commander" of the KPA Fourth Corps in an article citing

---

714   Kim Chun-sam dropped out of public view in April 2015, leading many Pyongyang-watchers to speculate that he had been purged and replaced by Ro Kwang-chol. However, he reappeared in August in photographs tied to the special meeting of the KWP CMC convened to handle the tensions following the explosion of the landmines along the DMZ. See "DPRK TV Shows Photos of Kim Jong Un at Emergency Expanded Meeting of Central Military Commission," *KCTV*, August 21, 2015.

715   "DPRK Leader Issues Order on Promotion of KPA Commanding Members," *KCBS*, October 7, 2000.

716   According to some sources, the position of first deputy chief of the GSD and director of the Operations Bureau may have been downgraded under Kim Jong-un to facilitate Kim's consolidation of direct control over the military. Kim Chun-sam is only a Lieutenant General, while other vice chiefs of the GSD are colonel generals. In addition, during Kim's tenure in the post, the First Vice Chief of the GSD has not accompanied Kim Jong-un on guidance inspections but has instead greeted the Supreme Leader on arrival—a major break with previous protocol.

criticism of then South Korean President Lee Myung-Bak. He later was present for Kim Jong-un's guidance of two KPA artillery-firing exercises in April 2014.

- **Lieutenant General Kim Yong-bok** is the commander of the 11th Corps (aka "Storm Corps"). He made his first public appearance with Kim Jong-un in December 2014 at a multiple-launch rocket drill, although in an unnamed capacity.[717] He was identified as the 11th Corps Commander when he attended and spoke at a meeting commemorating late leader Kim Jong-il's birth anniversary at Kumsusan Memorial Palace of the Sun on February 13, 2015. The 11th Corps is a special warfare command in nature but is much bigger and more diverse in the range of its mission. Experts estimate that it has a force size of 40,000 to 80,000. It has some ten brigades under its command, including a light infantry brigade called "Lightning," a combat air command called "Thunder," and a sniper brigade called "Thunderbolt."[718] Kim Yong-bok's formal chain of command runs through the GSD, although he most likely also has a line of communication to O Kuk-ryol, who retains responsibility for crisis operations within the NDC. Kim Yong-bok replaced Colonel General Choe Kyong-song, who has not been seen in public since October 2013, when he accompanied Kim Jong-un to a visit to the Kumsusan Memorial Palace.[719]

- **Lieutenant General Kim Rak-gyom** has been a member of the CMC and Commander of the SRF since 2012. Kim emerged very quickly on the leadership scene in 2012, replacing Choe Sang-ryeo, who had overseen the transformation of the Missile Command into the SRF in 2011. At the Fourth Party Conference, Kim Rak-gyom was the only Lieutenant General to be elected to the Party's CMC, a move which reflected the importance of the command within the armed forces, something made apparent with Kim Jong-un's speech on April 15th to

---

717   "Kim Jong Un Guides Multiple-Rocket Launching Drill; No Date Given," *KCNA*, December 29, 2014.
718   Lee Yong-Su, "Kim Jong-un's Right-Hand Man? 'Storm Corps' Unveiled," *The Chosun Ilbo*, December 14, 2011.
719   The rumors of change of command of the 11th Corps stretch back to 2014. It is not clear if Choe, who has personal ties to the Kim family, has migrated to another senior military position, has been sent away for temporary revolutionary education, or has been dismissed entirely. It is also not clear whether he retains his position on the CMC to which he was appointed at the Third Party Conference in 2010. See Michael Madden, "New KPA Special Operations Forces Commander," *North Korean Leadership Watch*, February 15, 2015.

the "bold soldiers of the People's Army, Navy, Air Force and Strategic Rocket Force." According to some sources, Kim Jong-un has a special attachment to the SRF in that it reflects the high-tech part of the armed forces. During the March/April crisis of 2013, Kim Rak-gyom was one of four military officers pictured briefing Kim Jong-un against a backdrop of a map showing the ranges of North Korean missiles. The SRF Command is a unified command of all short-, medium- and intermediate-range missile units under the NDC. Thus, Kim Rak-gyom most likely has direct channels of communication to a number of NDC members, including Kim Jong-un, the First Chairman, and the members who hold defense industry portfolios.

3. Government

- **Yang Hyong-sop (90)** has been a member of the Politburo since 2010 and Vice President of the SPA Presidium since 1998. Born in 1925, Yang is a member of the first generation of North Korean leaders. He is also tied to the Kim family through marriage.[720] His career has been spent in the SPA apparatus. He was elected Chairman of the Standing Committee of the SPA in 1983, after having been a Vice Chairman since 1962. In this capacity, he assumed the functions of de facto head of state after Kim Il-sung's death in 1994, as the post of President of the DPRK was never re-assigned. In 1998, a new Constitution passed the President's powers to the President of the Presidium, and Yang was replaced by Kim Yong-nam in that capacity. He occasionally receives foreign delegations and leads North Korean delegations abroad. He will likely be retired in the coming years, but for now he is one of the lynchpins within the regime that demonstrate continuity with both the Kim Jong-il and Kim Il-sung eras. His ties to Kim Jong-un are vague at best, and his communications with the senior leadership most likely were with Kim Kyong-hui and Jang Song-taek. Following Jang's purge and Kim's apparent incapacitation, his channel to the Supreme Leader is unclear, although he ranked 11th on Jon Pyong-ho's Funeral Committee list.
- **Ro Tu-chol (71)** has been an alternate member of the Politburo since 2012, Vice Premier since 2003, and Chairman of the SPC since 2009.

---

720   Yang Hyong-sop is married to Kim Sin-suk, who is the daughter of Kim Il-sung's father's sister.

His ties to Kim Jong-un and the senior leadership are evident in his recent rise through the ranks. He assumed the post of SPC Chairman in April 2009, shortly after Kim Jong-un was handpicked as successor. In November 2012, he was appointed as the Vice Chairman of the SPCSGC, a powerful "shadow leadership organization" headed by Jang Song-taek.[721] Ro has made frequent appearances at economy-related ceremonies. Along with Pak Pong-ju, he is one of the "young" technocrats who is well versed in external economic affairs. Like Pak, Ro built his knowledge of the economy through a number of government jobs and by working in the production field.[722] His appointments to the SPC and the Politburo have been interpreted by many Pyongyang-watchers as an effort by Kim Jong-un to increase the level of pragmatism in leadership deliberations on economic development. His line of communication to the senior leadership most likely went through Pak Pong-ju and Jang Song-taek. Although he was rumored to be close to Jang Song-taek, he was not part of the initial purge, as evidenced by his appearance as 23rd on Kim Kuk-tae's Funeral Committee list. His ranking rose to 21st on Jon Pyong-ho's Funeral Committee list.

- **Jo Chun-ryong** has been a member of the NDC and the presumed Chairman of the SEC since 2014. His first appearance in North Korean media was in March 2014, when he was elected as a deputy to the First Session of the 13th SPA. Jo's subsequent appointment to the NDC, presumably replacing Paek Se-pong, caught the Pyongyang-watching community by surprise. His direct ties to Kim Jong-un are opaque, but his position on the NDC would suggest some regularized contact. He was ranked 84th on Jon Pyong-ho's Funeral Committee list.
- **Kim Kye-gwan (72)** has been the First Vice Minister of Foreign Affairs since 2010. He is the leading figure in international talks over the country's nuclear weapons program, including the Six-Party Talks in Beijing. He played a major role in the shutdown of the nuclear program in 2007, which followed extensive meetings with Christopher Hill, the U.S. Assistant Secretary of State. He also met former U.S. presidents Bill Clinton and Jimmy Carter when they visited Pyongyang

---

721   "Report on Enlarged Meeting of Political Bureau of WPK Central Committee," *KCNA*, November 4, 2012.

722   No Jae-Hyeon, "The Group of Four Who Spearheaded the North's Economic Reform Are Making a 'Comeback' Under the Kim Jong Un Regime," *Yonhap News Agency*, August 20, 2012.

in 2009 and 2010 to negotiate the release of U.S. citizens. He was one of the officials sitting around the table in the January 25, 2013 photograph of the national security meeting. While he presumably has formal meetings with Kim Jong-un, it is probably not one-on-one, but in concert with Kang Sok-ju.[723] He did not appear on Jon Pyong-ho's Funeral Committee list.

- **Kim Chun-sop** has been a member of the NDC since 2015. He was first mentioned in the North Korean press in 1999, when Jon Pyong-ho put forth his name as a candidate for deputy to provincial (municipal), city (district), and county people's assemblies. At the time, Kim was a rolling steel worker at the Songjin Steel Complex.[724] He next appeared on the eve of the Third Party Conference in 2010, when he gave a speech proposing the election of leader Kim Jong-il as delegate to the Party conference. He was identified as the Secretary of Jagang Provincial Committee.[725] This speech no doubt marked him as a rising figure within the Party and tied him to a part of the country linked to the defense-industrial complex. He first accompanied Kim Jong-un on a guidance inspection of the Kanggye Precision Machine plant in 2013 in his capacity as Party Secretary of the Jagang Province. He spoke at an enlarged meeting of the Politburo in February 2015 before assuming membership on the NDC at the SPA meeting in April 2015.[726] Although Kim replaced Pak To-chun on the NDC, it is not clear if he has also assumed his role as Party Secretary for Defense Industry.

- **Ki Kwang-ho** has been the Minister of Finance since 2015 and is the Chairman of the Figure Skating Association. He first appeared in North Korean media in 2007 as North Korea's special envoy in the talks on the Banco Delta Asia issue with the United States. In 2012, Ki was identified as a Vice Minister of Finance and led negotiations on debt settlement issues with Russia. At the Third Session of the 13th SPA in April 2015, he was appointed Minister of Finance. He has

---

723   Ken E. Gause, "The North Korean Leadership: System Dynamics and Fault Lines," in *North Korean Policy Elites,* (Alexandria, VA: Institute for Defense Analysis Paper P-3903, June 2004). Kim Kye-gwan's relations with the Kim family are somewhat suspect. His wife served as a translator for Kim Song-ae, Kim Il-sung's second wife, and this allegedly undermined his standing with Kim Jong-il.

724   "Leading Party, State Officials Cast Votes," *KCNA*, March 7, 1999.

725   "DPRK Party Organ on Jagang, Yanggang Provincial Meetings for WPK Conference," *KCNA*, September 3, 2010.

726   At the time of his appointment to the NDC, Kim Chun-sop ranked 79th in the formal leadership rankings. "North Korean Power Politics: Kim Jong-un's Machiavellian Musical Chairs," *Nikkei Asian Review,* April 13, 2015.

the reputation as a savvy finance expert who gets results. He may also take a major role in helping to restructure the North Korean banking system. According to one Pyongyang-watcher, Ki is "reportedly in favor of greater cooperation with the Paris-based Financial Action Task Force (FATF) on Money Laundering through the work of the newly established Cabinet-level National Coordinating Committee on the Fight against Money Laundering and Financing of Terrorism, which he regards as a sufficient ground for Pyongyang to demand some relief from international financial sanctions."[727]

---

727   Alexsandre Mansourov, "The Third Session of 13th SPA: Business as Usual," *38 North*, April 15, 2015.

XIII. APPENDIX B: GIFT-GIVING UNDER KIM JONG-UN

According to defector sources, the act of gift-giving has undergone significant change during the Kim Jong-un era. The slow down in the Royal Economy has forced Kim to increasingly rely on beneficiary acts and expressions of gratitude as opposed to giving gifts. Below are examples of this phenomena and how the North Korean media has characterized Kim Jong-un's gift-giving.

Table 11: Examples of Kim Jong-un's Gift-giving and Beneficiary Acts

Date	Visit	Gift (as described in North Korean media)	Other Beneficiary Acts
April 10, 2012	Kim Jong-un Visits People's Theater	"People's Theater is a gift that our party gives the people who greet the 100th birth anniversary of the great leader"	
April 27, 2012	Kim Jong-un Attends Eunhasu Orchestra Concert	"...a grand and magnificent sanctuary of culture given to our people as a gift by the fatherly general on the occasion of the centenary of the birth of the great leader [*Suryong*]"	
April 30, 2012	Kim Jong-un Guides Rungra Pleasure Ground Development	"The pleasure ground is a gift to be presented by the [KWP] to the people"	
May 1, 2012	Kim Jong-un visits Daegwan Glass Factory and Machine Plant where Comrade Heo Cheol-yeong works		"...congratulated the working classes there on the occasion of May Day"

Date	Visit	Gift (as described in North Korean media)	Other Beneficiary Acts
May 24, 2012	Kim Jong-un Visits Changjeon Street		"There are in Changjeon Street 5 to 45-storied apartment houses for thousands of families"
May 25, 2012	Kim Jong-un Views Health Complex, Ice Rink Construction	"It is also a gift the [KWP] will present to the people"	
July 1, 2012	Kim Jong-un at Park, Cancer Institute		"…he impassionedly said that what he has done was necessary to implement the behest of the fatherly general who never lost sight of women in his mind's eye"
July 5, 2012	Kim Jong-un Visits Pyongyang Airport		"…Kim Jong Un expressed his great satisfaction over the fact that the soldier builders have built the Terminal 1 of Pyongyang Airport in a modern way in a short period of time"
July 25, 2012	Kim Jong-un, Wife Attend Rungra Park Completion	"The Rungra 888—which has been given to the working people as a gift by our motherly party"	

Date	Visit	Gift (as described in North Korean media)	Other Beneficiary Acts
January 19, 2013	Kim Jong-un Visits Daesongsan General Hospital Construction Site	"Daesongsan General Hospital is another gift of love given to the soldiers of the people's army by our party"	
March 5, 2013	Documentary on Kim Jong-un and military	Footage of expanded CMC meeting at which Kim Jong-un dispenses gifts to attendees	
March 12, 2013	Kim Jong-un's Inspection to Islet Defense Detachment	Photos show Kim Jong-un presenting an automatic rifle and a pair of binoculars as a gift	
March 24, 2013	Kim Jong-un Visits Restaurant Boat Under Construction	"…a gift of love given to the people by our party"	
May 26, 2013	Kim Jong-un Visits Masikryong Ski Resort		"firm determination of the Party to build the skiing ground into a world class one."
August 9, 2013	Kim Jong-un Visits Construction Site of Horse-Riding Club	"…Mirim Horse-Riding Club is our party's gift to people"	
August 14, 2013	Kim Jong-un Tours Housing Construction Site for Scientists	"…let us unconditionally complete the construction of houses for scientists of Kim Il Sung University by October 10, the party founding anniversary, and gift them to the scientists"	

Date	Visit	Gift (as described in North Korean media)	Other Beneficiary Acts
September 9, 2013	Kim Jong-un Looks Around Eunha Scientists Street	"The Eunha Scientists Street –a gift of love that the respected and beloved Marshal Kim Jong Un… gave to our scientists"	
September 15, 2013	Kim Jong-un Visits 3-D Rhythmic Cinema, Video Game Rooms	"The video games rooms are a gift the [KWP] presented to the people"	
September 22, 2013	Kim Jong-un Visits Construction Site of Mirim Riding Club	"…expectation and belief that the soldier-builders would unconditionally finish the construction of the riding club as scheduled as it is the [KWP]'s gift to the people."	
September 23, 2013	Kim Jong-un Visits Dental Hospital Construction Site	"The dental hospital is another gift of love that our party offers to the people on the occasion of the founding anniversary of the party."	
September 28, 2013	Kim Jong-un Visits Building Site of Educators' Homes	"…Kim Il Sung University educators' housing construction … completed by the anniversary of the party's founding to bestow it as a gift to instructors and researchers"	

Date	Visit	Gift (as described in North Korean media)	Other Beneficiary Acts
October 13, 2013	Kim Jong-un Visits Completed Munsu Water Park	"…he [Kim Jong Un] said with deep emotion how Kim Jong-i Il would be pleased if he had seen the wonderfully completed water park as he had made so much effort to provide a comprehensive water park to the people."	
October 14, 2013	Kim Jong-un Visits Mirim Riding Club	"…Mirim Riding Club, a gift of love from our Party to the people"	
June 2, 2014	Kim Jong-un Guides Development Work at Ssuk Islet	"…the scientific and technological study center to be built on the islet is another gift of the [KWP] for the people"	
October 14, 2014	Kim Jong-un Gives Guidance at New Satellite (*Wi-seong*) Scientists Residential District	"Kim Jong Un …energetically led the entire process of its construction so that it is completed by the 69th founding anniversary of the party and presented to scientists as a gift."	
October 21, 2014	Kim Jong-un Visits Completed Scientists Rest Home	"The rest home is one more gift provided by Kim Jong Un to the scientists with loving care."	

XIV. APPENDIX C: NORTH KOREAN MILITARY RANKS

A. KOREAN PEOPLE'S ARMY (조선인민군)

Insignia	Title/Name
Special Honorary Rank	
대원수 (*Dae-won-su*) Grand Marshal	대원수 (*Dae-won-su*) Grand Marshal
	공화국원수 (*Gong-hwa-guk Won-su*) Marshal of the Republic
장관 (*Jang-gwan*) General Officer	
	인민국원수 (*In-min-guk Won-su*) Marshal of KPA
	차수 (*Cha-su*) Vice Marshal

Insignia	Title/Name
	대장 (*Dae-jang*) General
	상장 (*Sang-jang*) Colonel General
	중장 (*Jung-jang*) Lieutenant General
	소장 (*So-jang*) Major General
영관 (*Yeong-gwan*) Field-grade officer rank	
	대좌 (*Dae-jwa*) Senior Colonel
	상좌 (*Sang-jwa*) Colonel
	중좌 (*Jung-jwa*) Lieutenanat Colonel

Insignia	Title/Name
	소좌 (*So-jwa*) Major
위관 (*Wi-gwan*) Company-grade officer rank	
	대위 (*Dae-wi*) Captain
	상위 (*Sang-wi*) Senior Lieutenant
	중위 (*Jung-wi*) Lieutenant
	소위 (*So-wi*) Junior Lieutenant
부사관 (*Bu-sa-gwan*) Non-commissioned officer rank	
	특무상사 (*Teuk-mu-sang-sa*) Sergeant Major

Insignia	Title/Name
	상사 (*Sang-sa*) Master Sergeant
	중사 (*Jung-sa*) Sergeant First Class
	하사 (*Ha-sa*) Staff Sergeant
병 (*Byeong*) Enlisted Ranks	
	상급병사 (*Sang-geup-byeong-sa*) Sergeant
	중급병사 (*Jung-geup-byeong-sa*) Corporal
	하급병사 (*Ha-geup-byeong-sa*) Private First Class
	전사 (*Jeon-sa*) Private

B. KOREAN PEOPLE'S ARMY NAVAL FORCE
(조선인민군 해군)

Insignia	Title/Name
장관 (*Jang-gwan*) General Officer	
	원수 (*Won-su*) Marshal
	차수 (*Cha-su*) Vice Marshal
	대장 (*Dae-jang*) Fleet Admiral
	상장 (*Sang-jang*) Admiral
	중장 (*Jung-jang*) Vice Admiral

Insignia	Title/Name
	소장 (*So-jang*) Rear Admiral
영관 (*Yeong-gwan*) Field-grade officer rank	
	대좌 (*Dae-jwa*) Commodore
	상좌 (*Sang-jwa*) Captain
	중좌 (*Jung-jwa*) Commander
	소좌 (*So-jwa*) Lieutenant Commander
	대위 (*Dae-wi*) Captain Lieutenant

Insignia	Title/Name
	상위 (*Sang-wi*) Senior Lieutenant
	중위 (*Jung-wi*) Junior Lieutenant
	소위 (*So-wi*) Ensign
부사관 (*Bu-sa-gwan*) Non-commissioned officer rank	
	특무상사 (*Teuk-mu-sang-sa*) Chief Petty Officer
	상사 (*Sang-sa*) Petty Officer First Class
	중사 (*Jung-sa*) Petty Officer Second Class

Insignia	Title/Name
	하사 (*Ha-sa*) Petty Officer Third Class
병 (*Byeong*) Enlisted Ranks	
	상급병사 (*Sang-geup-byeong-sa*) Able Seaman
	중급병사 (*Jung-geup-byeong-sa*) Seaman
	하급병사 (*Ha-geup-byeong-sa*) Seaman Apprentice
	전사 (*Jeon-sa*) Seaman Recruit

C. KOREAN PEOPLE'S ARMY AIR FORCE
(조선인민군 공군)

Insignia	Title/Name
장관 (*Jang-gwan*) General Officer	
	원수 (*Won-su*) Marshal
	차수 (*Cha-su*) Vice Marshal
	대장 (*Dae-jang*) General of the Air Force
	상장 (*Sang-jang*) Colonel General
	중장 (*Jung-jang*) Lieutenant General

Insignia	Title/Name
	소장 (*So-jang*) Major General
영관 (*Yeong-gwan*) Field-grade officer rank	
	대좌 (*Dae-jwa*) Brigadier
	상좌 (*Sang-jwa*) Colonel
	중좌 (*Jung-jwa*) Lieutenant Colonel
	소좌 (*So-jwa*) Major
위관 (*Wi-gwan*) Company-grade officer rank	
	대위 (*Dae-wi*) Captain

Insignia	Title/Name
	상위 (*Sang-wi*) First Lieutenant
	중위 (*Jung-wi*) Second Lieutenant
	소위 (*So-wi*) Third Lieutenant
부사관 (*Bu-sa-gwan*) Non-commissioned officer rank	
	특무상사 (*Teuk-mu-sang-sa*) Master Aircrew
	상사 (*Sang-sa*) Flight Sergeant
	중사 (*Jung-sa*) Sergeant

Insignia	Title/Name
	하사 (*Ha-sa*) Junior Sergeant
	상급병사 (*Sang-geup-byong-sa*) Corporal
	중급병사 (*Jung-geup-byeong-sa*) Senior Aircraftman
	하급병사 (*Ha-geup-byeong-sa*) Leading Aircraftman
	전사 (*Jun-sa*) Aircraftman

Insignia images illustrated by Kaidor [CC BY-SA 3.0
(http://creativecommons.org/licenses/by-sa/3.0)], via Wikimedia Commons

XV. BIBLIOGRAPHY

A. Books and Journal Articles

1. Baird, Merrily. "Kim Chong-il's Erratic Decision-making and North Korea's Strategic Culture." In *Know Thy Enemy: Profiles of Adversary Leaders and Their Strategic Cultures*, edited by Barry R. Schneider and Jerrold M. Post. Maxwell Air Force Base, AL: USAF Counterproliferation Center, 2003.
2. Bermudez, Joseph S., Jr. *Shield of the Great Leader*. St. Leonards, Australia: Allen and Unwin, 2001.
3. Cheong, Seong-Chang. *DPRK Leadership Under Kim Jong-un*. Seoul: Sejong Institute, 2012.
4. ———. "Process for Policymaking Regarding National Security." *Yonhap News Agency: Vantage Point* 36, no. 4 (April 2013).
5. ———. "Stalinism and Kimilsungism: A Comparative Analysis of Ideology and Power." *Asian Perspective* 24, no. 1 (2000).
6. Choi, Jin-Wook. "The Changing Party-State System and Outlook for Reform in North Korea." *International Journal of Korean Unification Studies* 18, No. 1 (2009).
7. ———. "The Dawn of the Kim Jong Eun Regime and the Choice for North Korea." *Korea Institute for National Unification: Online Series* 12, No. 17 (May 15, 2012).
8. Chong, Chang-Hyon. *Gyeoteso Bon Kim Jong-il* [The Kim Jong-il that I saw]. Seoul: Kimyongsa, 2000.
9. Cho, Young-Seo. "The Distinctive Nature of the Kim Jong-un Regime in North Korea and Prospects for its Change." *Yonhap News Agency: Vantage Point* 36, No. 9 (September 2013).
10. Clippinger, Morgan E. "Kim Chong-il in the North Korean Mass Media: A Study of Semi-Esoteric Communication." *Asian Survey* 21, no. 3 (March 1981).
11. Cumings, Bruce. *Korea's Place in the Sun: A Modern History*. New York: W. W. Norton & Co., 1998.
12. Eya, Osamu. *Great Illustrated Book of Kim Chong-il*. Tokyo: Shogakukan, 1994.
13. Gause, Ken E. *Coercion, Control, Surveillance, and Punishment: An Examination of the North Korean Police State*, 2nd ed. Washington, D.C.: Committee for Human Rights in North Korea, 2013.
14. ———. *North Korean Leadership Dynamics and Decision-making under Kim Jong-un: A Second Year Assessment*. Alexandria, VA: CNA Occasional Publication 2014-U-006988, March 2014.
15. ———. "The North Korean Leadership: System Dynamics and Fault Lines." In *North Korean Policy Elites*. Alexandria, VA: Institute for Defense Analysis Paper P-3903, June 2004.
16. ———. "North Korea's Political System in the Transition Era: The Role and Influence of the Party Apparatus." In *North Korea in Transition*, edited by Scott Snyder and Kyung-Ae Park. Lanham, MD: Rowman & Littlefield, 2012.
17. ———. *North Korea Under Kim Chong-il: Power, Politics, and Prospects for Change*. Santa Barbara, CA: Praeger, 2011.
18. Greitens, Sheena Chestnut. *Illicit: North Korea's Evolving Operations to Earn Hard Currency*. Washington, D.C.: Committee for Human Rights in North Korea, 2014.
19. Haggard, Stephan and Marcus Noland. "Follow the Money: North Korea's External Resources and Constraints." *2008 Korea's Economy*, Korea Economic Institute (2008).
20. Hawk, David. "National Security Agency." In *The Hidden Gulag*, 2nd ed. Washington, D.C.: Committee for Human Rights in North Korea, 2012.
21. Hirai, Hisashi . *Kitachosen no Shidotaisei to Kokei*. Tokyo: Iwanami Shoten, 2011.
22. Ho, Hye-il. *Bukan Yojigyeong* [Kaleidoscope of North Korea]. Seoul: Malgeun Sori Publishing, 2006.
23. Hyon, Song-il. *Bukanui Gukgajeollyakgwa Pawo Elliteu* [North Korea's National Strategy and Power Elite]. Seoul: Sunin Publishing, 2007.
24. Ino, Seiichi. *Kim Jong-Il's Will*. Tokyo: Asahi Shimbun Publications, Inc., 2009.
25. "Iran-DPRK Missile Cooperation, Role of Office No. 99." Tokyo: Japan Policy Institute, February 7, 2008.
26. Jang, Jin-sung. *Dear Leader: Poet, Spy, Escapee—A Look Inside North Korea*. New York: Atria Books, 2014.

27. Lee, Keum-Soon et al. *White Paper on Human Rights in North Korea 2008*. Seoul: Korea Institute for National Unification, 2008.

28. Lee, Kyo-Duk et al. *Study Series 13-01: Study on the Power Elite of the Kim Jong Un Regime*. Seoul: Korea Institute for National Unification, July 2013.

29. Lee, Sung-Yoon. "Engaging North Korea: The Clouded Legacy of South Korea's Sunshine Policy." *American Enterprise Institute*, April 19, 2010.

30. Lee, Yun-Keol. *The Contents of Kim Jong-il's Will: The Blueprint of Kim Jong-un's Regime and Possibility of Change*. Seoul: NKSIS, 2012.

31. *North Korea Directory*. Japan: Radio Press, Inc., 2004.

32. *North Korea: The Foundations for Military Strength*. Defense Intelligence Agency, October 1991.

33. Park, Hyeong-Jung. "The Demotion of Choe Ryong Hae: Background and Implication." *Korea Institute for National Unification: Online Series* 14, No. 5 (May 21, 2014).

34. ———. "North Korean Conservative Policy Since 2006 and Jang Song-taek: Looking at 2009." *Korea Institute for National Unification: Online Series* 08, No. 72 (December 23, 2008).

35. ———. "One Year into the '6.28 Policy Directives': Contents and Progress." *Korea Institute for National Unification: Online Series* 13, No. 18 (28 June 2013).

36. ———. "The Purge of Jang Song-taek and the Competition for Regency During the Power Succession." *Korea Institute for National Unification: Online Series* 14, No. 3 (February 27, 2014).

37. Seo, Jae-Jin. "Significance of Jang Song-taek's Visit to China." *Korea Institute for National Unification: Online Series* 06, No. 3 (March 31, 2006).

38. Seo, Jae-Jin and Kim Kap-Sik. *A Study of the North Korean Ministry of People's Security*. Seoul: Korea Institute for National Unification, 2008.

39. Shimizu, Atsushi. *An Overview of the North Korean Intelligence System: The Reality of the Enormous Apparatus that Supports the Dictatorship*. Tokyo: Kojin-sha, 2004.

40. "State Security Agency." In the *White Paper on Human Rights in North Korea*. Seoul: Korean Institute for National Unification, 2007, 2008, and 2009.

41. Suh, Jae-Jean. "Possibility for WKP to Take Back Role of Decision-making." *Yonhap News Agency: Vantage Point* 33, no. 8 (August 2010).

42. Suzuki, Masayuki. "Bukanui Sahoejeongchijeok Saengmyeongcheron" [The Theory of a Socio-political Organism in North Korea]. In *Bukanui Silsanggwa Jeonmang* [North Korea in a Changing World Order], edited by Han-Sik Park. Seoul: Donghwa, 1991.

43. Yun, Tae-il. *The Inside Story of the SSD*. Seoul: Chosun Monthly, 1998.

B. Press and Online Articles

44. "After Three Years of Kim Jong-un, Skyscrapers Popping Up on Pyongyang's Skyline." *Hankyoreh*, December 29, 2014.

45. Ahn, Jong-Sik. "Time to Take a Step Back on North Korea." *Daily NK*, February 8, 2014.

46. "Ancient N.Korean Propaganda Chief Bows Out." *The Chosun Ilbo*, April 17, 2015.

47. "Anti-Japanese Guerrilla Instigation." *Nodong Sinmun*, February 13, 1974.

48. An, Yong-Hyeon. "Kim Jong-il's Son Effectively Controls Security Forces." *The Chosun Ilbo*, April 13, 2011.

49. "Appearance of former Minister of People's Armed Forces Kim Jong-gak in Nodong Sinmun Photo Draws Attention." *Yonhap News Agency*, April 16, 2013.

50. "Austrian convicted for yacht sale to North Korean leader." *Reuters*, December 7, 2010.

51. "Brief History of Member of Presidium, Members and Alternate Members of the Political Bureau of C.C., WPK Elected to Fill Vacancies." *KCNA*, April 11, 2012.

52. Cathcart, Adam. "Thrice-Cursed Acts of Treachery? Parsing North Korea's Report on the Execution of Kim Jong-un's Uncle." *The Atlantic*, December 13, 2013.

53. "Central Military Commission of WPK Organized." *KCNA*, September 28, 2010.

54. "Central report meeting held to commemorate the 48th anniversary of Kim Jong-il starting work at the Party Central Committee." *KCTV*, June 18, 2012.

55. Cheong, Seong-Chang. "The Importance of Choi Ryong Hae." *Daily NK*, August 19, 2013.

56. "Choe Ryong Hae Called Ahead Of Hwang Pyong So: NK's Power Ranking Shift?" *Dong-A Ilbo*, October 30, 2014.

57. "Choe Ryong-hae, Close Aide to Kim Jong-un, Possibly Demoted to Only Member of Party Politburo." *Kyodo Clue IV*, March 8, 2015.

58. "Choe Ryong-hae to Second-in-Command with the Help of his Wife Who is Close to Ri Sol-ju – RFA." *The Chosun Ilbo*, November 6, 2014.

59. Choe, Sang-Hun. "Rodman Gives Details on Trip to North Korea." *New York Times*, September 9, 2013.

60. Choe, Sang-Hun and David E. Sanger. "Korea Execution is Tied to Clash Over Businesses." *New York Times*, December 23, 2013.

61. Choe, Seon-Yeong and Jang Yong-Hun. "Competition Between North's Power Organs To Show Loyalty to Kim Jong-un Intensifies." *Yonhap News Agency*, May 31, 2009.

62. ———."Kim Jong-un's Uncle Reported to be in Charge of Kim's Personal Security." *Yonhap News Agency*, September 22, 2013.

63. Choi, Yoo-Sik. "China To Invest $3 Billion in DPRK Special Economic Zone." *The Chosun Ilbo*, February 16, 2012.

64. Cho, Sung-Ho. "NK Leader Rushes to Defense Command After Gadhafi's Death." *Dong-A Ilbo*, October 26, 2011.

65. "Comrade Choe Pu-il: Alternate Member of the Political Bureau." *Nodong Sinmun*, April 1, 2013.

66. "Comrade Kim Jong Un, Supreme Commander of the Korean People's Army, Inspected the Artillery Company Under KPA Unit 963." *Nodong Sinmun*, December 2, 2014.

67. Corrado, Jonathan. "Part I: A New Approach." *Daily NK*, June 25, 2015.

68. ———. "Part II: The Path to Healthy Cash & Market Receptivity." *Daily NK,* July 6, 2015.

69. ———. "Part III: Helping North Korea find a better self interest." *Daily NK*, July 17, 2015.

70. "Covert Organization that Holds the Key to Finding Out the Whole Picture of the Abductions—Study of North Korea's Ministry of State Security." *Sentaku Magazine*, August 2014.

71. "Decision on Conferring Title of Vice Marshal of Korean People's Army on Hwang Pyong-so." *KCNA*, April 28, 2014.

72. "Defector: Kim Jong-un's Aunt Killed Herself Last Year." *Wall Street Journal*, November 26, 2014.

73. "Detour Route to China, South Korea Used for Illegal Exports to DPRK, Senior DPRK Official Directs Trade." *Sankei Shimbun*, February 3, 2010.

74. Dilanian, Ken and Barbara Demick. "Secret U.S.-North Korea diplomatic trips reported." *Los Angeles Times*, February 23, 2013.

75. "Does Aunt's Absence Weaken Kim Jong-un?" *The Chosun Ilbo*, January 7, 2014.

76. "DPRK Defector on Kim Jong-il's Family and Close Aides." *Gendai Weekly*, August 2003.

77. "DPRK Envoy's Trips to China." *Yazhou Zhoukan Online* 27, No. 29, July 28, 2013.

78. "DPRK Leader Issues Order on Promotion of KPA Commanding Members." *KCBS*, October 7, 2000.

79. "DPRK Leader's In-Law Gaining Power." *AFP*, November 11, 2008.

80. "DPRK Media Identify Ri Yong-chu as KPA Navy Commander 4 April." *KCBS*, April 7, 2015.

81. "DPRK Ministry of State Security Holds 'Special Military Tribunal' For Jang Song-taek." *KCNA*, December 12, 2013.

82. "DPRK National Defense Commission Decision No. 8." *KCBS*, March 16, 2011.

83. DPRK National Defense Commission Order No. 7. (1994).

84. "DPRK National Defense Commission Proposes 'High-Level Talks' with US." *KCNA*, June 16, 2013.

85. "DPRK's Office 99 Said to Have Played Central Role in Syrian Nuclear Project." *NHK General Television*, April 25, 2008.

86. "DPRK Party Organ Carries Full List of State Funeral Committee Members for Late Jon Pyong-ho." *Nodong Sinmun*, July 9, 2014.

87. "DPRK Party Organ Names Members on State Funeral Committee for Late Kim Kuk-t'ae." *Nodong Sinmun*, December 15, 2013.

88. "DPRK Party Organ on Chagang, Yanggang Provincial Meetings for WPK Conference." *KCNA*, September 3, 2010.

89. "DPRK TV Shows Photos of Kim Jong Un at Emergency Expanded Meeting of Central Military Commission." *KCTV*, August 21, 2015.

90. "Economic Reforms Stalled, Controls on Economy Tightened One Year After Death of Kim Jong-il." *Sankei Shimbun*, November 29, 2012.

91. "The Emergence of an Elite More Feared than the Supreme Leader." *New Focus International*, December 9, 2014.

92. "Enlarged Meeting of Central Military Commission of WPK Held under Guidance of Kim Jong Un" *KCNA*. February 3, 2013.

93. "Exclusive: DPRK Security Head Ryu Kyong Purged." *NKChosun.com*, May 20, 2011.

94. "Exclusive: Elite purges ahead, fracturing among N. Korea's power circles." *New Focus International*, September 1, 2014.

95. "Exclusive: Jang Song-thaek was executed following his letter to Chinese leadership." *New Focus International*, June 30, 2014.

96. "Exclusive: 'Kim Jong-un is a Puppet' in the Eyes of North Korean Elite." *New Focus International*, March 7, 2014.

97. "Explosion of Soaring Rage of Millions of Soldiers and People, Traitor for All Ages Firmly Punished—Special Military Tribunal of the DPRK Ministry of State Security Against Jang Song Taek, Unparalleled Traitor for All Ages." *KCBS*, December 12, 2013.

98. "Extensive Analysis of the Supreme Nerve Center of the Korean People's Army." *Shindong-A*, May-1 June 2006.

99. "Foreign Currency Earning Constructions in Africa." *Daily NK*, June 21, 2010.

100. Gale, Alastair. "Cash Crunch Hits North Korea's Elite." *Wall Street Journal*, October 8, 2015.

101. Gang, Byeong-Han. "Jang Song-thaek was Purged Because of Conflicts Surrounding Coal Mining Rights." *The Kyunghyang Shinmun*, December 24, 2013.

102. Gertz, Bill. "North Korea Elite Linked to Crime." *Washington Times*, May 24, 2010.

103. "'Jang's Confidant' Mun Kyong Tok Disappears From the North's Official Events…Has He Been Purged?" *Yonhap News Agency*, February 18, 2014.

104. "Jang Song-taek's Purge was Expected a Long Ago." *NKSIS*, December 10, 2013.

105. Jang, Yong-Hoon. "What Kind of an Organization Is North Korea's Kwangmyongsong Guidance Bureau?" *Yonhap News Agency*, December 3, 2002.

106. Jeong, Yong-Soo. "North Replaces Commander of Key Frontline Unit." *Korea JoongAng Daily*, April 30, 2013.

107. ———. "To Curb Jang Song-taek's Influence, Kim Jong-un Completely Reshuffles Core of the Military." *Korea JoongAng Daily*, July 3, 2012.

108. Haggard, Stephan. "Military Promotions in the DPRK." *North Korea: Witness to Transformation*, Peterson Institute for International Economics, August 13, 2013.

109. "Hamgyong Province: Can there be Factionalism in North Korea?" *New Focus International*, February 27, 2013.

110. Hann, Sung-Kwan. "North Korea, Getting Ready for Total Revolution and Opening in 2019, What's the Behind Story?" *NKSIS*, June 7, 2012.

111. Hong, Sung-Ki. "South Korea Needs New Policy on North Korea in Kim Jong Un Era." *Daily NK*, September 2, 2015.

112. "How Kim Jong Un Gets Rid Of Threats To His Power." *The Chosun Ilbo*, May 18, 2015.

113. "Inheritance of Wealth Among Children of People in Power in North Korea." *Dong-A Ilbo*, September 16, 2015.

114. "Interview: Unprecedented insights into North Korea's military structure." *New Focus International*, January 11, 2014.

115. Ishimaru, Jiro. "North Korean Authorities Distribute Jang Song-thaek 'Purge List' to Local Officials." *AsiaPress International*, January 28, 2014.

116. "Is Kim Jong Un Playing Musical Chairs At The Top?" *The Chosun Ilbo*, March 2, 2015.

117. "Is Kim Jong-un Throttling Back Personality Cult?" *The Chosun Ilbo*, July 8, 2013.

118. Jang, Cheol-Un. "Hong Yong-chil, New Face Who Frequently Accompanies the North's Kim Jong Un on On-Site Guidance Trips, Draws Attention." *Yonhap News Agency*, July 4, 2013.

119. Jeong, Yong-Soo. "Son of Kim Jong-un's Chief Secretary Undergoes Ideological Training After Stepping Down from His Position." *Korea JoongAng Daily*, February 24, 2014.

120. Jeong, Yong-Soo and Kim Hee-Jin. "Pyongyang Did China Business As It Purged Jang." *Korea JoongAng Daily*, December 12, 2013.

121. Kang, Cheol-Hwan. "Story of 'Mangyongdae Incident' That Led to Sacking of North's People's Security Minister." *The Chosun Ilbo*, April 9, 2011.

122. Kang, Cheol-Hwan and Lee Gyo-Gwan. "NK Report: State Security Department…Stops Even a Running Train." *The Chosun Ilbo*, March 12, 2002.

123. Kang, Mi-Jin. "Kim 'Repromotes' Choi Bu Il." *Daily NK*, June 11, 2013

124. ———. "New MPS Guidelines Portend Hard Times." *Daily NK*, January 7, 2014.

125. ———. "NK Adds Kim Jong Il to 'Ten Principles'." *Daily NK*, August 9, 2013.

126. ———. "Regime Pushing To Stem Defection Tide," *Daily NK*, January 15, 2014.

127. "Kang Sang-chun, New Director of the Secretariat for General Secretary Kim Jong-il." *Yonhap News Agency*, April 25, 2002.

128. Kang, Seung-Woo. "Choe Solidifies Power Base." *Korea Times*, December 24, 2013.

129. "Kang Sok Ju Meets European Politicians." *KCNA*, March 6, 2014.

130. Kim, Ah-Young. "Targeting Pyongyang's drug trade addiction." *Asia Times*, June 18, 2003.

131. "Kim Chong-il Inherits 'Great Leader' Title." *JoongAng Ilbo*, September 7, 1998.

132. Kim, Christine and Lee Young-Jong, "Kim Jong-un in charge of intelligence: Source." *Korea JoongAng Daily*, April 21, 2011.

133. Kim, Hee-Jin. "Before His Death, Kim Jong Il Wrote Instructions." *Korea JoongAng Daily*, April 14, 2012.

134. ———. "In First Year, Taming The Army Was Kim's Goal." *Korea JoongAng Daily*, December 17, 2012.

135. ———. "Inner Circle in Regime Mostly Stays Intact." *Korea JoongAng Daily*, April 11, 2014.

136. Kim, Hye-Rim. "Kim Jong-il Receives Medical Examination by French Doctors." *Open Radio for North Korea*, August 25, 2010.

137. "Kim Il-sung's Love Child Works for N.Korea's Foreign Ministry." *The Chosun Ilbo*, July 2, 2015.

138. Kim, Jeong-Eun. "Strengthening Close Guard on North's Kim Jong-un?" *Yonhap News Agency*, June 18, 2013.

139. Kim, Jeong-U. "A Full Account of the Purge of Jang Song-taek." *Chosun Monthly*, January 2014.

140. "Kim Jong-il Sends Wreath to Bier of Late Ri Song-bok." *KCNA*, May 21, 2001.

141. "Kim Jong Il's Statue Erected At Kim Jong Il University Of People's Security." *KCNA*, July 19, 2013.

142. "Kim Jong-il's Widow 'Purged'." *The Chosun Ilbo*, July 3, 2013.

143. "Kim Jong-il Visits Kwangbok Region Supermarket." *KCBS*, December 15, 2014.

144. "Kim Jong-un Declares War on Spread of Foreign Trends via Cell Phones, Computers." *NK Intellectuals Solidarity*, June 30, 2014.

145. "Kim Jong Un Gives Guidance at April 26 Cartoon Film Studio." *KCNA*, November 26, 2014.

146. "Kim Jong Un Guides Drone Attack, Rocket Drills." *KCBS*, March 20, 2013.

147. "Kim Jong Un Guides Meeting of WPK Central Military Commission." *KCNA*, August 25, 2013.

148. "Kim Jong Un Guides Multiple-Rocket Launching Drill; No Date Given." *KCNA*, December 29, 2014.

149. "Kim Jong Un Holds Operations Meeting March 29, Ratifies Plan for Firepower Strike." *KCBS*, March 29, 2013.

150. "Kim Jong Un Inspects KPA Air, Air Defense Unit 458." *Nodong Sinmun*, December 8, 2014.

151. "Kim Jong Un Marks Father's Death By Promoting Key Aides." *The Asahi Shimbun*, December 18, 2013.

152. "Kim Jong-un: North Korea's Supreme Leader or State Puppet?" *The Guardian*, May 27, 2014.

153. "Kim Jong-un Orders Agents Overseas to Return Home to Achieve Generational Change." *Sankei Shimbun*, December 22, 2014.

154. "Kim Jong Un Orders to Confer Rank of General Upon Minister of People's Security." *KCNA*, June 11, 2013.

155. "Kim Jong Un Pays Respects to Kim Jong Il." *KCNA*, December 17, 2012.

156. "Kim Jong Un Reorganizes North Korea's Foreign Currency Earning System; Kim Yo-jong to Oversee Party's Foreign Currency Earnings." *NK Intellectuals Solidarity*, January 10, 2014.

157. "Kim Jong-un's Aunt Critically Sick." *The Chosun Ilbo*, July 22, 2013.

158. "Kim Jong-un's Aunt Seriously Ill." *The Chosun Ilbo*, September 28, 2012.

159. "Kim Jong-un's Handwriting Shows Chip Off the Old Block." *The Chosun Ilbo*, January 4, 2012.

160. "Kim Jong-un's Order Number 0078 to Promote KPA Commanding Officer Ranks." *Nodong Sinmun*, February 16, 2015.

161. "Kim Jong-un's Secret Billions." *The Chosun Ilbo*, March 12, 2013.

162. "Kim Jong-un's Sister 'Given Key Party Post'." *The Chosun Ilbo*, July 22, 2013.

163. "Kim Jong-un's Sister Put in Charge of Regime's Coffers." *The Chosun Ilbo*, January 13, 2014.

164. "Kim Jong-un's three years in power, and what lies ahead." *New Focus International*, August 17, 2014.

165. "Kim Jong-un Still Trying to Get Control of The Military." *The Chosun Ilbo*, November 19, 2012.

166. "Kim Jong-un Visits Newly Built 'Village' in Rason." *KCNA*, October 7, 2015.

167. Kim, Ji-Hoon. "Kim Jong Un Says Recent High Level Inter Korean Meetings Could 'Bear Rich Fruit'." *Hankyoreh*, August 29, 2015.

168. Kim, Kwang-Jin and Choi Song-Min. "Border Security Goes Back to NSA. " *Daily NK*, April 22, 2012

169. Kim, Min-Seo. "When Its Investment is Defrauded by the North, China Says that It Can No Longer Put Up With North Korea." *Segye Ilbo*, February 16, 2015.

170. Kim, Myeong-Seong. "Kim Jong-un's Sister 'Married' Senior Party Official Managing Slush Funds." *The Chosun Ilbo*, October 29, 2014.

171. Kim, Seung-Jae. "Kim Jong Un's Closest Confidant U Tong-chuk Collapsed From Cerebral Hemorrhage." *YTN*, April 29, 2012.

172. Kim, So-Hyun. "DPRK Scraps Panel on Security Law." *The Korea Herald*, February 18, 2010.

173. "Kim Tong-un Named Kim Jong-il's Fund Manager." *Yonhap News Agency*, February 20, 2011.

174. Kim, Yong-nam. "Achieving Ultimate Victory of Juch'e Revolutionary Cause While Highly Enshrining Beloved and Respected Comrade Kim Jong Il at Top Place of State Is Firm Resolve of Party Members, Korean People's Army Servicemen, and People." *Minju Joson*, April 10, 2009.

175. Kim, Young-Gyo. "Return of N. Korean envoy in Geneva enhances Jong-un's succession." *Yonhap News Agency*, April 1, 2010.

176. Kim, Young-Jin. "N. Korean Leader's Aunt in Ill Health."*Korea Times*, September 7, 2012.

177. Kim, Yun-Sim. "The Life and Times of a Kingmaker: Kim Kyung-hee in Close-up." *Daily NK*, July 11, 2013.

178. Klingner, Bruce. "WebMemo #1389: Banco Delta Asia Ruling Complicates North Korean Nuclear Deal." *The Heritage Foundation*, March 15, 2007.

179. Koo, Jun-Hoe. "Mainichi Shimbun: Ri Su Yong Executed." *Daily NK*, December 11, 2013.

180. "The Korean People's Army [KPA] Supreme Commander's Order No 0046." *KCBS*, April 22, 2010.

181. "Korean People's Army Supreme Commander's Order No. 0036." *Nodong Sinmun*, June 10, 2013.

182. "Korean People's Army Supreme Commander's Order No 0029: On Promoting the Military Ranks of KPA Commanding Officers." *KCBS*, April 14, 2009.

183. Korean Workers' Party (KWP) Charter (*Jo-seon Ro-dong-dang Gyu-yak*). September 28, 2010, as published in *North Korea Tech*, January 22, 2011.

184. "KWP OGD Making a Clean Sweep of Key Posts in the Party, Military, and Provinces…Even Leading South Korea Policy in Reality." *Dong-A Ilbo*, June 26, 2014.

185. Lankov, Andrei. "The Shadowy World of North Korea's Palace Economy." *Al Jazeera*, September 3, 2014.

186. "Late DPRK Leader's Ex-Chef on Abduction Probe Committee Chairman." *Fuji Television*, August 6, 2014.

187. "Late N.K. Leader's Half Brother Named Ambassador To Czech Republic." *Yonhap News Agency*, January 21, 2015.

188. "Leading Party, State Officials Cast Votes." *KCNA*, March 7, 1999.

189. Lee, Beom-Jin. "Torpedo that Attacked Cheonan was Export Weapon of North Korea's Green Pine Association." *Weekly Chosun*, 17 August 2010.

190. Lee, Gyo-Gwan. "Kim Jong-il Secretariat, at the Center of Power although not Listed as an Official Organization." *The Chosun Ilbo*, April 15, 2001.

191. ———. "20,000 Receive Gifts from Kim Jong-il Every Year." *NKChosun.com*, January 12, 2002.

192. Lee, Mi-Young and Park Seong-Guk. "Defector Claims Jang-Choi in Military Battle." *Daily NK*, July 5, 2013.

193. Lee, Sang-Yong. "Elite Guards Form to Quash Anti-Kim Activity." *Daily NK*, April 24, 2015.

194. ———. "Kim's Hand-written Speech Sparks Debate." *Daily NK*, June 24, 2013.

195. ———. "Kim Yo Jong in de facto power of PAD." *Daily NK*, July 20, 2015.

196. ———. "Organization, Guidance Department '7th Group' Rises in Power" *Daily NK*, October 1, 2015.

197. ———. "SPA Session Offers No Substantial Policies." *Daily NK*, April 13, 2015.

198. Lee, Seok-Young. "Officer Families Just Like the Rest." *Daily NK*, December 2, 2011.

199. Lee, Yang-Su et al. "Analysis of the DPRK Power Group (2)—Route to the Heart of Leadership." *Korea JoongAng Daily*, January 5, 2007.

200. Lee, Yong-Su. "Exclusive: Jang Song-taek Gains Control of Kim Jong-un Guard Unit." *The Chosun Ilbo*, April 30, 2012.

201. ———. "Kim Jong-un's Right-Hand Man? 'Storm Corps' Unveiled." *The Chosun Ilbo*, December 14, 2011.

202. Lee, Young-Jong. "O Kuk Ryol, Who Returned Around the Time of Jang Song Taek's Downfall." *Korea JoongAng Daily*, December 25, 2013.

203. ———. "Report Details North Korea's Rising, Falling 'Stars'." *Korea JoongAng Daily*, December 19, 2013.

204. Lee, Young-Jong and Kim Hee-Jin. "Kim's Aunt Makes Appearance in State Broadcast." *Korea JoongAng Daily*, May 2, 2014.

205. Lee, Young-Jong and Lee Eun-Joo. "Weighing The Fall of Clique of U and Ri." *Korea JoongAng Daily*, July 23, 2012.

206. Lee, Young-Jong and Ser Myo-Ja. "Kim Yo-jong Grows In Clout As Brother Relapses." *Korea JoongAng Daily*, December 10, 2014.

207. Lee, Young-Su. "North Korea's Kim Jong Un Replaces All of the Military Gang of Four Who Escorted Kim Jong Il's Hearse." *The Chosun Ilbo*, November 30, 2012.

208. Lee, Yun-Keol. "Kim Jong Un and His Brother Kim Jong Chol Picked Their Uncle Jang Song Thaek as a 'Prey' to Maintain the 'Kim Dynasty Regime' in North Korea." *NKSIS*, December 10, 2013.

209. Levi, Nicolas. "A Big Day for the Elite Clans." *Daily NK*, April 10, 2012.

210. ———. "Analysis: Old Generation of North Korean Elite Remain Active." *New Focus International*, July 31, 2013.

211. ———. "Kim Kyong Ok and Ri Pyong-chol are dead?" *Elites et économie de la Corée du Nord*, November 3, 2014.

212. "List of Names on DPRK State Funeral Committee for Kim Jong Il." *KCNA*, December 19, 2011.

213. Madden, Michael. "Biographies: Hong Sung-mu." *North Korea Leadership Watch*, February 3, 2013.

214. ———. "Biographies: Kim Chang-son." *North Korea Leadership Watch*, May 14, 2013.

215. ———. "Biography of Hwang Pyong-so." *North Korea Leadership Watch*, September 14, 2012.

216. ———. "Biography of Kwak Pom-gi." *North Korea Leadership Watch*, September 25, 2012.

217. ———. "Biography of Ri Chol." *North Korea Leadership Watch*, March 30, 2011.

218. ———. "Choe Thae Bok Biography." *North Korea Leadership Watch*, March 30, 2011.

219. ———. "CMC Meetings Shown in DPRK Documentary on Kim Jong Un's Military Activities." *North Korea Leadership Watch*, March 18, 2013.

220. ———. "The Fall of Choe Ryong Hae." *38 North*, May 2, 2014.

221. ———. "Film Released to Mark 1 Year Anniversary of KJI's Death." *North Korea Leadership Watch*, December 13, 2012.

222. ———. "Jong Un Attends Guidance of SSD (MSS) Unit." *North Korea Leadership Watch*, October 26, 2010.

223. ———. "Kim Jong Un Chairs Meeting of Party Central Military Commission and KPA Senior Command." *North Korea Leadership Watch*, February 3, 2013.

224. ———. "KJI Youngest Daughter Working as Events Manager for KJU?" *North Korea Leadership Watch*, July 22, 2013.

225. ———. "The Organization Guidance Department." *North Korea Leadership Watch*.

226. ———. "The Personal Secretariat." *North Korea Leadership Watch.*
227. ———. "Third Floor." *North Korea Leadership Watch*, October 18, 2012.
228. Mansourov, Alexandre. "North Korea: Leadership Schisms and Consolidation During Kim Jong-un's Second Year in Power." *38 North*, January 22, 2014.
229. ———. "The Third Session of 13th SPA: Business as Usual." *38 North*, April 15, 2015.
230. "Massive N. Korean Crowd Takes Part in Rally Against S. Korea." *Yonhap News Agency*, July 5, 2011.
231. "Ma Won-chun: New Face Accompanying Kim Jong-un, 'North's Best Architect'." *Yonhap News Agency*, July 5, 2013.
232. "May Day Banquet for Workers Given." *KCNA*, May 1, 2014.
233. Melton, Alex and Jaesung Ryu. "Wanted: Handwriting Analyst." *North Korea: Witness to Transformation*, Peterson Institute for International Economics, February 5, 2012
234. "Members, Alternate Members of Central Committee, WPK." *KCNA*, September 28, 2010.
235. Min, Dong-Yong. "Kang Sang-chun Rumored to Have Been Arrested in China is Kim Jong-il's Butler—Manager of Slush Funds." *Dong-A Ilbo*, January 28, 2006.
236. Mo, Gyu-Yeop. "Kim Jong-un Replaces More Than Half of Corps Commanders Over Four Months in 2013." *Kukmin Ilbo*, August 8, 2013.
237. "NDC Decision on Dismissing People's Security Minister Ju Sang Song." *KCBS*, March 16, 2011.
238. "NK Leader Spends $650 mil. on Luxury Goods." *The Korea Times*, March 11, 2014.
239. "NK Leader's Sister Seen as Playing Key Role in Propaganda Work." *Yonhap News Agency*, June 3, 2015.
240. "N.K. Leader's Sister Serving As Chief Of Staff." *Yonhap News Agency*, March 30, 2014.
241. "NK Names Armed Forces Minister to Keep Army Chief in Check." *Dong-A Ilbo*, April 12, 2012.
242. "N. Korea Abolishes Secret Fund Organ for Kim Jong-il." *Kyodo World Service*, October 18 2012.
243. "N.Korea Desperately Seeking Cutting-edge Weaponry." *The Chosun Ilbo*, August 29, 2011.
244. "N. Korean Ambassador to Geneva Expected to Leave Office." *Yonhap News Agency*, March 10, 2010.
245. "N. Korean Purge All About The Money." *The Chosun Ilbo*, December 12, 2013.
246. "N. Koreans To Wear New Kim Jong Un Badges." *Korea Times*, July 8, 2015.
247. "N.Korea Promotes Power Elite Ahead of Anniversary." *The Chosun Ilbo*, April 14, 2011.
248. "N. Korea Purged Senior Intelligence Official: source." *Yonhap News Agency*, April 17, 2012.
249. "N. Korea Purges Deputy Spy Chief." *The Chosun Ilbo*, May 20, 2011.
250. "N. Korea purge sparked by mineral disputes: Seoul official." *AFP*, December 23, 2013.
251. "N. Korea Replaces Hawkish Armed Forces Minister." *Yonhap News Agency*, May 13, 2013.
252. "N. Korea's 'Bonghwajo' Club Doing Drugs, Counterfeiting." *Dong-A Ilbo*, April 18, 2011.
253. "N. Korea's Eminence Grise at Ease in Power." *The Chosun Ilbo*, February 1, 2013.
254. No, Jae-Hyeon. "The Group of Four Who Spearheaded the North's Economic Reform Are Making a 'Comeback' Under the Kim Jong Un Regime." *Yonhap News Agency*, August 20, 2012.
255. ———. "North Korea Replaces Vice Minister of Defense." *Yonhap News Agency*, May 17, 2013.
256. "North Korea Creates New Front Company to Supply Iran With Nuclear Technology." *Moscow Times*, April 27, 2010.
257. "North Korea Embarks on Full-Scale Economic Development with the State Economic Development Committee (Headed by Jang Song-taek) Taking the Lead." *NK Intellectuals Solidarity*, October 31, 2013.
258. "North Korea Integrates Maneuvering Organs Targeting the South and Overseas Into RGB." *Yonhap News Agency*, May 10, 2009.
259. "North Korea Purging Senior Officials Dealing With ROK?" *NK Focus*, February 16, 2008.
260. "North Korea replaces Vice Minister of People's Armed Forces." *The Chosun Ilbo*, May 17, 2013.
261. "North Korea Requiring Diplomats to Raise Millions in U.S. Currency." *UPI*, September 29, 2015.
262. "North Korea Says Certain Party Members Profiting from State Commodities." *Dong-A Ilbo*, August 10, 2013.
263. "North Korea's Kim Jong-un Executes 1000 of Jang Song-taek's Associates in 20 Days." *Free North Korea Radio*, January 3, 2014.
264. "North Korea's Power Trio Disappear From Public View." *Yonhap News Agency*, February 18, 2015.

265. "North's Kim Jong-un has Changed Everything at a Plant Related to Jang Song-taek." *Yonhap News Agency*, August 4, 2014.
266. "North's Security Command Commander Jo Kyong-chol Drawing Attention by Carrying a Revolver While Accompanying Kim Jong Un." *Yonhap News Agency*, May 14, 2014.
267. "'Notice to All Party Members, Servicepersons and People' on Kim Jong Il's Death." *KCNA*, December 19, 2011.
268. "No. 27 Bureau of the State Security Department Leads Crackdown on Cell Phone Use in North Korea." *NK Focus*, February 21, 2008.
269. "Obituary on the Death of Comrade Kim Kyok-sik." *Nodong Sinmun*, May 11, 2015.
270. Oh, Gwan-Cheol. "Keep an Eye on Premier Pak Pong-ju." *The Kyunghyang Shinmun*, December 19, 2013.
271. Oh, Se-Hyeok. "Jang Triggers Trials For Regional Traders." *Daily NK*, January 23, 2014.
272. "One of NK's richest men said to serve in assembly hall." *Yonhap News Agency*, February 19, 2012.
273. "On Organizing 'Special Investigation Committee' for All-Inclusive and Comprehensive Investigation Into All Japanese People." *KCNA*, July 4, 2014.
274. Park, Byong-Su. "N. Korea To Shuffle Senior Defense Figures Next Month." *Hankyoreh*, March 21, 2014.
275. Park, Chan-Kyong. "Kim Eyes Reform in Purge of N. Korea Old Guard." *AFP*, July 19, 2012.
276. Park, Jun-Hyeong. "Dangers Abound in Cutthroat World." *Daily NK*, September 2, 2011.
277. Park, Seong-Guk. "Lee Young Gil On The Rise." *Daily NK*, August 30, 2013,
278. "Photos of Kim Jong Un With State Security, Foreign Affairs Officials." *KCTV*, January 27, 2013.
279. "Power Struggle Said Behind DPRK's Uncompromising Stance on Missile Launch." *Zakzak Online*, April 10, 2012.
280. "Purge of Jang Song-taek Triggered by Supply Corruption." *The Chosun Ilbo*, December 12, 2013.
281. "Pyongyang Imposes Duty on Diplomats To Obtain Foreign Currency To Raise Funds To Celebrate 10 October 70th Anniversary of Founding of Workers' Party of Korea." *Sankei Shimbun*, September 29, 2015.
282. "Real Power of the State Security Department." *Economisuto*, October 1, 2008.
283. "Reception Given for Lao High-ranking Military Delegation." *KCNA*, July 11, 2015.
284. "Release Of U.S. Prisoners Baffles N. Korea Watchers." *The Chosun Ilbo*, November 11, 2014.
285. "Report on Enlarged Meeting of the Political Bureau of the Workers' Party of Korea Central Committee." *KCBS*, November 4, 2012.
286. "Report on Enlarged Meeting of Political Bureau of WPK Central Committee." *KCNA*, November 4, 2012.
287. "Ripples Still Felt From Jang Killing." *Korea JoongAng Daily*, November 17, 2014.
288. "The Rise of Moderate and Hardline Factions in North Korea." *Sankei Shimbun*, August 1, 2013.
289. "Ri Yong-ho 'Relieved' of All Posts at July 15 Party Meeting." *KCBS Pyongyang*, July 15, 2012.
290. "Ryu Kyong Had Actual Grip on North Korean Intelligence and Armed Forces." *NKChosun.com*, May 20, 2011.
291. "Second Meeting of Security Personnel of KPA Held." *KCNA*, November 20, 2013.
292. "2nd Session of 13th Supreme People's Assembly of DPRK Held." *KCNA*, September 25, 2014.
293. "Senior Party, State Officials Visit Kumsusan Palace of Sun." *KCNA*, July 8, 2013.
294. "Sharp Decreases in Gifts to Senior Officials Suggests Kim Jong-il's Influence May be in Danger of Waning." *Tokyo Shimbun*, April 2, 2010.
295. Snyder, Scott. "China-North Korea Trade in 2013: Business as Usual." *Forbes Asia*, March 27, 2014.
296. Song, Sang-Ho. "Absence of Kim's Aunt May Not Impact North Korea Leadership." *Korea Herald*, January 13, 2014.
297. "Source Says Purge Spreads to DPRK's Regional Areas After Jang's Execution." *Yonhap News Agency*, December 22, 2013.
298. "South Korean Government Confirms Top North Korean Security Official Dismissed for Mishandling China, North Korea Border Control." *Yomiuri Shimbun*, April 9, 2011.
299. "Statues of Kim Il Sung, Kim Jong Il Erected at Security University." *KCNA*, November 18, 2014.

300. "3 DPRK Men who Procured Luxury, Military Items for Kim Jong-il." *Uin Hatsu* "*Konfidensharu*," March 10, 2010.

301. "Top NK General Ousted For Debating Economic Reform." *Dong-A Ilbo*, July 31, 2012.

302. "Tracing the Whereabouts of Kim Jong-il's 'Secret Funds' –Kim Jong-un Inherits Huge Amount of Money Together with the Transfer of Power." *Bessatsu Takarajima*, Issue No. 1984 (April 25, 2013).

303. "Traitor Jang Song Thaek Executed." *KCNA*, December 13, 2013.

304. "Unidentified South Korean Government Official Says DPRK Kim Jong Un 'Removed' Two Aides." *NHK*, February 4, 2015.

305. "U.S. Doctor Visits N. Korea To Treat Leader Kim's Aunt." *Yonhap News Agency*, October 2, 2014.

306. "Who Is in Charge of N.Korea's Nuclear Weapons?" *The Chosun Ilbo*, December 26, 2011.

307. "Who Runs N. Korea?" *The Chosun Ilbo*, December 18, 2012.

308. "Why Did the North Appoint Party Vice Department Director Ma Won-chun as Director of National Defense Commission Design Department?" *NoCutNews*, May 19, 2014.

309. Winter, Caroline. "Mansudae Art Studio, North Korea's Colossal Monument Factory." *Bloomberg*, June 6, 2013.

310. "Wirepuller Kwon Yong-rok Behind Purchase of Luxury Yachts for Kim Jong-il." *Uin Hatsu* "*Konfidensharu*," July 28, 2009.

311. "Wreaths Laid Before Cemetery of Fallen Fighters of CPV." *KCNA*, July 26, 2013.

312. Yang, Sun. "Revealing the Mystery of North Korea's Investment Solicitation Office in Beijing." *Phoenix Weekly*, November 11, 2013.

313. Yi, Ji-Seon. "Kim Jong Un's 'Samjiyon Aides' In The Spotlight As The Rising Stars In North Korean Politics. " *The Kyunghyang Shinmun*, December 12, 2013.

314. Yim, Ui-Chul. "DPRK Missile Industry, Technology Examined." *Tongil Kyongje*, August 1999.

315. Yu, Shin-Mo, Bak Eun-Gyeong and Yu Jeong-In. "Kim Jong-un's Reign Of Terror: North Korean Military's Second in Command Purged." *The Kyunghyang Shinmun*, May 14, 2015.

316. Yun, Il-Geon. "Change in Seating of North's Security Commander Jo Kyong-chol…Has His Status Risen?" *Yonhap News Agency*, February 19, 2014.

317. ———."The Rise of Kim Chol-jin: North's Hidden Influence in Economic Development." *Yonhap News Agency*, February 2, 2014.